Béla Bartók

and Turn-of-the-Century

Budapest

The publisher gratefully acknowledges the contributions provided by the American Musicological Society and by the General Endowment Fund, which is supported by generous gifts from the members of the Associates of the University of California Press.

Béla Bartók
and TURN-OF-THE-CENTURY
Budapest

JUDIT FRIGYESI

UNIVERSITY OF CALIFORNIA PRESS

Berkeley   Los Angeles   London

University of California Press
Berkeley and Los Angeles, California

University of California Press, Ltd.
London, England

Library of Congress Cataloging-in-Publication Data

Frigyesi, Judit.
    Béla Bartók and turn-of-the-century Budapest / Judit Frigyesi.
      p.   cm.
    Includes bibliographical references and index.
    ISBN 0-520-20740-8 (cloth : alk. paper)
    ISBN 0-520-22254-7 (pb. : alk. paper)
    1. Bartók, Béla, 1881–1945—Aesthetics. 2. Bartók, Béla,
1881–1945—Sources. 3. Bartók, Béla, 1881–1945. Kékszakállú herceg
vára. 4. Ady, Endre, 1877–1919—Influence. 5. Modernism
(Aesthetics)—Hungary—Budapest. 6. Budapest (Hungary)—
Intellectual life. I. Title.
ML410.B26F75   1998
780'.92—dc21   97-19826
                                                      CIP

Printed in the United States of America
9 8 7 6 5 4 3 2

In memoriam Maestro Charles Bruck

Contents

Acknowledgments

Many friends and colleagues in the United States, Hungary, and elsewhere have helped me in my work. My teachers, colleagues, and students in the United States first made me realize the significance of the subject and encouraged me to explore it, among them Richard Taruskin, Michael Beckerman, Norman Smith, Pierro Weiss, Harold Powers, and Michael Steinberg. I owe special thanks to Leonard Meyer, who was the advisor for my dissertation and remains a faithful and encouraging friend and critic.

The background for this work draws on my knowledge of Bartók scholarship and Hungarian intellectual life and continued discussions with scholars and musicians, among others, Elliott Antokoletz, László Dobszay, Géza Fodor, Malcolm Gillies, Mary Gluck, András Hamori, Péter Hanák, Tamás Hófer, János Kárpáti, Géza Komoróczy, Sándor Kovács, György Kroó, Péter Laki, Vera Lampert, the late Ernő Lendvai, Miklós Lackó, László Somfai, Kálmán Strém, Miklós Szabolcsi, András Szőllősy, Tibor Tallián, József Ujfalussy, Iván Waldbauer, András Wilheim. My many conversations with György Kurtág and the late Charles Bruck were among my most inspiring experiences—I am thankful for their enthusiastic support. I am greatly indebted to those ethnomusicologists with whom I discussed problems of Hungarian folk music and gypsy music, among them Ferenc Sebő and, most important, Bálint Sárosi.

Some of the preparatory work included the study of archival material. I thank first the staff of the Bartók Archives for their support of my work at all stages, especially László Somfai, Adrienne Gombócz, Dorrit Révész, and László Vikárius. I am indebted to the staff of the Kodály Archive, especially János Kecskeméti, and to those of the Hungarian Academy of Sciences manuscript library as well as the New York Public Library. I wish to express my thanks to Peter Bartók, who was willing to send copies of Bartók's manuscripts whenever needed. I owe special thanks to my father, Dr. György Frigyesi, for assisting me in various ways in my research in Hungary, and to Pál Lővei of the National Board for the Protection of Historic Monuments for his expert advice and help in selecting and locating photographs of art and architecture.

Several of my trips to Hungary were supported by the University Committee on Research in the Humanities and Social Sciences, and by the travel fund of my Samuel Davies Presidential Preceptorship, both of Princeton University. My sabbatical leaves and the combined grant of the Joint Committee of the American Council of Learned Societies and Social Science Research Council allowed me to do research in Hungary and write parts of the draft.

The actual writing of this work was a solitary enterprise, in the course of which I discussed my ideas mostly with my students and often with nonmusician friends. The book's final form owes much to the criticism and suggestions of Mary Gluck, Elliott Antokoletz, László Somfai, and an anonymous reviewer for the press, who read the complete manuscript. Carl Schorske's criticism of the introduction and our discussions of various topics, and Robin Magowan's suggestions for style were of great help. I am greatly indebted to Péter Hanák and Miklós Szabolcsi for their support throughout the research and the writing of the book and their reading and, in the case of the latter, the careful and detailed comments on the manuscript.

I am grateful to Doris Kretschmer, at the University of California Press, for her encouragement since the inception of this project; Rose Vekony for her advice and control over the editing process; Edith Gladstone for her thorough reading and insightful editing of the manuscript; Rolf Wulfsberg for his excellent music setting; Barbara Roos for the preparation of the index; and Dr. Marianna Graf and Benjamin Laki for their help in correcting the proofs.

Many people helped me at the final stage of this project. I thank Gabriella Nyerges, Ida Kovács, and Csaba Gál of the Petőfi Museum of Literature as well as Zsuzsanna Turcsány and Zsuzsanna Farkas of the Hungarian National Gallery for their help in selecting and obtaining photographs.

As always, I am most grateful to my son, Benjamin Laki, for his inspiring suggestions and enthusiasm, and to my best friend and husband, Walter Feldman, who assisted me in my work on all levels with his insightful reading and good advice.

The examples from Bartók's First Concerto for Piano and Orchestra are based on the piano arrangement revised by Peter Bartók (Vienna: Universal Edition, 1992) and on the orchestral score, Philharmonia Partituren no. 463 (Universal Edition). The examples from *Duke Bluebeard's Castle* are based on the piano arrangement and the orchestral score of *A kékszakállú herceg vára* (Vienna: Universal Edition; New York: Boosey and Hawkes, 1963). The translations of all Hungarian poetry are my own.

Introduction

To most people outside Hungary, Béla Bartók is a lonely genius emerging from the gray background of an underdeveloped country whose capital, compared to the cultural centers of Western Europe, is at best second-rate. Hungary's language, its geographical position, and its lack of economic or strategic power, along with our own cultural orientation toward the territories of Romance and Germanic languages, all have kept other Hungarian artists out of the mainstream culture of Europe. Historians of European modernism deal exclusively with developments that occurred in cities in Western Europe and equate the culture of the Austro-Hungarian monarchy with that of Vienna. Consequently, Bartók is probably the only figure among the extensively studied composers of Western music who is not customarily looked on as part of an intellectual milieu. The reader interested in the intellectual trends current at the time and place of, say, Beethoven, Schumann, or Schoenberg can find substantial literature about their environment. But for similar information on Bartók's milieu we must turn to very specialized secondary sources and have no guidance as to how to create a coherent picture on the basis of this information.

The present book attempts to bridge these gaps. It addresses those who share my assumption that the turn of the century was a uniquely rich period of European history with ideas that touch on the problems we face in our lives. Taking up the intellectual milieu of Bartók and aspects of his music, the book complements cultural histories of the European mainstream modernism on the one hand and Bartók studies on the other. I focus on the question of why Bartók's music developed precisely in Budapest at this time by showing the developments that existed around his art and were connected with it.

I was led toward this topic very gradually, and the writing of the present book was a project that seemed to expand continuously. My original focus was Bartók's artistic development. I was intrigued by a sudden change in Bartók's artistic attitude that took hold some time around 1907 and remained, irrevocable, for the rest of his life. I was not surprised to find that a young musician from a partly puritan and partly nationalist bourgeois milieu became a political chauvinist and a somewhat conservative thinker when he arrived in the cosmopolitan, Jewish-German, "immoral" capital. But how did it happen, I asked, that within a few years' time the same person developed into a modernist artist? This change manifested itself in all spheres of Bartók's activities. In music, we see it clearly in the difference in style that separates the youthful compositions (such as the two suites and the Rhapsody op. 1) from the first pieces in the modern style (such as the *Fourteen Bagatelles* and *Duke Bluebeard's Castle*).

In musical studies of the twentieth century, the common great cultural heritage of Western Europe forms a primary unit of reference and so we would expect to relate such a development in a composer's style to Western European music. But in Bartók's case, coeval developments in German and French music do not explain some of the most significant aspects of his innovations. When I began to study Bartók's compositional decisions together with the emotional message intended by the piece, I increasingly felt that such decisions were not simply a matter of technique but reflected a particular worldview.

To demonstrate the connection between the style and the emotional "meaning" of these pieces, and of the products of Hungarian modernism in general, I recognized, I had to follow a very long road. Because Bartók's Hungarian cultural environment is not known to an international audience, I confronted the problem of having to produce at the same time a general and a more specific work: to show the link between a musical development and an intellectual tradition, and to base my argument on a general historical and cultural study. Furthermore, I needed a technique for approaching the cultural context to ascertain what the artist had intended to say. It is always difficult and sometimes foolhardy to reconstruct the purpose of an artist. But I found that Bartók's experiences and his artistic response to those experiences were not so different, after all, from those of his contemporaries.

SUBJECT AND METHODOLOGY

In turn-of-the-century Hungary, the attitude of the members of the radical circles was shaped by the difficult and controversial position of the intelligentsia within the society as a whole. The rapid and sudden development of a bourgeoisie in the modern sense and the emergence of a cosmopolitan capital were traumatic experiences that affected its life directly. At one time or another, all members of this generation found themselves opposing the ideas they had inherited from their parents, as well as the ideas they themselves had professed in their youthful years. The difficulty of their situation was aggravated by an anxiety over their national identity; they spent tremendous effort to assert their presence on the map of Europe as "Hungarians" while hoping to create a "truly European" society and culture.

It is difficult for our generation, which is both more skeptical and more disillusioned, to imagine the intensity of fights that characterized public life in turn-of-the-century Hungary. The historian Zoltán Horváth, who witnessed them, writes:

> In the middle of the 1930s, when under the pressure of the European events the Horthy regime clearly drifted toward fascism, it was officially encouraged to decry, slander, and stigmatize as criminals and traitors those creative minds—poets, writers, musicians, and scholars—who desperately fought for the democratization of Hungary at the turn of the century, and in part during the First World War. Theirs was a battle for the achievements of a never completely finished Hungarian bourgeois revolution against the defenders of a half-feudal society—in other words, against the big landowning nobility and the immeasurably wealthy clergy. If we consider that the fight against such powerful enemies arose in the years of impending crisis of the Austro-Hungarian monarchy, then we can perhaps imagine what heroic determination filled the hearts of those people who faced this fight. . . . [The generations born after the Second World War] do not and cannot know what the activity of these people meant to us. They don't know our excitement at the publication of a new poem by [Endre] Ady. . . . They did not live through the rebirth of Hungarian music, accompanied by storms coming to real disturbances at the performance of a new piece by Bartók. They don't know how it became the Word in the mouth of some intellectuals and how it led to the belief of the most radical of the masses that there should come a new, more genuinely true and free life in Hungary.[1]

Horváth describes the dramatic polarization of public life. In this polarization, on the one side stood the aristocracy and the middle nobility, who determined the country's politics and manipulated the majority to cooperate in the preservation of the half-feudal, backwards economic and social system. On the other side were these radical segments of the society, who found their ideological leaders in a handful of intellectuals, among whom a poet, Endre Ady, and a composer, Béla Bartók, were in the forefront. These radical segments gradually formed an alliance; they became somewhat a society within the society having their own subculture but still affecting the public consciousness of the country as a whole. In Hungarian cultural history, the group is referred to alternately as the "second reform generation," "the radicals," or "the modernists." In this book the terms "modernism" and "modernists" serve not as an evaluation or normative projection, but simply as labels for this specific intellectual tradition in postromantic Hungarian culture.

In a society as complex as that of turn-of-the-century Budapest, each sector within the society, or even each person, had a degree of cultural self-sufficiency. Horváth looks at Hungarian life from the angle of the radical intelligentsia. But in the approximately two decades preceding the fall of the Austro-Hungarian monarchy the traditional magnate aristocracy still flourished. Furthermore, the social climate allowed for the existence of a wealthy stratum within the middle class that was able to live without financial difficulties. If we leave aside the modernist movement, we can depict the story of Budapest at the turn of the century very differently. The city becomes a dream world of the happy middle class, whose members frequent cafés, balls, and operettas, listen to gypsy music at restaurants, watch the ladies dressed according to the new fashion of Paris or Vienna as they walk along the Korzó on the bank of the Danube, and spend the summer at the Adriatic Sea in Istria or in Italy. This happy life of Budapest (which is the focus of John Lukács's recently published book, *Budapest 1900*) is also a historical reality. It is true just as much as is our image of happy fin-de-siècle Vienna, with its inhabitants dancing to the waltzes of Johann Strauss and indulging in elegance. And just as this Austria was the land of *Kakania* for Robert Musil, this Hungary was the "fallow land" for the Hungarian poet Endre Ady.[2] For both, such a carefree life was absurd—it indicated the self-deception of a generation who remained indifferent to social reality.

What interested me most in the course of assembling material for this book was the formation of a group of intellectuals who could not accept the image of "happy Budapest." Rather than recount their accomplishments, I felt compelled to probe the motivation behind their activities and explain their frustrations, struggles, ideals, and beliefs. I wanted to see the world that surrounded them somewhat through their eyes.

As a result, the picture I present here is not a comprehensive treatment of Hungarian modernism. I ignore the cultural and intellectual life of the Hungarian provinces (even of such important centers as Nagyvárad [today Oradea, Romania]), the fascinating, original, and by any standard outstanding achievements of the visual arts and architecture, the developments in history, oriental studies, sociology, folklore, psychology, philosophy, theater, the sciences, and the entire domain of popular culture. The focus of this book is on music, literature, and aesthetics. In music I deal exclusively with the formation of Bartók's modern style and aesthetics, leaving aside the development of other modern composers, even of such prominent figures as Zoltán Kodály and Leó Weiner. In literature I focus on Ady, and to a lesser extent on Béla Balázs, placing some other major poets in the background and discussing developments in prose, journalism, and theater only in passing. In aesthetics the focus is on György Lukács's early theories and a few additional texts that complement them.

Besides Bartók's music, poetry was an obvious choice for my primary text of art to represent Hungarian modernism. From the middle of the nineteenth century to the present, poetry has played a uniquely important role in Hungarian public life; its importance cannot be compared to the role that any of the arts plays in the United States, or in other countries of the West. In the United States poetry is considered a matter of choice; many cultured people prefer nonfiction to fiction or prose to poetry, and lack of interest in poems would make no one an outcast in intellectual circles. In Hungary the opposite is the case. Poetry has been an ingredient of national self-identification, and familiarity with Hungarian poets is by no means optional for someone raised in that environment. In Bartók's time, as today, it was virtually unimaginable that an intellectual would not read (and enjoy) the poetry of Ady and of Sándor Petőfi, János Arany, Mihály Vörösmarty, Mihály Babits, Dezső Kosztolányi, and, later, Attila József.

There is another reason for my focus on poetry. As the quote by Horváth suggests, Hungarian public life at the beginning of the century had two main actors in the camp of the radicals: Ady and Bartók. Thus it is natural to present the story of Hungarian modernism as having not one main character but also another who is only slightly less significant than the first. This arrangement is a compromise between the historical reality—since Ady's role in the creation of Hungarian modernism equaled or perhaps surpassed Bartók's—and the needs of the readers of this book, to whom, understandably, Bartók's art is more important. Consequently, the central part of this book forms twin chapters, providing an analysis of the aesthetics of Bartók and Ady.

The time period covered in this book is essentially the first decade of the century, although I will point out, in each case, whether and in what way an idea remained significant for the following generations. The formation of modernist circles and the polarization of public life took place during the approximately one and a half decades that preceded the First World War. The war had a devastating effect on Hungarian social life and thinking; by its end several great figures of the first generation of the modernists had emigrated, and Ady died in 1919. The situation of the middle class and the political climate had changed significantly, and these changes influenced intellectual and artistic life. Nevertheless, it was the ideological opposition of the turn of the century that set the stage for the various developments in politics and culture.

The ideas of the radicals of the beginning of the century did not disappear but rather became integrated into new ideologies, permeating Hungarian thought throughout the twentieth century, even up to our time.

This book is in no sense a biographical account of the personal or intellectual development of Bartók, nor is it an attempt to explain the system of his modern style. It is devoted to five subjects: Bartók's aesthetics and its formation in the years between 1907 and 1911; the connection between this aesthetics and that of Endre Ady's poetry; the historical background, problems, and aspirations of the bourgeois segments of Budapest; the Hungarian modernists' ideals and artistic achievements; and finally, the attitude of the modernists to questions of existence. In all these topics, it centers on one specific question that will serve to establish the relation between Bartók's oeuvre and the ideas of the Hungarian modernists.

This question, which is spelled out most clearly in the first and fourth chapters, relates to the increasingly problematic relations of society and art and amounts, aesthetically speaking, to the issue of coherence. Is it still possible, this generation of Hungarian artists asked, to create coherent artwork in a world that is no longer whole? The realization of the "lack of wholeness" of social life made them question whether the very demand for coherence was relevant, and by questioning the validity of coherence in art they believed that they had challenged the possibility of art per se. All prominent members of this generation were preoccupied with this question and, in one way or another, created their aesthetics and ideologies in response to it.

Since I formulate my argument as one of tension between social reality and cultural ideals, their relation shows more clearly in differences and incongruities than in a simple paradigm. Consequently, I take as my context the dynamic and complex set of cultural practices that Bartók both shares with his contemporaries and shapes in significant ways. The parallel treatment of different topics in separate chapters—such as the aesthetics of Bartók and Ady, the literary background and musical structure of *Duke Bluebeard's Castle*—reflects my assumption that when different facets of life are considered in their own right, each as a coherent whole, they appear as reflections of each other, presenting varying combinations and projections of the same set of problems.

BARTÓK AND THE CULTURAL ENVIRONMENT

It would seem at first glance quite unnecessary to suppose that the environment had any direct contribution to the development of a man like Bartók, who became notorious for his individualism and whose style is highly personal. The story of Bartók's life during and after the First World War is basically the history of his disillusionment with society, with the intelligentsia, and with literature. Already years before the beginning of the war, he had moved to the outskirts of Budapest and limited his social encounters to a minimum. And it appears that, after his encounter with the poetry of Ady and the writings of Nietzsche during the first decade of the century, Bartók never again had a comparably significant literary experience.

Yet Bartók's isolation was by no means absolute. He continued to visit the Kodálys; he lived for some time in the house of the Lukács family; he participated in cultural events of literary circles and accepted invitations from friends.[3] Although the enthusiasm with which he was looking for company in his youthful years had disappeared, he continued to have a fair amount of contact with members of the modernist circles throughout his life in Budapest. And, like everyone else in this milieu, he had a huge library that he had built up gradually over the years. Besides his collection of musical scores, anthologies of folk music, and studies of music history, folk music, folklore, languages, and linguistics, he owned whatever works were considered the "classics" at the time. They included ancient Greek literature, French classical drama, romantic and modern novels, German literature, and a series of the Hungarian classics and works by modern writers, as well as the leading Hungarian literary journals. The marginal notes in his books and his references to readings in letters indicate that he actually read many of the works he owned, but often superficially; in the case of foreign-language books, usually for the sake of learning the language.

It is all the more interesting that during the interwar period, when we see Bartók retreating into his self-imposed "exile," he appears, nevertheless, to have been aware of the Hungarian political and cultural developments. He consistently allied himself with the circles whose ideals came closest to those of the radicals before the war (that is, with the literary circles that formed around the journals *Nyugat* [West], *Szép Szó* [Beautiful word], and *Ma* [Today]) and not with the mildly right-wing and somewhat racist "village-movement." Bartók made this choice in spite of the fact that his interest in peasant culture would naturally link him with circles focusing on the life of the countryside, and that he had seemingly little in common with the largely Jewish, urban-oriented, left-wing group of these literary journals. This attitude indicates not only that in Bartók's decisions the moral aspect took precedence but also that he was keenly aware of what was going on in Hungarian public life.

The relative social isolation and lack of enthusiasm toward new literary developments in his mature years, together with his continued leading position among the modernists, present a paradox that needs some explanation. If Bartók was uninterested in philosophy and literature, how could Nietzsche and Ady influence him so deeply in his early years and how could he respond so well to the poetry of Balázs? And if he was alienated from the social circles, how could he be aware of the current ideological and artistic trends, and why did he take sides?

Bartók's attitude should not be interpreted as a sign of indifference toward or incapacity to deal with intellectual issues. But unlike most people in his environment, Bartók was not particularly talented in debates. He always felt somewhat a stranger in intellectual circles, and similarly, the members of these circles often saw in him something like an unintellectual genius, a "big child." He gradually became accustomed to this situation and created a worldview and lifestyle in which his struggle with words gained a deeper meaning. His attitude rested on the assumption that there was a sharp dividing line between the understanding of an essence and its verbal-intellectual analysis. What probably irritated him most in the encounters of his intellectual friends was that their debates tried to analyze fundamental ideas that he felt were beyond explanation. This attitude defined his relationship to literature too. Whenever he felt that a work was able to express something essential, which was the case with writings by Nietzsche and Ady, he proved extremely quick in distilling the essence. It was precisely this quickness of mind that made it difficult for him to read a lot of literature attentively; he had no interest in variant elaborations of an idea that he believed he had already understood. He soon became bored with the writings of Balázs and read very little even of the works of Nietzsche. Ady was perhaps the only literary figure to whose works Bartók returned again and again.

This attitude in no way means that Bartók was incapable of dealing with abstract ideas: it was rather that he did not trust language to express the most important things in life. Nor does it suggest a belief that language cannot express anything at all; the existence of a large body of Bartók's writings obviously contradicts this supposition. Only things of the greatest significance were inexpressible. Bartók, like many other artists of the twentieth century, went through a crisis that made him question whether language was at all capable of expressing anything of the meaning of life. Bartók's situation is unique only in that he did not need to resolve this problem within the domain of language. His solution was simply to abandon language and concentrate on music as the sole medium for the expression of universal thoughts and great feelings.

However, between 1899 and 1909, that is, during the first decade of his life in Budapest, when his thoughts about language might have crystallized, Bartók was a very different person. He spent long afternoons with friends, especially with Emma Gruber and Kodály. He wrote detailed letters about his ideas and emotions and immersed himself in everything that seemed new and touched him emotionally. This period of intense involvement with all spheres of culture and social life coincided exactly with the decade when Hungarian modernism emerged. With the outbreak of the First World War, the intellectual life of Budapest began to decline, and the interwar period brought cultural developments that were less interesting for Bartók. By 1914 or perhaps even earlier, he no longer needed new artistic and philosophical impulses to resolve questions of life and art. He essentially resolved those issues that disturbed him at the beginning of his career—the meaning of art, the connection of art to life, the meaning of inspiration, the relation between technique and artistic essence, the Hungarianness of modern art.

Paradoxically, it is precisely Bartók's relative distance from intellectual life after the war that allowed him to remain—almost alone among the artists active at the turn of the century—the spiritual leader of the modernist circles throughout the first half of the twentieth century. His intense involvement with modernist ideas at the beginning of the century and his relative alienation from the following developments did not prevent him from orienting himself in the intellectual milieu of the interwar period but rather made that orientation easier. The new problems that disturbed the younger generation were not immediately important for Bartók. He was sensitive to the new situation only inasmuch as it related to the ideology he had already developed. Thus he was able to project an ideal that the younger generation found much harder to believe in. The ideas of the turn of the century are sometimes more transparent in pieces composed after 1926 than in the earlier ones: in the politically tense environment of the 1930s, Bartók felt the need to emphasize even more clearly the moral ideals of his youth.

THE IMPACT OF BARTÓK AND ADY ON HUNGARIAN MODERNISM

The change in Bartók's style took place exactly in those years when the first modernist developments occurred in the other spheres of Hungarian cultural life and at a time when his social encounters and literary experiences were the most intense. That there had to be a connection between his stylistic innovations and Hungarian modernism is hardly questionable. We cannot know exactly where and from whom Bartók heard a particular idea, for in the milieu of turn-of-the-century intellectual life in Hungary, the same problems and ideas recur again and again; the same questions are asked, and the same principles are stated by people who have little in common in their professional enterprises. Such echoes and refrains are hardly surprising, considering that in Hungary, as in Vienna, modern theories and works of art were the concern of people who used to meet and argue and who were familiar with one another's ideas. Bartók, Kodály, and Gruber met regularly two or three times a week for a number of years. We do not know what they discussed, just as we cannot reconstruct the conversations and debates among intellectuals that took place daily in cafés, at the homes of friends, during excursions, or after concerts. Because of the complex relation of interacting and overlapping circles, people were aware of the lives and concerns of many others they knew only casually. Ideas were generated by multiple and reciprocal influences.

In turn-of-the-century Budapest, intellectuals formed their ideologies without feeling the need to sort out their influences according to separate academic enterprises or learn established methods in fields other than their own. Not that such methods did not exist, but the products of various fields were thought to be part of an intellectual milieu within which they circulated freely. There was nothing unusual in Bartók's picking up Nietzsche without ever studying philosophy, and it was also not surprising that Nietzsche had a greater influence on him than did most musical works composed at the time in Hungary.

As long as we attempt to explain Bartók's innovations merely from within the study of music, some of the most striking aspects of his art remain inexplicable. We will not be able to deal with problems such as Bartók's insistence on the use of a dance-like, optimistic finale, his lack of interest in topics relating to the life of peasants in all his dramatic pieces (which had peasant music at their source), his tendency for expressing extreme emotional contrasts within a monothematic design. We will be equally perplexed by patterns of Hungarian art in general. Without considering spheres of life outside the arts we cannot explain why Ady's love poetry was regarded as a political act, why the names of Ady and Bartók were grouped together to symbolize social development and democracy, and why their figures were, then, associated with the nineteenth-century romantic aristocrat and politician István Széchenyi.

Was it merely a coincidence that Ady's first volumes of poems, Bartók's and Kodály's discovery of old-style folk music and their first pieces in the modern style, Lukács's first significant essays on aesthetics, Tivadar Kosztka Csontváry's revolutionary paintings, Ödön Lechner's modern architecture influenced by folk art, the establishment of the revolutionary literary journal *Nyugat,* and many other modernist endeavors all occupied their creators within a few years in the first decade of the twentieth century? Could it be only an accident that both Lukács (who was not interested in Hungarian poetry) and Bartók (who was not interested in poetry at all) were deeply moved by the poems of Ady and considered them to be among their greatest literary experiences? Is it likely that Nietzsche would have a decisive influence on people so different as Ady, Lukács, Bartók, and Balázs if it were not for a common intellectual milieu? Is it merely a superficial similarity that Lechner envisioned the use of folk motives in architecture in a manner similar to Bartók's use of folk song in music? And is it an insignificant biographical fact that, during his university years, Kodály was Béla Balázs's best friend (sharing a dormitory room with him), that Balázs became part of the Lukács circle, and that Bartók chose Balázs's text for his opera and ballet? Is it without any significance that Bartók dedicated one of his works to Béla Reinitz, a composer of cabaret songs based on the poems of Ady?

Bartók's choice of the poems of Ady for the text of his *Five Songs* op. 16, and his tribute to Reinitz, may seem to be an episode in the life of a composer devoted to "abstract music," until we find Bartók marking with red pencil many poems of Ady in his volumes and find his confession that "it is as if these poems had sprung from me—yes, were I not destined for music but for poetry, I would have written these poems."[4] It seems inexplicable to us today that Bartók was more enthusiastic in his praise for Ady than he was for most composers of his time. We encounter similar paradoxes in Bartók's writings about music. Most of these writings treat exclusively technical aspects of music, such as scales, rhythm, and form. But in a few letters and in some writings about modern music, Bartók appears before our eyes as a passionate person whose utmost concern is to convey feeling through music: "I cannot imagine that an artwork could be anything but the manifestation of the infinite enthusiasm, despair, sorrow, vengeful anger, distorting and sarcastic irony of its creator."[5] Given the romantic tone and the infrequency in Bartók's writings of such statements, they are usually regarded as peripheral. But should we exclude from the outset the possibility that such remarks had an integral connection with Bartók's art as a whole?

If all that Bartók left behind is taken into account, he appears not as an abstract musician whose art can easily be purified of cultural "background," but as a person who confronted the problems of a specific place and time. In the process of cleansing this art from all that connects it to its geographical location, we might easily impose on him an abstract expectation that reflects less the concerns of Bartók than the methods of today's scholarship. We arrive at a different image of Bartók if we take two factors into account. First, we have to consider seriously those comments that may sound "romantic" to our ears and do not fit with our image of a "modern composer." Second, we have to direct our attention toward his youthful years, during which his ideas developed and he struggled intensely with broad questions. We have to ask what problems Bartók faced and how he attempted to solve them before he began to develop his new musical language.

In explaining Bartók's art, we find three approaches: the English-language analysis, the Hungarian-language scholarship, and a view of Bartók common to the Hungarian intelligentsia. To English, American, and Australian scholarship Bartók is primarily interesting for his musical systems (particularly for his tonal systems); the study of Bartók's music in these countries is typically the task of analysts. The "Hungarian school" takes a different approach, focusing rather on Bartók's musical sources and on the compositional process. Of course, there are works written on Bartók in other countries and also studies in English and Hungarian that do not belong to these categories, but it is certain that these prominent trends define the character of the Bartók scholarship today.

But another tradition takes a very different view. This tradition goes back to the time when Bartók first appeared on the stage of Hungarian cultural life and remains the common view among Hungarian intellectuals. These intellectuals may be quite ignorant of the technical aspects of music and may not understand Bartók's musical innovations very well, let alone the complexities of his tonal systems. To these people Bartók is not merely a great composer. His oeuvre and personality signify much more: they are the symbol of political radicalism, of modern, democratic, "European" Hungary. And it is certain that if Bartók regarded himself as a national composer at all he did it also only in this sense—as being the representative of Hungarian social and artistic radicalism.

We are confronted thus with contrasting views about what constitutes the most significant innovation of Bartók's art. My assumption that there was a coherent and complex aesthetic view at the background of Bartók's compositional decisions and that this view was developed in connection with Hungarian modernism is new only in the domain of musicological studies. The Hungarian public of Bartók's music has never called into question the existence of such a connection. In Hungary, it is common to refer to the modernist culture of the beginning of the twentieth century as the era of Bartók and Ady. In the Hungarian political arena today, statements such as "We represent truly the ideals of Ady and Bartók" or "We act in the spirit of Ady and Bartók" are part of everyday discourse. It may be that such statements do more harm than good to political life and culture because they tacitly assume that art is capable of defining political objectives. But it is clear that the "Ady and Bartók" stereotype reflects an unquestioned belief on the part of Hungarian society about the meaning of the art of these artists. Yet despite the symbol's persistence there has been no study in Hungary or elsewhere addressing the problem of exactly how the works of these figures embody that content with which they are associated and why their art is grouped together at all. This study is the first attempt to discuss the artistic world of Ady and Bartók together and to superpose our discussion on current theories in aesthetics and on social and cultural history.

Nothing in this book casts doubt on the importance of any aspects of the prevailing scholarship. On the contrary: once we restore the context of Bartók's art and understand his preoccupations with art and morality, the significance of the existing studies becomes all the more apparent. But I believe that one consistent personality created abstract post-tonal music and aimed at expressing "spirit" and "feeling," and that we can understand each side only if we take both into account. In fact, we will understand that, for Bartók, a compositional idea was just as much a matter of "faith" as a technical musical invention.

FOCUS AND ORGANIZATION

A few explanatory remarks are relevant here. The fact that this book treats only the relation between Hungarian and German-Austrian culture should not be taken as a claim that artistic trends of other countries had no influence on modern Hungarian art. I choose to focus on this comparison because it shows most clearly the particular characteristics of Hungarian aesthetics. However, in general, the purpose of this book is not to situate Hungarian art in the European milieu but rather to explore the interrelations among the various cultural spheres within the country.

The discussion of the cultural climate of Vienna and the theories of Schoenberg and Webern in the first chapter, the interpretation of the aesthetics of Balázs and Lukács throughout the book, and the chapters on Hungarian social history are not intended as formal summaries of these historical situations or of theoretical and artistic oeuvres. Instead, they emphasize key issues that make my argument more intelligible. For summaries, the reader should turn to more specialized studies, for instance, Carl Schorske's *Fin-de-Siècle Vienna*, Janik and Toulmin's *Wittgenstein's Vienna*, or Mary Gluck's excellent work on Lukács's Sunday circle—books whose authors I am greatly indebted to for the inspiring and novel methods of their approach.

The sections on Ady and Bartók are quite another matter. Hitherto, scholarly studies of Bartók focused chiefly on issues entirely different from the topic of this book. My discussion does not in any way contradict the existing studies but expands their findings and combines them with an aesthetic interpretation. The case with the chapter on Ady is again different. The literature on Ady in English is minimal, and he is far from being extensively studied by modern scholars in Hungary either. In spite of the enormous weight Ady's name carries for Hungarian speakers everywhere, and in spite of the popularity of his poems, there has been no comprehensive study of his art since István Király's basic book of the 1970s. Ady's symbolism has not yet been treated for its philosophical and mystical implications, nor have these aspects been connected to the Hungarian intellectual tradition.

The first part of the book is devoted to the social, political, cultural, and conceptual framework of modernism: the first chapter is an introduction to the aesthetic context, the second describes the historical and social background, the third the modernist milieu, and the fourth the aesthetics of Hungarian modernism. The historical and social context, discussed in the second and third chapters, helps us explain the tension between the two opposing views of the modernists—their conception of life as something no longer coherent and their demand, nevertheless, for coherence. My aim is to show, first, that this contradiction was indeed a crucial one for Hungarian modernism and, second, that it meant something specific in the Hungarian context. If my findings are correct, in Budapest as in Vienna, the character of modern art at the beginning of the twentieth century was basically defined by concepts inherited from romanticism. Relying on the same artistic and conceptual tradition, the artists of both cities used the same rhetoric and even the same words but often meant radically different things.

The differences between the Hungarian and the Viennese modernists' conceptions of organicism, however, merit careful discussion, and the conclusion of this discussion appears only in the fourth chapter. To explain why a different interpretation developed in Hungary and how the modernist movement became implicated in social forces, the second and third chapters describe the social and cultural situation and the activities of the intelligentsia in Hungary: the second treats the historical background and the social situation of the middle class in general, while the third focuses on the development of the modernists' circles in particular. The subject of the fourth chapter is the basic notions of Hungarian aesthetics. This chapter discusses Bartók's ideas about organicism and folk music, the modernists' attitude toward "realism," and the concept of "the original facts."

The second part of the book forms two distinct parts, each containing two chapters. The central argument of the book appears in chapter 5. After discussing the basic principles of Bartók's aesthetics, this chapter analyzes the First Piano Concerto, which serves here as a case study of what Bartók attempted to achieve in his mature compositions. The analysis brings into sharper focus the question of how Bartók's compositional decisions express aesthetic principles he stated in his writings. The chapter turns then to Bartók's early writings (mostly hitherto unpublished in English) and to the writings of Balázs, Kodály, and Lukács. Most of these writings date from the first decade of the twentieth century and represent the period when these individuals were in the process of developing their ideologies. My assumption is that the conclusions Bartók and his contemporaries arrived at during these years were decisive for their entire careers. This is particularly true in the case of Bartók (and much less so in the case of others, especially Lukács). Readers might wonder at an attempt to explain the aesthetic beliefs underlying a composer's works by using his writings that date from years earlier. Yet Bartók's later writings—although they are infrequent and much less elaborate—are always in accordance with these earlier views, and the early discussions appear to deal directly with those issues that constitute the conceptual basis of the mature forms. The sixth chapter is a somewhat similar discussion of Ady's poetry, based on poems selected from three of his volumes. My focus is on Ady's symbolism, which I consider a primary example of the modernist philosophy that regarded the world as whole and also as a place of infinite tensions.

The last two chapters take a different approach by centering on one piece, Bartók's *Bluebeard's Castle*, as a key work of the period. Having presented in the previous chapters the main conceptual ideas of the aesthetics of Hungarian modernism, I attempt to show the connection of this aesthetics to a worldview, and to decisions about style, by focusing on the conceptual background of the dramatic concept of the piece in the seventh chapter, and on Bartók's stylistic innovations in the last chapter. The focus on the poetic idea of one piece may seem to limit the scope of discussion, but in this particular case it rather opens it up toward general issues. What the seventh chapter offers is not merely the interpretation of a work but rather the overview of varying social and artistic ideas that were in the background of this work and give us the means to understand it.

The final chapter is devoted to the musical style of *Bluebeard's Castle*. This chapter, again, is not intended to be an analysis in the conventional sense. The main issue here is to locate important aspects of Bartók's new style and to define their origins. If my supposition is correct, Bartók was inspired to develop his new style partly by his experiences with folk music and knowledge of traditional Hungarian popular and art music, and partly by his work with the conceptual ideas embedded in the dramaturgy of the play. This chapter is not meant to be a conclusion; Bartók's aesthetic ideas are outlined in a more general manner at the end of the fifth chapter. Whereas that chapter could be considered the basic treatment of Bartók's aesthetics, this last chapter answers the question of how Bartók arrived at that aesthetics. Accordingly, the fifth chapter considers a piece that is typical of the mature Bartók, while the eighth chapter deals with a piece that is in many ways exceptional, being the pivotal work in the development of Bartók's modern art.

In the course of writing this book, as I struggled to discover how poetry, music, and aesthetic writings reflect the same essence (as their creators believed), I gradually came to revise my ideas on the connection between art and "intellectual background." It became clear that many aspects of life unrelated to the creative process and even without direct influence on the artist could still assume an important role in his art. It became equally clear that the coherent and somewhat independent world that scholarship reconstructs as the intellectual context of an art is still not as general and comprehensive as what is usually found in cultural histories that do not focus on any one individual. The world *around* an artist is something in between the general cultural milieu and his immediate intellectual environment or influences. The fact that, in writing about Bartók, I had to provide a coherent picture of a milieu while treating his musical style forced me to write an unusual work that stands between musicology, cultural history, aesthetics, and literary criticism. But perhaps this problem is not unique to Bartók, and if this method were tried in the case of other composers, it could make their aspirations and ideals more understandable. It may be that after all we do not know, in the case of several composers, how to define the "intellectual milieu" that had bearing on their art; a milieu that was broader than their immediate experiences but more specific than the totality of the surrounding culture. Perhaps the real service of this work will be to provoke a better method to deal with the connection of different facets of life within the same environment.

PART I

History and Aesthetics

CHAPTER I

Organic Artwork or Communal Style?

Common Problems, Common Tradition, and the Viennese Response

MODERNISM OUTSIDE THE MAINSTREAM

Throughout the nineteenth and the twentieth centuries, three interrelated elements informed the process of intellectual and cultural change: an awareness of the disappearance of order, a renewed commitment to an ideal of coherence, and a search for self-identity. Within the social world of Western civilization, a perception of disorder and incongruity dates back to the Enlightenment, the first moment in Western history when the intellectual elite looked at their own social and cultural heritage with skepticism and searched for models outside its boundaries. The best known literary reflections of this attitude—which shifted the intellectual balance of the Western world—are the works of Montesquieu, Rousseau, and Voltaire. Within philosophy and the arts, the new awareness changed the social meaning of art and intellectual thought, and the relations between the individual and society.

Recognizing that social and individual life was no longer just and coherent and ordered, nineteenth- and twentieth-century thinkers felt it necessary in the same gesture to reject the old values and to search for a level of cohesiveness in life that was believed to characterize primitive societies and those of the past. Their explorations led to vast new considerations of what life and art might mean. But within the renewed attempts at modernism throughout these centuries, one impetus remained constant: awareness of the disintegration of order. Even though ideological attitudes and artistic styles differed greatly in various periods and local cultures, intellectual and cultural movements shared basic concerns and also basic responses to these concerns. For instance, what is "classical" in the works of Beethoven, Schubert, Brahms, and even Bartók is a matter not only of convention but of a determining common orientation toward art and life.

Because of shared orientations and problems, the new and the traditional, the local and the "mainstream" are often difficult to untangle. To judge by first appearance alone, we could explain almost any artistic development that took place in Europe during the first half of the twentieth century either as romantic or modern, as mainstream or peripheral, depending on which characteristics we took into account and how we interpreted them historically. We might argue, as several cultural historians do, that modernism began at the turn of the century with such radical changes as the introduction of abstract representation in the visual arts or the near disappearance of tonality in music.[1] Equally plausibly, we could argue that these developments, however original they may seem in terms of their structure, only intensified the romantic ideal that the artwork grows from the artist's passionate empathy with other human beings. Viewed in this way, then, modernism really started with the "new objectivity" of the period between the wars, with neorealism in the visual arts and neoclassicism in music. But we could also argue that neoclassicism was yet another effort to posit an ideal of order by separating art from the anxiety of modern life and turning to classicism, that is, to an order that was emphatically of the past. This trend, then, was not the beginning of modernism but part of the series of modernist endeavors in the first half of the century that preceded and overlapped the avant-garde tendencies of the 1950s and 1960s—yet another beginning. Moreover, even all these trends together do not describe the complex web of cultural developments in twentieth-century Europe: none of these developments affected all the artists and all the cultural spheres, and they were always part of other, sometimes contradictory, intellectual and artistic processes.

The presence of an underlying sociocultural problem together with the lack of an identifiable mainstream in European modernism is especially important to keep in mind when we deal with a cultural region that has been thought of as marginal. If we measure a particular cultural development against an imaginary yardstick of modernism, it becomes a matter of interpretation how and why we judge an artwork modern or conservative. For instance, if we take the atonal tendencies of Viennese composers or French neoclassicism, or both, as the mainstream of modernist developments and decide that folklorism was romantic—a common assumption of music histories—the historical place of Bartók's oeuvre becomes problematic. A superficial acquaintance with Bartók's work might give the impression that his interest in folk music was the continuation of romantic ideology and aesthetics. If we accept this view, his main achievement would lie in the creation of a truly modern and integral style without regard to nationalism; and this is, in fact, a common interpretation of Bartók's art. Alternatively, we could interpret folklorism as a variant of the expressionist movement's interest in primitivism. And if we look at folk music in this way—that is, as some original and primitive material—then folklorism becomes the expression of the Nietzschean demand to create art on the basis of the simple truth of the objective life. In this latter interpretation, folklorism is part of a common German-Austrian trend of modernism.

All these explanations may be relevant to some degree. But in reality the romantic and modernist tendencies offered artists an extraordinary range and freedom for ideology and musical style alike. Composers of the twentieth century not only were free to decide what would influence them but could entirely reinterpret a source, using it for a new purpose. For instance, Bartók selected the folk-music sources of his Hungarian national music in such a manner that his folklorism could not be used to support the nationalism of the political establishment; on the contrary, it undermined the basic tenets of contemporary nationalist ideology. For instance, consider the fact that he used Romanian, Slovakian, and Arabic music in pieces that he thought of as examples of Hungarian art music. Such a choice is difficult to appreciate without awareness of the political and cultural atmosphere of his immediate environment. But even those choices that seem to coincide with developments elsewhere are easier to understand if we observe them from the perspective of local tradition. Composers develop a style primarily from personal musical experiences drawn from the culture of their environment. Even artistic choices that appear similar to ones found in other cultures might be the result of an independent development determined by an immediate cultural and personal necessity. What influences artists is less some generic romantic or modern tradition than a concrete and unique cultural environment with which they are intimately familiar; it is the background against which they work. To create a new style on that basis or even to sustain an existing one is an artistic achievement regardless of whether it appears modern or conservative to us.

Attempting to locate Hungarian modernist art within a European modernism of the first half of the twentieth century is an unusually difficult task. The sources of Hungarian modernism were in part the same as those of Viennese modern art, and in several respects the social milieu was similar. But its aesthetics, its message, and its social function were radically different. The similarities were not simply influences from the mainstream, and the differences went beyond marginal local developments.

The crucial difference is often presented through the antagonism between the serialists and the folklorists—a rather artificial debate that, nevertheless, explains a lot about the differences between these two cultures. This debate was not really about folklorism but about a much deeper problem, namely the (real or imagined) contradiction between the truthfulness and the communal function of art. Arnold Schoenberg's rejection of folklorism illustrates a general attitude prevalent throughout most of our century.[2] Like Schoenberg, many composers and theorists saw art music and folk music as basically incompatible, and the merging of these styles as a serious problem that could not be conceptually resolved.

Bartók's oeuvre presented a challenge to this view. The harmonic and tonal integrity of Bartók's pieces, together with his emphatic use of folk music, carried implications that could not be explained in the context of German music aesthetics. For many, the greatness of Bartók's music contradicted the fact that he incorporated folk music into his compositions. In Theodor Adorno's eyes, Bartók's compositional achievement depended largely on his power to suppress his "nationalist instinct." In writing about the Third String Quartet, Adorno praised Bartók for his boldness in breaking the series of "folkloristic types" of the previous pieces and returning to his "true self."[3] The idea that the use of folk music is impossible in a true (that is, fully coherent) artwork remained unchallenged throughout the 1950s and 1960s and saturates discussions of modernism even in our time. In his essay "Nationalism and Music" Carl Dahlhaus concluded that the use of folk music in art music was a technique "no different in principle from the exoticism or historicism of the nineteenth century," and that both folklorism and exoticism were a "process of gathering heterogeneous material from exotic sources and incorporating it into the here and now in art."[4]

Why was the merger of folk music and art music so problematic for Schoenberg and Dahlhaus, and why was it so self-evident and natural for Bartók? We need not probe the political overtones of this debate, or its sociopolitical implications. What is important, however, is the conceptual difference between the Schoenbergian and the Bartókian interpretations of stylistic unity. By exploring it we may articulate the fundamental difference between the modernist conception of art in Vienna and that in Budapest. This subject is even more intriguing if we consider that Hungarian modern art was deeply rooted in the same philosophical tradition as the art of Schoenberg, a tradition that laid much emphasis on the integrity of style. Stylistic coherence was a focal point in Bartók's conception of art, and he used every opportunity to emphasize it in his writings: "[In our original compositions] neither peasant melodies nor imitations of peasant melodies can be found. . . . [In this case, the composer] has completely absorbed the idiom of peasant music which has become his mother tongue. He masters it as completely as a poet masters his mother tongue."[5]

Bartók's rhetoric suggests that he was familiar with the aesthetic problems folklorism raised. Folklorism is suspect; it involves the use of preexistent sources—therefore the composer relies on something readily available in place of invention. And the superficial nature of folklorism is nowhere more apparent than in the adapting of melodic turns. No doubt this chain of thought was familiar to Bartók. He wanted to guard himself against such criticism and hastened to assert that his folklorism was something other than the use of melodic fragments.

Schoenberg's dismissal of virtually all non-German music—"It seems that nations which have not yet acquired a place in the sun will have to wait until it pleases the Almighty to plant a musical genius in their midst"—sounds to our ears unbearably arrogant, resonating from the self-confidence and snobbery of a mainstream composer.[6] But Bartók was no less severe with the "folklorists" and was critical of the manner in which most nineteenth-century composers used folk music. Like Schoenberg, he condemned the empty display of folk characteristics at the expense of artistic integrity. He refused to accept the music of Ferenc Erkel, and even of Franz Liszt, as Hungarian art music because he maintained that the heterogeneous combination of elements found in their pieces not only failed to produce great music but also hindered the development of a national style.[7]

By devoting this discussion to the subject of coherence as it was understood by the German romantics and revitalized by Schoenberg and Webern, I do not want to suggest that this issue alone explains Viennese modernism. Viennese social and cultural life at the turn of the century was rich and extremely complex, with much interaction among the arts, social studies, and sciences, and it would be a great simplification to point to any ideology as being the determinant one.

In order to explore the character of Hungarian modernism, it is necessary to deal with its Viennese counterpart in depth for several reasons. First, the aesthetic demand for coherence affected all Hungarian artists throughout the first half of the twentieth century and even in the decades that followed. Second, it is in the conceptualization of coherence in art that Hungarian modernism comes closest to Viennese modern art (or to any modernist trend of the Western countries); this ideology was fully absorbed, becoming an inherent part of the Hungarian artistic awareness. But it is precisely because of this similarity that the issue deserves special attention: the divergent interpretation and application of this common ideology allows us to understand the unique character of Hungarian modernism. Finally, we have to remember that the idea of organicism is central to Bartók's art, and since Bartók is the most important (or perhaps the only) modern Hungarian artist who has been accepted into the mainstream, the interpretation of his endeavors and the debates around it determine, for better or worse, our view of Hungarian culture as a whole. The issue of organicism will serve as our mirror to reflect the general problems of turn-of-the-century artists in Central Europe.

THE ROMANTIC TRADITION OF ORGANICISM

Toward the end of his article "Folkloristic Symphonies" Schoenberg came to the conclusion that greatness in composition cannot be achieved a priori through the use of folk tunes.

> A composer—a real creator—composes only if he has something to say which has not yet been said and which he feels must be said: a musical message to music-lovers. Under what circumstances can he feel the urge to write something that has been already said, as in the case of the static treatment of folk songs? A real composer does not compose merely one or two themes, but a whole piece. . . . [His] musical conception . . . is one single act, comprising the totality of the product.[8]

In Schoenberg's view, there are two main reasons why compositions by a "real creator" cannot include folk music: first, the use of any precomposed material calls into question the originality of the conception "from inside," and second, the use of any outside material endangers the total coherence of the piece.

This view was central to the thinking of Schoenberg and the composers of the Second Viennese School. In their ideology, "unity" had a very special meaning that led to the "composition with twelve tones *related* to one another." As Anton von Webern said, "Unity is surely the indispensable thing if meaning is to exist. Unity, to be very general, is the establishment of the utmost relatedness between all component parts. So in music, as in all other human utterance, the aim is to make as clear as possible the relationships between the parts of the unity; in short, to show how one thing leads to another." Webern traced the origin of this idea back to Goethe, referring to his example of the "primeval plant": "What is manifest in this view? That everything is the same; root, stalk, blossom. And in Goethe's view the same holds good for the bones of the human body. Man has a series of vertebrae, each different from the others and yet similar. Primeval bone—primeval plant. And it's Goethe's idea that one could invent plants ad infinitum. And that's also the significance of our style of composition."[9]

Like Goethe, Webern viewed a work of art, in its genesis and final form, as endowed with organic properties. Goethe, strongly influenced by Herder, described a piece of art not as a teleological object constructed according to rules but as an organic product of growth in the mind of the genius, coming into being in a manner akin to the growth of natural organisms. The result is a totally coherent piece of art where every element is interrelated. In Goethe's words, "The number of art works of the first order still extant is much too small. But once one has seen them, one's only desire is to get to know them through and through and then depart in peace. These masterpieces of man were brought forth in obedience to the same laws as the masterpieces of Nature. Before them, all that is arbitrary and imaginary collapses: *there* is necessity, *there* is God."[10]

A closer look at these ideas will help us understand the controversy over folklorism. They reflect a conception of art—namely, the theory of organicism—which was at the heart of romantic aesthetics. It developed and traveled between countries and disciplines, informing the philosophies of such figures as Moritz, Coleridge, Addison, Young, and Herder, and of artists such as Goethe and Novalis, of music historians and musicians such as Hanslick and Busoni.[11] In the German cultural sphere by the end of the nineteenth and early twentieth centuries, the essential paradigm of organicist theory articulated nearly all discourse on art.

The theory of organicism became the common foundation for such divergent aesthetics as those of Nietzsche, Lukács, the Second Viennese School, and Bartók. Both the Viennese and the Hungarian modernist movements sought in organicism an aesthetic stance that was ethically and artistically relevant to the modern era. In doing so, they transformed the principal doctrines of the romantics into a theory of modernism. Only in the context of this philosophy could Schoenberg and Webern view composition with twelve tones as a logical and necessary step in the development of music. And as we shall see, Bartók relied on this same philosophical tradition when he asserted that modernity in music could be developed only from folk music in a natural and coherent manner.

A focal element of the theory of organicism was the distinction between "natural genius" or "genius of the first order" and that of the "second order." As Edward Young wrote, "An *Original* may be said to be of a *vegetable* nature; it rises spontaneously from the vital root of the genius; it *grows*, it is not *made*. *Imitations* are often a sort of *manufacture* wrought up by those *mechanics, art* and *labor*, out of pre-existent materials not their own."[12] In this view, artistic qualities could be grouped into two opposing categories: originality, nature, and growth from inside versus imitation, mechanics, and preexistent materials.

However simplistic Young's opposition of "geniuses" and "imitators" sounds to our ears, it expresses an essential element of romantic aesthetics, one that cannot be entirely transcended. We have to remember that romantic aesthetics was born from the realization that the earlier principle of imitation was untenable. Previous aesthetics conceived of art as imitating the surrounding world, "nature" as it were, the object of imitation being either visual experiences or emotions. This approach became increasingly unsatisfactory to nineteenth-century artists. Whereas earlier theories focused on the relation between the finished objects—that is, *objects* of nature and those of art—the emphasis shifted to the creator of the artwork and the *process of creation*. "The born artist is not content to observe nature, he has to imitate it, take it as his model, form and create as nature does," stated Karl Philipp Moritz, who was among the first to formulate this conception.[13]

The innovation of the romantics was a radical one even though the new aesthetics was also based on the idea of imitation. As Moritz explained, the difference lay in the fact that the object of artistic imitation was no longer anything in the surrounding world but nature as an abstract concept.

> No sooner does a beautiful image have to indicate and signify something outside itself than it approaches the status of pure symbol [= arbitrary sign], which does not really depend on beauty in the proper sense, any more than do the letters with which we write.—The work of art then no longer has its end only in itself, but rather outside itself.—True beauty consists in the fact that a thing signifies nothing but itself, designates only itself, contains only itself, that

it is a whole realized in itself. . . . To the extent that allegory thus contradicts this notion of beauty in the figurative arts, it deserves no place in the series of beautiful objects.[14]

Moritz's "beautiful object," the work of art, is a fully realized whole that requires nothing beyond itself. This thought is at the heart of the new aesthetics: if elements signified something other than what could be found in the artwork itself, we would fall back onto the older concept of imitation already transcended. This is also Goethe's and Young's approach to art. Goethe's "God" is not primarily a religious being but symbolizes the act of forming a perfect ("beautiful") object out of nothing, an artistic creation that is beyond human will and therefore transcendental and mystical.[15] Art is more than the imitation of nature; it *is* nature. The distinction lies not between good or bad works of art but between what is art and what is not: the artwork either repeats in itself the perfection of creation, or it is not art at all.

German theories of organicism thus concentrated on several strongly intertwined fundamental ideas, all interrelated and referring back to nature. First, nature expresses itself in an artwork through the unity of the elements of its structure. According to this view, nothing is accidental or of secondary importance in a coherent piece of art; no component can be altered or displaced, for all elements are totally interrelated. Second, such unity is not a mechanical construction but the result of a natural and uncontrolled growth from within the mind, that is, the evolution of an idea, obeying secret laws of nature. Finally, the paradigm invokes notions of truth and genius: truth manifests itself in unity and spontaneous growth, and these qualities are the sole property of the work of a genius.

The assertion that each work finds its end in itself has important implications. It means that the organicist paradigm of art refers typically to the individual piece and not to style and genre. Growth means the process through which a particular work comes into being in the mind of its creator rather than the development of a personal, let alone a historical, style. In this view, the emphasis is not on the creative process per se but on the fact that it is an integral development from a germ. An artwork is born when its original idea first presents itself, and that first idea already contains the entire piece. Any element that does not belong solely to the piece has a potential for pointing to elements outside the realm of the artwork. Consequently, representational aspect in art is not only unnecessary but a sign of mediocrity: only the lack of creative capabilities explains the need to turn to preexistent material.

The idea that the artwork is a fully realized whole in itself became significant also for another reason. For the romantics, true artistic experience meant transcendence; its power paralleled, or even surpassed, the power of religion. "The present sank away before him; his being was cleansed from all pettiness of this world"—this is how W. H. Wackenroder describes the response music elicited from his young hero, Joseph Berglinger.[16] The enjoyment of art is a spiritual experience that leads the individual to a higher and purer reality away from the everyday world. It is obvious why, in this logic, referential potential is in opposition to art's essence: it directs the mind toward the things of the empirical world and away from the abstract spiritual sphere. Transcendence is to be achieved solely by the "beautiful object" because only its compelling wholeness is able to possess our whole mind. In Moritz's words,

> As long as the beautiful draws our attention completely to itself, it shifts it away from ourselves for a while, and makes us seem to lose ourselves in the beautiful object; just this losing, this forgetting of the self, is the highest degree of the pure and unselfish pleasure that beauty grants us. At that moment we give up our individual, limited existence in favor of a kind of higher existence.[17]

Moritz's romantic affirmation that transcendental potentiality depends on the "truly beautiful" is by no means a mystification. On the contrary, since the beautiful equates with structural coherence, this theory rejected a vague and emotional basis for analyzing art. True art does not elicit fiery emotions; it is a cool and pure structure whose effect on the mind is not immediate but elevating and lasting. Novalis took care to distinguish between true art and mere fantasy: "The calm animating warmth of a poetic mind is the direct opposite to the wild heat of a morbid heart. This wild heat is poor, bewildering, and short-lived; but poetic warmth discriminates all forms cleanly, fosters the development of the most diverse relations, and eternally exists in itself."[18]

The notion that transcendence depends on the abstract nonreferential nature of art is by no means a universal belief, nor is it a necessary consequence of the organicist view. Yet this connection was made very early in romanticism and has been carried on with varying intensity to our day. In the history of music, this view led directly to the idea that instrumental music is superior to vocal music or, to state it on a more general level, that absolute music is superior to those musical forms with textual or visual references (such as program music).[19] But however essential the "structuralist" explanation of art was, the romantics took great pains not to explain unity in a simplistic and mechanical way. For Goethe's Wilhelm Meister, Shakespeare's *Hamlet* symbolizes the ultimate example of artistic unity; it can be likened to a full-grown tree from which no branch can be cut without harming the whole. And yet Wilhelm, somewhat contradicting himself, suggests cuts and changes in what he considers the background, to make the essence of the play more clearly perceivable in the context of German theater. He sees this essence not as some kind of a motivic germ but as an "inner spirit" that presents itself through tension (in this case, the tension between the character of Hamlet and his ethical responsibility).

For the romantics in general, there was no special merit in unity per se, but only in unity that was born from tension and manifested itself in variants and contrasts. As Coleridge expressed it in his *Theory of Life*, the value lies in discovering "unity in multeity," or "the principle of unity in the many," and the task of the poetic imagination is to balance or reconcile opposite or discordant qualities.[20] Similarly, when Herder viewed the work of art as a single whole in which no component could be altered, he referred primarily to a spiritual force, in his words, "one interpenetrating, all-animating soul."[21] (As we shall see, the Hungarian modernists gave greater emphasis to the presence of an "all-animating soul" in the artwork—what Lukács called the "transcendental center"—than did their Viennese contemporaries; this soul or center was the source of coherence, inexplicable and beyond anything shown through analysis of the structure.)

In music theory particularly, coherence was understood as something achieved through the mutual interrelation of various ideas rather than the evolution of one motive. In this sense the symphony was called a "musical drama," an "opera of instruments." Such characterizations of instrumental music, common in the writings of E. T. A. Hoffmann and Heinrich (Christoph) Koch, should not be viewed as attempts to put vocal music back in its former privileged place. They express rather the idea that in music a sort of "inner drama" unfolds, that pieces *achieve* coherence by unifying contrasting elements rather than by lacking contrast. Coherence does not mean the similarity of motives; it is the result of "poetic idea," that is, less a structural element than some spiritual force (character, mood). In his essay "Poetic Music" Dahlhaus wrote, "Like 'theme,' 'motive' is a dual category in a compositional and aesthetic sense: if 'theme' ranges variously, and sometimes lopsidedly, from an emotion captured in notes to an acoustic pattern devoid of emotional significance, 'motive' refers not only to the musical germ-cell that serves as the starting point of a piece of music, but also to what Wagner called the aesthetic raison d'être behind his cell."[22]

None of these conceptions is fully satisfactory: to understand the primary cell as the underlying spiritual idea is much too elusive, but to equate it with an isolated element of the structure leads to a mechanical conception of unity. Yet neither the romantic nor the modern aesthetic dispensed entirely with any of these interpretations, and the tension between the two has not been, and perhaps cannot be, resolved.

ORGANICISM AS MODERNISM

The organicist theory, already fully developed in the early romantic period, came to new life at the beginning of the twentieth century. This was not simply a continuation of the romantic philosophy. By the end of the nineteenth century, the organicist theory had long been overshadowed by new developments: a more positivistic approach dominated philosophy and aesthetics. The return to the organicist view was a reaction against the immediate past rather than a continuation of it. In music in particular, concentrated forms and a more structural approach to music became an antidote to the sentimentality of late romanticism, its tendency to recount a story or associate music with emotional or philosophical ideas—something paramount in the music of Richard Strauss and Gustav Mahler.

The tradition that concerns us here unfolds most clearly in the teachings of Schoenberg and Webern. As was true for discussions carried out by other artists at that time, theirs was not part of the discipline of philosophy or aesthetics in the strict sense; it did not grow directly from or contribute to a scholarly discourse. It was rather a "popular" philosophy of art, consisting of a set of assumptions that circulated among the intelligentsia.[23] True, its ideas did not represent the message of any particular work and only rarely illuminated concrete compositional decisions. Nevertheless, they generated an intellectual culture whose context allowed modernist endeavors to claim a part in the "great tradition," an issue of primary importance for Schoenberg and Webern. Developing an aesthetic along the lines of the romantics helped keep a sense of cultural identity at a moment when the formal, and therefore the more apparent, framework of artistic tradition seemed to be falling apart.

The emphatic affirmation of organicism in the twentieth century evolved into an ideology of modernism even though its roots were obviously in romanticism. The most apparent difference involved the concept of coherence, which shifted gradually from the emotional or spiritual aspect to the technical or structural one. Schoenberg explained:

A real composer does not compose merely themes, but a whole piece. In an apple tree's blossoms, even in the bud, the whole future apple is present in all its details—they have only to mature, to grow, to become apple, the apple tree, and its power of reproduction. Similarly, a real composer's musical conception, like the physical, is one single act, comprising the totality of the product. The form in its outline, characteristics of tempo, dynamics, moods of the main and subordinate ideas, their relation, derivation, their contrasts and deviations— all these are there at once, though in embryonic state. The ultimate formulation of the melodies, themes, rhythms, and many details will subsequently develop through the generating power of germs. . . . Thus a real composition is not composed but conceived, and its details need not be added.[24]

Schoenberg's position was clear: coherence was not to be achieved through mechanical construction as if working out the structure motive by motive. The direction of growth was predestined by the idea that already held, in a latent manner, every detail of the finished piece. The idea itself was the synthesizing power between tensions: "Every tone which is added to a beginning tone makes the meaning of that tone doubtful. If, for instance G follows after C, the ear may not be sure whether this expresses C major or G major, or even F major or E minor; and the addition of other tones may or may not clarify this problem. In this manner there is produced a state of unrest, of imbalance which grows throughout most of the piece, and is enforced further by similar functions of the rhythm. The method by which balance is restored seems to me the real *idea* of the composition."[25]

This thought is not entirely dissimilar to the romantic concept of unity through tension, the "musical drama" of E. T. A. Hoffmann. Nor is the emphasis on structural coherence entirely new; as we have seen, there was a strong inclination, already in the romantic era, to emphasize the cool emotionless beauty of art. But such predominance of a purely structural approach—one that had no place for qualities like character, genre, or style—was new. In this conception, it was no longer true that " 'theme' ranges variously . . . from an emotion captured in notes to an acoustic pattern devoid of emotional significance," as Dahlhaus put it. We are left with the latter interpretation alone. This view is apparent in Webern's lecture series as well as in Schoenberg's teaching. Webern remembered Schoenberg saying, "Our model in these matters is Nature. Just as in Nature everything develops from the primeval cell . . . likewise in music, large sound structures should be derived from a single motive which contains the seed of everything that is to come into being."[26]

It would be a mistake to associate this thinking with the Second Viennese School alone. Heinrich Schenker had the very same principle in mind when he established "a basis for describing and interpreting relations among the elements of any composition, from the moment-to-moment events at the surface of the music to the connections of longer range that ensure continuity and coherence over the span of the entire composition."[27] For Schenker, "coherence over the span of the entire composition" was the definition of true art that could be created only by a genius. If we accept that coherence is a synonym for the interrelatedness of structural elements and that such interrelatedness is an aesthetic value, the analysis that aims to discover structural relationships appears in a different light; it is not just the exegesis of the piece but a test of greatness. Or even more than that: for Schenker, the system of harmony and consequently the expression of the *Urlinie* was a "purely spiritual universe, a system of ideally moving forces, born of Nature or of art."[28]

The idea of coherence influenced the development of music theory after the Second World War, especially those analytical schools that focused on twelve-tone compositions. This attitude is inseparable from the last stages of Western music theory; it is deeply ingrained in our thinking and covertly expressed in our discussion of music.[29] It was clearly meant as praise, for instance, when Colin Mason wrote of Bartók's Fourth String Quartet that it was "almost as strictly and totally thematic, in every dimension of its musical structure, as a serial work."[30] The concept of structural interrelatedness took on supreme importance in the theory of the Viennese composers; they gradually relegated all other aspects—aspects of character, genre, style—to the background.

But why did this shift of emphasis occur? At the beginning of the century Schoenberg and Webern saw in the disintegration of musical genres and the dissolution of a common musical language a historically necessary process they could not and did not wish to stop. As Dahlhaus wrote in his article "New Music and the Problem of Musical Genre," twentieth-century composers regarded conventions of text, function, scoring, and formal model with increasing indifference or even disdain. Patterns of form and stereotypes of musical language lost their aesthetic credibility and degenerated into mere triviality; "art" was valid only inasmuch as it was an individual and original expression of the "infinite." In this context, the use of any preexisting pattern seemed not only unartistic but unethical. To conceive a work of art as an original creation as if out of nothing transcended matters of artistic decision; it was a moral issue. As Dahlhaus explains, Webern played a central role in this development:

Webern's procedure, seemingly a peripheral experiment, had a historical significance which no one was able to perceive in 1910. It meant nothing less than that the aesthetic, compositional, and technical basis of musical genres, and not of individual genres but of the concept of genres taken as a whole, had begun to crumble. In Webern's music there is no typical connection between form and scoring which corresponds to a genre norm, but a special individual nexus rooted in the unrepeatable character of the single piece. Both the forms and the scoring pursue a path toward individualization, the extreme consequence of which is the abolition of musical genres.[31]

MASS CULTURE AND THE PROBLEM OF STYLE

Webern's attitude was a direct response to the general social anxiety of the time. Especially in Central and Eastern Europe, the period around the turn of the century occupies a special position in the almost two centuries of intellectual struggle for coherence within an increasingly disintegrating society. What makes the cultural development of the period and the area, with its center in Vienna, unique is perhaps less the novelty of the underlying ideas than their consequences. To draw out all the consequences of a thought, perhaps even a relatively old one, can bring along an entirely new attitude, leading to the negation of the original thought itself. The modernity of the aesthetics expressed in the oeuvres of Schoenberg and Webern lies in the fact that it stretched romantic ideas to the point where those ideals virtually annihilated themselves. Already at the middle of the nineteenth century, artists and critics of art proclaimed that "the great mystery of being" was not expressible in the logical framework of language. Yet there is a great difference between the artistic consequences of such statements made by romantics and the experience of, say, Hofmannsthal, who arrived in effect at the point of not being able to use language anymore to express himself. Likewise, some of Liszt's remarks about the uselessness of imitating forms without expressing inner feeling may sound similar to Nietzsche's and other modernists' aesthetics, but we cannot forget that even such a revolutionary spirit and individualist as Liszt acquiesced without hesitation to the courtly life in Weimar for over a decade, living by a belief in the potential of continuing a traditional order in social life.[32]

There is something grand and moving in the intensity with which the intellectuals of Central Europe wrote of the disintegration of life. Their disillusionment—to Nietzsche, it is "decadence"—is not to be confused with the rebellious attitude of earlier artistic or literary youth. The decadence of the preceding generation, especially that of France, was a personal style, an expression of distance from the mediocrity of everyday life.[33] Decadent individuals refused the ordinary and the commonplace and self-consciously cultivated diverse eccentricities of behavior to mark their separation from the lifestyle of the petty bourgeoisie. In many of its expressions, this revolt against the emptiness of everyday life became a pose, one that the middle class was ready to incorporate into its own code of life.

The revolt of the modernists of turn-of-the-century Vienna, however, lacked that happy satisfaction in eccentricity; it was full of anxiety and pain. Perhaps in no other era were intellectuals so aware of the unreality of their social mission, and particularly of the mission of art, and yet so fervent in believing in it, so intent on proclaiming it. The list of prominent Austrians of the period who died by their own hand is long, and many others lost control of their mental faculties. Almost all creative minds lived through a crisis, one so deep that it sometimes made the continuation of work intolerable.[34]

At moments it seemed that the lack of wholeness in life eroded coherent expression. "What is the sign of every *literary decadence?* That life no longer dwells in the whole. The word becomes sovereign and leaps out of the sentence, the sentence reaches out and obscures the meaning of the page, the page gains life at the expense of the whole—the whole is no longer a whole. . . . The whole no longer lives at all: it is composite, calculated, artificial, and artifact."[35] For Nietzsche, the awareness of the collapse of all metaphysical and theological foundations, all sanctions for traditional morality—a sensation of meaninglessness—became a point of departure for a new philosophical theory. Hofmannsthal, a natural poetic talent, collapsed under the weight of this realization. In his youthful years he wrote as if his poetry flowed freely from some infinite source, but at the age of twenty-five he suddenly rejected all that had gone before. He became disenchanted with literature and with language itself, no longer accepting it as the means to express an essence: "[Previously] I, in a state of continuous intoxication, conceived the whole of existence as one great unit . . . in everything, I felt the presence of Nature . . . and in all expressions of Nature, I felt myself. . . . [But now] I have lost completely the ability to think or to speak of anything coherently. . . . I no longer succeed in comprehending [the separate elements of life] with the simplifying eye of habit. For me, everything disintegrated into parts, these parts again into parts; no longer would anything let itself be encompassed by an idea."[36]

Aggravating the modernists' anxiety over the incoherence of life was their fear that art would no longer be able to retain its higher moral aspirations as mass culture emerged and the broader public tried to set up its own version of elite art. The genre of the operetta, a popularized version of opera, exemplifies this development.[37] For those who insisted on the transcendental potential of art, the distinction between real art and pieces of entertainment posing as art was vital. In their eyes, light music in forms like the operetta only deluded the masses; it was the betrayal of the very essence of art. The disappearance of true art would mean giving up the last shreds of meaningful order and coherence.

It is irrelevant in this context that "high art" was never pure and that there had always been mutual interchanges between folk, popular, and art cultures. In the case of music, it would be difficult to say whether the crisis that took place at the beginning of the twentieth century was greater than, for instance, the crisis that resulted from the emergence of the *style galant* in the eighteenth century. It is certain, however, that the spread of what twentieth-century avant-garde circles labeled mass culture caused anxiety of unprecedented magnitude. With the dissolution of stylistic boundaries, particularly the boundary between art and entertainment, artists were cut off from the traditional forms and styles; in music, this meant the disappearance of the notion (and even the possibility) of a common musical language. The potential of a musical language that had become a mass commodity could not be trusted, and thus, there was no musical language at all. Art was deprived of its stylistic context, artists from their audience: the more such intermediate forms filled the gap between high art and mass culture, the more artists sought to guard the boundaries of serious art and thus isolate themselves.

This feeling of frustration resonates in the essay "In These Great Times" by Karl Kraus, a Viennese critic, poet, and satirist:

> Where all energy has been expended to make life frictionless, nothing remains that still needs such care [i.e., art and spirituality]. In such a region individuality can live, but can no longer be born. With its emotional desires it may be a guest where it will be surrounded by automata pushing past and forward in comfort and prosperity without face and greeting. . . . The tyranny of necessity grants its slaves three kinds of freedom; opinion free from intellect, entertainment free from art, and orgies free from love.[38]

Schoenberg experienced this cultural crisis in a similar way, as he wrote in the preface to his first edition of *Harmony*:

> Our age seeks many things. What it has found, however, is above all: *comfort.* Comfort, with all its implications, intrudes even into the world of ideas and makes us far more content than we should ever be. We understand today bet-

ter than ever how to make life pleasant. We solve problems to remove an un-
pleasantness. But, *how* do we solve them? And what presumption, even to
think we have really solved them! Here we can see most distinctly what the
prerequisite of comfort is: superficiality.[39]

It is not unlikely that the common source of the ideology of the Viennese
School and Schenker was indeed Karl Kraus.[40] Kraus disdained those pieces
whose purpose was to elicit a response from the audience. For Kraus, the essence of art had nothing to do with its social or cultural function; its value
could not be measured by its effect but by its "truthfulness." Art was a process
of self-realization coming from an inner spiritual force and bringing the artist
back to his origin.

> Where freedom became a meaningless phrase
> I was reactionary—
> where art they besmirched by their arty ways
> I was reactionary,
> backing all the way off to the origin.[41]

A basic category of this line of thinking, for Kraus as for Schenker, Schoenberg, and Webern, was "truthfulness." Truth lay only in what had not been
corrupted by society, that is, in the innermost soul and in the abstract perfection of nature. The individual must search for truth in those deepest areas of
the soul free of influences or allegiances to groups and to society. "Belief in
technique as the only salvation would have to be suppressed, and the urge for
truthfulness encouraged"—this is how Schoenberg summarized his principles
for the teaching of art.[42]

This inward-turning artistic credo bespeaks a heroic effort to justify artistic
existence in isolation. The phenomenon of mass culture discredited the idea
that the value of art had any connection to its effect on the public; it seemed
that works of the highest artistic quality were precisely those least appreciated
by the masses. Hence art was to be defined as something in opposition to the
public's opinion. This situation did not allow artists the luxury of feeling in-
secure about their own ideas: since the inner self alone was to be trusted, neither challenge nor justification could come from outside. The arrogance of
Schoenberg (and to a lesser extent Webern) in judging artistic tendencies different from their own follows from this circumstance. The Viennese modernists could not doubt their conviction. The refusal of lighter forms, neoclassi-

cism, folklorism, or whatever was not "from inside" was not, they believed, narrow-mindedness or elitism but a question of artistic ethic.

With the demand that the artwork be both totally coherent and original at each moment, Schoenberg attempted to achieve the impossible. Only that which had not been said before is "original," that is, artistically "true." This idea of truthfulness translates, in the musical form, into a flow of continually new ideas: the ideal of the Schoenbergian "obbligato recitative."[43] Structural coherence, however, requires a web of inner motivic repetitions and references; in a sense, the twelve-tone technique grew from the attempt to accommodate spontaneity while securing coherence. The architectural conception of form contradicts proselike linearity: this was an intractable problem, but the mere recognition of it, and Schoenberg's continued struggle to resolve it, was in itself an achievement.

To this way of thinking, the very notion of musical style was unacceptable. When Schoenberg used the term he referred strictly to the style of the individual artwork for, in his view, each piece demanded its own style growing exclusively from the mind of its creator: "Style is the quality of a work and is based on natural conditions, expressing him who produced it. In fact, one who knows his capacities may be able to tell in advance exactly how the finished work will look which he still sees only in his imagination. But he will never start from a preconceived image of style; he will be ceaselessly occupied with doing justice to the idea. He is sure that, everything done which the idea demands, the external appearance will be adequate."[44]

This thought was intimately linked to the defense of new music. Since critics rejected modernity in music because it did not conform to the language of traditional music, the very notions of tradition and common style became suspect. An idea for an artwork was by definition something entirely new and original and was thus the antithesis of style. In analyzing harmony and structure, Schoenberg categorically dismissed that he was teaching style.[45]

But the supposition that each artwork grows from nothing previously existent ran too obviously against what could be seen in practice. The fact that Schoenberg taught harmony and form on the basis of the classical and romantic repertoire, while he claimed that he was not teaching any tradition or style, needed to be explained.

The solution came from the organicist theory itself. If each work of genius expresses nature, then the structural rules of all true art pieces have to show some deep similarity. In this view, the similarity between compositions is understood not in terms of a continuous tradition but as the manifestation of some underlying law of nature brought to life by geniuses at various moments in history. What may seem to our eyes stylistic similarity results from the fact that the structures of different music are defined by the same natural laws. Schoenberg's teaching and Webern's lecture series "The Path to the New Music" explore this thought.[46] It is telling that Webern—following the suggestion of Schoenberg—chose to demonstrate the validity of the twelve-tone technique by discussing "the natural laws of music" as they were manifest in the music of preceding eras, rather than by introducing Schoenberg's or his compositions per se.[47] What he tried to convey was that music, like any other natural phenomenon, had its universal laws that demanded a particular path of development. Once the laws of music were understood, he argued, it would immediately become clear why the new music, represented by Schoenberg's and his pieces, had to develop the way it did, as if of necessity.[48]

All great pieces manifest the laws of nature, but the further we advance in history, the more we see human beings reaching a deeper understanding of this nature. The course of the history of music is gradual evolution: each artist strives to conquer ever richer possibilities of tonality and create ever higher levels of structural unity. Composition with the twelve-tone technique and with the use of the *Reihe* is a necessity in the course of musical history. These ideas derive from the same natural laws as the music of earlier periods, only they are a deeper expression of these laws: "Composition with twelve notes has achieved a degree of complete unity that was not even approximately there before."[49] Music has a predestined road; humanity proceeds on this road regardless of its will, out of necessity dictated by nature. "Man is only the vessel into which is poured what 'nature in general' wants to express."[50]

Webern thus reiterated, transposed to another level, the principal affirmation of the romantics on the subject of the work of art. The vision of a history of music as a continuous discovery of natural laws gave the issue of artistic creation another dimension. The genius was now entrusted with the power not only to create a perfect piece but also to advance the state of art in general. Modernity thus became the sine qua non of artistic creation; the genius was executing nature's will by uncovering the nature of art. Like the genius who discovered polyphony, Schoenberg and his circle had to pass through many "sleepless nights" to come to the discovery of the next predestined step in the history of music: the composition with twelve tones.[51] This self-tormenting thinking, which has to start anew with each piece in order to discover the laws of art, is the essence of the creative process. In Schoenberg's words, "It is indeed our duty to reflect over and over again upon the mysterious origins of the powers of art. And again and again to begin at the beginning; again and again to examine anew for ourselves and attempt to organize anew for ourselves. Regarding nothing as given but the phenomena."[52]

But how can we start anew? What is the meaning of the postulate "to create from inside," once this inside is deeply saturated with all that has already been composed, that is, in the case of Schoenberg and Webern, with the monumental repertoire of Western music? When Schoenberg said that with each piece artists should "begin at the beginning," he did not mean that they should erase all previous knowledge. Rather that they should direct all efforts toward the discovery of the unknown, suppressing conventional techniques to let the already internalized language find its way spontaneously. Similarly, Webern did not mean to imply that new discoveries in the realm of music would come purely through the intuition of the genius. Rather he suggested that after internalizing all that had been expressed in art, the genius withdraws into himself in order to create anew.

Clearly, there was a conceptual gap in these thoughts. They deliberately omitted the first step toward composition, namely, that any preoccupation with art begins with the internalization of a commonly known extant repertoire. It was a step so obvious that it did not need mention. To appreciate how deeply this idea had penetrated the thinking of musicians in the first half of the century we need only look at Schoenberg's *Fundamentals of Musical Composition*. For him, fundamentals of musical composition meant simply the study and analysis of the great pieces of the classical and romantic tradition of Western music. Such study was the prerequisite of composition, somewhat in the same manner as learning the language was the prerequisite of the art of composing poetry. Yet this omission is important. First, it reflects the unchallenged notion that the language of music was defined by the art tradition of Western Europe, the knowledge of which was the absolute and only necessary part of the craftsmanship of the composer. More important, this omission signals that the process of internalization had no part in the creative process but was only a preliminary step. Creativity and art resided exclusively with what was invented from inside.

The underlying aim of the Viennese was essentially romantic: to attain the maximum potential of art in expressing truth. But in creating an aesthetic framework for that goal, they reinterpreted the artistic theories of the classical and romantic eras in a manner alien to the very tradition they hoped to sustain. By renouncing the notions of genre and style, they gave up the possibility of communal art, that is, the primary aspiration of classical and romantic composers.

Paradoxically, this omission did not imply that they refused nationalism.

Schoenberg's explicit goal was to sustain German culture and "effectively oppose Latin and Slav hopes of hegemony."[53] But his nationalism had little to do with serving a real community of "here and now." The whole aesthetic was directed toward an abstract ideal of "art," and he believed that German art alone reached the level of abstraction when art rises above the national to become universal. At its best, Schoenberg's commitment to society was an abstract one based on the belief that the moral value of art transcends the artistic needs of specific communities.

MODERNISM AND THE
SOCIAL CONTEXT OF AUSTRIAN ART

Schoenberg's and Webern's expansion of the organicist aesthetic was not merely the outcome of analytical thinking and not even a purely musical development. In order to see clearly the artistic issues involved, we must consider their social-historical perspective and the larger Viennese intellectual milieu. The cultural source of this aesthetic lies in the separation of art and society that characterized Viennese life at the turn of the century.

For the Austrian middle-class elite, a garden was the symbol of the ideal and imaginary territory where morality and an order of life could develop free from social obligations and conventions. The idea of this garden was based on Adalbert Stifter's work, *Der Nachsommer* (1857), which inspired Hofmannsthal and others;[54] in Schorske's interpretation, the garden was the locus for Viennese art. For Stifter, the garden is a place where life is lived to its best potential. In the garden the anarchy of life and the disorders of passions are transformed into a world of beauty and order; feelings are channeled and refined, sublimated in art. Moral and cultural education raises the individual to this state beyond and above society. In essence, it is social withdrawal.

To associate art with this image of garden may seem to contradict the fact that in Austria, art was closely bound to social status, especially in the representational arts, theater, and architecture, all central to the tradition of the Catholic aristocracy. But although Vienna prided itself on being an art city, it was, as Hermann Broch wrote, "far less a city of art than a city of decoration par excellence. In accordance with its decoration, Vienna was cheerful, often idiotically cheerful, but with little sense of indigenous humor or even sarcasm and self-directed irony. . . . Decorativeness was legitimate in Vienna; only it was more or less that kind of legitimation which befits the establishment and maintenance of a museum. In fulfillment of its duty to tradition, Vienna confused culture with 'museumness' and became a museum to itself."[55]

Art was decoration and social display and, at its best, embodied the ideal that its practice might help build an ethical personality. But this latter notion of art only reinforced its separation from the reality of everyday life. Morality was not a social issue but a matter of the soul, that is, it might have consequences for the society but could not be created by it. Stifter thought that "whoever is morally free can be politically free and always is so; not all the powers of the earth can make the others free. There is but one power which can do so: *Bildung.*"[56] *Bildung* was the cultivation of mind and soul, by an individual alone.

The gap between morally developed individuals and the rest of the society was to be bridged by an education within the ideological framework of the process of *Bildung*. This idea reverberates in what Webern, following Karl Kraus, called the "moral gain" of the study of music. Through knowledge and respect for the material (language for Kraus and music for Webern), individuals learn to respect other values in life: "the need awakened or satisfied in the striving after perfection of language" is more than an aesthetic one.[57] This ideology could lead toward participation in social life but did not regard art as an essential means of such participation, for art was to remain the sphere of individual expression. As Schorske wrote, "Austria's garden of beauty was a retreat of the *beati possidentes*, a garden strangely suspended between reality and utopia. It expressed both the self-delight of the aesthetically cultivated and the self-doubt of the socially functionless."[58]

In turn-of-the-century Vienna, art had increasingly become the ruling conventional culture of an intellectual and social elite within the middle class. The modernists rejected the empty conventionalism and the beautified order of this garden, and this rejection in itself was liberating. But, however much they detested the aristocratic decorativeness and the seclusion of the artistic milieu, they had neither the historical precedents nor the social potential to transform this framework. On the whole, their opposition to the existing system led to their further alienation from public life. As Schorske wrote, "The shock the newcomers caused produced social rejection; that rejection reinforced their alienation. Alienation in turn became the basis for their adventure into new realms, spiritual and artistic. The two anti-bourgeois bourgeois, Kokoschka and Schoenberg, found the forms to express the soul of men whose culture had prevented their irrational private experience from finding public expression."[59]

With the acceptance of isolation as the only possible context for artistic expression, the Viennese cut themselves off from art that had meaning in a broader social context. They believed that the individualism of modern art precluded the formulation of social visions—even though all their efforts to create true art were ultimately born from a desire to serve humanity. They recognized this contradiction but could not overcome it. It would dissolve only, as happened in Schoenberg's case, with a shift from the idea of society as a concrete and objective unit toward an abstract idea of humanity. Several of Schoenberg's pieces, the *Jacobsleiter, Moses und Aron, Survivor from Warsaw,* and *Kol Nidre,* manifest the belief in finding the way toward an imaginary public by the force of the expression of a human pain that cries out for sympathy and compassion.

CHAPTER 2

The Historical and Social Context of Hungarian Modernism

SEARCH FOR IDENTITY
IN A FRAGMENTED SOCIETY

One of the first novels about modern urban Hungary, Tamás Kóbór's *Budapest* (1901), presents the tragedy of individuals who cannot come to terms with their identity. The book opens in the inner city as the heroine, Éva, a working-class girl dressed up as an elegant middle-class woman, bumps into her sister coming out of a factory. The conflict of the modern city symbolically captured in this meeting becomes the theme of the book. The motivation behind Éva's fight for social advancement is not just greed and anger but hope for a better, more human, and moral life. But as she struggles, she loses her morality.[1]

In Frigyes Karinthy's serious but ironic short story "Loneliness" (A magány), written between the wars, a nondescript man wanders into a city looking for his son (the writer of the story), who he says is almost identical to himself.[2] As he begins to talk to people, encountering bureaucrats who require precise information, he realizes that he is unable to explain who his son actually is and how he looks; or who he himself is and where he is from. The streets and the people look familiar and at times he feels like one of them, but something always disturbs that feeling. He goes to the outskirts of the city to end his journey (his life) in the knowledge that he will return ("five more times, at most") somewhere at some time.

The elusive nature of identity and the stylized and absurd stage of the surrounding world are the main theme of Jenő Rejtő's mystery novels of the interwar years.[3] No individuals in Rejtő's mysteries are what they claim to be, but everyone takes the others' appearance at face value. The plot is a labyrinth with no way out; the climactic "solution" comes with the eruption of a violent scene in which everyone is fighting everyone else and acting entirely out of character. For all their fresh humor, Rejtő's novels—which were written, sold, and read as popular mystery stories (and at the same time as caricatures of such stories)—are a deep satire of alienation from everything, even from the medium of the novel.

In Dezső Kosztolányi's novel *Cornelius of the Evening* (Esti Kornél [1933]), the hero is introduced by the writer as a friend he has known since a time he cannot even remember. He has always been around him and close to him, as if inside him, contradicting and challenging whatever he does, someone he adores and hates at the same time.[4]

In *Duke Bluebeard's Castle* (1911), Bartók depicts the personality of Bluebeard through antagonistic images, as if several contradictory worlds existed within him without reconciliation: they are the seven chambers of the castle. In *The Miraculous Mandarin* (1919), passion—the original driving force of life that is beyond humanity, morality, and feeling—concentrates symbolically in the character of the mandarin, who is, however, emphatically alien, even grotesque and frightening. In the *Cantata profana* (1930), the sons of the old man find both morality ("the clean spring") and their true selves only by transforming themselves from humans into stags and returning to their origin, to Nature.

Common to these works from the first half of the century is an anxious search for identity and morality within a disintegrating and confused society. Although their underlying similarity is apparent, to mention these pieces in one breath blurs significant differences of genre, artistic quality, personal attitudes, and social and individual topics; more important, it ignores the contrast between the aesthetic of the era before the First World War and that of the interwar period. The artists in turn-of-the-century Hungary focused on the pressing issue of identity; the generation of the first decade of the century could still project the idealistic demand for coherence into the personality and the world. As Europe approached the Second World War, the search for identity became both immeasurably more intense and hopeless.

In a society in transition, decisions about loyalties to conflicting forces are never easy to make, especially if, as was the case with turn-of-the-century Hungary, that society is an uneasy collection of segments, each of which feels threatened by the others. The contrast between the wealthiest and the poorest segments was extreme, and they lived in separate worlds. For the majority of the population, the life of the higher aristocracy was practically unknown and certainly unimaginable; its seclusion in immeasurably rich palaces kept the aristocracy unaware of the life of the rest of the country.

At the other extreme of the social continuum were the millions of industrial workers and agricultural and domestic servants (*cseléd*) who owned barely more than their lives. During the period between the Compromise (1867) and the First World War, the working day for industrial workers could be as high as sixteen hours and averaged around twelve.[5] A contemporary survey describes the circumstances of work as harsh: out of 530 factories, only about 20 had any facilities for washing hands, and measures to prevent work-related accidents were almost unknown.[6] In 1901, 36 percent of the population of Budapest lived in what was considered at the time "worrisome bad conditions," that is, six or more persons per room; and among another 30 percent four to five persons shared the same room. On the basis of contemporary statistics Zsuzsa Ferge concluded that around the turn of the century approximately 65 percent of the population—that is, nearly 9 million people of a country with a population of 13.5 million—lived at the edge of or below the level of what was officially labeled poverty. Acsády's view of the feudal Hungarian society of the early nineteenth century as a country of "two nations" that "face each other with deadly hatred and abhorrence" in many ways reflected the situation of the beginning of the twentieth century as well.[7]

Of course, neither poverty nor the rigid separation of classes was a new phenomenon. What was new was that they came to the notice of educated segments within the middle class. The awareness of social problems is not to be seen as an inevitable attribute of an "objectively" bad situation; societies with great inequities may appear fairly peaceful and "democratic" as long as they can isolate certain segments and exclude them from the notion of society and nation. Furthermore, the period between the Compromise of 1867 and the First World War was generally progressive. The economic and social conditions were certainly not worse in Hungary than before, or worse than those in many other European countries. The increasing anxiety arose partly from the visibility of these contradictions in the context of urban life, and, more important, from a new set of expectations for society's potential to improve human conditions. The abolition of feudalism in 1849 and the relatively favorable position of Hungary within the Habsburg Dual Monarchy after the

Compromise, paralleled by rapid economic progress and relatively liberal politics, gave rise to the belief that the social and economic problems were destined to disappear automatically and that Hungary was going to elevate itself to the level of the most developed Western societies within a short time. In the framework of the newly emerging ideologies in the West, chasms between different social groups no longer seemed natural or tolerable.

In Hungary, the awareness of social problems was a basic impetus for the creation of the radical movement and artistic modernism. Because these developments occurred primarily among the educated segments of the middle class, an overview of the class is necessary here. The extensive literature on the problem of the bourgeois development in the countries of Eastern Europe uses terms such as "middle class," "urbanites," "urbanization," "bourgeoisie," "educated classes," "intelligentsia," "professionals," or even "citizens" to discuss social segments in situations that overlap but differ from one country to another and from those in the Western countries.

EMERGENCE AND STATUS
OF A BOURGEOIS MIDDLE CLASS

As in several other countries of Central and Eastern Europe, in Hungary until the latter decades of the nineteenth century the bourgeoisie was a minority in both a political and an ethnic sense.[8] For the most part, the inhabitants of the cities were ethnically different from the majority of the population and thus, in a sense, outside the nation, even though the urban bourgeoisie was an accepted national estate (*rend*) of the feudal system. Some of these urbanites shared the culture of other social segments, but others had a background that differed greatly from that of the aristocracy and middle nobility.

There is no English equivalent for the Hungarian terms *polgár* and *polgári;* "bourgeois" and "urbanite" are only approximations. The notion of the *polgár* included the *civis* (a specific type of bourgeois) of the *mezőváros* (a typical Hungarian formation of large urban-like areas with a basically agricultural population), the German and Jewish urban bourgeoisie, and the impoverished middle nobility in the bureaucratic apparatus. In a broader sense *polgár* applied to all people who were not engaged in agriculture. These various middle-class segments lacked a common ideology and economical interest to enable them to assert their rights against the feudal establishment.

In this historical context, *polgár* began to assume a meaning that had less to do with actual social formations than with a social and cultural ideal, and this ideal became synonymous with the notion of civilization. It emerged in the romantics' expression "civic virtue" (*polgári erény*), a state of being educated, enlightened, and rational, and projected back onto the word *polgár*, to connote a particular ideology, culture, and lifestyle. It did not unite the bourgeoisie, but the ideal behind the notion became clearer as the century wore on.

The historical differences between the various bourgeois groups did not disappear with the era of industrialization. On the contrary, they intensified into a rigid system of hierarchy within the framework of the bureaucratic apparatus of state-supported institutions. Even though the greatest dividing line still separated the higher (educated) classes from the underprivileged masses, this new and more complex hierarchy added a series of titles for addressing individuals, indicating precisely to which salary category they belonged.[9] The rules were a grotesque contrast to the relatively liberal atmosphere of the capital. The young generation began to feel increasingly uncomfortable among the *Spiessbürger*—Bartók's slighting term for conventional bourgeois citizens—and dismissed their social protocol as absurd.[10]

The differences in ethnic origin, religious allegiance, and family lineage further divided the middle class, and the various sets of ranks and inherited wealth often caused enormous tension. Among the artists of the emerging modernist circles, it is difficult to find two with similar background and education. The most important poet of the era, Endre Ady, was born in a thatch-roofed cottage in a little village where his maternal grandfather was a Protestant pastor. His father, an impoverished noble from a Protestant family, sent him alternately to Protestant and Catholic schools to provide whatever he considered the best education available in the region. Another leading poet, Mihály Babits, the son of a judge, was raised in a highly sophisticated intellectual environment where the knowledge of and admiration for European culture and Greek literature were the norm; he studied at the Cistercian gymnasium. To the writer Zsigmond Móricz, his family tradition meant a legendary past and held in its microcosm the essence of Hungarianness: on his mother's side he came from an impoverished but ancient noble family, while his father was the descendant of serfs who gradually ascended to the rank of the village intelligentsia. Another aspect of Hungarianness was emphasized in the family tradition of Gyula Krúdy. He was an illegitimate child with a grandfather and paternal uncle who were both in the Hungarian army in the 1848 war of independence; his uncle was among those few who refused to surrender and organized a guerrilla group after the defeat of the revolution. Gyula Illyés's father belonged to a rich gentry family, but his mother came from the most deprived segment of society, agricultural servants. The noble family of Margit Kaffka had once held high rank but had become impoverished, so that for years she was educated in a convent. Zoltán Kodály's father worked for the Hungarian railroad and represented the intelligentsia of little towns that used its limited means to keep up a modest but respectable cultural life with an orientation toward classical music. During his university years, Kodály (together with Balázs) belonged to the Eötvös college, a group of students who lived in the same dormitory and formed an intellectual elite. Bartók's family background gave him a dual legacy: in his father, who was the director of an agricultural school in the countryside, he could find a model of the traditional Hungarian middle class who worked toward the progress of the country, while his mother, who was German by origin, taught in the public school system and transmitted the ideal of a somewhat rigid morality and devotion to work.

There were tensions even among what may seem to be a fairly homogeneous group. For instance, the young intellectuals who formed around György Lukács and became known as the Sunday circle were mostly assimilated Jews, but among them too there were significant differences in wealth, rank, and ideology. Lukács's father was a self-made man who rose to become a wealthy and influential banker in Budapest. Béla Balázs (German on his mother's side and Jewish on his father's) came from the world of the provincial Jewish intelligentsia. Anna Lesznai's parents were wealthy landowners who embraced the values and lifestyle of the Hungarian landed nobility.[11]

As the young generation of the turn of the century began exploring modern urban life, their thinking was colored by the experiences they brought from their families. Each ideological legacy held a confused but specific system of values that included a vision of Hungary's history and expectations for the country's future. It offered little guidance in modern life yet had deep roots in the young intellectuals' consciousness. When these youth moved away from home—in both the literal and figurative sense—they left behind a tradition they abhorred and loved at the same time, and most of them took many years to come to terms with and understand the value of their heritage.

Moreover, the character and ethnic composition of the newly emerging modern bourgeoisie that they were to join did not accord with the popular romantic image of "modern Hungary." Reformers at the beginning of the nineteenth century had envisioned a Hungarian bourgeoisie that was to develop organically from the enlightened Christian aristocracy and the middle nobility of the countryside (partly Catholic, partly Protestant). A new society formed after the principles of the French revolution was to be based on Christian morality and social equality. This idea, most clearly expressed by István Széchenyi, who led the Hungarian reform movement during the first half of the nineteenth century, was virtually sanctified by the novels of Mór Jókai, the most widely read author at the end of the century. Jókai's idealistically depicted Budapest was an all-Hungarian city containing the palaces of the nobility and populated by diligent and righteous workers. Jókai's heroes were either modern-minded aristocrats who concentrated in themselves all imaginable human values or righteous and happy craftsmen and housewives who radiated modesty and dedication to hard work.

The sudden emergence of cosmopolitan Budapest, with its overwhelmingly Jewish and German intelligentsia and its petty bourgeoisie and growing mass culture, hardly accorded with these expectations. The gap between the semifeudal countryside and the capitalist city seemed unbridgeable, and little in the culture of Budapest resembled a coherent high culture or something truly Hungarian. The misery of inhabitants in the rapidly growing industrial capital, along with their cultural displacement, frightened even those who belonged to the circles of the modern urban intelligentsia. Confused and angered, Bartók and other members of the young generation responded to the situation with a renewed affirmation of unrealistic dreams, turning first toward conservative and nationalistic ideologies.

What made the situation of the Hungarian modernists especially uncomfortable was that they wanted to break away from the traditional lifestyle of their parents but felt skeptical about modernization as well. In a position similar to those in today's more developed third-world countries, they recognized that Hungary had arrived at a stage of social and economic development whose benefits they found more and more difficult to believe in. Unlike the reformers of the romantic era, the generation of the turn of the century could not proclaim capitalism to be the dawn of a new and happier world. They could see the deep problems of the capitalist phase in the experience of the more developed European countries.

Similar contradictions presented themselves in other spheres of life. The generation of the turn of the century felt itself to be Hungarian and aspired to create Hungarian art, yet it had to refuse the traditional form of Hungarianness in culture and lifestyle because that was monopolized for chauvinistic and antidemocratic political aims. Under the label of "Hungarian art," an institutionally codified set of outmoded classicizing topics and forms was being propagated. But if the modernists turned toward an ideal of uncommitted art whose aim was only to please, they would seem to approve of the ideology of mass culture that they abhorred. When they aspired to sustain a moral attitude, they realized that for most people morality translated as mediocrity because it meant adherence to the lifestyle and value system of the petty bourgeoisie.

THE BACKWARDNESS
OF THE POLITICAL ESTABLISHMENT

The impetus to organize these heterogeneous segments into a more or less coherent group came from their recognition that conservative political tendencies were undermining their very existence. During the last decade of the nineteenth century the political situation in Hungary greatly deteriorated.[12] The
political fights that marked the first half of this decade brought victory to the
liberal factions; the sanctification of the law of civil marriage, religious freedom, and legal acceptance of the Jewish religion all occurred by 1905. This result incited the conservative circles to launch their battle in the name of religion. In 1895 after much preparation and propaganda the Catholic People's
Party (Katolikus Néppárt) was formed. Beginning with the government of
Dezső Bánffy (1895–98), the political leadership turned openly against liberal
ideals. Bánffy changed the tone of nationalism into one of open chauvinism.
He proclaimed the politics of the "strong hand," suppressing any attempt to
ease the problems of the lower classes and using armed force against peasants,
workers, and members of socialist organizations. Parliament became increasingly an empty facade, its debates theatrically affirming the political power
structure but ignoring the issue of much-needed economic reform.

The drift toward more conservative, clerical, and chauvinist ideas on the
part of the leading political institutions did not happen entirely unexpectedly,
but it nevertheless meant a departure from the liberal ideology of the reform
generation of the 1830s and even that of the political groups of the 1870s and
1880s.[13] This turn proved to be irrevocable. None of the governments that followed were able or willing to foster the democratization of the country. During most of the first half of the twentieth century the political establishment
remained conservative, although the political system was unstable. It changed
from a constitutional monarchy to a democratic republic in the fall of 1918,
under the government of Mihály Károlyi, and then became a Bolshevik republic of councils in the spring of 1919 under the Communist party leader Béla
Kun. At the beginning of 1920 a conservative government suppressed what it
interpreted as the liberalism of the Bolshevik republic. The government's conservatism only increased during the era of the semiconstitutional kingdom
without a king under the regent, Admiral Miklós Horthy, and led directly toward Hungary's shameful role in the Second World War and the fascist terror
regime that began in the autumn of 1944.

On the whole, Hungary's politics were no more conservative or nationalist
than those of the other European countries. In fact, compared to the parallel

developments in Italy, Germany, or Austria, the general atmosphere was still relatively liberal. But because Hungary fell behind the West European development economically and socially, the conservativism of the leading segments had a more destructive effect—at least before these countries embraced racism in the 1930s. In Hungary, conservativism was directed toward the reinstallation of the feudalist manner of thinking. Lacking the power to change the course of economic and social modernization, the conservative political establishment could at least slow its pace and make it despicable in the eyes of the masses. Those segments who wished for more rapid progress were fearful that the gap between "Europe" and Hungary would widen. To relapse into feudal patterns would make the slowly emerging bourgeoisie even more fragile and virtually unable to function.[14]

The objective historical problems described above—that the bourgeoisie in the modern sense was still in the state of formation and that it found itself in opposition to a conservative political leadership—made the development of a modern art and intellectual life extremely difficult. The intelligentsia's social position was weak and ambiguous, because the traditional middle nobility took only a small part in modernization but supported the conservative government. Underlying the beliefs and attitudes of this powerful and established middle nobility—the gentry—and all those segments who allied themselves with it were images of a legendary past and the historical supremacy of the Hungarian nobility. A look at their beliefs helps us understand why artistic modernism became a political issue in Hungary and why the modernist circles insisted on the public and politically radical nature of modern art.

NATIONALISM AND THE GENTRY

Before the April laws of 1848 that sanctified the abolition of feudalism, Hungarian nobility was more than a social stratum: it formed the entire Hungarian nation.[15] Nobility, of course, had not been homogeneous for centuries; the chasm between the aristocracy and the middle nobility was almost insurmountable. Although many members of the middle nobility sank into poverty and their life hardly differed from that of the serfs, the nobles represented an integral unit, legally and in the minds of the people.

Even when the legal basis for the feudalist ideology disappeared, the myth that only nobles were real Hungarians remained in the public consciousness throughout the nineteenth century and beyond. According to legend, the land of Hungary was acquired through conquest "by right of our Hun ancestors" and on this conquest "Hungarians were an original and totally free noble nation (*nemes nemzet*)." Only cowards who refused the duty of a soldier became slaves. The descendants of these slaves became serfs, along with the inhabitants of other occupied lands. Serfs were not regarded as part of the nation, for—as the axiom went—the Hungarian nation consisted only of nobles (*nemes*) and brave warriors (*vitéz*).[16] Out of an almost mystical belief in the power of the conquest of Hungary arose the idea that the supremacy of the nobility was "natural" and "in accordance with the genuine Hungarian spirit."

Hungarian feudalism was different from that of most other East European countries in that the nobility here included a large and diverse segment of the population. Although the total number of nobles accounted for a very small percentage of the country's inhabitants, its lower segments were numerous enough to be regarded as a separate class within the nobility. As a result, instead of the serf peasantry, the middle and petty nobles came to be considered the "folk." They were "the people of the nation," and in the bureaucratic language they were called the *populus*.[17]

At the time of the abolition of feudalism, the nobles were entirely unprepared for a transformation of the country's economic system. Employing inefficient and outdated agricultural techniques, suddenly deprived of statute labor and subject to taxation, middle-sized estates rapidly collapsed. But the deeper their noble owners sank economically, the more they clung to their outmoded way of living, which in turn drove them even further toward impoverishment. Although many among them had lost their wealth by the end of the nineteenth century, they showed no inclination to engage in any productive occupations, for these were not thought to suit a nobleman. For these landless noblemen, lacking the economic status that belonged to the ownership and administration of estates but preferring to be called "gentry," the only alternative was to take positions in the government or in county administration. Such positions brought power and financial security and helped them avoid a merger with the despised nouveau-riche bourgeoisie and intelligentsia. The gentry's social status relied more and more on bureaucratic power.[18]

However, the gentry needed some moral basis to justify its claim to the powerful position it held. Having lost its economic privileges, the gentry created an ideological one: the privilege of genuine patriotism. Gradually, the middle nobility transformed itself from an economic class into a political class, "vying for the proprietorship of the state" by monopolizing the concept of patriotism.[19] It proclaimed itself the prototype of the Hungarians and by the end of the century virtually personified the nation in the public mind. Its doctrine was by no means new. As we have seen, the equation of nobility with Hungarian nation, and the ranking of the middle nobility as the *populus* (now called "the core of the Hungarians"), was a deeply rooted historical belief. The gentry had nothing to invent; it only gave an old set of beliefs new vitality.

In this sense, the gentry played the role that the peasant had played in the romantic notion of "folk." Instead of the peasantry, the gentry passed for the best guardians of national identity. The real character of the peasants had no place in this concept of Hungarianness. As a class, the peasants were of little importance in public life, and the peasant question was believed to have been solved forever with the abolition of serfdom. Yet in reality the lifestyle and the standard of living of the peasantry had hardly changed. As we can read in a historical study from 1903, "The proletariat of Hungary, especially the rural one, has remained deprived of political rights in spite of the 'glorious liberation of serfs.' It has no representatives in legislation to act as a true advocate of its interest. Parliament continues to be the representative body of the ruling class by property, the 'nation' in the pre-March sense."[20]

Against the class of peasant stood that of "gentleman" (*úr*)—as members of all noble and non-noble segments of the middle class were called. Between peasants and "gentlemen" the barrier was insuperable; the higher classes despised the peasants, who in turn regarded them with deep suspicion, if not with hostility. A local informant from Transylvania warned a folklorist before his field trip around 1904: "You, the gentleman, will stand before the Székler [peasant]. . . . The 'gentleman' is something hateful to the Székler. . . . Not surprising. The sheriff is a gentleman, so are the inspector of forest, the parish clerk, the bailiff. The parish clerk establishes the tax, and as a result, the bailiff puts the house under the hammer. And so on, with all the other gentlemen, they are there only to make life bitter. It will be difficult to collect data, for you are gentlemen and alien to the people."[21] In the eyes of the gentry the peasants were a miserable, dirty, and uncultured mass. To call someone "a peasant" was an insult; it implied a lack of education, good manners, and sensibility. Nor did most of the intelligentsia sympathize with the peasantry: in their view peasants embodied the provincialism that hindered the cosmopolitan progressive cities. Bartók and Kodály carried out their ethnomusicological work amid such hostilities.

In spite of the general indifference toward the peasant's real existence, the romantic image of the peasant persisted. In fact, there was a growing interest in peasant culture, especially since peasant art was expected to infuse new blood into national art. However, this interest focused on an ethnographic surface. Popular images of relatively recent or foreign origin, such as the baroque tulip, were believed to harmonize with the Hungarian character and—with no basis in history or folklore—prized as originally Hungarian. The most characteristic slogan of this trend was "The embroidered peasant felt coat contains the ten commandments of Hungarian taste."[22]

Even though destructive nationalist feelings were whipped up at the end of the century in order to control an internal social situation, their effect on the other nations of the Carpathian basin was equally damaging. Before the First World War, the territory of Hungary held at least eight major and several minor ethnicities, including Hungarians, Slovakians, Romanians, various German groups (e.g., Saxons of Szepes and Transylvania and other places; Schwabians of mainland Hungary), Serbians, Croatians, Slovenians, Bulgarians, Armenians, Ruthenians, Jews, and Gypsies.[23] Among Hungarians' ancient ethnic groups were the Székler (Székely), Kuman (Cuman, Kún), As (Alan, Jász), and Palots (Palóc). Although these groups had lost their original language, culture, and history, they preserved subtle linguistic and cultural differences and remained conscious of their different ethnic identities until the twentieth century.

During most periods of Hungarian history, to be Hungarian meant simply to be an inhabitant of the Hungarian state and had no ethnic implications: a Hungarian (*hungaricus*) was not necessarily of Hungarian ethnicity (*magyar*). For some of the intellectuals of the twentieth century, including Bartók, such a traditional image of the state remained a political ideal. This thought was at the background of his ethnomusicological and compositional aspirations: for him, "Hungarian national music" had to be based on the folk music of all major ethnicities of the country.

However, by the late nineteenth century such an attitude clashed with the opinion of the majority, who asserted the Hungarian's natural right to supremacy among the surrounding nations. Conservatism in the legal system and in social questions merged in this ideology, and the oppression of the nationalities was an integral part of it.[24] This nationalism proclaimed the Hungarian gentry's "original right" for leadership of its "original territory," which it had conquered in the tenth century and ruled since the state of the first Hungarian king, Saint Stephen. Nobility now became the "historical class" (as if the peasantry had not been "historical" as well), and Hungary became the "empire of Saint Stephen." Just as the various nationalities were deemed alien to Hungarian territory, the newly developed classes were alien to traditional Hungarian society. Industrialism, urbanism, and in general all bourgeois values and modern ideologies came under attack as anti-Hungarian: none of these had a precedent in history, so they were considered incongruous with the Hungarian character.

With the collapse of the Dual Monarchy at the end of the First World War, the political basis for the ideal of multiethnic Hungary collapsed entirely: Hungary lost two thirds of her territory, including almost all the multiethnic lands. This territorial loss was considered unjust by virtually everyone (and not entirely without reason), but the government magnified this national grievance to veil its inability to deal with internal problems. To regain these areas became the sole object of political aspirations. Territorial loss was the national tragedy and the cause of all problems. In this situation, chauvinism and racism flourished. Because of the deteriorating economic situation, political programs that purported to lead the country back to "the good old days" (that is, to feudalism and to a Hungary of larger territory) appealed to the population, although in reality this was yet another way to disguise antidemocratic social ideals.

"NATIONAL" MUSIC: *VERBUNKOS*, GYPSY MUSIC, AND *MAGYAR NÓTA*

It was unique to the situation in Hungary that the ideal of national unity could be matched with forms of art, in particular with romantic poetry and gypsy music. The case of poetry was indeed complex because what was considered to be characteristically *magyar* included nearly everything written in Hungarian, from simplistic sentimental poetry to the best pieces of romantic literature. The generation of modern writers at the turn of the century brought from home an almost "religious cult of Hungarian literature."[25] Young children acted out in their games the heroic fight of the Hungarian against "the enemy" as they were running around reciting patriotic poems. Members of the middle class wrote poetry in a classicizing style modeled on the heroic romantic tradition.[26]

Even more than in poetry, the Hungarian soul was believed to express itself in gypsy music. The case of gypsy music exemplifies the intermingling of historical facts and beliefs that saturated the cultural atmosphere of the turn of the century. The belief that gypsy music was a commonly shared national tradition was not entirely an illusion. During the nineteenth century several popular musical styles developed and spread throughout Hungary and often beyond its borders. One was the *verbunkos* (literally, "recruiting dance"), a national style of instrumental dance music. Its antecedents are the "Ungaresca" dances of the sixteenth and seventeenth centuries, preserved in collections both within and outside of Hungary, and the continuous existence of the type was attested in later written sources.[27] The eighteenth-century *verbunkos* shared certain features with contemporary Western music (e.g., period-structure, triad and tonic/dominant-based harmonies and melodic turns) but had some unique characteristics as well (predominance of dotted rhythms, descending note-pairs, cadential syncopation, ornaments attached to long notes). We know very little about the early development of the *verbunkos* of the romantic era. It is not clear with which segment of the society and in which geographical area it originated, and it is uncertain how much of a role the growing number of Gypsy musicians had in its evolution. By the end of the nineteenth century the *verbunkos* appears to have been known to all strata of society. Several modern folk dances derive from the *verbunkos*, and its characteristic ornamental, rhythmic, and melodic figures are recognizable in virtually all forms of instrumental music among the peasantry. *Verbunkos* penetrated into Hungarian and foreign art music; it was a style well known in the West, as can be seen in the *verbunkos* topoi in Haydn, Mozart, and Beethoven. In Hungary throughout the nineteenth and twentieth centuries, the list of Hungarian composers who wrote piano compositions, symphonies, and chamber pieces in the *verbunkos* style includes Bihari, Csermák, Lavotta, Rózsavölgyi, Mosonyi, Erkel, Liszt, Bartók, and Kodály.

The nineteenth century also brought a new wave of song composition that soon became overwhelmingly popular. Its first branch was composed mainly by amateurs for the urban middle class and is usually called "art song," "folk-song-like art song," or "Hungarian song" (*műdal, népies műdal, magyar nóta*). Coeval with the spread of the *magyar nóta*, a repertoire of "new-style folk songs" (*új stílusú népdal*) developed among the peasantry, perhaps partly under the influence of the composed urban songs.[28] Notwithstanding stylistic differences between them, both groups share some main characteristics. They typically have four musical lines arranged symmetrically, the last line often being the exact repetition of the first. The first and last lines usually employ a lower range, and the second or third line reaches the melodic climax. The lines are usually longer than those of the old-style folk songs and use a much larger ambitus. *Magyar nóta* is less symmetrical than new-style folk song, and its melody is often based on a harmonic progression similar to those in romantic music. Even though *magyar nóta* belonged mostly to the urban middle class and new-style songs were to be found more frequently among the peasants, both groups of songs circulated throughout the country.

The reason for the sudden emergence and popularity of the modern song styles is not completely understood, but it is clear that the process began no earlier than the middle of the nineteenth century. Even in the first decade of the twentieth century the styles were unfamiliar to some older people and unknown in the more isolated villages. In some other areas, however, the new style almost entirely replaced the older repertoire. It is likely that the war of independence of 1848–49 and sympathy for soldiers had some role in the growing popularity of these melodies, which in contrast with the older styles were typically in metric rhythm and performed in chorus. The increased migration of peasants (as soldiers or temporary agricultural and industrial workers) may also have contributed to their distribution.

The peak of the *verbunkos* and the creation of a new popular song culture in the nineteenth and twentieth centuries coincided with a change in social context and performing styles of instrumental music among the peasantry. Along with solo instrumental music by amateur musicians, ensembles of three to five instruments by professional Gypsy groups began to play for peasants.[29] Among the middle class and the aristocracy, Gypsies had established themselves centuries earlier as the musicians of the Hungarian repertoire. But by the end of the century, they had become the primary professional musicians in many of the villages as well, gradually replacing the peasant musicians of more traditional and more typically amateur solo instruments, such as the bagpipe. The repertoire of the Gypsy string ensembles included mainly dances and instrumental renditions of vocal pieces.

Thus several developments coincided: the use of professional ensembles became regular and almost indispensable for social gatherings in the more wealthy villages and in urban restaurants; and Gypsies came to monopolize instrumental music, passing it on as a hereditary profession. By the end of the century, professional music making—that is, music making for remuneration as a service to patrons practiced by a trained and more or less closed group—was associated almost entirely with Gypsies in the domain of popular music to the extent that the designation "gypsy" (*cigány*) became a synonym for professional musician. As professional entertainers, Gypsy musicians were extremely flexible, and their style naturally depended largely on the taste of their patrons. But however great the differences might have been, there existed—or so it was thought—an idiosyncratic gypsy manner of performance that was best represented by the style of the urban ensembles. For Hungarians, this *cigányzene* (gypsy music) embodied quintessential Hungarian music.[30]

To the nineteenth-century public, the musical traditions from which urban gypsy music drew its repertoire—*magyar nóta*, modern popular dances such as the *csárdás* and *verbunkos*—were both ancient and national. If *verbunkos* played a role in connecting popular music to a "historical Hungarian style," the songs of the nineteenth century linked the different social groups.

Magyar nóta was transmitted orally, usually without the name of the composer, and for turn-of-the-century Hungarians its popularity justified the label of folk song. And to be sure, in the nineteenth and twentieth centuries there were probably very few Hungarians who did not know dozens of these songs and have a favorite tune.[31]

Without *verbunkos* and gypsy music, Hungarian romanticism is unimaginable. The sad-faced lad, sitting and drinking among a company of friends in a pub where gypsy violin music played in the background, personified one side of the Hungarian soul. Symbolizing the other side was the wildly dancing, intoxicated young man, who represented the vigor, passion, and strength of "the Hungarian." The slow and fast gypsy pieces matched these two aspects of the Hungarian character. Though both images were stereotypes, Hungarians took them seriously, since they symbolized feelings that seemed both individual and communal. *Verbunkos*, gypsy music, and their associated images also saturated the highest forms of art, including the poems of Csokonai, Arany, and Vörösmarty. The dark passion and exuberant joy of the drinking-dancing Toldi, the eponymous hero of János Arany's epic poem, strike the reader even today as being genuine and sincere, with the author depicting an almost childish simplicity coupled with frightening strength and determination.

Against this unique historical background, a grandiose theory of unified national music seemed inevitable. Bence Szabolcsi captures what the Hungarians of the romantic era might have felt at the discovery of a national style:

> In Hungary "high" and "low" emanate from the same national music: *verbunkos* expresses the soul of the villages as well as the soul of the towns. This is not only the historical heritage of the nobility, not only of the elite but also the music of the simple folk. Could we hope for a better justification, a more powerful source for our reform? We can now approach those who remained indifferent [to our national cause] since the village is our supporter. . . . At this [historical] moment we see new roads in front of our eyes; we have arrived at a height where we can grasp the music of the whole nation as an enormous, unified manifestation of emotions, where we can easily set the next task of an already victorious, integral Hungarian music culture. The nation has created, as a sign and proof of its one and unified spirit and awakening will, its heroic and glorious music.[32]

Although Szabolcsi's pathos has more than a touch of irony, his text is a faithful imitation of both the thoughts and the style of the romantic rhetoric. But the glory of the *verbunkos* soon began to fade, for its intoxicating power was also seen in a negative light at the moment it became popular. For Arany, the portrayal of Toldi would not have been complete without a scene of danc-ing and drinking—but in the *Gypsies of Nagyida*, another of his epic poems, he caricatured the *verbunkos* mania.

The more realistically thinking nobility of the nineteenth century realized that "all of this is mostly illusion that evaporates at the first touch of reality." The "unified spirit of the nation" turned out to be nothing more than a fash-ionable performing style of popular music. Szabolcsi's description summed up the history of romantic national music: euphoria and disenchantment (*mámor és kijózanodás*).[33] The historian Gyula Szekfű described this disillusionment:

> The feudal warrior spirit of the baroque era [that originated in] the system of estates was successfully transplanted [into the nineteenth century] with the help of music. . . . Hearing [these gypsy melodies], the public literally shed tears remembering its national greatness and its centuries-old spirit of opposi-tion. But already [in this era], Kölcsey, who abhorred superficiality in nation-alism, dismissed this music with harsh terms and László Szalay castigated . . . his youthful enthusiasm for national music as an "unspeakably empty enter-prise." Széchenyi never ceased to caricature this new dance music, which he considered the symbol of national self-conceit. For him, the generation of [gypsy music] was the generation that indulged in rhetoric but was incapable of action.[34]

Burdened with such a heritage, how were composers to conceptualize a program for the creation of modern national music? If not the *verbunkos*, then what music could represent adequately the Hungarian nation? In his excellent work on Hungarian romantic music, Kornél Ábrányi painted with dark colors the gradual decline and eventual disappearance of serious Hungarian music. He was deeply disappointed with the achievements of both the nobility and the growing bourgeoisie and doubted that gypsy music had potential for de-velopment. He poured his contempt into angry comments like the closing re-mark of his chapter about Gypsy musicians: "To live in a reasonably economic manner and save money was not characteristic of the . . . Gypsy musician. . . . Even in this regard, the Gypsy assimilated into the Hungarian middle and high nobility . . . whose majority became also the victim of this ancient habit!"[35]

Ábrányi's sarcastic remark summarizes in a nutshell the place of gypsy mu-sic in the social life of turn-of-the-century Hungary, its direct association with the gentry lifestyle. This lifestyle was not a personal matter, it was the corner-stone of the nationalist ideology. To understand this phenomenon, we have to recall that the pretext of the middle nobility's refusal to participate in capitalist enterprise was that such occupations did not fit its traditional patterns of life. By the end of the century the gentry lifestyle had little substance. Participating in card games and in political discussions, socializing in cafés and casinos, and addressing other members of this clique in the second person singular were its typical activities. Food, drink, card games, and gypsy music—these were the truest manifestations of the "weeping-rejoicing" Hungarian character.[36] In Szekfű's words, "The rural residences [of the nobility] turned into pubs where you did not have to pay, as if they had been still supplied with free goods, as was normal in the feudal system. It was at this time that the passion for gypsy music emerged as the property of the 'gentleman': 'Let's poke a banknote of fifty or of a hundred or of a thousand into the favorite Gypsy's hand!' "[37]

By the end of the century gypsy music was invested with enormous emotional and political energies. From the fact that it was an inherent part of gentry lifestyle followed that it was Magyar music par excellence: not simply national music but the original and spontaneous expression of the Hungarian soul. Gypsy music was talked about almost as an anthropological feature of the true Hungarian, and this accorded well with Hungarian chauvinist ideology. National identity required a certain facial type, spontaneous and uncontrolled gestures, mercurial temperament.

The case of gypsy music was symptomatic of the Hungarian situation of the turn of the century where the discourse about culture had long transcended purely cultural matters.[38] The romantic scenario had repeated itself: the modern period brought new waves of euphoria and disenchantment. But this time the political ideas related to culture became more polarized and the voice of nationalism more strident. As the century wore on, it became increasingly difficult to enjoy gypsy music and much of the heroic romantic tradition for its artistic value alone and forget about its latent political potential.

CHAPTER 3

The Romantic Roots and Political Radicalism of Hungarian Modernism

NATIONALISM AND REFORM IN THE NINETEENTH CENTURY

Romanticism's enormous force underpinned the modernist movement and gave its ideology a sharper focus. Recognizing the similar character of the reform generation of the 1830s and the modernists of the twentieth century, Zoltán Horváth called the modernists "the second reform generation."[1] In the social awareness of Hungarians today the legacies of these two radicalist movements represent the idea of "modern and truly European Hungary"; these are the main historical sources of a national self-identification that finds its symbols in the figures of Petőfi, Kossuth, and Széchenyi on the one hand, and Ady and Bartók on the other.

The legacy of romanticism in Hungary was markedly different from that in Austria or Germany. Stifter's attitude of leaving "the scene of contemporary social action for an idealized rural-aristocratic past"[2] was alien to this tradition. The Hungarian romantic ideology contemporaneous with Stifter's work posited a directly opposite worldview; instead of retreating into the garden of artistic and moral sophistication, it entered the arena of political battles. The leaders of this movement were mainly aristocrats.[3] Among them, the most important figure who almost single-handedly created the ideological basis for this development was Gróf (Count) István Széchenyi—the hero and model for virtually all Hungarian modernists. His famous work *Hitel* (Credit), completed in 1830, undertook a merciless critique of the Hungarian social and economic system. In his eyes the underdeveloped countryside was not the symbol of ancient Hungarian spirit; it was land left fallow. Széchenyi proclaimed that the nobles' ancient privileges were a prison for national development, that the peasants' servile state degraded the whole country, and that the system of forced field labor as well as the exemption of nobles from taxation harmed even its supposed beneficiaries. From then on, Széchenyi devoted his life to the idea of reform in Hungary. In 1825 he offered his total income of one year for the establishment of the Hungarian Academy of Sciences; in 1827 he established the Hungarian Casino, a forum of the aristocracy for political and social discussions; between 1832 and 1842 he organized the building of the first bridge to connect the separate cities of Pest and Buda; and in 1845 he began a project to create a railroad system in Hungary.

The radicalization of political life in Hungary, that is, the shift from the idea of slow reform (whose main advocate was Széchenyi) toward the idea of bourgeois liberalism, owed much to Lajos Kossuth's talent as a writer and speaker. From 1832 in his *Országgyűlési Tudósítások* (Congressional reports), which presented the parliamentary opposition's view and circulated as handwritten copies of uncensored personal letters, and after 1841 in the popular *Pesti Hírlap* (Pest journal) with unflagging intensity, he castigated the backwardness of the nobility and passionately denounced serfdom. By the late 1830s the social program of Széchenyi appeared to be conservative; many desired a more radical change and Hungary's complete political independence from the Habsburg empire. These movements, which culminated in the abolition of feudalism with the April laws of 1848 and in the revolution of 1848–49 (crushed by Austrian and Russian military forces), left a determining mark on the national consciousness.

Although Széchenyi participated in the first free Hungarian parliament in 1848, he was overcome by anxiety at the outbreak of the revolution. He feared the worst. He did not doubt that the revolution would be defeated and the Hungarians annihilated in both the political and cultural domains. He blamed himself for the impending catastrophe because he thought that his reform plans had contributed to a situation entirely out of control. After a suicide attempt, he was sent to the mental hospital of Döbling. Recovered and active by the second part of the 1850s, he informed the foreign press about the miserable situation in Hungary and the Habsburg police's cruel retaliation against revolutionaries. His home became a virtual publishing house for the foreign press, and the secret police put him under observation. In 1860 they searched his home and the homes of his friends and confiscated all manuscripts, including his personal diary, as possible evidence in a planned trial for capital treason. A month after the house search, Széchenyi committed suicide.

To his compatriots, Széchenyi's life became the symbol of "Hungarian fate." Mihály Babits, a leading Hungarian poet of the first half of the twentieth century, believed that Széchenyi's life was the mirror of the nation's consciousness: a monumental self-tormenting agony over the existence of the Hungarian nation.[4]

Behind all the reform generations' programs was the idea of patriotism. Its two central tenets were first, to direct attention toward the nation as a whole, including the legally excluded segments, and second, to modernize the country in both the social and economic sphere, following the road to capitalism and liberalism like the countries of Western Europe. Even though the reformers were by no means in agreement on all questions (the main antagonism being between Széchenyi and Kossuth), in one way or another the ideals of social awareness and modernization were at the background of all activities. True patriotism—as József Eötvös, another aristocratic member of the reformers, argued—was not the conservation of outmoded habits and lifestyle but active work toward the elevation of the nation into the ranks of the most developed countries of Europe. This goal could be accomplished only by granting freedom to each individual: "The fatherland is not that piece of land where we were born. . . . It is something more: it is the place where we feel ourselves free. . . . Patriotism is not the virtue of slaves, it can have its roots only in freedom, . . . it is the affection of people to that place where they can feel themselves happy and free. Only if we give constitutional rights to everyone who lives within the borders of our country can we awaken patriotism; only those who, living according to their rights, can feel themselves happy and proud of their state as citizens, only those, will be loyal to their nation."[5]

Like their Austrian contemporaries, the Hungarian reformers held that progress meant the perfection of the moral soul. Characteristically, the issues of social modernization arose first in small aristocratic societies whose immediate aim was to foster the members' moral development.[6] What Széchenyi and his aristocratic friends meant by moral development is closer to what we would call today development of a coherent and ethical worldview, in other words, a capacity for responsible judgment in moral, social, and cultural matters. They referred to this as the "civic virtues" (*polgári erények*). In their vocabulary, "civic" was the synonym for modern-mindedness; it meant a noble existence in the figurative sense of the word and not in the spirit of old-fashioned feudal customs. Their ideal was a society that allowed and expected individuals to think and act in a moral and reasonable manner.

But while in Vienna Stifter and the followers of his ideology maintained that moral development was the prerequisite of social freedom, the Hungarian reformers claimed that the opposite was true: only human freedom, together with the amelioration of social and economic conditions, would bring the people to a higher moral standard. As Széchenyi said, "To give civic existence to all inhabitants of Hunnia!—this is what I regarded in 1832 not only as a timely aspiration for our country but already a belated one. . . . The inclusion of all the inhabitants of our country into our nation would bring life for our fatherland, but the exclusion of nine million from it will bring its death. This is the confession of my consciousness."[7] With this thought the reformers believed they were acting in the spirit of a Christian morality, by which they meant personal responsibility for public action. Their insistence on morality and on the Christian character of this morality resonated with the commonly held belief that only the European Christian societies had arrived at a level where the human dignity of the individual had value in social life. In this sense, for instance, Eötvös argued for the emancipation of the Jews on the basis of a Christian morality; for he maintained that the proper guide for a person's actions was the spirit of Holy Scripture, not its isolated sentences.

THE POWER OF LOGIC AND REASON

The ideas of social liberalism and nationalism were natural allies because they opposed the staunch conservatism of the Habsburg court. Modernity of thought and liberalism were in themselves modes of national opposition, uniting many Hungarians. Already during the Napoleonic Wars, and even more after the conclusion of the second peace treaty of Paris in 1815, Austria's leading diplomatic position was anchored in Metternich's ability to establish a common conservative platform acceptable to east and west. The theoretical foundation of this conservatism (characteristic also of Prussia) exploited a somewhat romantic view of social inequities as an organic and natural development. This argument was based on the supposed connection between the nature of human beings and that of society. The relations between individuals and the government, so the reasoning went, could not be determined by constitutions drawn up in a haphazard manner guided solely by rational argument. The present order, based on differences in rights and duties that reflected differences in birth and tradition, evolved organically, its existence itself being the proof of its inevitability. An enduring government could be built only on the traditional institutions of society: the throne, the church, the nobility, and the army.

The Hungarian reformers, however, insisted that their program derived from logic and reason and not from ambiguous beliefs, for they maintained that only logical thinking and debate could lead to correct conclusions. With this argument, they found themselves in opposition to the conservative ideologies of both the Hungarian nobility and the Habsburg court over liberation of the peasants and emancipation of the Jews (reformers in Parliament brought up the latter question as early as the 1840s). They regarded reason and controlled passion as the appropriate behavior of "mature man." In their writings we frequently find expressions such as "manly sensibleness," "manly wisdom," "manly will," and "manly determination." Here "man" refers less to the contrast between woman and man (which it implies) than to the contrast between immature youth and mature adult. "Manliness" meant the capacity to listen to the voice of reason and form a critical judgment according to principles of morality. From a reformer's realistic viewpoint, the self-congratulating patriotism of the nobility was an empty facade behind which stood backwardness, fear, and indifference. As Széchenyi wrote, "In my mind, the true love of the fatherland has to be based on noble and constant inclinations and not on blind love. . . . The reason that I do not praise everything in my country is the following: I am not tied to my fatherland by such weak means as was Venus to Psyche—that is by the lack of sight."[8]

Rationalism did not mean the lack of passion. Kossuth was held to be a great leader because of his power of persuasion. Here was a leader who "could capture his compatriots both with his pen and with his [spoken] word, who could turn their icy indifference into passion, who could break the traditional immobility of the historical forces. He was the leader who forced the people to reject the outmoded and the old, but he did this not simply with arguments but through evoking emotions, awakening in them the feelings of horror and enthusiasm."[9] The political speeches and writings of some reformers came to be viewed as an art; the name of Széchenyi, for instance, can be found in Hungarian histories of literature.

As we shall see, the modernists of the twentieth century founded their ideology on this attitude. They admired the reformers for their ability to conquer their passion for the sake of realistic thinking, and to "escape," as the writer Zsigmond Móricz said, "into strict realism from the intoxication of fantasy."[10] The late-nineteenth-century literary critic Jenő Péterfy described "the art" of Eötvös: "There is perhaps no other political pamphlet that had been written with more enthusiasm and less hastiness (*több hévvel és kevesebb hevességgel*), deeper conviction and less empty passion. . . . Eötvös believed in the power of ideas, in their consequences and invincibility, but he was never the follower of abstract logic—he was not what the Germans call a *Principienreiter.*"[11]

The fact that the ideological outlook of the reform generation was first shaped by an aristocratic nobility with a cosmopolitan orientation had far-reaching consequences. The generation of aristocrats active around the 1830s did not yet think in terms of the unconditional nationalism that was common toward the end of the century; for them, service to the nation was by no means the first in a series of loyalties. Nor did they need nationalism to come to terms with their identities or justify their social status, as was the case with much of the middle class at the turn of the century. Their determining spiritual experience was the French Enlightenment, and their purpose, in the spirit of the Enlightenment, was the "elevation of mankind." For them patriotism had validity only as long as it did not clash with humanistic ideals.

In theorizing about nationalism as part of a universal ideal, the romantics drew on the organicist conception of nature. Just as there is no such thing as "flower," but only many individual flowers that occur in nature as part of a species, there is no such thing as "human" in a general sense, only individuals and communities. To this way of thinking, which the modernists revived as the basis for their interpretation of organicism, human nature always manifested itself within a communal framework. Thus when a man works toward the elevation of his nation, he works for the elevation of the whole of humanity because the survival of each nation, even the smallest one, enriches mankind. As Gábor Egressy (a famous actor and friend of Petőfi) wrote in 1848, "Some people think that this principle [i.e., of nationalism] is in contradiction with the principle of humanity, of duty toward mankind and of cosmopolitanism: they think that it means isolation, misanthropy, and that it is impossible to exist among other nation-families; they think that nations should rather move toward fusion. What nonsense! This is nothing else than to desire that the individual should disappear from nature, that colors should blend together . . . whereas it is precisely in the variety of individual existences that the infiniteness of God expresses itself."[12]

THE POWER OF POETRY

The impetus for nationalist feeling in Hungary came from the fear that the Hungarian nation would dissolve into the surrounding German and Slav cultures.[13] It emerged in literature as the theme of "national death" and became, in turn, the symbol of cosmic loneliness, of the death of civilization, of humanity, of morality. The best expression of this feeling can be found in the strikingly modern, even surrealistic images of the poetry of Mihály Vörösmarty. In his poems, "man is the wound and sorrow of the earth" (*Az ember fáj a földnek*); "the race of man was bred from dragon's teeth" ("Men" [*Az emberek*], 1846).[14] These images were the reflection of Vörösmarty's agony over the tragedy of civilization, that neither good intent nor knowledge could change the human condition. In this feeling of hopelessness Vörösmarty captured a general attitude of the reform generation and of Hungarian romanticism. His dark images were preceded by Széchenyi's vision of the country as a barren and deserted fallow land, and this topic was explored in Imre Madách's *Tragedy of Man.*

It is against this bleak background that Széchenyi and Vörösmarty forced on themselves the optimism of action, the first through projects of reform and the second through works of poetry. Skepticism could not be the reformer's or the poet's final vision because it justified withdrawal from an active life and, for both men, passivity was immoral. The synthesis of these two reactions—despair caused by the futility of art and knowledge, and a contradictory belief in their mission—led to the proclamation of a heroic imperative. Those who possessed knowledge must work and fight for the elevation of humanity against all odds. Vörösmarty asked: "What is our task on earth? Always to fight, / As best we can, for all the noblest things." In Vörösmarty's poetry, in accordance with the attitude of the romantics in general, this imperative is a tragically heroic gesture. It symbolizes the commitment to social action in the full knowledge of the hopelessness of such action—their " 'and yet' morality," as Péter Hanák called it.[15] It is a moral stance that, like morality itself, has no justification.

The idea that the literati of society are responsible for the rest of humanity is rooted in the thought of German romanticism. Hungarian romantics and their foreign contemporaries did not consider art an entertainment, an ornament to life; nor did they see it solely as a means to express emotions and ideas. Art had the power to reveal the truth that is the deepest meaning of human existence. According to this ideology, true art was always democratic and was comparable in that potential only to religion. As the leading poet of the century, Sándor Petőfi, wrote, "Poesy is not a social hall, / Where fancy people . . . / Go to prattle; / Poesy is more than that! It is a building / That is open to happy and unhappy ones. / For everyone who yearns to pray, / In other words: It's a church, where it is allowable / To step in with boots or, for that matter, barefoot."[16]

Poetic truth thus had a dual meaning in Hungary: the artwork was an original work created from inside the soul and represented social problems faithfully in harmony with the artist's actions. The art and persona of the poet Sándor Petőfi illustrate this stance. In his monumental poetic oeuvre, he showed himself to be a revolutionary spirit with uncompromising devotion to social liberty and justice. His ideas, if expressed with some naïveté, had an enormous influence on the public. Petőfi lived up to the role he prescribed for himself in his poetry: he was one of the leaders of the Budapest uprising on 15 March 1848 and lost his life on the battlefield in the war of independence. In Petőfi's activities, the notion of the prophet-poet became a historical reality.

THE BIRTH OF THE RADICALIST AND MODERNIST MOVEMENTS

When Bartók began his career at the end of the century, the legacy of these historical figures defined the public discourse. Everyone in the middle class and many members of the lower classes knew many details about their lives and deeds and had read their major works. Statues of Széchenyi, Petőfi, and Kossuth, erected throughout the country, depicted them in theatrical heroic poses that were often quite at odds with their characters but corresponded to the image the nation held of them. People looked up to them as role models, even writing patriotic poems in the style of Petőfi or modeling their prose style on Széchenyi's writings.

The young Bartók was no exception. He cherished a copy of the patriotic poem his father wrote, and his youthful letters read like copies of romantic nationalistic prose.[17] As an example we might take the oft-quoted passage from a letter written in 1903: "Everyone, on reaching maturity, has to set himself a goal and must direct all his work and action toward this. For my own part, all my life, in every sphere, always and in every way, I shall have one objective: the good of Hungary and the Hungarian nation. I think I have already given some proof of this intention in the minor ways which have so far been possible to me."[18] Anyone familiar with the writings of Széchenyi and other romantic politicians would find these lines strikingly similar to—virtually the copy of— Széchenyi's prose. The phrase "on reaching maturity" alludes to Széchenyi's concept of the "mature man." The emphasis on "work and action," the dramatic intensification ("all my life, in every sphere, always and in every way"), and finally the ideal of the nation's elevation were all romantic clichés.

The myth surrounding the great figures of the preceding era cast its shadow on political life. Each party wanted its share of the romantics' inheritance. The reading of newspaper reports about parliamentary battles over the legacy of the romantics amounted to a virtual mass ceremony.[19] As Gyula Szekfű wrote in his *Three Generations* (1920): "We heard the name [of Széchenyi] day after day from the leaders of the nation, from those who generated public opinion. Everyone who labored to elevate the Hungarian to a higher state of power and culture swore by his name. His name reverberated in scholarly societies, in aristocratic clubs, and in the modest associations of university students. . . . But almost all of these depicted Széchenyi as they themselves wanted to see him. . . . Everyone created his own Széchenyi in whom he could admire his own image."[20]

The political establishment began to feel increasingly uncomfortable with the universalistic aspects of the romantic tradition and sought ways to exploit the romantic themes for the sake of political nationalism. For the reform generation, nationalism was meaningful only if it took into account a broader humanistic context and emerged in social action. As a result of the political establishment's nationalist propaganda, discussed in the previous chapter, the postromantic era began to see nationalism as a purpose in and of itself. The active attitude of the reformers gave way to passive nationalism, mystifying and indulging in the "eternal" qualities of "the Hungarian." This ideology tried to put art into its service, demanding that its foremost purpose be to incite patriotic feeling.

Against such a nationalism a strong radical opposition developed among the intellectuals at the turn of the century. As they confronted both the conservativism of daily life and the problems of the emerging modern capitalist world, at first they began to withdraw from public life. Artists proclaimed an aesthetic of *l'art pour l'art* and the self-imposed isolation of the artist, reacting against the political atmosphere that penetrated deeply into the spheres of art to condemn anything "modern" and "bourgeois" as anti-Hungarian.

Yet compared with other countries, Hungary in the twentieth century remained singularly unaffected by the idea of "art for its own sake" that lies at the base of the aestheticist movement. It is true that the first impetus to modernism came from aestheticism and certain ideas related to it—most significantly, organicism—had a continued role in the sustenance of the modernist culture. For decades, art's separateness from politics had remained in debate, the topic of ever-renewed battles as the century wore on. But the authors influenced by aestheticism usually turned away from it within a short time.[21]

What members of the emerging modernist movement decided to do instead was enter public life. Such an attitude was more natural in Hungary, where art has traditionally been part of movements of national dimensions. The decision did not involve endorsing a political ideology or rejecting individualism. But artists realized that by its very nature, art affected society and had a potential to change the public consciousness. Even works with intimately personal topics could affect the public's thinking in social matters. Artists could not evade responsibility by withdrawing from society because such isolation would in itself convey a message with potentially damaging consequences to the development of cultural life. As a minimum requirement, the acceptance of a public role meant an awareness that such a connection existed. But in fact, most members of the emerging radical movement aspired to much more; they wanted to integrate their moral and political convictions into their aesthetics and expected the public to recognize and respond to such a message embedded in art.

The acceptance of a public role resulted mostly in affiliation with ideals of the political left wing—although not always or even typically with left-wing parties. In Hungary, a leftist orientation was unavoidable. When at the turn of the century artists intrigued by the problems of modern life and society were trying to create space for themselves within society, they confronted the semifeudal tradition. Their very existence forced them to oppose it and look for allies within the context of the movement of social radicalism.

It is symbolic that the movement started with the establishment of a sociological journal called *Twentieth Century* (Huszadik Század) in 1900. A year later the contributors and editors of the journal established the Society for Social Studies (Társadalomtudományi Társaság, or TT). The first president of the society was Ágost Pulszky, a scholar of the positivist study of law, and the next was Gyula Pikler, a scholar of the philosophy of law and a sociologist. The society counted among its members writers, literary critics, journalists, linguists, and historians such as Lóránt Hegedűs, Bódog Somló, Gusztáv Gratz, Ármin Vámbéry, Rusztem Vámbéri, Ignotus (Hugo Veigelsberg), and Oszkár Jászi. With the support of members among the Hungarian freemasonry, the Society of Free Thinkers (Szabadgondolkodók Magyarországi Egyesülete), an anticlerical and atheist independent society, was established in 1905 under the leadership of Samu Fényes. Soon there were two more masonic lodges formed with members of the radical intelligentsia, named after Comenius and Martinovics; the latter included several members of the TT and also artists such as Endre Ady and Béla Reinitz (the future composer of songs based on Ady's texts, and the dedicatee of Bartók's *Five Songs* op. 16). In 1908, with the help of the Martinovics lodge, a new association of "liberal-minded university students with social and radical views" was established and named the Galileo Circle (Galilei Kör). Its members were students of medicine, engineering, and social studies. Besides organizing lectures and debates about artistic and scholarly issues, the Galileo Circle published pamphlets summarizing the recent achievements in various fields.

In painting, the break with conservative ideas took place in 1896, when Simon Hollósy left the Academy of Arts and opened a painting school in Nagybánya together with his students (including important figures of modern Hungarian art such as János Thorma, Béla Iványi Grünwald, Károly Ferenczi, and Pál Szinyei Merse, who joined the group later). They objected to artistic cliques, politicized institutional art, and the academic style of painting. This development was followed in 1906 by the creation of the Circle of Hungarian Impressionists and Naturalists (Magyar Impresszionisták és Naturalisták Köre, or MIÉNK), including István Csók, Béla Czóbel, Adolf Fényes, Károly Ferenczi, Károly Kernstock, and József Rippl-Rónai, under the leadership of Szinyei. A year later, those painters who found the association of MIÉNK insufficiently modern separated from the group to form the Eight (Nyolcak).

In literature, by the end of the nineteenth century the weekly called *A Hét* (The week) brought together several of the more modern-minded intellectuals. It published articles by almost all the individuals who were active in modern art: writers or literary critics like Endre Ady, Sándor Bródy, Milán Füst, Géza Gárdonyi, Jenő Heltai, Ignotus, Mór Jókai, Gyula Juhász, Margit Kaffka, József Kiss (the editor), Dezső Kosztolányi, Tamás Kóbor, Gyula Krúdy, Kálmán Mikszáth, Ferenc Molnár, Ernő Osvát (the future editor of the literary journal *Nyugat*), Árpád Tóth; painters, art historians, or scholars of aesthetics like Pál Szinyei Merse, Károly Lyka, and Lajos Fülep; and music critics like Emil Ábrányi, Aurél Kern, and Géza Molnár.[22]

Much of the modernist development occurred without any formalized framework; ideas were discussed among friends at private gatherings and around café tables. The debates of the young intellectuals who gathered regularly at the home of György Lukács and became known later as the Sunday circle generated many ideas that influenced the movement.[23] In 1904 Lukács and some of his friends created the Thália, an experimental theater whose aim was to break with the national theaters' formalism and elitist isolation to bring dramatic works to the masses. At the first organizational meeting, which took place at the home of Lukács, there were about thirty people, including Béla Balázs (who provided the texts of two Bartók stage pieces), Zoltán Kodály, the literary critic Marcell Benedek, and the assistant director of the National Theater, Sándor Hevesi.

But the breakthrough came with Endre Ady's publication of the collection

New Poems (Új versek) in 1906. His entry onto the stage of Hungarian cultural life meant the beginning of a new epoch. The integrity of his art and life and his all-encompassing vision of social reality found expression in a poetry that was both uncompromisingly modern and of the highest quality. A parallel work also published in 1906, Bartók and Kodály's collective arrangements of *Hungarian Folksongs*, became the symbol of the new stylistic orientation in music. Their work was a manifesto of modern Hungarian style, positing a new ideal of the connection between folk and high art, between modernity and national culture.

The year 1908 marked the publication of the first issue of the literary journal *Nyugat* (West). The journal soon became the leading organ of modern art, accommodating virtually all significant literary figures of the era. It contained articles treating social, cultural, and philosophical issues, as well as reviews of theater productions, exhibitions, and Hungarian and foreign works of history, philosophy, and the arts. Its regular contributors included, besides those who published in *A Hét*, Mihály Babits, Béla Balázs, Lajos Hatvany (a Jewish baron who also financed the journal), Frigyes Karinthy, Menyhért Lengyel (the author of the text of Bartók's *Miraculous Mandarin*), Anna Lesznai, György Lukács, Zsigmond Móricz, and Géza Csáth (one of the first music critics of Bartók and Kodály). *Nyugat* welcomed novelty, quickly disseminating information about cultural developments in the West; its editors, especially Ernő Osvát, insisted on quality. The journal and the cultural evenings organized around it (where Bartók performed several times) constituted a real alliance of the modernists who were called the *Nyugat* circle. More than a forum for literature, *Nyugat* became a magnetic force and the symbolic center of modern culture.

The appearance of Ady, Bartók, Kodály, and the *Nyugat* circle was not simply the continuation of the modernist trends of the 1890s but a new modernism. The previous generation of modernists broke with the conventions of romantic forms, but their art was still somewhat decorative and light. The members of this new wave of modernism built on the achievements of their predecessors, creating an art whose depth and power of expression superseded theirs. For instance, the idea of eliminating the difference between essential material and ornament by making the circular lines of an ornamental surface part of the global design originated with the artistic movement called *Jugendstil* or art nouveau. But the new generation saw in circularity a deeper symbolic meaning and reinterpreted it for the sake of dramatic expression, indeed in order to render the basic contradictions of existence.[24]

Many of these developments were connected with programs of public education. In 1906, the TT established a series of free educational lectures directed toward the working classes and organized as a free university with a four-year curriculum. The faculty, consisting of scholars, artists, and art historians, taught without financial compensation and managed to continue the lectures until the beginning of the First World War. In the fall of 1906, within a more institutionalized framework, another independent university opened under the name Free School of the Social Sciences (Társadalomtudományok Szabad-iskolája), under the direction of Oszkár Jászi and Bódog Somló. Clearly there was a need on the part of the intelligentsia to reach out to a broader public and to fulfill thereby their responsibility as literati. Also, many believed that a new and less elitist audience could perhaps better appreciate modern art than the traditional middle class. The desire to reach out to a more spontaneous audience underlined the plan of the Lukács circle's experimental theater, the Thália. Years later a similar spirit led Kodály to launch a program of musical education and choral singing that Bartók also supported and led them both to provide pieces for young people and the less musically educated public.[25]

A casual look at the activities of the second reform generation reveals such diversity that it is hard to understand what united them and how they projected a coherent ideology. Groups associated with the movement ranged from small circles of friends to broad cultural networks, and the character of their activities might have been political, scholarly, or cultural. In the cultural sphere, modernity could not be associated with the high arts alone. A considerable amount of popular art was in fact modern and accorded with the ideologies expressed by the radicals. Among Ady's closest friends was Béla Reinitz, whose cabaret chansons based on Ady's texts were a most effective means of popularizing his poetry.[26] And Reinitz's chansons inspired Bartók to compose his *Five Songs* op. 16 for the poems of Endre Ady, and he dedicated the piece to Reinitz. For the recordings of his and Kodály's folk-song arrangements Bartók chose singers who moved easily in the domain of urban popular music. One was Mária Basilides, a great alto singer of classical repertoire and the interpreter of Reinitz's songs; another was Vilma Medgyasszay, who performed operetta and classical music but was primarily a cabaret singer and the leading actress (later director) of the famous Endre Nagy cabaret.

Socially, the radicals were a most heterogeneous group. Its center was the intelligentsia of Budapest, with the prominent participation of assimilated Jews and substantial support from assimilated Germans but also from members of the aristocracy and the working class. And still, the majority of the bourgeoisie and the conservative middle nobility dreamed of holding the traditional ranks of a feudal system, and many Jews joined the conservative middle nobility as well. As an establishment the Catholic church was clearly on the side of the conservative ideology, but the Catholic population on the whole was probably not more conservative than the Protestants and the Jews.

In general the opposing camps of the ideological war between modernism and conservativism did not form along the lines of religious or ethnic allegiances or historically developed groups and economic classes. For that reason, the definitions of "radicals" and "modernists" are both loose and circular: they include all who thought and acted in terms of the radical ideology and associated themselves with these circles at one time or another, in way or another. Like any other cultural phenomenon, the second reform generation was not a rigidly defined, stable entity; personal relations were multiple and complex, with concentric and overlapping circles of friends and constantly changing alliances and ideologies.

THE POLARIZATION OF PUBLIC LIFE

And yet the varied activities of these heterogeneous and loosely defined groups elicited a solid front of opposition. The consensus and clear public stance of the radicals was possible because the central issue of their ideological battle was concentrated in one desire: change. This issue overrode all others, or better, the acceptance or refusal of the idea of modernization determined the attitude toward all other issues. The radicals opposed the politics of conservativism by reclaiming the romantic heritage. In their eyes, the conservatives had betrayed the romantic tradition because they resurrected meaningless remnants of a half-forgotten past without understanding its essence. They maintained that theirs was a "more true Hungarianness" because it focused on the real and existing needs of the nation. The radicals saw themselves as the heirs of the reformers first and foremost because they too fostered the idea of modernization.

The objective of the reformers at the beginning of the nineteenth century had been to establish the possibility of capitalist development with the abolition of the feudal institution; the second reform generation at the beginning of the twentieth century aimed at the elimination of all remnants of feudalist society and a full acceptance of the capitalist economy and liberal legal system. By interpreting the tradition of the reformers as one of modernization, the new generation could posit the ideal of progress as a national heritage against the conservatism of political nationalism. As Ady wrote with angry passion,

"Whoever is the enemy of progress, of striving for the better, of uncompromising freedom of spirit, is a traitor to the nation even if he does nothing in his entire life but sing the national anthem."[27]

Ady was among the first to reiterate the ideology and the images of the nineteenth-century reform movement, using it to confront the modern situation. Just as for Széchenyi, for him the "Hungarian fallow land" (as he called it in the volume *New Poems*) is the metaphor for backwardness. It is the land of winter and abandonment that "dreams without dream," where every new idea is drawn to the ground by the weeds that reach up to the sky:[28]

Csönd van. A dudva, a muhar,	There is silence. The burdock and mallow
A gaz lehúz, altat, befed	Draw me to the ground,
S egy kacagó szél suhan el	They lull and cover me.
a nagy Ugar felett.	And the laughing wind flies by
("A magyar Ugaron" [1905])	Above the Fallow Land.
	("On the Hungarian Fallow Land")

Ady's words deliberately echo Széchenyi's and Vörösmarty's apocalyptic visions of "national death," a death that would be caused not by an enemy but by the nation's incapacity to "continue along the road" to liberalism:

> Those men who learned to think in the light now put their heads together with terrified whispers and say that this darkness sheds its shadows over everything, and woe to those who do not learn to go backward like crabs. . . . The world created the myriads of wondrous machines and now it proclaims that man, the man who owns his own self, is not needed anymore. . . . [In this little country] live and reign a hundred thousand persons, but there are millions who, just born, sweat blood, suffer, and die. Here those who pray to their gods in another manner than is wished by the lords of light and luxury are barely tolerated. . . . Woe to the children of Moses, woe to the descendants of the Maccabeans, woe to those who are really the followers of Christ, woe to the followers of Luther, and woe a thousand times to those who dare to believe in . . . the great work of Voltaire, and thus—continue along the road.[29]

The ideology of the Hungarian romantics that posited as a moral demand the active will of the individual against hopelessness became central to the ideology of the radicals of the twentieth century; it was their " 'and yet' morality." For the modernists, the legacy of the romantics provided an example of a moral commitment to society. Referring to the romantics, Ignotus wrote in

1906, "Our only hope for the clearing of our sky springs from the knowledge that such [greatness] did exist not long ago, so there could be soon [again] people able to live up to their responsibility."[30] The belief that an artwork has to point toward a positive acceptance of life, with the full awareness of a tragic reality and in spite of it, animated the attitudes of Ady and of Bartók and became a cardinal tenet of their aesthetics. This legacy was the source of the moral stance of those modernists who stood up against the country's growing racism during the interwar period. As Babits wrote, "Even if we had no hopes at all, and one had all the reason to lose faith in the power of morality and justice, still, the heroism of the lighthouse is more worthy of the literati: it stands faithfully marking the direction, even though no bark turns its prow toward it—until the Deluge drowns its lamps."[31]

The two radical movements were similar in spirit and in their historical function. In both cases the majority of the political leadership and the population was on the side of conservativism. Against such overwhelming power, a few people tried to raise interest in ideas of social, economic, and cultural progress. The reform generation of the nineteenth century had a great advantage: several of its leading members came from within the establishment, and the battle between the reformers and the conservatives was played out in the sphere of politics with the support of art, especially poetry. Also, the public the reformers had to gain for their ideas was limited to the politically active elements of the nobility. Moreover, several of the movement's leading personalities, such as Széchenyi and Wesselényi, enjoyed great respect as members of the traditional aristocracy and had the economic means to back up some of their programs.

The situation of the radicals of the twentieth century was much more difficult. The movement was created and sustained by scholars, university teachers, and artists, along with members from the bureaucracy and occasionally individuals from the industrial aristocracy and, more rarely, from the traditional agricultural aristocracy. Even though the radicals had a few wealthy supporters, on the whole they were economically marginal people without power or status. Their method of fighting was merely persuasion.

And yet the effect of their work was enormous. By 1908—within the few years between Ady's emergence on the Hungarian scene and the formation of Nyugat—the attitude embedded in Ady's art became the cornerstone of a political and cultural battle. József Révai explained the context:

> When Ady appeared on the stage of Hungarian literature, immediately a passionate fight arose around him. This was not only an aesthetic war but a political war to death whose participants did not conceal that much more was at

stake than just the battle of literary trends. Ady's poetry struck hard, touching on the sore point of Hungarian reality. It was such a conscious declaration of war that the political and literary reaction could not have been content, even if it had wanted to be, merely with the mere aesthetic analysis of Ady's poetry. . . . Before the First World War, the boundaries of the opposing factions of the battle around Ady were clear and obvious. . . . Everyone took it for granted that Ady belonged to the camp of bourgeois transformation and that [for this reason] the literary representatives of the conservative reaction expelled and condemned him.[32]

Modernists and conservatives alike understood how deeply the bourgeois transformation was to affect the power structure, and with it everyone's life. The spread of bourgeois art was more than a cultural issue. It undermined the hegemony of a feudal lifestyle and values. "It is treason and slander," wrote a conservative journalist, "what they do in *Nyugat* under the pretext of civilizing the barbarian Magyars. They want to ruin our morals, they want to disillusion us of our faith, and they want to crush into pieces our national pride. A storm of outrage should sweep away all those who commit such deep offenses against the nation." Cultural issues gained such significance in the battle for political power that they drew the Hungarian prime minister, István Tisza, into the action.[33]

It was not merely the politically sharp observations Ady put forward in his articles that shocked the conservative majority, but the totality of his art. Ady's poetry, and modernist art in general, irritated the public even when it was private and intimate. As the denunciation of *Nyugat* illustrates, this art opposed the conventional idea of the "nation" simply by focusing on topics that were emphatically personal. Themes of love and sensuality, loneliness and estrangement in the modern world were all topics stripped of sentimental happy endings and thus revolutionary in themselves. All those themes—without political overtones for readers today—struck the majority with the force of a manifesto against the conventional image of the Hungarian spirit. But the most rebellious aspect of this art was simply its modernity. Matters of technique, like the use of a new brush stroke in painting or the introduction of a new poetic form, became evidence of opposition.

THE DISCOVERY OF PEASANT MUSIC

Within this context of controversy, Bartók's discovery of peasant music has political significance.[34] Bartók's attitude was by no means intentionally political.

His ethnomusicological thesis was presented in a scholarly manner and the results of his research were, in essence, independent of aesthetic and political considerations. In turning toward peasant music in his original compositions, his decision was based on aesthetic grounds; in his eyes, gypsy music was the paramount example of romantic sentimentality, the very style from which he struggled to liberate himself. But we can imagine how deeply the following lines might offend most of the Hungarian middle class: "That this Hungarian popular art music, incorrectly called gypsy music, has more value than [much similar] foreign trash is perhaps a matter of pride for us, but when it is held up as something superior to so-called 'light music' . . . we must raise our voices in solemn protest. . . . On the other hand, we cannot indulge in the desire . . . that shallow musical taste be changed overnight. . . . The role of this popular art music is . . . to satisfy the musical needs of those whose artistic sensibilities are of lower order."[35]

As Bartók's correspondence shows, at the beginning of the collecting project he only envisioned a large number of new melodies in the style of the *magyar nóta,* and the role of the peasants was merely to provide further new examples. This project would have been in accord with official politics. But Bartók and Kodály discovered that certain elements of peasant music—particularly the old-style song and its characteristic performing style—were idiosyncratic to the peasant culture and did not form part of any generally known national music.[36] Not that collectors before Bartók and Kodály had missed all these tunes. But it was a discovery that there existed, among the peasants, not just a few more examples of tunes in a shared Hungarian style but a repertoire and performing style entirely dissimilar to those of gypsy music and *magyar nóta.* The fact that these old-style songs were rapidly going out of fashion did not diminish either the scholarly or the political significance of their finding. However relatively small this repertoire was, it led to a new conceptualization of folk music.

The emphasis, for Bartók, was on the fact that the national culture was not unified: "There is considerable confusion about the concepts of folk music and folk song. The public at large generally believes that a country's folk music is something homogeneous although this is by no means the case."[37] He realized that, even within the peasantry, there existed various styles and substyles. What mattered, however, was that there did exist a style known only to the peasants: "Within peasant music in the broader sense there is a distinctly separate layer [group], at least in Eastern Europe, which we may call *peasant music in the narrow sense.* . . . Taken in this narrower sense, peasant music includes those melodies that belong to one or more coherent styles. In other words, peasant music in the narrower sense consists of a large repertoire of melodies of similar structure and character." And as Bartók explained elsewhere, some of the songs of the old style represented the oldest layer of Hungarian music; they might have originated in the music culture before the Hungarians conquered the land.[38]

In the political context of turn-of-the-century Hungary, this discovery seemed nothing less than high treason. It undermined the myth of a unified national musical style, thus subverting one reason for belief in national unity. Bartók's and Kodály's work called into question important tenets of the official, gentry-centered nationalism. First, they claimed that among Hungarian peasantry there existed a homogeneous and distinct musical style. Second, they called it a collective creation of the people. And third, they traced certain of its features to historical periods before the conquest of Hungary. This new theory of peasant music called attention to the existence of a Hungarian art known only to the peasants, and hence independent of the upper classes, the nobility, and the gentry. The claim that features of Hungarian peasant songs could be traced back before the conquest of Hungary challenged the traditional view of the conquest as the very moment of the nation's birth—the origin of everything truly Hungarian. In a sense, Bartók and Kodály were taking whatever was valued as "national" in gypsy music and transferring it to an unknown type of peasant song. They undermined the notion that national character inhabited a single class and gave that class its ultimate measure of value.

The fundamentally new element in Bartók's attitude was the recognition of the "otherness" of peasant society. The awareness of the peasantry as a social entity of its own, with a culture alien to the upper classes, made Bartók place the emphasis on the separateness of his art from folk music. Its difference from any style he had known forced him—unlike any composer of the romantic era—to approach folk music as a resource for reshaping his own style. Hungarianness in musical style could no longer be considered a given, a birthright. It belonged to the culture of "the other," and an outsider had to approach it with respect and had to labor to understand it.

From the perspective of the gentry-centered ideology, how absurd to claim that a genuine Hungarian had to come in "direct contact with the peasants" in order to feel the spirit of this music and needed to "absorb the idiom of peasant music" in order to make it into "his mother tongue."[39] Was not folk song by definition the mother tongue of the Hungarian, and was not its spirit felt spontaneously by anyone genuinely Hungarian? The majority of the middle class refuted bitterly Bartók's new scholarly and artistic ideas. The conservatives did not want to hear of "peasant music in the narrower sense," nor could they agree with Bartók that their *magyar nóta* was merely composed urban folk song. But they were most hostile to the idea that national music could be modern and dissonant, and that its Hungarianness would not be overtly expressed.[40] The issue of folk music became even more politicized as the century wore on. In order to illustrate the fusion of political and musical attitudes, it is worth quoting from Emil Haraszti's 1929 "Gypsy music, peasant music, official music" at some length:

> The most characteristic and at the same time most unresolvable problem of Hungarian musical culture is the case of gypsy music. Village and town, aristocrats and socialists, the peasant and the gentleman, the intelligent and the uneducated, the Christian and the Jew (today the gypsy-Jew is a type of its own), in other words the entire Hungarian society becomes united as one in the cult of the gypsy [music]—with the exception of a single percent, the segment of the educated musicians, although even among them there are fans of gypsy music. We witness thus a distortion [of normal development], a unique and unparalleled phenomenon to which nothing similar could be found in the cultural development of other nations. The whole nation is unanimously on the side of the gypsy because it is [our nation's] faith that this music expresses the collective soul of its race. The foreigners too surrender because there was never another folk music that so powerfully captured them. Yet at the same time the learned musicians renounce [this music]. . . . The peasant music should also be disseminated—but, if possible, not with modern harmonies. . . . [But we have to realize that] Hungarian gypsy style . . . stands closer to the atavistic thinking of the Hungarian people than all the music of Kodály's *Háry János* with all its faithful folklore and artistic primitivism. . . . We have greater need for gypsy music now than ever before, for *the gypsy is Hungary's own militant irredentist, whose like as an artist cannot be found anywhere else in the world.* Hungarian sighs are carried to the four corners of the world by the gypsy violin, and Hungarian hearts are heard beating in his music.[41]

We find here the euphoric tone of romantic nationalism revitalized, indulging in the praise of the atavistic, spontaneous, and "militant" (!) power of gypsy music that unified the Hungarians and made foreign nations surrender. Nationalism cannot tolerate the idea of progress: it refutes even the mildest forms of artistic modernism in Kodály's *Háry János* and Kodály's and Bartók's folk-song arrangements.[42]

This passionate defense of gypsy music illustrates how desperately the conservative circles wanted to save the illusion of an all-encompassing, original national style. At one time or another, they labeled all who associated themselves with modern art or the radical movement "traitors," "cosmopolitans," "enemies of the nation," or "Jews." The Jewish question, the questions of modern art, of social progress, and of urbanization were intertwined. The accusation that Budapest and its bourgeoisie lacked Hungarianness resulted in violent quarrels between two groups that came to be known as the urbanites (*urbánusok*) and the villagers (*népiesek*). The dispute raged at varying levels of ideological fervor until the end of the Second World War. Gyula Illyés's criticism illustrates the main argument: "Budapest is not in Hungary. It is above it, below it, next to it, God knows where it is exactly if we have to find its place according to its spirit."[43]

Although the quarrel over Budapest was most intense between the two wars, its conceptual background and political significance were already present during the first decade of the century. Many similar accusations came both from inside and outside the intellectual circles, creating tensions and enmities of wild and bewildering complexity. The territory at issue was not the countryside and Budapest; the accusations never came from those who lived outside of the spheres of modern urban bourgeois life. Rather, the conservative middle class used the euphemisms "Budapest" and "urbanite" to attack what they considered the Jewishness, rootlessness, cosmopolitanism, corruption, and shallow culture and immorality of the city. In their eyes, the modern bourgeoisie of Budapest was Hungary's "ahistorical middle class."

In fact, this characterization was apt. As in other Eastern European capitals, the assimilated Jews had a prominent role in creating the modern intellectual life of Budapest. They included university professors like Henrik Marczali, Ignác Acsády, Dávid Angyal, Bernát Alexander, Ignác Goldziher, and Bernát Munkácsi, as well as the psychoanalyst Sándor Ferenczi, who introduced many of Freud's ideas to the Hungarian public. Many Jews created and supported modern Hungarian literature and the arts, as performers, publishers, critics, and patrons, among them the families of Gruber, Arányi, Kohner, Hatvany, and Lukács, whose salons of modern art offered a context for informal concerts of modern music. Bartók had contact with all of them; from the circles of these Jewish salons came his first supportive audience. The financial backer of *Nyugat* was Lajos Hatvany, and its first organizers and editors were also Jewish: Miksa Fenyő, Hatvany, Ernő Osvát, and Ignotus. Ady's most faithful supporters and closest friends were two Jews, Béla Reinitz and again Hatvany. Many among the first generation of modern writers were Jewish: József Kiss (the editor of the journal *A Hét*), Sándor Bródy, Jenő Heltai, Tamás Kóbor, Menyhért Lengyel, Béla Balázs, Ferenc Molnár, Dezső Szomory, Ernő Szép, József Vészi, Béla Zsolt, and Anna Lesznai (who was also a painter). Jews were important as well in the visual arts: in painting most notably Róbert Berény (the painter of the well-known Bartók portrait), Adolf Fényes, Béla Iványi-Grünwald (the director of the Nagybánya school), Izsák Perlmutter; and in sculpture Fülöp Ö. Beck. Sándor Hevesi was the founder of modern Hungarian theater and instrumental in the creation of the Thália, whose other leading members, György Lukács, László Bánóczy, and Marcell Benedek, were also Jewish. The publishing houses established or owned by Jews included Révai, Wodiáner, Singer and Wolfner, and Deutch. All important music publishers were founded by Jews: Rózsavölgyi, Kálmán Nádor, Ferenc Bárd, and Zipser and König.

Budapest was the only environment in Hungary with which assimilated intellectual Jews could fully identify. But even though some Jews and most other segments of the intelligentsia had roots in the countryside, they too realized that the cultural life of Budapest was the sine qua non for their existence. Analyzing this period in the 1950s, Pál Ignotus wrote, "The spiritual revolution that began around the turn of the century . . . was the revolution of urban existence against the oppressive and petrified country mentality."[44] To defend Budapest meant to accept this revolution. It meant to fight not only for the acceptance of Jews and radicals, of Budapest and modernity, but, most important, for a larger conception of Hungarianness.

In reality, the traditional concept of a "unified Hungarian nation" now excluded most of Hungarian society. Modernists fell outside it partly because they were often of German or Jewish origin and partly because their lifestyle and taste did not accord with the stereotypical image of the Hungarian. The Hungarian hero, even in modified Jókaian form, did not resemble the inhabitants of the rest of the country either: the proletariat, the capitalist banking and industrial aristocracy, the conservative (partly also Jewish and German) middle class, the landless agricultural workers, the domestic servants, not even the petty bourgeoisie.

As long as it was defined in historical terms, Hungarianness would oppose any progressive endeavor: by the nature of things, a concept cannot be at the same time new and traditional. As Ignotus wrote in 1908,

It would be useful to collect how many things were deemed non-Hungarian in the past decade. . . . Budapest is not Hungarian. The dialect of Pest is not Hungarian. The stock exchange is not Hungarian. Socialism is not Hungarian. Internationalism is not Hungarian. The organization of agricultural workers is not Hungarian. Capital is not Hungarian. Secession and symbolism are not Hungarian. It is not a Hungarian idea to exclude the religious institutions from public education, or to eliminate religion from the curriculum. Caricature is not Hungarian. Greater tolerance toward love is also not Hungarian. General suffrage is not Hungarian. Materialism is not Hungarian and it is not Hungarian to suppose that people may change their institutions . . . rationally, according to their needs. But most of all: whoever is not satisfied with the existing situation is certainly not a Hungarian and such a person should have the sense to leave the country with which he is unsatisfied.[45]

A new conceptualization was needed, one that dispensed with the old expectations and accepted as being "Hungarian" everyone and everything that existed de facto in Hungary. In 1904 Ignotus described this idea of tolerance by using Budapest as its symbol:

Mikszáth with his charming bias loves his village more than the jungle of houses he cannot associate with, and we have to accept this with patience, the more so because our literature is much beholden to such bias. . . . I became one with Budapest . . . it is my business and my feeling that I let spill into my poetic works, if I know how to do it. But I have no right to order other writers to follow this feeling as the only way of salvation under the penalty of being expelled from the nation and literature.

Either we design a uniform standard for literary thought, feeling, interest, and expression, and in this way force writers to lie or at least produce bad things, or we regard everything that is de facto written by Hungarians as literature and as Hungarian, and in that case we have to give up this persecution aesthetics that would measure literary value by political standards.[46]

Despite their love for Budapest, emotional identification with the city was not easy even for the intellectuals. The chasm between the Hungarian countryside and a cosmopolitan—or at least differently Hungarian—Budapest was disturbing: "Here are gathered all kinds of shoddy, good-for-nothing German and Jewish rabble, who make up the majority of Budapest's population," wrote Bartók impatiently in 1905.[47] Kodály, who arrived in Budapest from the countryside at about the same time as Bartók, had similar impressions: "If it had not been for the fact that the program notes were written in Hungarian, the music played at concerts would have made one think that one was in a small German town."[48]

Like most other members of his generation, Bartók could overcome his ambivalence. Not that he felt entirely comfortable in the urban Jewish intellectual milieu, but he had no doubt that this was the only segment of society from which he could expect support for his art, and he accepted the fact that intelligentsia in the modern sense could develop only in the city. Whatever his criticisms of city life, Bartók did not hold up the ideal of the village or of an idealized past as alternatives. In his *Miraculous Mandarin*, it is not a peasant figure who opposes the inhuman life of the city but someone who is alien; the mandarin is the symbol of an imagined primordial, abstract morality. The fact that Bartók chose to write one of his most monumental works about modern urban life illustrates the emotional energy he invested in thoughts about the city. The social implications of the stances for or against the city were obvious to him.

For a number of reasons, their commitment to urban culture and particularly to Budapest became increasingly difficult for several artists during the interwar period. The movement of "village research" (*falukutatás*) grew in part from the renewed need of some of the modernists to affirm their connection with an older image of Hungary (and to replace the earlier idealizing ethnographies with a more faithful account of the realities of peasant life). Although at some point the movement had clearly racial overtones (against Germans and Jews), it did produce valuable studies and literary works.[49] The Jews and many others who came to view Budapest as their only real environment, but who did not want to isolate themselves from the rest of the country, felt trapped in an impossible situation. Outside this circle and even within it, to remark on the city's immorality, rootlessness, and Jewishness was fashionable, even among those who were deeply attached to it. István Vas remembered his ambivalence toward the city:

> When this love first burst from me, I realized that I already felt Budapest in my pores, that I knew it in the same way a man knows a woman. I loved her smell, the cool and stale smell that came from the gated arcades of large buildings on hot summer days, the smell of acetylene lamps at the Teréz district fair, of boiling bitumen to fix the asphalt. . . . [Earlier, I was unaware of my love for Budapest] or better, say I did not accept my city. I did not accept it as sometimes a man does not accept a woman even though he is in love with her. He does not acknowledge this relationship in front of others because this woman is not liked in some circles, because it discredits him. But he would

not admit this love to himself either. Perhaps because he did not like her smell, even though unconsciously he fell in love with it. Or he did not like her voice. In Pest, for instance, the sound of the street-organ, the beggars' violins you often heard in the morning from the courtyards of the Teréz district, and on summer nights, the tunes and words of popular music that reverberated from the brick walls of Pest. . . . [So, for a long time, I insisted I did not love the city] and I did not draw the consequences even from the fact that whenever I came home from vacation or from Vienna, or when I came home after even the shortest trip, I could not begin my life here before I quickly ran to the Korzó [the walk at the edge of the Danube] to indulge again in this panorama that was so familiar but still always new.[50]

MODERNISM AS SUBCULTURE

Clearly, a feeling of insecurity characterized the life of the intelligentsia in Budapest's new milieu as well. Yet on a certain level, the formation of the modernist circles resolved or at least eased its members' anxiety over social identity. Being part of the modernist circles meant belonging to a group based on ideological and cultural allegiances, and in turn-of-the-century Budapest such identification proved more meaningful than traditional ethnic, religious, or class distinctions. To the survival and development of Hungarian modernism the social interactions of these people, the discussions within circles of friends, were as crucial as their actual scholarly and artistic production.[51] Belonging to a marginal group in constant opposition, the radicals needed to reinforce their status and identity by keeping up a social life. The art historian Károly Lyka described their life:

> More or less the same stratum of the Budapest public went to all the exhibitions, performances at the opera house, concerts of the Philharmonic, and all the performances at all the theaters, this public bought the new literary works, this was the audience for lectures at literary societies. That stratum of the public from whom culture demanded so much support was actually not small but still it was not large enough to sustain the artistic life of the entire country.[52]

The central circle of the modernists was indeed rather small. For those who witnessed it, this milieu was something with an obvious character, almost a nation within the nation. It was "*A közeg*," as István Vas called it, the active milieu, the vital context of the radicals' whole lives. For the inner circles the nation was not Hungary but "the City," by which they meant the modernist

FIGURE 1.   The *Nyugat* circle of friends: an evening at the Academy of Music, 1930. *Left to right,* Menyhért Lengyel, Biró (the concert's organizer), Oszkár Ascher (actor and reader of poetry), Aladár Schöpflin (literary critic), [?], Ernő Szép (with cigarette), Oszkár Gellért, József Erdélyi, Zsigmond Móricz, Aladár Tóth (music critic), Sophie Török Babits, Milán Füst, Mihály Babits, Dezső Kosztolányi, Frigyes Karinthy. (Photo by Szécsi of Turul Photos. Courtesy Petőfi Museum of Literature, Budapest)

milieu of bourgeois Budapest. As Lajos Hatvany said to the representatives of the conservative aristocratic forces, "For me the Hungarian nation does not mean the same as for you. For me the Hungarian nation means Endre Ady and Béla Bartók."[53] This attitude of the modern-minded intelligentsia, and especially its Jewish members, persists in an excerpt from *Nine Suitcases*, a documentary book by Béla Zsolt, a Jewish writer and journalist of the interwar period. He wrote the following lines in 1944 when, after escaping deportation from Nagyvárad (now Oradea), he returned with forged documents to hide in the big city.

> I have sinned against everything and everyone, but not against this City, into which I must now steal in disguise and where I would be shot down, if recognized, like a rabid dog. . . . Still, it is my home. This city was built by my urban predecessors; to each one of its bricks the city-founding heroism of urban workers and day laborers and bourgeois, or their crimes, if you will, are attached—and I take the city upon me together with its crimes, even today! But what have these strangers to do with it, these strangers who in the provinces have always been irritated, been made suspicious or spiteful, by the pace, the attitude, the way of dressing, the dialect, the press, the literature of the city that with its crimes and frivolity represented for them the West to which they were averse. They thought it offered them an intellectual challenge they might well meet one day, but they were unwilling to tackle it because of their spiritual laziness. . . . Did they have an idea what our bridges meant to us emotionally, or a new house built on an empty lot, or an old house with a history and artistic value—or even our hideous petty-bourgeois neighborhoods and miserable slums . . . everything that was Budapest. . . . And now we natives will be rounded up—not only the Jews, but all those who wanted this city to resemble the big, beautiful, healthy, and civilized cities of the world, differing from them only in those things that are really worth differing in.[54]

Artistic and scholarly achievements alone cannot change social systems and economies, and the activities of the second reform generation did not culminate in monumental national deeds. But the persistence of its members in proclaiming the need for the recognition of modern art, democratic rights, and a capitalist economy, transformed the thinking of many of the middle class and, at the very least, created a strong, modern-minded intellectual elite. The activities of this segment affected everyone who had some connection with Hungarian art or intellectual life. No cultural movement between the wars could ignore the activities of Bartók, Kodály, Babits, of the circle of *Nyugat* and other organizations. Their names reverberated in political discussions as well.

This circle of intellectuals embraced anything it judged meaningful to modern life. It was the only milieu in Hungary that accepted Bartók, Ady, and later Attila József, giving them a context for their art in spite of and emphatically against the leading opinion of the country as a whole. Because of the polarization of public life, these artists lived in an environment of condemnation and adoration. Rarely did a "national composer" meet with such hostility and unfair criticism as Bartók did from the official cultural establishment in Hungary. But nowhere else in Europe could he find such an enthusiastic, almost fanatically devoted and supportive audience as the one that surrounded him in Budapest.

CHAPTER 4

Hungarian Modernism and the Organicist Theory of Art

UNIVERSAL OR NATIONAL ART

Summarizing the relation of art to reality, in 1926 Ignotus gave readers of *Nyugat* a strictly organicist view of artworks:

> Even the faithful copy of [the surrounding] reality cannot affect us as real [in the artistic sense] unless it is presented as necessity, as the "only must," something that could not be otherwise. . . . The copy of a person is not a sculpture . . . it needs something to become [art]. And this is necessity. . . . The sculpture is a sculpture only when it is structured, when all its elements are related in an organic manner, when it is saturated by the same idea of motion or motionlessness. . . . The sculptor, the painter, the poet has all the freedom to add thousands of details [to the essential thread] but all has to amount to one thing: necessity. Organicism, credibility, logic, balance, structure: all of these are variants, or governing forces, or equivalents of this same thing. . . . How to create a piece of such qualities is a secret. . . . [The artist] works somewhat in a manner so that while he creates the art piece with pain and inspiration he can see an invisible model, as it were. Whatever comes to mind is either in harmony with this model and thus "good," or is not and thus "bad." And he is working somewhat in this way . . . as long as, in his work, every detail corresponds to the model. And at that point [when he finishes the artwork], there is only the piece, as if no model ever existed.[1]

Written after eighteen years of work with the central journal of Hungarian modernism, Ignotus's words represent the aesthetics of the movement in general. To appreciate its emphasis on organicism—which is by no means self-evident—we must take into account the complex and contradictory forces at the background of the modernist aesthetics.

Hungarian artists at the beginning of this century encountered a set of contradictory and idealistic demands for works of art. Like their Viennese contemporaries, they wished to revolutionize art and at the same time perpetuate its great tradition. Modernity itself imposed a dual demand: uncompromising originality in expression on the one hand and response to the reality of contemporary life on the other. Relating to current social life and expressing the emotions of the individual, an artwork was nevertheless to carry on the tradition. As we have seen, Schoenberg and Webern believed that they had found the answer to these challenges in one concept: the organic nature of the artwork.

The other contradiction was a particularly Hungarian phenomenon, resulting from the legacy of Hungarian art, which drew on the European tradition and on Hungarian romantic art. Only the most extreme nationalist aesthetic could construct an image of the art of the Western European countries as "other" and as completely separate from Hungarian artistic developments. In fact many more artists held the opposite opinion, underestimating the achievements and uniqueness of Hungarian art during the previous centuries. With the exception of Hungarian romantic poetry, which the young generation held in high esteem, its members considered it their task to "invent" Hungarian art.

An art that had the ambitious aim of being both truly Hungarian and European was not without problems. Although Hungarian romanticism was influenced by contemporary foreign movements, its legacy was considerably different from the aesthetics that Hungarians distilled for themselves from the intellectual tradition of the German cultural sphere. The public nature of Hungarian art opposed the abstract, philosophical, and individualist worldview transmitted by artworks and by the teachings of Goethe, Schopenhauer, Nietzsche, and Freud, to name only the figures who were most influential around the turn of the century.

In this context the renewed interest in the literature of the West and the revival of the organicist theory meant less the continuation of prevailing concepts of art than a break with them. As we have seen, artistic life at the beginning of the twentieth century was monopolized by state institutions that promoted the ambitious conception of a "national art" able to sustain and create empires by the mere force of its all-Hungarian character. From the suffocating world of Hungarian academic literature, the young literati looked up to the modernist developments of Western Europe with admiration and jealousy; they were ready to embrace everything that seemed to offer a more universal and at the same time more individual conceptualization of art. As Mihály Babits remembered,

> Our teachers saw barely anything else in the great Hungarian works than some patriotic or folkloric "content." And whatever modern poets we had access to seemed to regard this aspect as the most important in poetry. We, the critical young people, had a rather straightforward judgment of this whole contemporary literature. In our eyes it was nothing but the empty rhetoric of cheap sentimentalism. From the one side we got preaching, on the other we were bombarded by *magyar nóta*. But the public was not even looking for anything else in literature than for empty phrases and *nóta*. . . . Whoever was chased by the decadent thirst for real literature looked toward the West. He raved about English and French poets, about modern and supermodern poems, in order to keep himself ostentatiously away from the banal truisms of the poetry of empty phrases and the [*magyar*] *nóta* of incriminating simplicity. The names of Baudelaire and Verlaine, Poe and Swinburne, Mallarmé and Rilke circulated among the fuzzy-haired youth of the *Nyugat* circle.[2]

The whole of the modernist movement represented, consciously and intentionally, a new ideal set against the officially promoted image of national art. The first step toward the new conception was not merely to reject the notion of "national art" but to refute any limits or preset rules on content, style, and form. Reflecting their belief in the organicist concept of art, the modernists left the old institutions for Simon Hollósy's school of painters in Nagybánya or set up other independent associations such as MIÉNK (circle of Hungarian impressionists and naturalists), Nyolcak (the Eight), Thália, *Nyugat*, and Bartók's and Kodály's UMZE (new Hungarian musical society). On the surface, these movements meant the liberation of artists from the institutional establishment, the expression of their dissatisfaction with the traditional way of looking at art, which had focused on technique and style. But at a deeper level they involved an exodus from style itself, an active move of the avant-garde to free itself from any external constraint and return to its fundamental elements, that is, to nature. Lajos Fülep wrote about the Nagybánya school, "The strength of their individuality and the greatness of nature is completely sufficient for their art; they have no need of an academy or of foreign examples; they paint out of their own emotions and their innermost souls."[3]

And the motto of MIÉNK, on the catalogue of their first exhibit, stated, "We are believers in nature, but no longer do we copy it with the eye of the academies; we dip into it with out intellect."

The new artistic attitude pointed toward a conception of art whose strength and moral commitment came from within. In the framework of organicist theory, artists had no allegiances to ideals outside the domain of art, such as nationalism or any other political ideology. Morality rested in the artwork itself. The responsibility of the artist, the modernists claimed, should be "merely" to create art of the highest quality. By the force of its truthfulness, such art would affect social consciousness and advance the national cause.

Paradoxically, in Hungary the emphasis on organicism was itself a political statement. It was the declaration of the liberation of art from political propaganda and a clear stance against both artistic conservativism and the emptiness of mass culture. As Ignotus wrote, "What is occurring here is not simply a revolution but . . . [a true] war of independence; a war for the freedom of the writer from the ignorance that seeks to elevate its laziness and narrowness to the rank of a demand claiming that these were Hungarian characteristics and tradition; it is a war against politics that attempts to justify its intrusion into literature with the catchword that it is protecting the national character of Hungarian art."[4]

REALISM AND THE
HUNGARIAN MODERNIST AESTHETIC

But even though organicist theory was essential to the creation of modernism, it was not fully satisfactory in the Hungarian context. Because of their intimate interaction with the day-to-day destinies of Hungarian society, artists could not be satisfied with an ideology that aimed at maintaining the high aspirations of art alone, not even if it underpinned their opposition to the establishment. While there were some who cultivated a sense of isolation and disdained the world that distracted them from the purest forms of art, the majority were developing an ethos more appropriate to the struggle of the country that was on the slow road to modernization and democratization.

Although they subscribed to the organicist view, they did not believe in the existence of art outside communal culture. In Vienna, the accent was on the artists' honesty to their own beliefs and work even at the expense of the community's artistic needs. Success meant work that responded to the public's tastes, necessarily mediocre. In contrast, Hungarian modernists stressed the reconciliation of art's honesty and its public effect. The demand to create an art with public significance and—as Bartók said—"specifically Hungarian" character ranked high.

In fact, the modernists maintained that a work that did not show communal characteristics was not really true; it was the imitation of fashion, or speculative and arbitrary. To invent something that appeared to be new was not difficult; the real task was to create an original style that was at the same time modern, Hungarian, and of high aesthetic quality in organicist terms. For them, artistic quality and modernity were inseparable from the issue of Hungarianness: we have noted Bartók's desire to "create" Hungarian music because, according to him, no earlier pieces that sounded Hungarian were of the highest quality. It was this postulate that disqualified Liszt as a national composer because, as Bartók saw it, Liszt's most Hungarian pieces were not his most serious compositions.

The modernists' attitude called for a different reading of, and ultimately the transcendence of, organicism. The first problem the theory raised was that of style. The conceptualization represented by Hofmannsthal, Kraus, Schoenberg, and Webern tended to strip all conventions from art to fit their demand for the honesty of expression. In this way they eliminated the notion of style as a common language or tradition, equating it rather with the unique language of each individual piece on the one hand, and with the eternal natural rules on the other. These eternal rules had nothing to do with local tastes. They were universal, obeying only the necessity of nature—thus Schoenberg and Webern presented twelve-tone composition.

This conceptualization of style fell short of explaining art's potential to express communal identity, a crucial point for modern Hungarian art. But as the Hungarian modernists saw it, this interpretation was not necessary: the organicist theory did not preclude the possibility of multiple styles and multiple roads toward new art. As the individual is always part of a species in the natural world, in art too the individual finds expression in the context of communal style. According to this idea, the notions of "individual" and "universal" are only abstractions: in reality, all natural phenomena appear in classes and types, the constraints of which no individual entirely escapes. The universal potential of art is not to be found in what is similar in all artworks but often in what is different; it is the totality of the multiple and complementary forms of expressions that is universal.

In the political sphere this reasoning took on new urgency. Joining a heated debate about ethnic identity—particularly Jewish identity—during the 1930s, Béla Tábor wrote:

> It is the destiny of every human being to be an individual different from everyone else, a different expression of the one [and only] spirit. But this dissimilitude should not aim at isolation, rather its subjects should complement and enrich one another. It should express the fact that each individual color is irreplaceable. The individual's self-awareness could subsist only on this irreplaceable character, and it is also the source of ethnic consciousness. Ethnicity is the historical prerequisite of individuality, that is, it is the historical prerequisite of both real differences and real similarities among people. The first means that all those essential factors that make it possible for humans to participate in reality according to their own individual character penetrate the historically constrained individuality in man through the filter of a concrete ethnicity. The second means that all those essential factors that make communication among different people possible also come through the filter of ethnicity. The word "human" is an empty abstraction as long as we separate it from the reality of ethnicity.[5]

In Hungary, most people within the modernist milieu and even outside it embraced this chain of thought. Many social groups felt marginalized by a stronger group within a fragmented society: the assimilated Jews by the Christians, non-Hungarian ethnicities by Hungarians, the modern bourgeoisie by the gentry-minded political establishment. More important, in the context of Europe, the whole of Hungarian society seemed marginal and its members had reason to embrace an ideology that emphasized multeity. In fact, Tábor's remark was the continuation of the romantic argument for the necessity of patriotism. We noted Gábor Egressy's words in 1848: "[To desire that] nations should rather move toward fusion . . . is nothing else than to desire . . . that colors [of the natural world] should blend together."

The modernists saw the individual and communal nature of art in dialectical opposition, as necessary forces that continuously act with and against each other. They did not challenge the view that art was true to itself only if it was original. Like their Viennese contemporaries, Hungarian artists believed themselves to be geniuses who created from within their soul through suffering. The following lines from Balázs's diary are illustrative of their self-image: "I can work only with difficulty. Everything is torn out from me with pain, because I do not use resources already exploited but try to reach for some new depth. But I can say that [whatever I write] I find it in the innermost depth of my soul . . . I feel physical pain and weariness." But Balázs realized that even the most individual expression in art had value only if it was also communal: "The eternal law of every art is that it can reach greatness only from the soil of a nation through the characteristics of an ethnicity. And this is what matters in theater too."[6]

The anxiety to achieve greatness *and* Hungarianness—although a bit exaggerated in Balázs's mind—mirrored a common concern: in Hungary, the only justification for the existence of modern art was that it was national art, that it expressed something that was relevant for the people "there and then," in a way that foreign works or those of an older Hungarian tradition were not. But the communality of art was a cardinal issue for aesthetic reasons as well. First, it meant coming to terms with art as a social object, that is, attending to its communicative power. More important, however, the communality of art related to its coherence and transcendence. These demands were not exclusive; on the contrary, they could be realized only through each other. It is telling that, in György Lukács's opinion, the structural coherence in drama was a result of its functioning as a communal form.[7] Transcendence, whether in art or ritual, was not a lonely experience but intimately linked to a feeling of togetherness. As Balázs put it, "The Jewish service requires the presence of ten persons. There is a deep psychological reason for that. . . . The more people are together, the more intense is the feeling of the reality of transcendence."[8]

Furthermore, if art aimed at capturing a deeper essence in reality, it could not ignore the most immediate experience of reality—that is, social life. Coherence had meaning because and only if it captured all of reality, not only the depth of the soul and the abstract harmony of all-encompassing nature, but also all the common aspects of everyday life.

The urge to confront reality was the motivation behind new art already in the first phase of modernism in Hungary. In 1890 the editorial of the first issue of the modernist journal *A Hét* (The week) announced its hope to be a forum for writings that are "only literature, and not the great force to form and create state and nation." But what Bernát Alexander demanded was not aestheticism but realism: "I have to confess that I find little actual realism in our new literature, little sensitivity toward the reality of our lives. It shows no sign of profound observations and at the same time leaves much to be desired in its form; it lacks that artistic urge that ripens the work with caring devotion and forms it with strict diligence. . . . If the nation does not recognize its face in a literature, it turns away from it. One can buy books out of patriotism, but one will read them only for pleasure."[9]

On a basic level, the emphasis on the real assessment of life generated a feeling of insecurity—not only about the place of art in society, as was the case with the Viennese, but also about the potential of art itself. To put it differently, while the Viennese circles responded to the crisis of art with the affirmation of what they knew art should be, the Hungarians questioned the postulates of art. Nothing could be taken as given; modern artists had to start anew, redefining the relationship of art with reality and the place of the artist in society and nation. Even the issue of being a Hungarian was unclear: personal letters and diaries as well as literary journals and pieces reflect the hesitation of the intelligentsia when it came to the question, What is it to be a Hungarian?

In order to create new art, the modernists recognized, they had to address basic questions concerning life, they had to descend to "the origin," the "essential facts" of existence. The inspiration for this thought came partly from German-Austrian tradition, particularly from Nietzsche's philosophy. In his copy of Nietzsche's *Human, All Too Human,* a work that was well known among the literati in Hungary and had a great influence on him, Bartók marked several passages.[10] One such passage expresses the idea that true creation could be born only from one's search for phenomena (the idea often recurs in the book):

> It is the mark of a higher culture to value the little unpretentious truths which have been discovered by means of rigorous method more highly than the errors handed down by metaphysical and artistic ages and men, which blind us and make us happy. . . . That which has been attained by laborious struggle, the certain, enduring and thus of significance for any further development of knowledge is nonetheless the higher; to adhere to it is manly and demonstrates courage, simplicity and abstemiousness. . . . Formerly the spirit was not engaged in rigorous thinking, its serious occupation was the spinning out of forms and symbols. That has now changed; serious occupation with the symbolic has become a mark of lower culture. As our arts grow ever more intellectual, our senses more spiritual, and as for example we now adjudge what is pleasant sounding quite differently from the way we did a hundred years ago; so the forms of our life will grow ever more *spiritual,* perhaps to the eye of earlier ages *uglier,* but only because it is incapable of seeing how the realm of inner spiritual beauty is continually growing deeper and wider, and to what extent we may all now accord the eye of insight greater value than the fairest structure or the sublimest edifice.[11]

Nietzsche disdains the shallow imitation of tradition, indeed he disdains tradition as a whole, because it brings us only the forms and not the essence. New art has to aspire to a "deeper and wider" "inner spiritual beauty." But we attain this spiritual beauty only if we value the "little unpretentious truths which have been discovered by means of rigorous method" and "attained by laborious struggle." It is not hard to see that this line of thought accords well with Schoenberg's and Webern's ideology, since they often refer to the natural laws of music, to the phenomena (clearly the same as Nietzsche's "little unpretentious truth"), and to that "laborious struggle" from inside the mind that leads artists to new discoveries. Of course, when Schoenberg reminds us that it is "our duty . . . to examine anew for ourselves. . . . Regarding nothing as given but the phenomena," he takes for granted that the phenomena are the structural elements of the great works of Western art.[12] His *Fundamentals of Musical Composition* is, in a sense, a collection of such phenomena.

But Hungarians viewed this issue differently. To renew art from within the boundaries of the great tradition made little sense. Are the natural laws of art to be found only in the pieces of the genius and are they to be found necessarily within the domains of traditional art at all? Could there not be a way to find the sources for art in a new reality—perhaps a new Hungarian reality?

We have seen that artists in Hungary were trying to reconcile various artistic traditions with one another and with their desire for modernity and hoped to resolve the contradiction between individual expression and communal art. All these problems now seemed to center on the search for what they called "the phenomena." The phenomena had to do with the unchanging and permanently valid reality that transcended the subjective ego of the artist. Discovery in art had to emerge from a search to see deeper into reality, to recognize what is objective and essential. In the words of Lukács, "Today we again seek order in what surrounds us in the world. To see what is there and see in ourselves what truly belongs to us. We seek what is constant, we desire that our deeds have weight and our statements have meaning. . . . We seek meaning in all of our things, that they have consequences and that it would be clear what they exclude."[13]

As Lukács clearly stated in the article, with this new Weltanschauung Hungarian modernists "proclaimed war against any ideology and art whose first and last words were 'I.' " They were not rejecting individualism but were convinced that the universality of art lay in its capacity to grasp what is essential in life. The idea resonates in the diary of Anna Lesznai (a prominent member of the circle of Lukács and Balázs): "What are the phenomena existing in society and the individual psyche, which have retained strong magical tendencies? These are art, certain facets of religion, erotic love, a whole series of spiritual experiences such as presentiment, telepathy, déjà vu, suggestibility."[14]

The phenomena are not simply material facts. They are the constant elements of various facets of human existence, of behavior, religion, art—feelings, attitudes, experiences, actions, ways of dealing with things that can be understood only through the individual experience. People have to live life fully in order to see what is essential: the subjective individual experience leads to the discovery of what is objective and universal. As Bartók wrote to Stefi Geyer: "You really do not want to struggle, to have emotional shocks, even life-threatening feelings and situations? Then how are you going to feel the Ninth symphony, the *Faust*, Nietzsche's *Zarathustra?*"[15]

The idea that understanding comes from exploration of the inner self was not a novelty after the late romantic trends and in an era of psychoanalysis. But the Hungarian modernists insisted that the discovery of the phenomena of life came from an active involvement with matters of everyday life. Intent on seeing lives distant from theirs, intellectuals set out to travel abroad and into the Hungarian countryside. Lukács devoted much energy to the organization of theater, Ady to journalism, Bartók and Kodály to field work, Balázs to the Communist party. All these activities led them away from their immediate environment and professions to a territory where they could not feel entirely at home.

THE AESTHETIC CONCEPTUALIZATION OF FOLK ART

Although "life" meant the totality of the empirical world, including all aspects of modern life, there was a consensus that the basic phenomena of existence manifested themselves more clearly and immediately in a "primitive" communal culture whose framework appeared to be more constant and enduring. The thought led artists directly to folklorism. Folklorism kept alive "national" tradition and expressed the romantic "spirit" of the people. But now folk art came to be significant for another reason: it witnessed the individual's primordial oneness with society. Paradoxically, the modernists believed that specifically Hungarian themes and forms of folk art revealed the essential and universal aspect of life in the simplest and yet most expressive manner.

Simplicity was both at the beginning and at the end of the road in the development of artistic expression. At the beginning of the road stood folk art, as the expression of a primordial, oceanic consciousness of oneness with the universe, a feeling of wholeness without conflict. To the circle of Lukács, the paradigm of primordial art was the tale, which unlike most art forms takes the totality of life as its theme for stylization in art: "The goal of [stylization for] every literary form is to render one [single] potential of the essence of life as something concrete and possible to live through. . . . The [folk] tale, however, takes as its central motive of stylization the entire life, that is, life in its broadest sense, which means the metaphysical essence of the soul as well as simple existence, an existence that has not separated itself from nature."[16]

Opposed to this primordial stage of expression stood the simplicity of artworks. The artist was supposed to arrive at a higher level of simplicity through the increasing sophistication and complexity of feelings; this simplicity was the final outcome of a complex process. With this idea, which played a central role in Bartók's aesthetic, Hungarian modernism paralleled certain artistic tendencies of the West. The impetus for abstract geometrical representation that appeared in the paintings of Braque and Picasso reflected the belief that in "primitive" constructs the artist reaches down to something primeval—not to copy primitive art but to use their forms to achieve a higher level of concentration. Of course, during the first decade of the twentieth century the Hungarians could not know that these trends in the visual arts were just about to develop in the West too. But they were certainly aware of a general artistic tendency toward simplicity and intense expression. In their case the tendency merged with the desire to create national culture. They hoped to capture an original feeling that emerged also in folk art and recreate it in a manner that was relevant to the complexity of modern life. Lukács believed he had found the realization of this ideal in Balázs's poetry:

> The fundamental feeling [of Balázs's poetry] is a primitivism that has been achieved after having gone through [stages of] sophistication. It is a primitivism that is imbued with all possible ways of sophistication. [His simplicity is] expressed also in the primitive nature of the form. The events of the soul are reduced to one moment, to the very moment when fate appears transparent and encompasses the entire stage of the soul. This moment is given weight, color, and shape, in the emotional sense, by the intimacy that finds its focus and expresses itself in the most extreme concentration. It is for this reason that some of his poems are so close to [Hungarian] folk song both in their language and rhythm, for the most monumental effect of folk song also involves such concentration and the economical use of words. There is something prophetically intellectual in these poems; their language is endowed with wonderful sensuality precisely because of its intense emotionlessness, formulaic precision, and concreteness. The moments reflected here are the most exalted moments

of life, they encompass in themselves the totality. These short and cold words are able to contain something more and deeper than all the superficial sensuality of most of life."[17]

The idea of creating a modern and national style with the stylistic integration of folk art proved most fruitful in the domain of architecture, at least around the turn of the century. Ödön Lechner, the leading figure of the secessionist movement, envisioned new Hungarian architecture in much the same manner as Bartók envisioned new Hungarian music. Like Bartók, Lechner considered it the task of his generation to create a specifically Hungarian style within the high arts. He too thought of folk art as a distinct "language" whose principles were to be learned so that a synthesis could be achieved between these and the demands of modern architecture:

> The Hungarian language of [architectural] forms is something that was missing in the past but will exist in the future. This is the conviction that leads me in my creative work, whose sole purpose is to cut a path for the creation of a Hungarian style [in architecture]. . . . Hungarian style does exist, it can be found among the Hungarian people and it is a distinct style and can be recognized [as Hungarian]. . . . We have to learn this Hungarian folk style as if it were a language, as we have learned the Greek folk style [of architecture]. We have to discover its rules, we have to immerse ourselves into its spirit so that we are able to integrate the spirit of these forms into the larger, more developed, and monumental architectural demands of our era.[18]

In collaboration with Gyula Pártos, Lechner designed several buildings in Budapest, Pécs, Kecskemét, and other cities of Hungary. After a period of eclectic use of various historical styles, beginning in the 1890s, he began to devote special attention to the coordination of functional designs of forms and ornamental elements inspired partly by folk art. He took advantage of modern technologies in the creation of ornamental surfaces, especially of the facades of buildings. He developed an ornamental style through experiments in the Zsolnay china factory. The Zsolnay factory produced some of the most inventive pieces of turn-of-the-century china and experimented with the synthesis of folk themes as well as the curved designs and exciting colors of art nouveau patterns. Among the most successful buildings of Lechner using this ornamental folk style are the Institute of Geology (designed 1896, built 1897–99) and the Hungarian Postabank (1899, built 1900–1901; Figures 2, 3).[19] Several members of the following generation continued the path of Lechner. Among them,

FIGURE 2. Ödön Lechner, entrance hall of the Institute of Geology. (Photograph by Lajos Dobos. Courtesy National Board for the Protection of Historic Monuments, Budapest)

FIGURE 3.   Ödön Lechner, Postabank. (Reproduction by Gábor Barka from *Budapest, Neubauten* (II) [(Vienna:) Verlag Anton Schroll, 1910]. Courtesy National Board for the Protection of Historic Monuments, Budapest)

Károly Kós used Székler architectural patterns in the geometrical shapes of his buildings (Figure 4).

In spite of a number of inventive and artistically successful experiments, the infusion of folk style into Hungarian art remained, on the whole, a peripheral movement in architecture. The merger of folk and modern styles was even less successful in literature. Few shared Lukács's high esteem for

FIGURE 4. Károly Kós and Dezső Zrumeczky, building in the Budapest Zoo. (Reproduction by Gábor Barka from *Magyar Építőművészet* [1912]. Courtesy National Board for the Protection of Historic Monuments, Budapest)

Balázs's poetry. Most of the modernists as well as the Hungarian public at large found his folkloristic-modernist fusion artificial.

Ady chose an altogether different solution. His art reflected the problems of all segments of Hungarian society as well as the many contrasting images of modern existence. But rather than integrate these feelings into a coherent personal style, he expressed the multiplicity of social experiences through multiple styles and poetic forms. His topics ranged from intimate expression in love poems to perspectives of misery in the lives of peasants and the proletariat. Stylization was an important part of Ady's socially committed art: when he spoke of something that he had not lived through totally, he chose to express compassion by maintaining distance. The most successful examples of such stylization are his *kurucz* poems. In order to express the underprivileged people's suffering and feelings of abandonment, Ady revived and stylized the Hungarian *kurucz* poems, choosing as his symbol the partly historical and partly legendary figure of the *kurucz*, the poor "fugitive" (*bújdosó*).[20] The positive message of Ady's art, embracing the entire society, cannot be overestimated. But neither Ady nor anyone else in literature integrated folk poetry into a coherent, modern, and personal style. Perhaps such fusion of styles is impossible in literature, since its elements are tied to precise meanings. Whatever the reasons, literature and the visual arts both failed to realize the grand idea of modern Hungarian art—to express within a single form the phenomena of life, the spirit of modernity, and the essence of the Hungarian character.

BARTÓK'S ORGANICIST FOLKLORISM

The only artist in Hungary to use folk culture for its motivic resources *and* as "original material," a source for the "phenomena," and the only artist able to integrate it entirely into his personal style within the framework of organicism, was Bartók. The enthusiasm of the modernist circles for Bartók's art sprang from the recognition that it encompassed their ideal of folk-based, organicist, Hungarian modern art.

The Bartókian stylistic synthesis is so complex that we cannot summarize all of its aspects here. But in order to understand Bartók's central place within the modernist movement and give a background to the development of his aesthetics, we must explore one aspect of his folklorism: its deep connection to organicist theory. Perhaps Bartók did not set out for his first field trip with the pretentious demand to draw it out into a grand organicist vision. But he interpreted his folklorism in this manner very early on, as evidenced by virtually all his writings on the subject from the late 1910s. Like several artists in Hungary, he understood the search for the phenomena somewhat as a scholarly undertaking, a continuous preoccupation with reality. Such preoccupation was not part of artistic creation per se, which he conceived in organicist terms—that is, from inside the mind alone. It was rather some preliminary study, similar to the study of a language in which an author plans to write poems.

Bartók's entire ethnomusicological oeuvre was in a sense a search for phenomena, that is, a search for those basic forces that governed the inner life of the musical organism. In his ethnomusicological studies, he concerned himself above all with exploring the resources of music, developing subtle and comprehensive ways to express it. Folk music, Bartók believed, was music in its primordial original form. The compositional principles of folk music were a priori legitimate because they came from nature. As Somfai wrote, Bartók "felt more confident in his compositional innovations when they seemed to him to have some justification in the various kinds of folk music he studied scientifically. Just as Schoenberg justified his innovations by appeals to the great German tradition, Bartók had a decisive, really ideological belief in the example provided by what he called the 'natural phenomenon' of folk music."[21]

To conceive of the study of folk music as a search for phenomena gave a new dimension to the concept of modernity and also to the organicist theory. In their path to the new music, Schoenberg, Webern, and Bartók faced the same essential problem: after having internalized the repertoire, how should a composer progress in renewing the language of music? The answer was clear: he had to turn to the original source, to nature. But nature was something different for Schoenberg and Webern than it was for Bartók. For the Viennese, nature meant the return to the individual's own self, reaching down to the innermost spheres of the mind and soul. In contrast, for Bartók, nature meant the return to the phenomena that are to be found in the "original facts" of music—evidently most clearly present in folk music. Looking at modernity from this angle, Bartók understandably found the inward-turning attitude of the Viennese composers artificial. To his logic, the development of a new style exclusively from inside did not mean turning to nature but rather avoiding reality:

> Of course many other (foreign) composers, who do not lean on folkmusic, have met with similar results [that have been described in my music] at about the same time—only in an intuitive or speculative way, which, evidently is a procedure equally justifiable. The difference is that we created through Nature, for: the peasant's art is a phenomenon of Nature. . . . As a negative example of what I mean, the works of Schoenberg may be mentioned. He is free from all peasant influence and his complete alienation from Nature, which of course I do not regard as a blemish, is no doubt the reason why many find his work so difficult to understand.[22]

Bartók, in contrast, believed that he had come to his discovery by reaching out for a reality closer to nature. It is hard to miss his emphasis on the fact that his experience of folk music was "real"—that he had to move away from his environment, come into contact with something more primitive and natural, and internalize it in its original form: "It was of the *utmost* consequence to us that we had to do our collecting [of folk songs] ourselves, and did not make the acquaintance of our melodic material in written or printed collections."[23]

For Bartók, it was of supreme importance that every stage of his study, internalization, and compositional use of folk music accord perfectly with the organicist theory. First of all, folk music in itself was an organic whole, whose elements were totally interrelated; the whole and its parts grew from inside following the laws of nature:

> Within peasant music in the broader sense there is a distinctly separate layer [group], at least in Eastern Europe, which we may call *peasant music in the narrow sense.* This could be characterized in a more precise manner. Taken in this narrower sense, peasant music consists of those melodies that belong to one or more coherent styles. In other words, peasant music in the narrower sense consists of a large repertoire of melodies of similar structure and character. . . . *Peasant music of this kind actually is nothing but the outcome of changes wrought by a natural force whose operation is unconscious in men who are not influenced by urban culture.* The melodies are therefore the embodiment of an artistic perfection of the highest order; in fact, they are models of the way in which a musical idea can be expressed with utmost perfection in terms of brevity of form and simplicity of means. . . . A melody of this kind is *a classic example of the expression of a musical thought in its most conceivably concise form, with the avoidance of all that is superfluous.*[24]

Bartók's logic is significant. From the outset it defines real peasant music as an organic whole: the category of "peasant music in the narrower sense" follows the criterion of stylistic unity (a justifiable standpoint in musicology). Even more important is the concept of stylistic coherence. Being the result of natural laws ("outcome of changes wrought by a natural force"), it came into being spontaneously ("whose operation is unconscious"). This art comes strictly from inside: peasant music in the narrower sense is "not influenced by urban culture." Bartók does not miss the opportunity to connect artistic quality and spontaneous growth: the melodies have artistic perfection *because* they came into being through organic growth ("the melodies are *therefore* the embodiment of an artistic perfection of the highest order"). And finally, they manifest natural phenomena: in folk music, the basic structural aspects of music appear in the simplest and clearest form ("brevity of form and simplicity of means," "most conceivably concise form").

Folk music thus achieves a coherent, organic whole; it is on the same level as the greatest compositions of Western culture. In fact, folk music is superior to art music in one respect: it came into being without an individual creator, a composer. Being the outcome of spontaneous, communal creation, it shows the nature of music in its most immediate form: "Peasant music, in the strict sense of the word, must be regarded as a natural phenomenon; the forms in which it manifests itself are due to the instinctive *transforming power* of the community entirely devoid of erudition. It is just as much a natural phenomenon as, for instance, the various manifestations of Nature in fauna and flora."[25] Far from looking down on the simple folk as if he were looking at flowers or insects, Bartók compares folk music to natural phenomena to insist that nature expressed itself in folk music. To regard folk music as fauna and flora was similar to Young's assertion that the "originality of the genius" was of "vegetable nature."

In order to bring his ethnomusicological observations into harmony with the organicist ideal of art, Bartók went so far as to advance a rather unlikely theory that recent research does not support. Bartók rejected the idea that individual peasants might compose folk songs: "The view that particular melodies were invented by particular peasants . . . has never been substantiated by a single observed instance, and besides, is scarcely acceptable on psychological grounds."[26] That folk music came into being collectively and spontaneously was a cardinal point of his theory. For Bartók there were only two manifestations of natural growth, either from the mind of the genius (as is the case of the entirely original individual pieces of high art) or from the spontaneously and coherently functioning mind of the traditional community untouched by the corruption of mass culture. What fell in between these two was unacceptable. "In any event it is interesting to note that artistic perfection can only be achieved by one of the two extremes: on the one hand by the totality of the peasant community, completely devoid of urban culture, on the other by the creative power of an individual genius. The creative impulse of anyone who has the misfortune to be born somewhere between these two extremes leads only to barren, pointless, and misshapen works."

It was of primary importance to Bartók that the composition derive from "pure" (that is, artistically perfect) sources. Bartók might have refuted the organicist criticism of folklorism by asserting that it was not the source but the quality of the completed piece that mattered. This was a logical and in fact quite correct statement, one he could have supported with countless examples from the history of music. But Bartók did not use this argument, precisely because he believed in the organicist theory. Popular music was for him evidence of banality; it could not serve as the starting point for a great piece because if such a mediocre idea was developed organically, it would necessarily result in a mediocre piece. That art came only from a pure source—"from clear springs," as the stags of the *Cantata profana* remind us—was indeed a deep Bartókian conviction.

Bartók thus superposed a second organicist paradigm on the idea he shared with Schoenberg and Webern. He thought not only of the individual artwork but of style too in organicist terms, as if style were an artwork. He conceived of it as a structurally coherent whole, its elements an organic growth from nature. Here nature equated with folk music, and growth meant the organic development of the composer's new and personal style from folk music.

A logical consequence of the development of style as organic process, the organicist model now expanded to include all stages of learning and composition. This idea did not hold for original compositions alone; Bartók even thought of folk-song arrangements in these terms. A piece in the genre of folk-song arrangement had to grow coherently from an idea just like any work of art, only in this case, the idea was the folk song. That is, the composer could not simply combine the folk song with some other material; instead, he was supposed to sense and obey its nature: "But in every case it is of the greatest importance that the setting that serves as a frame to the melody should be derived from the musical character of the melody, from qualities which are openly apparent or latent in it, that is, the melody and all additions should create the impression of complete unity."[27]

The theory Bartók devised for his folklore-based style is no less artificial than Schoenberg's and Webern's thesis claiming the universal necessity of twelve-tone music. Similar to theirs, Bartók's concept intellectualized a highly personal artistic style in a manner that could be seen as part of a common European aesthetic tradition.

The originality of Bartók's concept lies in the fact that he drew folk music into the sphere of the personal compositional process. What is important here is not the various techniques of integration but the novelty of the concept itself. Now folk music was the seed from which the new style grew in a coherent manner. Bartók believed that his modern tonal language derived from ideas latent in the folk song, often involving the projection of their linear structures into vertical ones within the composition—a method he regarded as a coherent process of development.[28] The germ of the piece (or style) was not the folk song as a finished object but rather its inherent tonal potentialities, which gave rise to further melodic and harmonic devices.

Here we recognize Schoenberg's and Webern's idea of the *Reihe*, which Webern called "an attempt to remain 'thematic,' to derive things and partial forms from the principal theme . . . the theme unfolding not only horizontally but also vertically—that is to say the reappearance of polyphonic thinking."[29] Of course, the *Reihe* in twelve-tone technique has a very different function from folk song in Bartók's compositions. But these rather dissimilar compositional procedures were articulated theoretically in a strikingly similar manner. Like Bartók, Webern and Schoenberg presented their technique as a method to achieve utmost coherence in an organically conceived structure, the under-lying idea being that the basis of the work was a linearly conceived melodic progression from which all further tonal and harmonic ideas could be de-rived.[30]

In fact, it would be misleading to say that Bartók's aim was to integrate elements of folk music or even to organically derive the new style from it. What he wanted to achieve was a profound understanding of the material of music. His preoccupation with folk music was a way to learn the most funda-mental elements, not simply of folk music, but of music as such—elements more basic than any particular style. When Bartók uncovered such ele-ments—for instance, the transposition of themes by a fifth (a technique fun-damental to Hungarian folk music and Bach's fugues)—he consciously ex-ploited them in his pieces.[31] He often noticed techniques in folk music that he had encountered many years before in art music. Such findings gave him proof that he had found something basic and constant—the "phenomena" of music.

COHERENCE AND REALISM

Bartók's stylistic synthesis, born from the idea of the "phenomena," resolved one basic problem of the organicist model: the issue of style. Organicist theory, however, contained another, even deeper contradiction: its organic image of reality did not accord with the modern experience of chaos. In his poem "Cartway at night" (Kocsi-út az éjszakában [1909]), Ady captures the intensity of his contemporaries' fear that the world was falling apart:

Milyen csonka ma a Hold,	The Moon is a broken plate,
Az éj milyen sivatag, néma,	The night is silent, a desert,
Milyen szomoru vagyok én ma,	What sadness has come over me,
Milyen csonka ma a Hold.	The Moon is a broken plate.
Minden Egész eltörött,	Every Whole has broken to pieces,
Minden láng csak részekben lobban,	Every flame flares up in fragments,
Minden szerelem darabokban,	Every love has fallen apart,
Minden Egész eltörött.	Every Whole has broken to pieces.
Fut velem egy rossz szekér,	A broken carriage is running with me
Utána mintha jaj-szó szállna,	As though a woe-cry flew behind it,
Félig mély csönd és félig lárma,	Half moan and half deep silence,
Fut velem egy rossz szekér.	A broken carriage is running with me.

The disintegration of life was a basic experience, a phenomenon in its own right that one writer of this generation found beautiful in its absurdity and incoherence. Gyula Krúdy does not "accept" this world; rather, he sees in its fragmentation, unreality, and confusion the real face of life. The nostalgia his novels express is for a world that has no precise space or time, as if it had fallen apart long ago, leaving behind only sad and beautiful dreams, fragments of lives, passions, beliefs, and pains that float within an indifferent cosmos. He wrote to József Kiss, the editor of *A Hét*, about his novel *The Red Mail Coach* (A vörös postakocsi [1914]):

> You ask me what the topic of my novel that I am writing for *A Hét* is going to be? . . . Everything that is dear to me . . . things that have lived in me for decades . . . thoughts that are born in the solitude of the night of a man living a bit like a hermit, toward dawn when they start to clean the cafés; apparitions that happen on the street, at a ball, and at the theater when we are standing half-hidden next to a column, human faces and shapes that flee by us, familiar and unfamiliar, the meeting of the stupids and the clevers, . . . the market of Pest like the one I can see from the window. Gentlemen and ladies come and go without clothes, the lame devil looks through the roof; the dead did well to flee the city. . . . Someone is playing a serenade on the cello and geese shriek loudly in the spring night under the stars' beams. Hear pain and murderous bitterness; a cynical glance at little joys and great sorrows; sighs, walks in the forest; actresses, real and false courtesans, mothers and schoolgirls; corrupt man and married woman; children who are brought up in cafés; words spoken softly, memories thought to be forgotten, sufferings at which we smile today; the worthlessness of fulfilled dreams and hopes that no longer exist; the early autumn and the startled awakening in a dark room; soft plans for suicide; dark thoughts of robbery, murder, vengeance; the anticipation and desire for death when the sun rises.[32]

Krúdy's attitude was unique; no one in Hungary could experience the contradictions of the modern world in such a peaceful manner, without anxiety. For his contemporaries, his art seemed alternately a betrayal and a revelation. He was admired and rejected, praised as the greatest novelist of his time and ignored. His ease in confronting the modern world raised the most disturbing issue of art: is coherence at all a valid response to this new reality? All artists at the turn of the century explored this problem and turned out many talented and interesting (if not always successful or finished) pieces. In the cases of Ady and Bartók, the contradictory demands of capturing reality and expressing an ideal and coherent order were not easy to resolve. The ambivalence emerged in Ady's lack of a coherent poetic style, and in Bartók's lifelong struggle to compose a convincing, optimistic finale for the final movement of his compositions.[33]

We see similar anxiety reflected in the fears of Kraus and Hofmannsthal that art and language might be unable to express anything at all. One attempt to meet this problem was unconditional belief in the power of art. In Hofmannsthal's aesthetic, poetic beauty in itself—the power of language, its sonority and rhythm—is able to reconcile the contradictions of the fragmented society. In Schorske's words, "The poet must accept the multiplicity of reality, and, through the magic medium of language, bring unity and cohesion to modern man. . . . Where others saw conflict or contradiction, the poet would reveal hidden ties and develop them by bringing out their unity through rhythm and sound."[34] But can language be trusted to bring about a coherent vision of an incoherent reality? What makes us believe that coherence in an artwork is the revelation of truth behind the fragmented everyday reality and not merely a matter of technique? At first glance, Lukács's view seems to accord with Hofmannsthal's: "Every great art is the revealing of the empty and fragmented nature of the empirically sensed reality, and the creation of an utopian integrity that has a demanding and obligatory force [on life]."[35]

There is a crucial difference between Hofmannsthal's and Lukács's concepts. As Lukács sees it, the poet's work does not simply accept but "reveals the empty and fragmentary nature of empirical reality." Implied in this formulation is a tragic view of life ("empty and fragmented"), and the recognition of people's tendency to overlook this tragic state of being—the poet has to awaken them to this deeper vision of reality. Furthermore, integrity does not come about simply through the "magic medium of language." Lukács's vision of art comes close to the Hungarian romantics' heroic stance, their " 'and yet' morality": even though it grows from the fragmented life, art must create a feeling of integrity.

Lukács opposes the "utopia" of integrity to "empirically sensed reality." Utopia does not mean here a constructed model that people believe, wrongly, to be a goal for social reality. It connotes rather an emotional and conceptual ideal, one that, although it exists only in art, reflects back on life.

ART AND MORALITY

To understand the modernists' emphasis on the inevitable and inexplicable "must" that overlays an ideal coherence upon an incoherent reality, we need to take into account the social experience from which Hungarian modernism was born. The complexities of modern life, together with shifting social and moral codes, compounded the problem of defining morality itself. The radicals hoped to separate truth from lies within the existing social conditions, but they emphatically insisted that judgment would not follow conventional moral codes. Skeptical of the social conventions of both the semifeudal Hungarian system and the capitalist world of the West, they would not rely on any authoritative framework in judging human behavior.

The search to understand the nature of morality was thus not an attempt to resolve some abstract philosophical problem, but an intense experience of day-to-day existence. Responding to this situation, many modernists arrived at the realization that instead of rules, they followed their "sense" of morality, an abstract ideal impossible to circumscribe with words. But moral behavior could rely neither on an abstract ideal of morality nor on a narrow set of social rules and guidelines. Morality should bring individuals up to the threshold of empirical reality, helping them when they crossed over it alone to meet, one by one, the problems of everyday life.[36]

The modernists of the turn of the century hoped to explore above all the possibility of creating an art that would reflect the moral nature of the individual. At the center of their system of nature they posited a "truth" that would connect the ego, the society, and the universe. The demand that art express this sense of morality as an imaginary center of life, a "metaphysical consciousness," superseded any other demand, even that of structural coherence. It was a cardinal point of Lukács's aesthetics:

> All psychological depth, social breadth, and cosmic expansion is in vain: if something is not born [integrally] in and from [its own] form, if it is not the expression of the idea of form, it does not exist [as art]. And yet: beyond the extreme artistic awareness, there is another voice, the soft, barely audible but clear voice of bad conscience, as if the really complete forms have forgotten something they cannot pronounce but should not keep in silence. It is as if they have forgotten their real home that gives them sense and weight, as if they have left behind the colors and smells of this home that cannot be measured and forced into concepts, as if they have not brought with themselves the only possible manifestation of the eternal longing for the lost home: the metaphysical conscience of the artist.[37]

The first sentence of this passage expresses a basic tenet of Lukács's aesthetics, that coherence is essential to art. But he goes on to state that there is something even more important than coherence: a "metaphysical consciousness," a sense of center in life. Morality is an ideal impossible to achieve, but we must fix our mind on it, in constant "longing for the lost home." Lukács connects this longing—which is something like a feeling of an essence—to mysticism and to the essence of art. This essence is impossible to codify or prescribe and cannot be found once and for all; it is something that the artist strives to discover always anew through creation:

> It is the belief of Jewish mysticism that an angel is born out of all our deeds: a perfect and beautiful angel from miserable and worthless deeds. The uninitiated are not to blame for [the fact] that, by spoiling their very self, they spoiled the complete and true world, that, because of them, the Messiah cannot come. But every creation [of art] stands in front of the tribunal of eternity, and its sin is even more serious because of its "artful" perfection if its word—because it did not speak from the true depths—is found trivial and empty. For the poet came in order to dig out (in the form of artwork) and by this digging out, to call it by its name, and by this calling awaken to life the essence of the soul. He came so that behind his perfectly complete words there would emerge, with mysterious and clear transparency, what cannot be pronounced in any other way, the only real truth: the essence.[38]

We encounter here the duality of the visible but complex and uncontrollable reality of life on the one hand, and the invisible but clearly felt abstract moral center on the other. It is not this abstract ideal but real life that is out of focus. Each situation demands a unique response that cannot be fully planned in advance, and the decision is always the inalienable property and responsibility of the individual. True morality eludes regulations, whether communal or religious; it has its roots in a deeper existential reality. But paradoxically, it is precisely the abstract nature of truth and morality that ensures their effect on life. Life exists in possibilities and compromises, it operates by usefulness and reward. Morality is true to itself only as long as it is indifferent to such demands. Because "religious morality" holds out the promise of punishment or reward instead of responding to inner need, it is not really "moral." In his "Two hexameters" (1936) the interwar poet Attila József catches the essence of this idea: "Why should I be righteous? / They'll stretch my corpse anyway! / Why should I not be righteous! / They'll stretch my corpse anyway."[39]

The search for moral essence was at the heart of the Hungarian modernist literary movement. It pervaded the attitude of Ernő Osvát toward anyone involved with *Nyugat*. Osvát, who himself wrote little, was a legendary editor, admired for his insistence on quality and his keen eye for talent. Generations of writers were grateful to him. His continued effort to maintain the high standard and the total autonomy of *Nyugat* was the driving force behind the vitality of literary life. No other oeuvre exemplified as clearly as Osvát's life the intensity of the search for an art that would express moral essence, and that only in the most concentrated form of art. Osvát's anxiety over the issue resulted in his incapacity to produce literature, for he could never believe that he had met the standards he set for himself. As one of his friends, the writer Milán Füst, said half-jokingly and half-critically: "If the entire universe, all our experiences and thoughts could be compressed into one ironical, light, and at the same time deep[ly expressive] word, into a word that would shine like a giant diamond and would glow like the sun: maybe Osvát would consider this word worthy of being written down."[40]

The central issue for Osvát was the opposition of intellect and morality—the impossibility of pure thought in a life of actions and consequences: "Which is the most unpoetic characteristic? Rationality: the slave of facts that accepts fate; the Pyrrhic victory of the soul, which submits without opposition to the nonsense of reality, over the noble desires."[41] Osvát attempted to break down the boundaries between art and morality, even at the expense of "dethroning and humiliating art." He strove for the totality of both, for an absolutely pure morality that would avoid every conservatism and for an art that "smiles at the life of all things, which is a judgment over [all] judgments."

Perhaps Osvát "strove for an artificial ideal," as Füst was quick to suggest.[42] But this uncompromising attempt to achieve the utmost potential of art, to illuminate life's moral essence—in Lukács's terminology, the "transcendental center"—paralleled the quest of many artists in Hungary.[43] Lukács theorized that "every creation [of art] stands in front of the tribunal of eternity." But the artists of the period really felt this responsibility to express a "spirit"—together, against, and beyond structural perfection. As Karinthy humorously wrote,

> A thought or a feeling or an impulse I could never capture in its completeness. . . . A sentence I could never compose for myself in a way that would make it entirely valid and final. The gymnastic exercise of my soul, some nice production I had to start over and over again because it was imperfect either in its form or in its content. . . . Is that what is called being a writer? In that case, I have been a writer since the age of six. I can say it is a rather awkward state to be in—nervousness, that you should be ready for something, the ambiguous feeling of an affair unresolved, the fear before an exam throughout your entire life. Whatever happened to me always had a faint taste of an exam, of having to answer something—not even always in front of someone in particular, not even in this life but over there, somewhere. I was given a task in the cradle and I forgot what it was, I had to watch everything with a keen eye in order to remind myself.[44]

As Attila József's and Karinthy's examples show (and there are many others), artists between the wars also felt the challenge to understand and connect artistic truth and morality. But they did not want to create moralizing art. On the contrary, they disdained works that preached about morality and themes conventionally considered to be moral issues. The aim was to grasp an essence behind the incongruities of everyday existence. The search for identity, the phenomena, the essence of life and art and morality now coincided—artists realized that an attempt at understanding the meaning of one brought them closer to understanding the others.

Bartók's *Cantata profana* expresses this fusion. The old man's sons are searching for "the clear spring"—that is, truth, existential essence, the deepest realm of the soul. This search brings about their metamorphosis: they become stags, they become nature. Finding the center of all things demands the annihilation of everyday life. It is transformation into a symbolic existence.

PART 2

Poetry and Music

Ady and Bartók

CHAPTER 5

The Formation of Bartók's Aesthetics

FOLK MUSIC AND THE REFLECTION OF SPIRIT AND EMOTION

Twentieth-century textbooks use various terms to describe the distinctive cultural traits that shaped Bartók's art. They call him a "folklorist" or an "almost serialist" composer and place him under the rubric "East European School," "Nationalist Composition," or "Independent Trends." Most such characterizations are appropriate in one context or another. Bartók's artistic decisions were obviously the result of a common historical and cultural tradition, and the stylistic traits of his art naturally show similarities to other modernist developments. Yet none suggests the essential feature of Bartók's aesthetics: a highly individual choice of elements from the common stylistic-aesthetic tradition and their articulation in a coherent personal style. The particular blend of modernist tendencies and his unique manner of interpreting them for his own purposes created an aesthetics that in its totality was without parallel even in Hungary.

Among the most important elements in the background of this aesthetics was a dual conception of the artwork's "spirit." As Bartók understood it, the artwork was to express a communal spirit (the spirit of folk music) and yet arise from the inner urge of the artist to express his emotions. "Spirit" was something beyond the material of music; in the case of folk music, it expressed the totality of lived experience. This attitude is best illustrated by the statement Bartók wrote in 1928:

> It was of the *utmost* consequence to us that we had to do our collecting [of folk songs] ourselves, and did not make the acquaintance of our melodic material in written or printed collections. The melodies of a written or printed collection are in essence dead materials. It is true though—provided they are reliable—that they acquaint one with the melodies, yet one absolutely cannot penetrate into the real, throbbing life of this music by means of them. In order to really feel the vitality of this music, one must, so to speak, have lived it— and this is only possible when one comes to know it through direct contact with the peasants. . . . I should, in fact, stress one point: in our case it was not a question of merely taking unique melodies in any way whatsoever, and then incorporating them—or fragments of them—in our works, there to develop them according to the traditionally established custom. This would have been mere craftsmanship, and could have led to no new and unified style. What we had to do was to grasp the spirit of this hitherto unknown music and to make this spirit (difficult to describe in words) the basis of our works.[1]

Bartók's commitment to expressing "the spirit" of folk music is much more familiar to us than his individualistic approach toward art because he described the latter in letters mostly unavailable in English. In a letter to his wife during a field trip to Darázs (Slovakia) in 1909, he wrote:

> I strongly believe and profess that every true art is manifested and created under the influence of "experiences," those impressions that we absorb into ourselves from the surrounding world. He who paints only in order to paint a landscape or writes a symphony only in order to write one is no more than a good craftsman at best. I cannot imagine that an artwork could be anything but the manifestation of the infinite enthusiasm, despair, sorrow, vengeful anger, distorting and sarcastic irony of its creator. Before I experienced it in myself, I did not believe that one's works could signal—more precisely than one's autobiography—the important events, the governing passions of his life. Of course, I am talking here only of a real and true artist. It is strange that in music the basis of motivation has so far been only enthusiasm, love, sorrow, or, at most, despair—that is, only the so-called lofty feelings. It is only in our times that there is place for the painting of the feeling of vengeance, the grotesque, and the sarcastic. For this reason the music of today could be called realist because, unlike the idealism of the previous eras, it extends with honesty to all real human emotions without excluding any. In the last century, there were only sporadic examples for this, for instance, in Berlioz's *Symphonie Fantas-*

tique, Liszt's *Faust*, Wagner's *Meistersinger*, and Strauss's *Heldenleben*. There is another factor that makes today's music [the music of the twentieth century] real: that its impressions come, partly subconsciously and partly intentionally, from folk music, that is, a music that saturates everything in the great reality.[2]

In these writings Bartók makes two demands on art that seem at first glance contradictory. If the artwork expresses the spirit of folk music, how could it at the same time express the personal feelings of the artist? Yet it is clear that Bartók envisioned precisely such a synthesis. In his view, only by living up to this dual demand could the artwork be "true" and "real." Realism, in Bartók's conception, is not the imitation of empirical reality but "honesty"—what is true both to the grand totality of life and to the artist's deepest feelings. Bartók envisioned an ideal connection between two realisms in art: the realism that means the artist's truthfulness to his own infinite passion, and the realism that results from his capacity to relive, so to speak, the "great reality" of life, remaining faithful to its basic and original manifestations—which is, musically speaking, folk music.

Bartók insisted on this synthesis throughout his career. The original plan of the Harvard lectures from 1943, the last attempt to summarize his style and artistic belief, restates the aesthetics that he explained in the letter from 1909. In summarizing the structure and character of his music, Bartók planned to discuss nine topics in the following order:[3]

1. Revolution, evolution
2. Modes, polymodality (polytonality, atonality/twelvetone music)
3. Chromaticism (very rare in folkmusic)
4. Rhythm, percussion effect
5. Form (every piece creates its own form)
6. Scoring (new effects on instruments), piano, violin as percussif [*sic*] instr. (Cowell) (*hegedű kellene* [a violin would be needed])
7. Trend toward simplicity
8. Educational works
9. General spirit (connected with folkmusic)

Because of his illness, Bartók had to interrupt the lecture series after the third lecture. By that time he had written part of the fourth lecture and an autograph draft containing the above outline, but nothing survived of lectures five through nine. Thus the Harvard lectures as we know them today give the impression that Bartók attempted a purely technical analysis of his style. As this draft illustrates, his intention was different: he planned to progress from structural aspects (outlining even their relation to originality and folk music) toward aesthetic issues and hoped to end the series, in a final message, with the discussion of the "general spirit (connected with folk music)."[4] Since Bartók had great difficulty verbalizing anything that was not purely technical, it is remarkable that he considered devoting a full lecture to the issue of simplicity and another to "spirit." The inclusion of educational works is also significant. First, it indicates his emphasis on the social aspect of art music, his belief that the composer had to find channels through which he could reconnect his art to a broader community. Second, with the emphasis on separating the topic of educational pieces from "simplicity," he apparently wanted to emphasize that, in his understanding, "simplicity" meant something other than easily accessible or popular. Most important, the lecture series concludes with the same idea he had expressed years earlier: the title "General spirit (connected with folk music)" reaffirms the dual demand of spirit on the artwork.

But how could the spirit of folk music manifest itself in a composition that is no longer folk music? Only at the beginning of his career did Bartók view folk song as a self-contained entity and a representative type that could evoke, at least symbolically, folk music.[5] Later he came to the realization that spirit cannot be connected in any direct manner to technical aspects of the music. This realization came gradually, and the process of distancing the thematic material of the original compositions from the actual appearance of their folk-music models was by no means absolute. While the sources of Bartók's compositions became gradually more abstract than an actual piece or type, some works reiterated obvious surface features of the folk song.[6] Yet typically, at least in the mature compositions, his point of departure was not an actual piece or type but a complex web of dissociated musical elements, variational procedures, and other structural ideas. He treated the dissociated elements of folk music, together with elements of art music, as a collection of rough material that he could draw on as he wished, to create his style.

The accent here is on the separation and reconnection of spirit and material. Elements of folk music permeate the composition but no longer appear in the surface form. Yet the composition retains the feeling of folk music and even intensifies it, filtering it through a personal interpretation. Moreover, the complex design of the large-scale form conveys this spirit, even though its dimensions are incongruous with the conciseness of folk music.

Bartók's mature compositions have great variety of structural designs and yet share a certain orientation. All the mature pieces achieve maximum integrity in the thematic material and create, at the same time, the maximum polarization of thematic characters. During the process of thematic-motivic transformations, themes of similar-sounding materials diverge while ones that began by sounding different merge. No parts of the music, not even those themes that sound somewhat like folk songs, have direct connections to any particular piece or type of the actual folk-song repertoire.

THE FIRST PIANO CONCERTO

Bartók's first concerto for piano and orchestra illustrates this technique. For his point of departure in creating the thematic material, Bartók took a commonly known rhythmic and melodic scheme of East European peasant music (Example 1). The songs of this type have symmetrical structure, combining two-measure units whose characteristic basic rhythmic scheme is ♪♪♪│♪♪│ . The melodies move typically in stepwise motion and often use scalar patterns and note repetitions, sometimes almost in an ostinato-like manner. Less frequently, they combine motives in narrow stepwise motion and contrasting motives with wide leaps. In Hungary, this rhythmic type is associated with the swineherd dance that Bartók thought was derived from the *kolomeika* rhythm of the Carpathian Ukraine.[7] Bartók considered the swineherd songs to be the source of the popular *kurucz* song repertoire and also of the instrumental *verbunkos*—which is indeed often based on *kolomeika*-type melodies (Example 2). Since Bartók believed that the new-style folk songs developed from the *verbunkos*, he was able to draw connections among virtually all the rhythmic schemes of Hungarian metric (giusto) music.[8] Moreover, Bartók also encountered relatives of the *kolomeika*-type in Romania and Slovakia in a variety of genres including lyric songs, children's songs, instrumental dances, and colindas (Romanian Christmas carols). It is telling that more than one quarter of all giusto folk songs that Bartók arranged have *kolomeika* rhythm or a variant of it.

Choosing this rhythmic scheme and the corresponding melodic style as the basis for the theme of the concerto, Bartók relied on what he regarded as "original" musical material, a kind of *Urmusik*. But the *kolomeika* type was appealing also for another reason: it suited particularly well the needs of a concerto. Its association with both the most basic peasant dance and the instrumental and improvisational style of the *verbunkos* allowed the extension of the thematic material in different directions. By intensifying the repetitive rhythms of the *kolomeika*, a composer could evoke the image of barbaric and "original" dance. At the same time, he could develop its association with the *verbunkos* into ornamental, virtuoso material in the style of both folk

EXAMPLE 1.   The *kolomeika* type and related pieces from the Hungarian folk tradition, after the original notation. Bartók collected and used all these songs in his compositions. (Vera Lampert, "Quellenkatalog der Volksliedbearbeitungen von Bartók," in *Documenta Bartókiana* 6 [Budapest: Akadémiai; Mainz: Schott's Söhne, 1981], 15–149)

a.

b.

c.

EXAMPLE I   *(continued)*

d.

[Tempo giusto, ♪ = 154 acc. 180]

E – gyik ágy – ban   pet – re – zse – lem,   a má – sik – ba   zel – ler,

Kocs – má – ros – né   szó – gá – ló – ját   meg – tosz – ta   ja   kel – ler.

I – há – ni,   ci – gá – ri,   jó   be – lő – le   pi – pá – nyi,

Ha – ja   dá – ri,   ma – dá – ri   jó   be – lő – le   pi – pá – nyi.

e.

Tempo giusto, ♩ = 80–90

I – šlo dieu – ča – tko ho – re   dra – ha – mi,   ňie – slo _____

instrumental music and the Western concerto. Indeed, it is likely that Bartók chose this type precisely in order to join the styles of folk and art music.

All themes of the concerto derive from *kolomeika* in one way or another. Behind the complicated structure of the first theme (Example 3), we recognize the symmetrical *kolomeika* song as a latent ideal (Example 4). Although its *kolomeika* structure and character are evident, this latent song—reconstructed hypothetically in the upper staff of Example 4—is a rather strange combination of elements of the type: in folk music, syncopation and standard *kolomeika* rhythm do not typically occur in the same piece, and the tonal displacement of the cadential line would sound "out of tune." Compression of rhythmic patterns and addition of elements foreign to the style move this latent song even further from the model. Some aspects of the rhythm and melody point outside vocal folk music: syncopation is more common in the urban popular instrumental dance tradition; ornamenting a melody with scale figu-

EXAMPLE 2. *Verbunkos* piece based on *kolomeika*. (János Bihari, "Magyar tánc vagy verbunkos" [1807], in *A magyar zenetörténet kézikönyve*, by Bence Szabolcsi, ed. Ferenc Bónis [1947; reprint, Budapest: Zeneműkiadó, 1979], 218)

rations is a technique that may derive from a virtuoso instrumental concerto tradition as well as from *verbunkos* but be alien to vocal folk styles; and the use of upbeat is common in *verbunkos* and classical music but entirely missing from Hungarian folk song. Thus Bartók superposes multiple styles in a quasi-polyphonic conceptual design—and collapses them into one melody.

The result, nevertheless, does not strike us as an artificial, abstract condensation of ideas. On the contrary, the theme sounds spontaneous, almost improvisatory, as if depicting a quasi-ecstatic moment of bursting emotions. In a theme that generally uses eighth and quarter notes (except for ornaments), the upbeat should logically be an eighth note, but the upbeat is here shortened to a sixteenth note, as if, immersed in the energetic introductory scale, the virtuoso soloist would almost miss his thematic entry (see Examples 3–4). The syncopation suggested in the second measure of the latent song merges with the beginning of the next motive. The rhythmic asymmetry thus created has the same effect as the shortening of the upbeat: the soloist seems to run ahead

EXAMPLE 3.   First theme.

EXAMPLE 4.   The latent folk song and the first theme.

impatiently, merging three eighth notes into one quarter note and the subsequent eighth notes into sixteenth notes. This same exuberant feeling also characterizes the last gesture of the theme: the grand upbeat of a descending scale replaces the syncopation and ostinato-like eighth notes.

Bartók's version of the *kolomeika*-type dance music entailed not just minor modification but distortion of the folk-music model. "Distortion" does not mean that a listener experiences the result as something contorted or grotesque. Nor does the word refer to the compositional process. There is no sign that Bartók arrived at this theme (or at other similarly conceived folk themes of his compositions) by the gradual process of modifying a folk song; it probably came to him more or less completely in a moment of inspiration, and if anything he changed only minor aspects. In fact, there is no sign that his themes evoking folk music had actual folk models.[9]

Yet the relation between Bartók's theme and the folk-music model *is* a kind of distortion. Despite all differences, the folk-music examples of the *kolomeika* type had a common element, namely a continuous quarter-note motion arranged symmetrically, with one structural unit metrically corresponding to the other. Bartók destroyed precisely this basic aspect of the rhythm. He twisted the structural parts of the type out of their natural relation, thereby changing the form and character—in a sense, to the disadvantage—of the original form.[10] Both the technique and the result are remarkable and no doubt intentional: the composer destroyed the form precisely in order to express—and concentrate—the optimism and excitement of these dance pieces. Clearly, Bartók considered the driving, exuberant energy of this music more essential than its surface form; the distortion of the form became the vehicle for expressing its emotional essence.

The expression of overflowing exuberance is in fact one underlying theme of the concerto; it is the governing principle behind the large-scale form. This energy is almost self-destructive: at important points of the piece its force almost blocks the road to intelligible expression, toward the formation of self-contained symmetrical units. The five-measure "structural upbeat" preceding the theme proper already manifests this heightened state of expression (see Example 3). As if stammering with an uncontrolled expressive urge, the music cannot break away from the energetic ostinato on A, searching, with each motivic unit, for its proper final form. Each measure brings metrically different melodic units (counting in eighth notes, successive units of three, four, six, five, and four), and the melody that breaks forth from the note repetition constantly "corrects itself" in search of the proper scale (F to F sharp; restatement of C sharp an octave higher as C natural; see Example 3).

This theme functions as a "theme" in the Beethovenian sense. Its patterns, which appear at this point improvisatory, are in fact entirely structural and provide the basis for complex thematic transformations. For instance, the ascending motive that closes the first melodic line (F sharp, G, A) appears to be a momentary, improvisatory idea that brings about the diminution of the eighth notes to sixteenths. Yet this three-note motive will serve, in the course of the movement, as one of the most constant motivic elements, used in the background, either building to a polyphonic, dense texture or as a counter-theme, superposed on the primary thematic idea of a section (see, for instance, the orchestral part in Example 10b).

The motivic fragmentation begins immediately after the thematic statement, with the use of the three-note motive and scalar patterns distilled from the main theme. Against this development the second theme brings a strong contrast, a moment of calm with a recognizable folk-music atmosphere (Example 5). The symmetrical nature of the theme alludes to the eight-measure

EXAMPLE 5.   Second theme: piano and strings.

(continued)

EXAMPLE 5   *(continued)*

antecedent-consequent structure of classical music but evokes even more obviously the new-style Hungarian folk songs. Yet nothing functions here as it
does in folk music. The melody is a compression of a fragment of a tune, as if
it were outlining the "main notes" of what could be the first two melodic lines
of a four-line song (Example 6a). But the melody of the first phrase would be
more likely to appear as a cadential line of a folk song (last measure of Example
6b). Compression destroys the continuity of the melody and rhythm: instead
of continuous melodic motion, there is something like a grotesque dialogue
between the right and left hands.

The character of this theme is not immediately apparent. It is clearly a
more lyrical and lighter moment, despite the allusion to folk dance in the full,

EXAMPLE 6. Folk-song sources of the second theme. (Vera Lampert, "Quellenkatalog
der Volksliedbearbeitungen von Bartók," in *Documenta Bartókiana* 6 [Budapest:
Akadémiai; Mainz: Schott's Söhne, 1981], nos. 61, 184)

a.

b.

homophonic ostinato accompaniment of the strings. But its skeletonlike bareness, strangely large melodic leaps, arpeggiated octaves, and grotesque ornaments (almost like the rattling of bones) turn it into its own caricature. This theme has two characters at the same time: it is grazioso and the grotesque caricature of grazioso. To compress such complexity of feelings into a simple musical gesture is a typically Bartókian technique, and the idea of capturing these two specific qualities in one theme had occurred to him many years before the composition of the concerto.[11] As though the pianist had no more patience to endure this calm, an energetic reiteration of the three-note motive interrupts the second theme (see Example 5, rehearsal number 13). The almost theatrical gesture shows that the second theme was but an interjection and suggests the impossibility of turning the elements of the first theme into something calm and symmetrical.

Bartók's recapitulation is at the same time consolidation and deconstruction. It stabilizes the form by bringing back the themes of the exposition (after the development built on different themes). But thematic return coincides with thematic decomposition. The five-measure introduction to the main theme here becomes developmental, improvisatory preparation leading to the theme. Whereas in the exposition Bartók placed the "Allegro" tempo marking at the beginning of the five-measure introduction—thus considering it part of the theme—here "Tempo I," the mark of the formal recapitulation, occurs *after* the introductory measures (see Examples 3 and 7). Capturing the energy of the soloist, the five-measure introduction explodes, bringing new improvisatory variants at each new occurrence in the course of the retransition and recapitulation (mm. 338, 346, 356, 371, 373; see Example 7 for mm. 371–75).[12]

The treatment of the second theme is similar: its symmetrical patterns are compressed into asymmetrical rhythmic formations (Example 8). This is again a soloistic gesture, as if the performer could not wait until the end of the motive in order to move on to the next one. But this decomposition is humorous rather than dramatic. The pianissimo pastorale-like string ostinato that we heard in the exposition continues here. This accompaniment and the grazioso ornaments—reminding us somewhat of Bartók's "tipsy" characters—along with the still perceptible symmetry of the theme, prevent us from hearing this "destruction" as something really serious: it is the caricature of the self-destructive exuberance itself.

All these structures and processes are similar in one respect: they are extremely complex both emotionally and structurally. It is important to realize that neither the development nor the decomposition of motives lead from simple forms toward more complex ones or vice versa. The first theme is al-

EXAMPLE 7. Retransition (end) and recapitulation (beginning).

ritornando al _ _ _ _ _ _ _ _ _ _ _ _ _ _ _ _ _ 40 _ _ _ _ Tempo I

EXAMPLE 8. Recapitulation of the second theme.

ready an example of utmost concentration—this is obvious even without taking into account its tonal plan and the polyphonically conceived orchestral parts. The decomposition of this theme leads to a new complexity by continually reusing its elements in new combinations. In this respect Bartók's conceptualizing of theme is entirely classical. With him, as with Haydn and Mozart (and to a lesser degree Beethoven), the theme of a piece has a dual function: it is both a self-contained entity and the source of the musical material from which and against which the dramatic form evolves.

Bartók had yet another plan in this concerto. It is as if he thought of the organic development of themes in terms of concentric circles: he superposed on a more or less classical design a deeper layer of thematic material and a more extreme manner of development. If the first theme is a "theme" in the sense of the "first theme of a classical sonata," then the "introduction" functions as a theme in the sense of the original material. It presents the piece's basic musical ideas, its real themes—the inarticulate elements that precede coherent speech. Unlike the slow introduction in classical forms, this introduction does not create dramatic material to which the actual movement will be a contrast in tempo and character, rather it is a kind of "creation-music" (Example 9).

EXAMPLE 9.   Introduction (orchestra).

Bartók's design reminds us of the thought with which Thomas Mann begins his Joseph tetralogy: the well of the past is deep. Each musical idea or musical form carries many ideas or forms; below each thought there is always another, a more primary and ancient layer. The introduction reaches down to the deepest level. The seeds of the music exist here as three primary ideas: sustained note, ostinato, and stepwise melodic motion. In the course of the piece, Bartók develops all motives from these markedly "primitive" elements, and in fact, he presents them already here as if they were deriving from each other. The two themes on the winds are both circular—at the time, circularity was seen as the symbol of original, ritualistic motion—and end with an attempt to break out of their circles in ascending melodic lines. The two basic rhythmic ideas of the Bartókian *kolomeika*—syncopation and even eighth notes—appear here as variants of the same idea.

We could interpret every moment of the large-scale form in accordance with an ideal classical formal model. But the potential of this model expands to its limits in order to give place to other more unusual formal processes. The development section merges the formal functions of development and trio: it brings a dramatic intensification of previous themes but is also a self-contained unit whose central sections strike the listener as an insertion of some monumental, barbaric dance. This central developmental section is preceded by an introduction within the development: the cadenza-like virtuoso passages of the piano are interpolated by the ascending version of the introduction's syncopated theme on the winds (in Somfai's analysis: part 1 of the development).[13] It is followed by the pseudo recapitulation (functioning also as retransition) that brings fragments of the first theme (Somfai's part 4). The central part of the development has two sections (Somfai's parts 2 and 3), each based on the varied repetition of a motive derived from the introduction. The first of these sections is somewhat restrained, almost a sidetrack to a gentle and static mood after which the second brings formal and emotional climax.

The dramatic energy derives here from the continuous varied restatements of a few motives rather than from motivic elaboration, which would be typical in a development. These motives come not from the exposition but from the introduction, as if searching back to something deeper and less articulate than complex themes (Example 10a, c). This barbaric dance functions as the counterforce to the idea of classical, articulate expression and control: maddening repetitiveness, drumming ostinato, and constant accelerando depict the eruption of energy. Here is the emotional center of the movement, and it is no accident that Bartók's first thematic idea for the movement appears to be the one he used in this section.[14]

EXAMPLE 10. Themes of the development.

a. Theme of first section.

b. Baroque theme.

Variants of the syncopated theme of the introduction recur also in the ex-position and the recapitulation. Being based on the introduction, like the the-matic material of the central part of the development, they have a common seed but their formal function is different. Played on the brass or the wood-winds, these themes signal the beginning and end of sections usually announc-ing—almost like stylized horn signals—a new theme or the entry of the soloist (m. 94 trumpets, trombones; 152 trumpet, trombone; 162 woodwinds; 195 and 221 clarinet, bassoon; merged with the main theme: 339 brass, woodwinds; 400 horns, trumpets, woodwinds; 449 horns, trumpets, trombones; 456 trombones [= Hungarian variant on Example 11]; 472 brass, woodwinds).

EXAMPLE 10   *(continued)*

c. Theme of second section.

EXAMPLE 11.   The Hungarian theme of the recapitulation.

Thus in the course of the movement, the many themes derived from the introduction become gradually more and more distanced from their common thematic origin and from one another; each assumes a specific character and formal function and undergoes its unique series of transformation. The direction of these transformations is positive, leading from shapeless and neutral motives toward themes of definite character and form. Because the technical aspects of these themes change very gradually, the listener experiences each change of character as surprising and yet somehow unavoidable. Thus, in the development, the nonsyncopated theme of the introduction and development becomes a baroque-sounding theme (see Example 10b). The syncopated motive returns in the recapitulation with an unmistakably Hungarian character, alluding to the style of heroic symphonies of the romantic era (see Example 11).[15]

These transformations occur against an ostinato background from which they emerge and to which they connect thematically. The ostinato is the most extreme aspect of the distortions of the folk-music model: Bartók isolated the idea of steady eighth-note motion of this type and made it an absolute, individually functioning aspect of the musical texture. The ostinato holds together all the diverse musical materials of the movements; it is the cohesive, centrifugal force that balances the destructive, centripetal energy of overflowing passion. At some points, it is "faceless" background material—an accompaniment—but at other times it assumes a precise character. It functions as the original material from which any theme and character may evolve. Characteristically, the introductions to the first and last movements depict the formation of rhythmic ostinato. But the ostinato also connects the piece to a classical model. Bartók was very likely inspired by Beethoven's Piano Concerto in G major, which is likewise based on themes connected by the idea of note repetition. In this manner Bartók was able to create generic musical material in which virtually any theme may transform into another yet keep its link to distinct styles of the folk and Western idioms.

Ostinato emerges again as the central idea of the second movement whose underlying theme is the percussive sound of continuous eighth notes. Against the monotonous background chords and clusters of the piano and the beats of the percussion, the woodwinds play—in polyphonic elaboration—a theme that is essentially the varied repetition of one motive. Similar in concept to the first movement, the restatements of this melody lead to climax. But while the ostinato is integral to the themes in the first and last movements that are mostly in double meter (alluding to folk dance), in this movement, ostinato and melody are superposed on each other without merging together—the triple-meter ostinato continues throughout the movement with an almost inhuman (or superhuman) stubbornness. There is something mysterious—even mystical or ritualistic—about the continuity of one melody against the exuberance of multiple percussive sounds of the persistent eighth-note beats in the background—Bartók never again composed a slow movement similar to this.

In the cyclic plan, this Andante functions as center (in the sense of the Bartókian bridge form) and as an extended introduction to the last movement leading naturally to the ostinato-based finale. The attacca transition from slow ritualistic ostinato to fast barbaric ostinato at the end of the movement is among the most structurally conceived and yet, in its effect, most spontaneous and powerful of Bartókian passages.

Bartók's conception of the third movement as a variation of the first meant not only thematic variation but also variation of the dramatic idea. The complex thematic material of the first movement is decomposed to its basic motives, and these motives are recombined in a novel manner. For instance, the first theme of the first movement is reduced here to its minimal elements—rhythmic ostinato, repetition of the three-note motive, and scales—but this musical rough material is presented as a symmetrical four-line theme, which, however, soon dissolves in scattered scalar motives (Example 12). The rhythm of the opening line of this theme is the retrograde of the rhythmic pattern of the closing measures of the second theme and those of the "latent song" of the first theme. It is as if the last movement attempted to project a "withdrawal" of the thematic material.[16]

In the last movement, the thematic transformations move toward an even more extreme polarization of characters. In a series of transformations, the theme of the introduction of the first movement becomes first the theme of the transition, then secondary theme a, secondary theme b, and the closing theme. What is most remarkable about this section is not the monothematic design, nor the highly skillful techniques with which Bartók manipulates this very simple theme, but the fact that he is able to express entirely different characters through these four variants and yet create themes that carry out their role in the sonata form. The first variant, the theme of the transition, leads away from the preceding obsessive ostinato and introduces a milder, more melodic motion (Example 13). However, the second variation on the trumpet and the muted trombones (functionally, the first secondary theme) is of a grotesque, almost wicked character (Example 14). The motivic fragmentation that follows leads to repetitions of chords in the orchestra and the piano, bringing the music to a virtual halt—a gesture reminiscent of preparations in classical sonata forms before the entry of the second theme. It is at this functionally highlighted moment that the third version of the theme, obviously a pseudo-folk song, appears, evoking an unexpectedly grandiose, almost sentimental mood (Example 15). The fourth variation is an imitative, stretta-like version of the theme, connecting it back to the idea of the mesmerizing dance (Example 16).

Bartók's plan is hard to miss: instead of compressing complex feelings into one theme, which was the idea behind the second theme of the first movement, here he breaks them into their component parts. The music grasps that unique moment when the two aspects of one thing become suddenly

EXAMPLE 12.   The first theme of the third movement.

EXAMPLE 13.   The theme of the transition to the second themes.

EXAMPLE 14.   Second theme A.

EXAMPLE 15.   Second theme B.

EXAMPLE 16.   The theme of the transition after the second themes.

irreconcilable. The extremely grotesque and the extremely emotional stand side by side, without connection or reconciliation. The polarization of characters is even more unexpected and unusual because both fulfill the function of secondary theme.

The introductory section of the development builds on the first theme, decomposing its elements into fragmented motivic ideas (mm. 210–55). Against this decomposition, the central section (mm. 256–319) brings a series of reiterations, often polyphonically as fugue entries, of a clearly Hungarian-sounding theme based on the second theme of the exposition (m. 254 horns, 272 piano; fugue entries: 284 strings, 290 piano, 297 trumpet, 300 woodwinds, 302 trombone). Thus the development intensifies aspects of the exposition by further separating them: the theme in the introductory section moves in a negative direction, becoming more and more fragmented and agitated, while the development of the second theme becomes the affirmation of a positive, communal spirit. However, the dramaturgy of the development is not unidirectional. Superposed on the Hungarian fanfare themes, the barely articulated, exalted motivic transformations continue, providing a countervoice throughout the entire development. This voice could be called background were it not, for the most part, played by the solo piano displaying great virtuosity.

The recapitulation, then, is an almost incomprehensibly compressed statement of the preceding musical ideas: it is at the same time a second development—breaking down all the themes into their basic elements in a demonic, whirling dance—and a synthesis, through its reinstatement of all the main thematic ideas of both exposition and development in close succession. The final gesture of the piece, nevertheless, is a sarcastic statement of a version of the introduction's theme.

In a sense, the underlying idea of the concerto is a search for structure itself; it is designed to explore the potentials of material and form, the "phenomena" or original facts of music. At the same time Bartók expanded the limits of the classical form by using all its basic aspects functionally. In this piece he confronted several significant questions of the era: what is the elemental and most minimal source of music? How can this source be organically developed into themes and forms that keep their traditional formal functions (and traditional connections between patterns and form) and yet express something unique and new? What are those elements of music where all "sources" meet—that is, where the distance among the varieties of musical styles disappears? And finally, to what degree can emotional expression be polarized to the point of even becoming primitive, wicked, or sentimental? How can an emotionally convincing coherence be reached nevertheless?

In this piece Bartók explored the possibilities of musical language and expression with rare intensity. In certain respects the design of the First Piano Concerto is unique; it illustrates, nevertheless, the basic ideas that recur in virtually all Bartók's mature pieces:

- The choice of some basic melodic-rhythmic idea, a kind of *Urmusik*, which nevertheless has clear folk-music associations. A melodically and rhythmically "minimal" element is used as the cohesive force that symbolically and structurally unites the styles of classical and folk music and has the potential to connect an infinite number of themes.
- The recapturing and intensifying of the "spirit" of folk music in a complex theme, through the distortion and/or superposition of unrelated elements of folk and art music.
- The dissolution of a theme into its most minimal motivic (tonal, rhythmic) elements at formally accentuated points (such as the introduction, the recapitulation, or the corresponding section of another movement).
- Monothematism and the polarization of themes—continuous transformation of themes into variants that are structurally logical but unexpected in character (typically either a caricature or an almost sentimental nationalist symbol) and have a basic thematic continuum.
- The concept of bridge form—the design of the large-scale form around a central movement in a symmetrical fashion, with the last movement being the recomposition of the first (in the case of five movements, the fourth also being the recomposition of the second).

What is the meaning of this design? Could this process of thematic transformations be "translated" into a meaningful narrative? Why did Bartók feel it necessary to destroy the themes of the first movement, which already achieved a complex and in a sense perfect representation of the spirit of folk music, and why did he recompose its more balanced thematic contrasts into something more demonic and grotesque in the last movement? Why did he save the caricature of a "serious" theme for the last gesture of the piece?

Bartók's use of the positive direction of the thematic transformation is no less problematic. Somfai described these moments in Bartókian form as a characteristically and emphatically "Hungarian-[sounding]" culmination point as a type that appears toward the end of the movements in Bartók's large-scale instrumental compositions.[17] For Somfai, these moments are the "confessions" that, in spite of his decidedly international musical language, Bartók felt himself to be closest to a Hungarian folk style—and this interpretation is certainly correct. But it does not answer our question as to why Bartók used a theme of such an extreme and easily recognizable Hungarian character in a work that transcends such simple associations, or included characters ranging from extreme caricature to extreme expression of Hungarianness in works that also contain more sophisticated integration of these themes. How do these formal decisions reflect Bartók's aesthetic belief that his aim was "to grasp the spirit of folk music"?

THE ROAD TOWARD A NEW AESTHETICS

These structural ideas consistently recurring in Bartók's instrumental pieces after 1920 (and occasionally before that date) reflect a conception that began to develop around 1907. Because of our limited access to crucial documents of this period of Bartók's life, we know little of how the composer developed his new aesthetics. But we can trace the conceptual discovery to a period of disenchantment and depression. It was in Bartók's character to hold on to an ideal until he realized that it was untrue, at which point he turned against his former belief with equal vehemence. He was aware of the exclusiveness of his opinions, his sudden and total conceptual changes. In his letters to Stefi Geyer in 1907, he confessed that he had believed with his full heart in a conventional morality and described how he became within a few years just as passionate an opponent of those ideas. In his letters he bitterly and sarcastically described his former self, the naive "believer" in Christian values, accepting all the assets of a popular morality of mediocrity and superficial appearances. In Bartók's library, there are a number of books designed for the young that he received as presents during his middle and high school years. If he read these or similar sentimental and moralizing books—which is very likely—we can understand why he spoke with such anger and irony about the era when he was under the influence of such "teaching."[18]

As Bartók recalled in his letter to Geyer, his first doubts arose at the age of fifteen or sixteen, when he attended the sixth and seventh grades of the Roman Catholic Main Gymnasium of Pozsony (now Bratislava). After he came to Budapest in 1899 at the age of eighteen, he could for the first time think seriously about such problems. In these years he was desperately searching for other ideals that would, in a simple and unambiguous manner, reconnect him to a broader community and to moral ideals. The years between 1899 and 1905 (the beginning of his studies at the Academy of Music) were a time of futile attempts to find such an ideology in the nationalist trends of the time.[19] Bartók's expectations were high and rather naive. So when he saw through the slogans of political nationalism, his disappointment was immense. Partly as a result of his trip to Paris, and partly through exposure to other views on social matters, he came to a more realistic but also more depressing view of Hungarian society. The reality he experienced around 1904 was so far from his vision of an ideal, modern, democratic, and yet somehow still Christian and deeply national community that he saw modern Hungarian society and his place within it in bleak colors. He was fully aware of Hungary's backwardness; he despaired at the tragic disintegration of its society, the incoherence and cultural indifference of the emerging bourgeois middle class, and the destructive force behind the empty slogans of political parties. His depression was aggravated by personal failures, his lack of success as a pianist, problems in composition (at times, mental blocks), loneliness among friends, and, during a crucial year of emotional development, hopeless love for Geyer.

In Bartók, a sensitive individual, the intense fixation on one thought—which later he understood to be superficial and even false—generated an overwhelming moral force molding his whole personality. The series of disenchantments with concepts that were all one-faceted and somewhat simpleminded forced him to search for a more complex vision of truth. During this time his varied experiences, and especially his feeling of loneliness, gradually transformed themselves into aspects of an authentic conception of art: Bartók's own identity and artistic task came into sharper focus. In order to come to this new understanding, he needed distance from his former roles, in which he was constantly provoked to show achievements, as he was during his student years and when he sought to establish himself as a pianist. The acceptance of loneliness opened up the possibility of a deeper, more philosophical look into questions of life, a shift to focus on the inner world.[20]

The most telling documents of his philosophical and aesthetic discoveries of the time can be found in letters to women: to his mother and sister, to Irmy Jurkovics, Stefi Geyer, Emma Gruber, and Márta Ziegler. Bartók never wrote about emotional matters in any serious way to his male acquaintances—or at least no such correspondence is known—and the tone of the letters to women is invariably didactic and simplistic. Bartók's verbal style reflects the assumption that his knowledge of philosophical and psychological matters equipped him to guide these women in such difficult matters. Of course, it is precisely for that reason that he preferred to discuss such issues with women, since he himself lacked the intellectual sophistication and verbal eloquence to carry on philosophical discussions.

But there was also another, deeper reason. Partly following the spirit of the time, but even more likely reflecting his personal character, Bartók revealed his feelings only to women. The notion that the discovery of the self was intimately connected to the discovery of the Other (and to love) infused the intellectual milieu of that time. The war between man and woman was thought to epitomize the basic questions of human existence. This attitude was natural for Bartók, perhaps more so than for several of his contemporaries—even though he was occasionally puzzled by the fact that all his close friends were women. Bartók related to life more through emotions than through the intellect; he instinctively felt that understanding was possible only through insight, in a mental activity where mind and soul were not separate. In order to think about his own self, Bartók needed to have an emotional connection with someone; it had to grow from love and with the hope of being loved, at least during this period of his life. Thus he came to an understanding of his own personality and emotions at the time of his great love for Geyer.[21]

In Bartók's case, it is not the complexity but rather the naïveté of his writing that makes it an ungrateful task to try to grasp the depth of his thinking. Yet hidden in his somewhat simplistic writings is a complex philosophical thought that becomes transparent once we relate the many scattered ideas he sketched haphazardly in letters to his life experiences and his readings of Nietzsche, Ady, and Balázs. The most significant documents are the letters to Geyer, most of them written during his folk-song-collecting trip in the mountains of Csík county in 1907—especially the one of 27 July, which contains several pages on his approach to music and composition. Bartók begins by explaining the immediateness of the musical experiences in his childhood:[22]

> Pieces whose content does not rise above certain heights can be understood by children just as much as by those who "suffered a lot." In such pieces, the emotions expressed are more general and much less complicated, they are emotions that could be appropriately expressed more or less by one word: pain, maddening pain, gentleness, and so on. Because a child already has experienced all such things, he is able to feel it. For instance, Mendelssohn's Violin Concerto is such a piece. I accompanied this piece many times when I was eleven years old and I remember very well how I could feel it; in fact, much better than now because at present I find it boring. . . . [I suppose that] perhaps you too subscribe unconditionally to the idea that a child cannot comprehend much from the masterpieces of the other arts, as the entire lack of child prodigies suggests in those cases.

The starting point of Bartók's aesthetics is an immediate and direct relation between music and emotion. Such direct connection—which for Bartók was not a theoretical supposition but a personal experience—was art's most important potential. In this sense music ranked above the other arts, because music elicited even a child's spontaneous emotional reaction. Here was the original state of aesthetic response, which Bartók considered only a few works capable of evoking—only some of the best pieces and, as Bartók hints in another letter, folk music.[23]

The task of art was to create immediate, direct connections to the emotions, but the emotions reflected in the greatest works of music were far more complex:

> I still remember well: I was fourteen when I first heard Beethoven's String Quartet in C sharp minor. I became passionately fond of it, I wanted to get to know it. Of course, this was not so easy: we had little money and I had to wait till the next Christmas and even then I did not get the score but the four-hand arrangement because that was cheaper. I studied it, within a short time, I learned it by heart and kept playing it with two hands on the piano—and still I could not feel it at that time as I feel it now. The [allegro] theme[24] is something so magically deep, it paints an inexpressible feeling that a child could feel at best as charming "grazioso," but that is much more than that. Today I cannot think of this theme without enormous emotion (affection), at the time this was not the case. [And] how could a child feel the shattering, infinite pain that is expressed by [the Tristan chord]? I am very grateful to you for challenging me to this discussion because, as an afterthought to it, the question emerged before me: what is the relation between such a chord as a physical phenomenon and the emotion signified by it? For the time being I cannot answer this question. . . . Could you?

A child cannot understand the emotion expressed in the theme of Beethoven's quartet because it cannot be reduced to simple and common feelings such as pain or happiness. In the most concentrated moments, music—and music alone—takes hold of deep feelings and makes them transparent in a precise and clear manner that words cannot equal. As he wrote to Geyer, "With me, you can know everything with absolute certainty. I do not only write words but also musical notes. And what is expressed in an ambiguous manner in the former is the most exact and clear speech in the latter. A musician can understand it."[25]

In Bartók's vocabulary, complexity (of feeling) meant depth and not tangled confusion. A feeling no longer expressible in words was still one single coherent thing, a grand sensation. It was not possible to "decompose" this complexity, to "translate" it into various simple feelings. Art rendered such complex emotion in the simplest manner—by a gesture: a chord, or a melody.

The expression embedded in such musical ideas could not be analyzed, only felt. In Bartók's judgment, Strauss's music fell short of the demand of great art precisely because it decomposed a deep feeling into many simple emotions and laid them out, so to speak, in the form of narrative. The tonal-rhythmic inventions—that is, the structural complexity of the music—did not compensate for the fact that it was not able to concentrate into one gesture the great feeling to which the title alluded: "In spite of its promising title, Strauss's *Zarathustra* does not express these highest emotions: its second half is excessively joyful, painting a feeling that everyone could have had and thus has access to. . . . This is not a dismissive criticism, only the stating of certain facts. Nevertheless, I regard *Zarathustra* very highly."[26]

NIETZSCHE AND FOLK MUSIC

Bartók had no doubt that complex emotions were the only means to communicate the reality of life. For him, these complex emotions were not "feelings" in the common sense of the word but rather sensations or realizations. In these uniquely concentrated moments of the mind and the soul, the realities of the world (and of the inner self) became suddenly transparent. In explaining this feeling, Bartók would use the word *átélés*, which is an understanding of things from inside, through feeling or empathy. By 1907 the inseparable connection between such intuitions of life and the expressive potential of art was an unquestionable fact for Bartók. As he wrote to Geyer in another letter, "Do not wish that fate would always treat you as its favorite child! In that case, the doors of your heart would be closed on most human emotions. You really do not want to struggle, to have emotional shocks, even life-threatening feelings and situations? Then how are you going to feel the Ninth symphony, the *Faust*, Nietzsche's *Zarathustra?* Whoever wishes to entirely feel ideas born from suffering must have suffered too. Don't you think so?"[27] This belief remained with Bartók for the rest of his life. The reason for his disappointment with the music of many contemporary composers—even Stravinsky's, especially from his neoclassical years—was that in his judgment it did not transmit this grand sensation of existence.[28]

How, then, was Bartók to conceptualize large-scale form, when he placed the notion of a single great feeling at the center of the artwork? How could he cut himself off from the idea of music as narrative? For Bartók, the answer clearly lay in the rejection of linear moment-to-moment interpretation itself. He began to search for a method by which to express the essence (a feeling or spirit) in some other way than a one-directional process where "resolution" follows the "problem." The fundamental idea that led him toward the formal designs of his mature pieces came to him in 1907, when he saw in polarized images the means to capture the essence of something coherent (in this case Geyer's personality): "One day last week I suddenly came to this apparently indisputable necessity, as if by some magic impulse, that your piece could only consist of two movements. Two opposing images: that is all. Now I am just amazed that I did not see this truth before. One's eyes are so rarely opened."[29]

An essence cannot be depicted or explained, it is like an invisible center, a point of gravitation apparent only in its contrasting realities. Music cannot render such essence, it can only make reality transparent through a complex play of polarized ideas. Influenced by Nietzsche, Bartók here envisioned musical form, at least potentially, as a direct outgrowth of the great feeling of life, a sensation in which opposites become part of one and the same great feeling. To be able to feel life in this way, an individual has to rise above all things to reach a state of complete independence. Bartók understood, from his own experience—and took great pains to explain it in a letter to Irmy Jurkovics—that this higher state of detachment was in fact the most intense feeling. After (freely) quoting Nietzsche ("Each must strive above all; nothing must touch him; he must be completely independent, completely indifferent. Only thus can he reconcile himself to death and to the meaninglessness of life"), he wrote, "It needs a gigantic struggle to rise above all things! How far I am yet from doing so! What is more, the further you advance, the more intensely, it seems, you feel!"[30] Just as detachment from the world did not mean a lack of feeling, the realization of the aimlessness of human existence did not involve a pessimistic attitude toward life. "What!! You are rebuking me for being a pessimist?!! *Me*, a follower of Nietzsche?!!"

These spontaneously written lines signal what Bartók already sensed in 1905: the Nietzschean demand on the soul does not necessarily lead toward negative feeling. As opposed to many contemporaries, for whom the philosophy of Nietzsche was essentially a destructive force, Bartók took from it another attitude. As he explained to Geyer, an awareness of the purposelessness of existence served to counterbalance a great enthusiasm for the ever-present richness of life: "In a thousand years, I am sure that my whole work will be lost without a trace. The same fate awaits the work of every one of us. It would not be a pleasant thing to work with only this depressing thought in mind. To be able to work, one must have a zest for life, i.e., a keen interest in the living universe. One has to be filled with enthusiasm."[31]

Bartók describes here a spiritual state, a basic attitude toward life that must

underlie artistic creation. It is significant that Bartók drew this aesthetic demand not from a philosophical theory but from a personal problem. To train
himself to experience life in its totality meant to come to terms with his own
self, his failures, and, most important, his deepening problems with musical
composition. The notion that artistic expression depended on life experience
is Bartók's most original, as well as most central, artistic conception. To be
sure, this idea has its roots in romanticism, but the seriousness with which Bartók insisted on it, and the manner in which he worked it into his life and aesthetics, was something quite specific to him, even though it had parallels in
Hungarian modernism (especially in Ady's attitude, as we shall see).

It could be said that, in these years, the compositional problem he struggled with was primarily not one of technique or style; it was one of feeling.
Bartók understood that, in order to move away from his earlier nationalistic
and romantic music, it was necessary to distance himself also from his previous
simplistic vision of reality. The sudden, and for him quite uncharacteristic, enthusiasm for literature of philosophical depth, such as the works of Nietzsche
and the poetry of Ady, and his subsequent insistence that he had to train himself to learn to feel life in a new way, are indicative of the stages of this development. But how could he learn this new feeling? And what if he were unable
to learn it in time? Bartók was perplexed by these questions: "How far I am
from doing so [being able to rise above all things]! . . . My mother tries to console me and says that the future holds brighter days in store for me! Yes, to be
sure. But what if those brighter days come too late?"[32]

The breakthrough came with his field trip to the mountains of Csík in
1907. "The days I spent in the village among peasants were the happiest days
of my life," Bartók exclaimed.[33] What did his comment mean? Our very different anthropological consciousness distances us from Bartók's enthusiasm
for collecting folk music. Bartók's letters did not reveal an idyllic, Rousseauian
retreat to the countryside. Nor did Bartók see the peasants in an idealized, romantic light; he saw their life from close enough to be aware of its misery and
brutality. His letters were full of complaints about physical conditions and
about a community's often indifferent or unfriendly reception. Once he had
to sleep in a damp room without heat and woke up soaking wet the next
morning.[34] Another time he barely escaped from the house of a drunken man
and, to avoid wandering the streets for the whole night, had no choice but to
return to the same place—arming himself with a dagger. He had to endure
living on minimal and boring food (once there was almost nothing besides raw
meat). One man threatened to beat him if he continued "this coming and going"—an incident that made him want to order a revolver.[35]

FIGURE 5.   Béla Bartók on his field trip in Transylvania, 1907. (Reproduction by István
Kováts. Courtesy Bartók Archives, Institute for Musicology, Hungarian Academy
of Sciences)

In the social context of the beginning of the century, a meaningful relationship between peasants and the visiting gentleman from the city was almost unthinkable. And the idea of such closeness never occurred to Bartók. In his eyes, the peasants were somewhat like children whom he admired but with whom he had little in common. The peasants were more "primitive," meaning that they ranked both lower and higher than members of his society: they were closer to an original understanding of life but less developed intellectually and emotionally.[36]

Of course, peasant music made an indelible impression on him. Bartók was amazed by the conciseness of musical expression characteristic especially of the old-style songs. Even more than its technical aspects, he admired the utmost intensity of expression within the simplest form—no sentimentalism, no exaggeration. Without diminishing the importance of this experience, we have to recognize that Bartók regarded folk music as he did the peasants who sang and played it. In his view, folk music represented an original state of musical culture—it ranked higher than even the greatest pieces of art music. Yet it lacked the sophistication necessary to hold the complex feelings of the best art music. In one letter to Geyer, he wrote that his interest in folk music was on the whole less a musical than a scientific matter; at another time he complained that these melodies became after a while somewhat boring.[37] Yet throughout his life Bartók emphasized both the importance of folk music and the fact that its real spirit, and thus the spirit of his own compositions, could be understood only by those who experienced the music in its "natural context." Listening to recordings did not transmit the experience: Bartók insisted that whoever wished to understand his compositions had to come with him to the village. Thus he took along Egisto Tango, the conductor of the first performance of the *Wooden Prince* and *Bluebeard's Castle*, to Romanian villages in 1917. Later, trying to establish contact with Delius, he suggested the same thing to him.[38]

For Bartók, being in the village was neither a purely anthropological nor a purely musical experience. It surpassed both. Surrounded by the most magnificent natural landscapes, hearing songs of the utmost simplicity and intensity, seeing the life of the peasants, and knowing that he was fulfilling a mission (preserving the remnants of an old culture)—the composer was truly happy:

> [For all these physical sufferings] I am rewarded only by the joy of hearing with my own ears those melodies of unusual mood that we find in our [written] collections as the remnants of the poetry of an era that sank into oblivion long ago. When I read these for the first time, I hardly could believe they all live today in the songs of the peasants. I hear this strange, archaic speech that is about to disappear and I cannot help being moved when I think of the fact

that the last remnants of a disappearing era are now in front of my eyes, an era that no living being will be able to find coming here forty or fifty years after me. I am somehow moved when I hear how an old woman, in her shaky voice, chants an ancient melody.[39]

Bartók's attitude toward folk music was by no means unusual for the time. His contemporaries viewed the peasantry in more or less the same manner and probably had similar emotional experiences during fieldwork. Nor was the conceptual basis of these experiences peculiar to Hungarian ethnology. Folk art was generally thought to be an integral whole existing in and of itself, a remnant of an otherwise extinct common national culture of which the peasants were only carriers. Folk culture was something "natural," something close to earth: peasant art was part of a country's natural landscape and, like natural life, material for careful objective research.[40] Such was the ideological basis of virtually all ethnographic research at the time, including the famous Berlin Phonogramm-Archiv directed by Erich von Hornbostel.

Yet research gave Bartók the framework for reaching a deeply personal solution to questions of life, communication, and art. In Bertalan Pethő's interpretation, Bartók liked to be in the village because among the peasants, and only among them could he become really himself.[41] The distance between him and the villagers freed him from the burden of communication. There he could remain distant, silent about his thoughts and feelings, but share in a communal life that had more integrity than his existence in the city. This interpretation is probably correct. However, the experience of the village went beyond compensation for his psychological and social problems. It gave Bartók the feeling of being one with all—with nature and society—and at the same time above and distanced from everything. The archaic life of the village, its amazingly complete communal life, was in some sense unreal; it was as if he had a glimpse of the past, of a life that perhaps did not even really exist any more. But this life was also more real than the life in the city: people's daily activities in the country were tied to the simple and most basic aspects of human existence, governed by a true communal consciousness.

Bartók's time in the village was time out of life: everything that happened in the village was in parentheses and had no effect on the course of his normal life. Yet there he could feel really alive, precisely because of the enormous physical difficulties: his worrying about food and heat, about threats by villagers—these brought him closer to earth than the sheltered life of the urban intelligentsia could. In the village Bartók experienced a great excitement and detachment from everyday life, a feeling he called happiness:

I feel so strange here in Karcfalva. As if everything were more beautiful here than down there in Csíkrákos—I don't know whether this is caused by the more beautiful landscape or by something else. I come and go with fiery excitement. I would like to continue working here but I would also like to go home to my peaceful house to continue composing, I would like to travel to Venice to those Venetians—just now. . . . If I wanted to analyze this feeling, I might even claim it was happiness. Something I've not felt for a long time.[42]

Bartók integrated, through a uniquely personal experience, an essential aspect of Nietzsche's worldview. After the field trip of 1907 he no longer mentioned in his letters that he was unable to attain a Nietzschean detachment. Bartók's "feeling of life" comes into sharper focus if we complement his partial descriptions with those paragraphs of Nietzsche that influenced him in envisioning this feeling. The crucial relevant passages are aphorisms 33 and 34 from *Human, All Too Human;* Bartók marked these sections, underlined certain sentences, and added an exclamation mark in the margin:[43]

The great majority endure life without complaining overmuch; they *believe* in the value of existence, but they do so precisely because each of them exists for himself alone, refusing to step out from himself as those exceptions [of greatly gifted and pure souls] do: everything outside themselves they notice not at all or at most as a dim shadow. . . . *He,* on the other hand, who really could participate [in the others' fortunes and sufferings] would have to despair of the value of life . . . for mankind has as a whole no goal, and the individual man when he regards its total course cannot derive from it any support or comfort, but must be reduced to despair. If in all he does he has before him the ultimate goallessness of man, his actions acquire in his own eyes the character of useless squandering. But to feel thus *squandered,* not merely as an individual but as humanity as a whole, in the way we behold the individual fruits of nature squandered, is a feeling beyond all other feelings.—But who is capable of such feeling? Certainly only a poet: and poets always know how to console themselves.

During field trips Bartók was able to, as Nietzsche put it, "step out from himself" and "really could participate" in others' fortunes and sufferings. The cardinal point of this philosophy is transparency: man has to distance himself from everyday reality in order to get a true view of this reality, because the real events of life always intimately relate to him, they close him into his own self—to be involved in everyday events amounts to selfishness. Only by turning his face away from his own self, becoming aware of his smallness and aimlessness, is man able to really see life. This distancing is the renouncing of empirical life; one no longer lives life, one only looks onto it. To feel life in this way is a transcendental experience, it is like a sensation or inspiration: "a feeling beyond all other feelings" of which only poets are capable.

Such orientation in life is not a momentary revelation and its result need not be negative. Even when this experience is a more or less transitory event, it is enduring in relevance; the real value of such exaltations is in their aftereffect, a vision of life that is "much simpler and emotionally cleaner." The varied facets of life no longer need to be justified and explained in relation to each other; they are no longer causes and results—they simply *are*, and their value lies simply in existence alone:

> Is it true, is all that remains a mode of thought whose outcome on a personal level is despair and on a theoretical level a philosophy of destruction—I believe that the nature of the after-effect of knowledge is determined by a man's *temperament:* in addition to the after-effect described I could just as easily imagine a different one, quite possible in individual instances, by virtue of which a life could arise much simpler and emotionally cleaner than our present life is. . . . In the end one would live among men and with oneself as in *nature*, without praising, blaming, contending, gazing contentedly, as though at a spectacle, on many things for which one formerly felt only fear. One would be free of emphasis, and no longer prodded by the idea that one is only nature or more than nature. For this to happen, one would to be sure, have to possess the requisite temperament, as has already been said, a firm, mild and at bottom cheerful soul, a temper that does not need to be on its guard against malice or sudden outbursts and in whose utterances there is nothing of snarling or sullenness. . . . He is happy to communicate his joy in this condition, and he *has*, perhaps, nothing else to communicate.

His involvement with this thought of Nietzsche's and especially his capacity to feel it, had a decisive impact on Bartók, determining his entire lifestyle in the years to come. In his peculiar way, Bartók remained devoted to the idea of living life as fully as possible. He desired activity even to the point of taking up public responsibilities in Hungarian music life. He was part of the Music Directorate during the Communist regime, participated in various events of the *Nyugat's* circle, and contemplated becoming the director of the Hungarian Opera. He wanted to create, with the help of Kodály, a forum for modern music and never really overcame the fact that this plan did not succeed. Once he mentioned to his wife that, in fact, even folk-music collecting was a substitute for some more real activity: he poured his energy into collecting and transcribing because there was no real modern musical life in which he could have taken an active part.[44] Bartók had an urge to do things, to accomplish: he was proud of how many folk songs he could collect in a day and how fast he was able to transcribe. He loved hiking, loved to travel, loved to see the lives of other people and discover new things. Fieldwork was appealing because it allowed him to face ever new and unexpected situations. He did not even mind the hardship; on the contrary, he enjoyed being able to overcome enormous physical difficulties: "I am compelled to accept these many miseries because of the desire to search and discover and it is better to fulfill this desire through hardship."[45]

Bartók wanted to root all knowledge firmly in an individual experience; however, he also wished to retain the idea of Nietzschean distance—that is, the belief that the capacity to grasp the essence of life is the fruit of a momentary inspiration that comes only in isolation, away from life. There was a clear pattern in Bartók's life that corresponded to this ideal. As soon as he was able to, he moved out of Budapest to one of the suburban villages; from then on, he commuted to the Academy of Music by train. He gradually developed a pattern of dividing his time on a yearly basis, drawing a rigid line between the time reserved for composing and that for all other activities. He spent only a surprisingly short period each year with composition, essentially only the summer months. And he set about the task with particular intensity. As he once noted, "I do not like to mix works. If I begin something [i.e., a composition] I fully devote myself to it until I finish it."[46] When he composed, Bartók suspended all other responsibilities; he tried to isolate himself completely from life, did not respond to letters, and when possible sent his family away. During the time set aside for composing, Bartók stepped away from life, so to speak. This pattern corresponded to his belief that composition was not "work" in the same way other activities were; it needed a special, inspired state of mind. As he wrote to Geyer in 1907, "For some time, I have been in a strange mood. . . . This is exactly what is needed for work (for composition)."[47] It is characteristic that during his field trip in Transylvania—far away from real life—he felt for the first time, after a long period of interruption, that he was able to compose again.

Bartók's sketches are revealing documents of belief in the ideal that "the artwork had to be born from inspiration." Normally, he worked out his compositions in his head, conceptualizing a fairly long section of the music before he began to play it at the piano. What he then put down in notation was usually already a complete movement, a continuous draft. As he once said to the poet Dezső Kosztolányi, he composed his pieces *between* the writing desk and the piano.[48] However, Bartók did sketch up themes. There is reason to believe that he notated them in a moment of inspiration; they usually contain a full-fledged melody with some indication of harmonic context, a potential theme.[49] The fact that Bartók—who was able to work out an entire movement in his head—felt it necessary to notate these themes reveals how highly he valued ideas that came to him in an inspired moment. He might have regarded these ideas as something original and perfect—the germ of a composition. Indeed, the themes preserved in these sketches are often almost identical with the theme as we know it from the finished work, as is the case with the thematic sketches for the beginning of the Sonata for Violin and Piano no. 2, for the theme of the second movement of the Violin Concerto (no. 2), for the *Cantata profana*, and for many others.

THE CONTEXT FOR BARTÓK'S AESTHETICS

How did Bartók transfer this attitude to life to the formal principles of musical composition? Nietzsche's text alone might have given him the idea for the structural design of his mature pieces. In the Nietzschean worldview distinct aspects of reality were not linear events in a temporal sequence but existed as contrasts and variants laid out without hierarchy in a metaphysical entity. The fact that Bartók experienced life in this manner and began to transmit this idea to art around 1907 was the result of an inner development. But it cannot be an accident that Lukács and Balázs developed similar views around the same time. These ideas are also the basis of Ady's symbolic poetry and could have reached Bartók through various channels. He had just read Nietzsche and Ady attentively; their works were among the most widely read and discussed literature of the modern-minded intelligentsia. The copies Bartók used were given to him by friends, and so they probably came up in conversations. During this time, Bartók spent his afternoons—at one point, almost every other afternoon—with Emma Gruber and Zoltán Kodály, not only wonderful musicians but also well read and intellectually and emotionally developed individuals. Through them, Bartók came into contact with a broad circle of musicians and intellectuals, among them Kodály's best friend, Béla Balázs, who was in turn a link with the young aesthetes and literati of the Sunday circle who gathered around György Lukács.

Gruber was among those few people who had a decisive role in helping Bartók and Kodály develop their concepts of life and art. Her generosity and encouragement were great resources for both composers as they came to terms

FIGURE 6.   Béla Balázs and Béla Bartók walking on the highway, 1917. (Photo by Edit Hajós. Courtesy Bartók Archives, Institute for Musicology, Hungarian Academy of Sciences)

with personal problems. Perhaps she generated several of their ideas, inspiring them intellectually and artistically. Unfortunately, Gruber's letters and diary (if she had one) are not yet available, and at this point we cannot say anything concrete about her intellectual influence.[50]

We know, however, that Balázs and Kodály struggled with problems very similar to those of Bartók—in particular the problem of how to live and feel life, and how to then grasp the essence of the great feeling of life in art. Kodály began to advocate physical exercise, cultivating an outdoor life, walking, hiking, and swimming. He tried to win Bartók over to this idea so that he would also learn to have "more joy in the mere existence" of his physical being. Kodály viewed Bartók as someone who was unable to live fully: "It pains me that someone who can write such things [i.e., compose such great music] is able to grasp life only to such a small extent."[51] But he in turn complained of the same problem: "I am so impatient sometimes. In spite of everything, I feel as if I were only walking on the banks of the sea of life, instead of jumping into it

FIGURE 7. Zoltán Kodály, Emma Kodály, and Béla Bartók on a field trip, 1912. (Courtesy Bartók Archives, Institute for Musicology, Hungarian Academy of Sciences)

and even dying if I were unable to swim through. Half-pleasures, half-pains, nothing full . . ." Similar thoughts troubled Balázs: "The road to the discovery of life goes in two directions (although at the end they come together): out to the world and into my own self. Until now, I have been traveling almost entirely on the latter."[52] Both Kodály and Balázs were searching for the great experience of life, and Kodály found it in folk-music collecting. In a letter to Gruber, Kodály tried to analyze this unique feeling, only to conclude that his many feelings about the village amounted to one great emotion: "The whole thing is some great emotion that can be compared only with the effect of art or of love—if anything could be compared to these at all."[53]

Balázs and Kodály, like Bartók, connected the idea of living fully to an artistic demand. The demand had a dual and seemingly self-contradictory meaning: devotion to the experience of life and renunciation of life. As Balázs put it, the aim of all great art was to make one feel reality, but the prerequisite for creating such art was the loss of a sense of reality.[54] He took the idea seriously to the point of making it a life program: in his diary Balázs repeatedly hints at the fact that, in order to be able to create, he imposed solitude on himself even by artificial means.[55] The moment of inspiration was something ecstatic, the great experience of the feeling of life without being part of life any longer. It was the moment when "having reached the edge of intellect, having wandered all over the world and wandered through everything reaching the end—one looks into the void of space from which everything is created (*onnan néz be a mindenszülő űrbe*)."[56] The three men often discussed the idea that art had to grasp the sensation of life, something beyond words, and Balázs, reflecting on some recent conversation in his diary notes, came back to this issue again and again:[57] "Every thought that burst out from the soul has a radiant, vibrating atmosphere, something that the word signifying the phenomenon cannot contain in itself. And this is the task of art: to grasp this atmosphere through forms." In the same spirit, he reproached himself for being unable to capture in his short stories anything beyond "problems:" "A short story of problems. That is, there are problems in it, whereas [its topic] should be the mystery of life itself. . . . This is not 'greatness.'" And a few weeks later he noted, "The ultimate goal of all art is to make it possible for people to grasp through feeling the nature of life and their own selves as a miraculous and mysterious great event."

As if Kodály and Balázs had been influenced by the same lines of Nietzsche that captivated Bartók (as is not at all unlikely), they were seeking clarity—a vision of life as something transparent, where all elements simply coexist without judgment or hierarchy: "Where is the truth that is but fact, that is reality?

. . . Something that is not necessary to proclaim, to defend, to prove, that simply needs to be pointed at [in order to be seen]."

This chain of thought was now conceived more and more in terms of an aesthetics, as a demand on musical structure. A piece should not impose feelings on the listener, for instance, by means of heavy orchestration and calculated effects; it had to be strict and precise, and capture by such clarity a great feeling. By 1907, Kodály had become skeptical about the music of Strauss for reasons very similar to those of Bartók. He wrote after having heard Strauss's *Salome*, "Yesterday: Salome. Interesting, interesting (at least it is not so overorchestrated), a bit more fine, often boring, empty. Sometimes it is annoying that [it is composed of] series of cleverly calculated (*raffinált*) 'baby effects' ('*hatásocskák*') without having one great effect. Afterwards I do not feel anything: it is quite the same whether I am coming from the pub or from Salome. Nevertheless I listen to Strauss always with a spirit of discovery, I like to discover for myself new territories of pleasure."[58] That already by 1906 Kodály, Bartók, and Balázs connected their ideas about life and reality to a conception of musical form without narrative is indicated by one of Balázs's diary notes, in which he contemplated a potential opera libretto for Kodály: "Zoltán told me that he would need a tale. . . . I am going to do it! Just as I said at the time, [it is going to be] a lyric drama, without epic—so that there would be no need for program music."[59]

Many elements of this thinking were rooted in a common Central European intellectual tradition, which in turn perpetuated ideas of German romantic aesthetics. For all the common ideas emerging in the aesthetics of Balázs, Kodály, and Bartók, each artist reacted to and interpreted the German romantic tradition in his own way. Unlike Balázs, Bartók and Kodály had great difficulty speaking about themselves. Balázs was constantly frustrated with Kodály for his resistance to analyzing feelings and human relations. Balázs associated with Kodály the view that the "[analytical] dissecting [of feeling] is pointless . . . it does not clarify anything—a spontaneously found word is more fruitful."[60] But for all his interest in analyzing emotions, Balázs also knew that the soul has secrets deeper than what could be seized by the intellect. And for his part, Kodály also desired to communicate his feelings and was particularly frustrated that he and Bartók, supposedly the best of friends, were unable to speak to each other about anything beyond objective, practical matters.[61]

Yet silence could mean very different things. Behind Bartók's shyness was an enormous passion and expressivity, and, we gather from his letters, he wanted to cultivate them by pouring the passion and expressivity entirely into music, not into words. Kodály, a very different character, resolved his problem in a different manner. His interpretation of the same ideas about the great feeling of life led toward what Balázs called his "artistic materialism."[62] His stance was closer to a kind of neoclassicism; he viewed music more as a craft, with the composer's task being to continue the tradition at the highest level. The three artists realized how personal their ideologies were. Kodály contemplated the reasons for his ascetic attitude, asking himself whether it was a conscious artistic decision or simply a matter of character.[63]

THE THEORETICAL PARALLEL IN
THE EARLY WORKS OF GYÖRGY LUKÁCS

The letters and diaries of Kodály, Balázs, and Bartók show us a complex web of ideas that characterizes the thinking of young intellectuals in their era. From these heterogeneous elements, a core aesthetics began to emerge around the end of the first decade of the century in the writings of György Lukács. Lukács's early writings are important for our understanding of Bartók and Hungarian modernism even though they had little direct impact on Bartók. But they crystallize ideas that all the artists felt and discussed and scattered among letters and diary notes.

By 1911 Lukács arrived at a coherent aesthetics that set drama as the paradigm of the connection between reality and art. Tragedy, according to Lukács, does not depict the experience of everyday life; rather it grasps the essence of life in an intense form. In tragedy, the gestures and words of everyday life become at once symbols of a deeper reality and, as a result, lifeless forms: "Drama alone creates—'gives form to'—real human beings, but just because of this it must, of necessity, deprive them of living existence. Their life is made up of words and gestures, but every word they speak and every gesture they make is more than gesture or word; all the manifestations of their lives are mere ciphers for their ultimate relationships."[64]

Real empirical life is the collection of arbitrary things, of "chaotic coincidences," with no deeper meaning. Against this chaotic existence stands a deeper and truer reality—the never realized complex web of potentialities. The source of tragedy is life, but tragedy does not show the colorful richness of life; rather, it uses elements that reveal its own essence and necessity: " 'Lived experience' is latent in every event of life as a threatening abyss, the door to the judgement chamber: its connection with the Idea—of which it is merely an outward manifestation—is no more than the conceivable possibility of such a connection in the midst of the chaotic coincidences of real life." The notion of the tragic therefore "knows no space or time; all its events are outside of the scope of logical explanation, just as the souls of its men are outside of the scope of psychology."[65] From this thought Lukács arrived at the negation of linearity by envisioning a conceptual timelessness in drama:

> Tragedy is only a moment . . . and the technical paradox contained in trying to give temporal duration to a moment which, by its very nature, is without such duration, springs from the inadequacy of expressing a mystical experience in terms of human language. . . . Tragic drama has to express the becoming-timelessness of time. . . . Not only is the empirically real sequence disturbed and destroyed by turning the present into something secondary and unreal . . . even the way in which these moments follow one upon the other is no longer a sequence in time. . . . Its moments exist in parallel rather than in series, they are no longer a line within the plane of temporal experience. . . . Drama interrupts the eternal flow of time not only at its beginning and its end, bending the two poles toward each other and melting them together; it carries out its same stylization at every instant of the drama; every moment is a symbol, a reduced-scale image of the whole.

The pillars of Lukács's aesthetics were those uniquely important ideas that we glimpsed also in writings by Balázs and Bartók: first, that the ultimate aim of art is to grasp the totality of life, and second, that this totality has to be made transparent not through a linear process but by the coexistence of elements in their simple and pure being. But Lukács went further: he conceived of this clarity of elements in a dramatic manner, as the playing out of the maximum contrast of the material versus an overpowering unifying force. Here lay the meaning—and the only meaning—of form in art. Lukács's conceptualization of form is so similar to the aesthetics manifest in the pieces of Bartók and expresses it so perfectly and beautifully—almost poetically—that it is worth quoting at some length.

> Every culture is the conquering of life, the unification of all manifestations of life (that is, of course, never the unification of concepts) with such force that whatever part we approach from a totality of life, we have to see, deep down, the same thing. In real culture, everything becomes symbolic, because everything is the expression—and everything is equally only the expression—of the only important thing: the manner of reaction to life, the manner with which the total self of the individual turns toward the totality of life. . . .
>
> The essence of art is form: it is to defeat oppositions, to conquer opposing forces, to create coherence from every centrifugal force, from all things that have been deeply and eternally alien to one another before and outside this

form. The creation of form is the last judgment over things, a last judgment that redeems all that could be redeemed, that enforces salvation on all things with divine force.[66]

For Lukács, coherence is not a structural aspect at all—it could not and should not be manifested in the unification of elements or of concepts in the piece. On the contrary, the elements of the piece should display the greatest possible disparity. Form is the painful realization of the alienation of things, the stage where the extreme and unresolvable opposites of life come to the foreground, expanding to the maximum their potentialities to be different—suggesting in this way the infinite. Coherence is meaningless if it results from apparent similarity; it should be an invisible demand, acting from behind with enormous force. This coherence need not and cannot be shown or proved through structural connections in the form because its source is not structure but belief. At the foundation of that belief there is a vision of life similar to Nietzsche's, according to which elements of life belong together not because of their relations but simply because they *are* life.

Thus, for Lukács, there is only one true symbolism: the artwork as a whole is the symbol of an attitude toward life. This symbolism affects the smallest elements of the work, not for what they mean in a world outside the drama but for their concrete and precise shape that stretches the potential of the material: the characters act as a force against unity. The symbolic meaning of the technique of presenting precise characters in drama lies in the insistence on contrasts and differences, counterbalancing the belief that they all come from and will return to the same source:

> The form is the maximal display of strength within the potentialities of the given situation: this is the real ethic of forms. The form is circumscribed from the outside but opens everything toward the infinite within itself. . . . Everything happens in the atmosphere of the soul, but this is not the weakening of things but their deepening, their transformation into something inner, this is the struggling through and the suffering through of all paradoxes of the soul. Because everything is ours, everything is of the soul, and everything that is tragic can happen only within it, all dissonances become sharper: precisely because they all become part of the inside and it is not possible to push them out, nor is it possible to transfer them to anything else outside of it. And the salvation—the redeeming power of form—is only at the end of all roads and all sufferings, it resides in this belief, which is impossible to prove and which lies vividly beyond all proofs, in the belief that the scattered multidirectional

roads of the soul do meet at the end; they have to meet because they departed from the same center. And the form is the only proof of this belief, because it is its only realization, a realization more vivid than life itself.[67]

By conceiving of coherence as a demand that an artwork include all potentialities of the soul, Lukács creates a framework in which form becomes an ethical issue. Ultimately, the work is only about the soul and is responsible to the soul alone. This limitation opens up form toward the infinite in depth because now it has to represent all the potentials of the soul, everything that is possible to imagine and feel. The demand for honesty brings suffering: what comes to light is full of paradoxes and inconsistencies; things that have been "deeply and eternally alien to one another." But it is only through displaying the elements' alien character that form is able to act as a redeeming force: salvation is "only at the end" of all roads. It is as if Lukács reworded Bartók's letter to Márta Ziegler quoted at the beginning of this chapter: the realism of art means the honesty of the soul to *all* its feelings, even the "feeling of vengeance, the grotesque, and the sarcastic." In Bartók's eyes too, the aim of the artwork is this realism—the representation of the "infinite enthusiasm, despair, sorrow, vengeful anger, distorting and sarcastic irony" of its creator—and it is through this realism that the piece connects with the "the great reality," the "spirit of folk music." For Bartók the perception of form (and also of the piece as a whole) is a sensation—it is the moment when all connections become transparent.

Bartók's idea of polarizing themes and motives—often almost to the point of absurdity or banality—and his idea of counteracting this chaos with a quasi-monothematic design gain deeper meaning in the light of this aesthetics. The duality of polarized contrast and unifying force defies narrative interpretation: this duality is present throughout in a timeless form. Timelessness, of course, should not be understood as the elimination of time in the auditory experience. It is obvious that Bartók, a practicing musician always concerned about a piece's immediate effect, was deeply interested in how the piece would work in context. None of the Bartókian formal inventions, not even the bridge form, intend the negation of time for an actual performance—nor did Lukács intend a parallel negation for drama. The only question is how we are to interpret this temporality for the artistic message of the piece. The polarities of the themes usually remain; in fact, most pieces move toward ever greater polarization of characters. If we think of form in terms of direction at all, it is more circular than unidirectional. Various directional plans overlap one another: one aspect of the thematic material may develop toward symmetry, while another may break up; one theme may develop toward more polarized characters while differentiated themes may merge with each other later. The interpretation of these superposed functions is necessarily ambiguous; they point toward directions that are polar opposites. The message of the last movement of the First Piano Concerto might be a retreat into nothingness, leading toward ultimate destruction—against which rises an optimistic, heroic Hungarian theme. Or we could see the movement as a return to the origins: the decomposition of the material reaching back to the neutral ostinato suggests a new beginning, projecting the idea of circularity, of the infinite.

In the Bartókian form, except for rare instances, sections have multiple and contrasting functions; for this reason a narrative interpretation is difficult. For instance, at the beginning of a movement, thematic exposition and creation-like introduction often merge: Bartók's introductions typically strike the listener as something themeless, yet they present all thematic ideas in a concentrated manner. Or a recapitulation may be entirely without clear statement of the theme—functioning thus also as disintegration—or bring extreme transformation of the theme—thus superposing the functions of apotheosis and recapitulation.[68] Bartók merges classical functions to express polar opposition: the themeless material (symbolizing the original nothingness) is actually the basis of all themes (symbolizing a real life manifest in characters).

Correspondence between musical structure and aesthetics is never entirely direct: an aesthetic demand does not translate in any straightforward manner into principles of structure. The artwork is always more than just the realization of an aesthetics: Bartók's pieces have many other aspects that would be difficult to draw into the Lukácsian theory of drama. Moreover, when trying to interpret Bartók's musical choices, we have to keep in mind that Bartók never formulated an aesthetics, simply because he was not interested in working out any ideology apart from music. It is likely that, for the most part, he did not think over these issues in a verbally expressible manner at all. Certainly, after the emotional experiences that culminated in his trip to the mountains of Csík in 1907, Bartók did not need further verbal elaborations to gain a vision of what his modern art could be: the problems after that point were no longer philosophical but musical. And since Bartók generally thought in music, he spelled out the solutions to aesthetic problems, then as well as later, strictly as compositional issues.

It would be wrong to imagine the development of Bartók's modern style as a process from aesthetics toward musical solution. Yet in a sense this was the case. Around 1907 he already had a philosophical understanding of life and a vision of modern art but had not yet found the technique and structure to match them in composition. With his first large-scale piece in the modern style, *Bluebeard's Castle*, Bartók came to a deeper understanding of this aesthetics, realizing its relevance and potential as a governing force in musical form.

CHAPTER 6

Ady's Mystical Symbolism

ADY'S ROLE IN THE HUNGARIAN
RADICALIST AND MODERNIST MOVEMENT

> No one ever will be able to measure the impact Ady made on an entire generation of young people and on the continued work of that generation in our time. Endre Ady cast a . . . wondrous magic spell on the souls, his impulse lifted them into inexpressible extremes so that, during the "Ady-years," our generation jumped ahead a whole era. . . . Endre Ady was the concentration of the burning and flaming creative passions that lived in the soul of the people. His poetry became the reflection and the inciting sparks of flame and fire and, with his Word, the seed of a new will fell into every soul.[1]

Virág Móricz's reminiscences reflect Ady's mesmerizing effect on the generation of the turn of the century. Writings about Ady burst with enthusiasm, and all who attempted to convey the atmosphere of the "Ady years" invariably spoke in extremes—in an almost romantic, poetic manner. Ady's personality embodied truth, and his poetry was a declaration of faith in that truth. He was a prophet, a seer: he was the indefatigable castigator of the sickness and corrupt selfishness of Hungarian society.

Ady had a stirring and lasting influence on all his contemporaries in

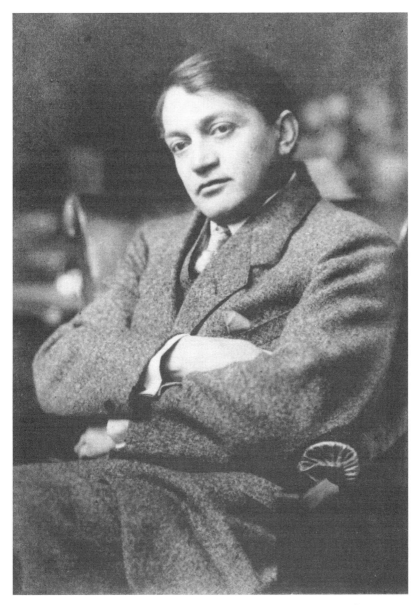

FIGURE 8.   Endre Ady, fall 1915. (Photo by Aladár Székely. Courtesy Petőfi Museum of Literature)

the intellectual milieu, including Lukács, Balázs, Kodály, and Bartók.[2] Bartók described his encounter with Ady's poetry in enthusiastic terms like Móricz's. The discovery came in the spring of 1908—with perfect timing— along with his other significant life experiences, the love for Geyer and the first trips to collect folk music. In a letter from 1916, Bartók told how he was given the volume *Vér és arany* (Blood and gold) by "his only friend"—obviously Kodály—who one day brought it up to his apartment.[3] Since in general Bartók was not interested in poems (as he noted in this letter), scholars normally assumed that he made a rather superficial assessment of Ady's poetry, the influence of which was temporary and peripheral (limited essentially to his composition on the basis of Ady's texts, *Five Songs* op. 16, for voice and piano [1916]).[4]

In fact Ady's effect on Bartók was enormous. He started to read the volume the same day and could not tear himself away from it until late after midnight. He later recalled that at the first reading it was Ady's "prophetic poetry" that affected him the most, because in those poems he found a reflection of his own anxiety about society, art, and the role of the artist. The pencil markings in the margins of the volumes he owned indicate an interest also in the symbolic and intimate side of Ady's poetry. But even these pencil notes do not give us an image of all the poems he actually read or how deeply they moved him. Some markings appear to be notes to himself, perhaps made on the first reading, but others appear to be directed toward another reader, as if trying to guide someone through Ady's world.[5] As Bartók confessed, "in these two volumes [*Szeretném, ha szeretnének* (Longing for love) and *Minden titkok versei* (Of all the mysteries)], I've marked those strophes that speak to me—speak from me— the most. But there is one of them that was [so close to me that it] was impossible to mark: 'My bed calls' (Az ágyam hívogat). . . . I cannot tear myself away from it."[6]

Not only individual poems, but Ady's poetry as a whole appealed to Bartók. Naturally so. Particular poems cannot evoke Ady's world—only the volumes in their entirety transmit an atmosphere, an attitude, the poet's personality. Like his contemporaries, Bartók instantly understood this aspect of Ady's art: "with Ady, the order of poems is important because his poetry is virtually a biography, or at least diarylike writings, in verse."

By 1908 the cardinal points of Bartók's worldview and aesthetics had crystallized around an ideal that aimed at drawing all life's diverse and polarized aspects into an intensely unified vision. He found the ideal expressed clearly in Ady's work. For this reason Bartók felt closer to Ady than to any other contemporary artist, despite their differences of lifestyle and personality: "What sensation of my life was the first Ady volume, *Blood and Gold*! ... As if these poems had sprung from me—yes, had I not been destined for music but for poetry, I would have written these poems—this is what I felt."

Why did Ady's poetry have such an enormous impact on the young generation, an impact so deep that the intellectuals remembered this period as "the Ady years"? First and most important because of his moral stance, which for Ady was a question inseparable from the idea of poetry. The only binding responsibility Ady recognized was to draw all activities into the same sphere, to look at all things with the liberating and unifying demand of a poetic ideal, which for him meant the demand of uncompromising honesty toward all things and toward one's own self.

Even before his first volumes of poetry appeared, Ady had made a name for himself as a journalist; his reportage fills several volumes and is compelling reading even today. Journalism, which for most literati meant drudgery acceptable only as a way to earn their living, was for Ady a vocation. He worked for several years with amazing energy, often around the clock, reporting on the most diverse events, from workers' strikes to cases in criminal court.[7] Journalistic activity trained Ady to deal with reality. It forced him, or rather gave him an opportunity to force himself, to learn to see and feel the life of others, to test his capacity for empathy and his strength to stand up for what he believed.

Ady's worldview, inasmuch as complex and diverse opinions and emotions form a worldview, grew from his refusal to accept any conceptual framework on the basis that it was "traditional" or "Hungarian" or that it fit the leading view of the social group he belonged to. His attitude of open-minded liberalism without a preconceived agenda revived the ideals of the reform generation of the first half of the nineteenth century. Ady was aware of new trends in sociology and political studies, yet the political outlook that emerges from his writings does not confine itself to any existing political theory. In forming his opinion, he relied less on an ideology than on his conviction that every member of society had the right to live fully and in accordance with the spirit of the times. It was an ideal of democratic social justice by which he could measure every action. To say that Ady firmly alienated himself from racial prejudices is an understatement. He almost stammered with shock and amazement when writing about racism.[8]

Ady had a keen eye for social injustice and the courage to take sides, along with the strength and talent to profess his opinion with passion and anger. Most of Ady's articles would be rejected by newspapers today for their subjective viewpoint. Ady did not want to be neutral. In his eyes, neutrality was yet another way of betrayal; he loathed the coolness of objectivity when confronting misery. Showing anger and showing his full personality were part of the truth he wanted to express:

> Yes, most honorable right reverend, we do castigate our social conditions. We are bitter, irascible, restless people always ready to pick quarrels and we get out of the bed every day on the wrong side. We are rarely satisfied, least of all with social conditions. We maintain and proclaim that today's social conditions are untenable. We maintain and proclaim that Hungarian society, if there is such a thing, is immature, uneducated, superstitious, and sick. We maintain and proclaim that almost all the relations of today's society are unjust and dangerous. We maintain and proclaim that in this society, the few secular and religious despots own everything: and that we keep the millions . . . in the slavery of superstitious traditions. We maintain and proclaim that, if we are to stay alive, the walls of militarism, clericalism, and feudalism must be pulled down.[9]

Ady never justified his opinions. He knew he was right—and knew his anger too was right—and, in his view, this was enough. Even in journalism he was a poet, not only because of the poetic style of his articles but, more telling, because of their deep empathy for all things. The intensity of his rhetoric angered the conservative majority, but it became prophecy for those who envisioned a new social system and culture: "My writings, especially the poems, simply outraged the people: I was called a madman, a comedian, a senseless un-Hungarian, traitor—in other words, I achieved everything that a new poet could achieve in Hungary. But I did not die."[10]

Anyone attempting to grasp the meaning of Ady's poetry, even at its most abstract and philosophical, has to remember that all his work was rooted in a real experience of life, including tiresome, down-to-earth, daily work that made constant demands on his social and moral sensitivity. In poetry, Ady's influence rested on a dual poetic achievement. No Hungarian reader could fail to perceive his clairvoyance and energy in social matters; Ady had fierce enemies among the conservative-minded, but they opposed his work precisely because they understood only too well the ideals he stood for. But his second achievement, the invention of an entirely new kind of symbolist poetry, puzzled several of his contemporaries and lost something of its appeal for the following generations. Yet in the development of the aesthetics of Hungarian modernism, and with particular reference to Bartók, symbolism and social message had equal importance. And, as we shall see, Ady's symbolic poetry—even when it strikes us today as entirely personal and devoid of social implications—is intimately connected to all the other spheres of his artistic and human activities.

THE EGO AS MIRROR OF THE UNIVERSE

Ady's unique symbolism combines elements of the Hungarian romantic tradition and the European symbolist movement.[11] Within the Hungarian romantic tradition, a poetry of intimacy that aimed at capturing moments of personal life was part of a broader trend toward simplicity, and it implied a style similar to folk poetry. Ady's sources in this genre include János Arany and Sándor Petőfi as well as the late-eighteenth-century poet Mihály Vitéz Csokonai. In another trend of romantic poetry, especially in Vörösmarty's visionary poems, Ady found a model for a different type of expression that uniquely suited his character. The monumental apocalyptic visions of Vörösmarty's poems were not poetic exaggerations of reality and did not derive from images of the empirical world at all. His fantastic, even surrealistic, images were metaphors for an intense feeling, most typically pain, evoked by the human condition.

In Ady's poetry, the two trends of nineteenth-century poetry merge: cosmic vision and the intimacy of the moment become one and the same thing. Ady's poems are always visionary. Even seemingly insignificant moments of life glow with the utmost intensity. For Ady, each kiss is fire and ice, every moment is the first and the last moment of life, every experience is birth and death, every woman is eternal love and hate, joy and torture. The grandness and intensity of his expressive style transforms every event into a metaphor for human existence. Being lost in the park at night becomes a metaphor for the aimlessness of existence and the joy in this aimlessness; getting up and going to bed stand for the eternal circularity of life and of the universe.[12]

In spite of this intensely romantic outlook, Ady became the founder of the modernist movement in Hungary. The modernists sought to create an art of simplicity far from the exalted imagery of the romantics. Ady's solution was unique. He intensified aspects of romantic poetry in order to express a modernist aesthetics that posited the multiplicity of real and intense life experiences against a vision of oneness.

The first step toward this conception was to diminish or even annul the opposition between the ego and the world, as in the poem "Because you love me" (Mert engem szeretsz):[13]

Áldott csodáknak	Your eyes are mirrors of
Tükre a szemed,	Blessed miracles,
Mert engem nézett.	Because they looked at me.
Te vagy a bölcse,	You are the wisdom,
Mesterasszonya	Masterwoman
Az ölelésnek.	Of embraces.
Áldott ezerszer	Be blessed a thousand times
Az asszonyságod,	Your Womanliness,
Mert engem nézett,	Because it looked at me,
Mert engem látott.	Because it saw me.
S mert nagyon szeretsz:	Because you adore me:
Nagyon szeretlek	I adore you
S mert engem szeretsz:	And because you love me:
Te vagy az Asszony,	You are the Woman,
Te vagy a legszebb.	The most beautiful.

"Seeing" emerges here as central to—or even identical with—love. "Eyes," "looking," and "seeing" are metaphors for the boundary between the subjective and the objective, between the inner and the outside world. They are metaphors for objectivity: one looks and sees the world in its naked reality. Yet they are also metaphors for an understanding beyond empirical reality and logic: one sees and understands without questioning, words and explanation. "Your womanliness looked at me and saw me": seeing the Other is the metaphor for love.

The Hungarian original puts emphasis on all those words that relate to the first person singular. An exact translation of the first and last phrases would be, "Your eyes are mirrors of / Blessed miracles / Because it's me they looked at," and "And because it's me you love, / You are the Woman, / You are the most beautiful." The immense egoism on display here was the basis of Ady's compassion and broad understanding of life. The paradox it embodies reminds us of Nietzsche's view (he had a tremendous impact on Ady).[14] But for Nietzsche, it was the individual's alienation from the world that led him toward compassion and understanding; for Ady, it was man's projection of the world into the ego, a way of looking at everything through the soul. Love was the sensation of the sameness of the outside and inside worlds. In love, the objective and the subjective collapsed into each other: love becomes objective truth only because the subjective ego experienced it as true. As we shall see, Ady based all knowledge and true lyricism—not love alone—on erasing the antagonism between objective and subjective worlds.[15]

Along with repeated emphasis on "I," the use of words with associative power conveys this attitude. The first two lines bring together words whose symbolism is at the same time positive and mysterious. They move from the miraculous toward the earthly; the words appear in the Hungarian in the following order: blessed, miracle, mirror, eyes. They evoke unknown and secret things beyond the power of humans to understand or control. In their mystery, however, these symbols point toward a world that is reassuring and good.

Complementing this imagery, a series of nouns alludes to a feeling of peaceful heaviness of a fully lived life; master, woman, wisdom, embrace—these words connect back to an "objective" reality of life, not in the sense of the everyday modern world but rather that of "original" human existence. These words concentrate in themselves the notions of knowledge, feeling, and the original movement of one person toward the other. It is significant that, among the two Hungarian words that denote "woman," Ady chooses the one less connected to sexuality (woman as opposed to man) than to the idea of fertility and maturity.[16] Associated with the concepts of knowledge and understanding of life rather than ownership and authority, "masterwoman"—a word Ady invented for this poem— evokes an almost pagan image of a woman goddess.

Ady's poetry associates and draws invisible links between simple feeling and the great sensation of existence. In this way, it connects gestures to feeling, and feeling to metaphysical thought:

Karollak, vonlak s mégsem érlek el:
Itt a fehér csönd, a fehér lepel.
Nem volt ilyen nagy csönd még soha tán,
Sikolts belé, mert mindjárt elveszünk,
Állunk és várunk, csüggedt a kezünk
A csókok és könnyek alkonyatán.

. . . .

Megállt az élet, nincsen több sora,
Nincs kínja, csókja, könnye, mámora,
Jaj, mindjárt minden, minden elveszett.
Fehér ördög-lepel hullott miránk,
Fehér és csöndes lesz már a világ.

("A fehér csönd")

I hold you, I draw you toward me and I
    cannot reach you,
Here is the white silence, the white veil.
There had never been such silence
    before,
Cry out or we will be lost,
Standing and waiting, our hands hang
    limp
In the twilight of kisses and tears.

. . . .

Life halted, it has stopped its course,
It has no more pain, kisses, tears, ecstasy,
Soon all, all will be lost.
A white devil-veil has fallen on us,
And the world will be silent and white.

("The white silence")

This poem captures a moment of terror and amazement. The lovers stand in embrace, and yet somehow they feel nothing at all, as if love had slipped away. "White" and "silence" here are not merely descriptive words but metaphors of "death" as a quasi-philosophical concept (not physical death but the negation of all motion). "White silence" is the metaphor for the abstract idea of absolute stillness, implying both human and cosmic dimensions. It is the negation of gesture, of feeling, of screaming—that is, the negation of life. On the cosmic level, it symbolizes the motionlessness of everything: the end of the orbiting of the planets, the end of the universe. The unique achievement of this poem is to project multiple momentary sensations into one basic feeling. It captures the fear of death, of nothingness—in love.

To perceive this meaning, we must consider Ady's general attitude toward feeling on the one hand, and his expanding symbolism on the other. The generation after the First World War was already puzzled by Ady's insistence on the associative power of poetic imagery, on words loaded with grand and monumental concepts. But the exalted language, replete with words like "fire," "ice," "deafening silence," "crying," and "tears," was not only a matter of style; it was the true reflection of the intensity of the poet's feelings. In Ady's poems, tears really mean tears; the embrace in which a lover faints means real embrace and real fainting—nothing is just metaphor. The point was precisely that real experience and metaphoric meaning had to become one and the same. Ady saw no reason to turn a grand vision of the universe into blocks of words. Poetry had to make transparent the connection between the feeling of the soul and the understanding of life, but it could do so only if its base was an authentic experience.

Exaggeration and distortion, even to the point of self-destruction, become integral elements of this aesthetics. Ady is not interested in the form of things as they appear to the eye but in the hidden essence they hold. Even the most common feeling of everyday life has a deeper essence behind its typical appearance. Only exaggeration shows the essence by testing the limits of every feeling and every gesture. For instance, what an "embrace" really means can be grasped only through an embrace that transcends, "leaps out" from what it normally is: an embrace that is fainting, suffering, murder, and death.

Ady's personality backed up his message of poetic exaggeration. The reminiscences of his contemporaries fill thick books, transmitting an Ady legend about a self-destructive lifestyle, long nights spent at a favorite café, love affairs, immense sensitivity, energy, and passion in absorbing and reacting to everything he came across. But for his contemporaries, the most important aspect of his personality was not what appeared in enticing anecdotes, and not even what they viewed as novel sensual and "immoral" aspects of his poems, but that he was in all of his deeds intensely involved, fully himself, and capable of reflecting this intensity in his poetry. To grasp the essence by experiencing everything to its limits, and bring that essence into his writing, was more important for Ady than classical beauty of language, clarity of expression, and consistency of thought and personality. To this aim he sacrificed everything, including his own public image. It did not matter to him that his poetry did not project a consistent and lovable personality, for he knew that his devotion to experiencing life precluded consistency anyway. As Lukács realized, "The poems of Ady are almost impersonal even though hardly ever had deeper and clearer confessions been written; still one could not draw from them the 'imaginary portrait of Ady.' "[17]

For Ady, the central experience was love—physical sensual love between man and woman. In Ady's poetry love becomes the metaphor for life, and on a broader level for cosmic reality. He saw an intimate connection between sensual love and every manifestation of greatness; love was wisdom, prophecy, and poetry:

Valami szent, nagy éjszakán
Vad nászban megfogant az élet
S azóta tart a nász örökké,
Minden kis mozgás csókba téved.
Csókok világa a világunk,
Csókban fogan a gondolat,
Kicsi kis agyvelő-csomócskák
Cserélnek tüzes csókokat.
S a legforróbb csókból szület meg
A legszebb, legnagyobb ige,
Mely hódítóan csap belé
A végtelenbe, semmibe.
. . . .
Nincs vad párzás, nincs tüzes csók ma
S nincs a világnak Messiása.

("A csókok átka")

At some great sacred night,
In wild lovemaking, life was conceived,
And since then, lovemaking is forever,
Every motion ends in a kiss.
Our world is the world of kisses,
In a kiss is conceived thought,
Little brain-knots
Exchange burning kisses.
And from the most burning kiss was born
The most beautiful, the greatest Word,
Which flies out to conquer
Eternity, the Nothing.
. . . .
Today, there are no wild lovemakings, no burning kisses,
And the world has no Messiah.

("The curse of kisses")

EXPANDING SYMBOLISM

Ady developed his language in two directions—and unfortunately both resist translation. One was toward spontaneity of expression. His language is full of everyday usages that lack elegance and are emphatically unpoetic—at times even rude, silly, or primitive. Ady uses the language to its full capacity and improvises words and syntax, sometimes taking the context as inspiration for a neologism. As we shall see, this insistence on spontaneity reflects his mystical attitude toward life. But his language often captures a complex image with few words. Hungarian allows such conciseness because it uses a conjugation and declension system in addition to prefixes and suffixes and thus puts into one word what other European languages must express in several. In the poem "The white silence," the Hungarian *karollak* corresponds to the phrase "I hold you," and *vonlak* translates as "I draw you toward me." At times, as here, Ady's preference for basic words gives his style an almost biblical simplicity and strength.

While Ady exploits the full potential of the language, his list of key words—ones that recur often with rich symbolic associations—is short and contains the most basic words. Here is the other direction of Ady's language. Instead of trying to express an idea by the use of many varied expressions and words, he uses the same word to express many meanings, projecting a complex imagery into a relatively limited vocabulary. Rather than expand the language, he concentrates it. By consistently focusing on words' associative power, simple words such as "blessing," "woman," and "white" transform themselves into vessels that can absorb, through associations, a potentially endless layer of thoughts.

Ady's invention rests on the belief that poetic associations hold a message that goes beyond anything that is communicable in the words' literal sense. It is not to be confused with the musical quality or the linguistic beauty of poetry. The source of this message is less the rhythm and sonority of the words (although these also have an important role) than their inherent symbolism. In some words symbolism is more evident, but most of them suggest a whole range of images and meanings that, superposed and interacting, create an atmosphere. Even when a word's symbolism is more or less obvious, the imagery has a "surplus" that goes beyond the composite of these associations.[18] This is true for all poetry, but in the case of Ady this "surplus" or atmosphere carries the message to a much greater extent than is usual. Ady exploits the associative potential of language to the maximum, often at the expense of its logic or commonsense meaning. Indeed, some lines appear to avoid everyday meaning entirely.

With Ady, key words appear typically in contrasting pairs, pointing toward a basic symbolic opposition between (e)motion and (e)motionlessness. For instance, the words "color/dark/blood/red/brown" often contrast to the word "white," or "flame/fire/burning" to "water/ice/lake." "Cry/shout/scream/

weep" stand against "silence"; "falling down" against "flying," or "pale/cold/tears" against "gold/light/king/life/desire/light beam." The complex symbolism of each word evolves gradually around a polar axis. The symbolic meaning of whiteness in the poem "The white silence" is reinforced by the function of this word in various other poems. In the poem "In vain you haunt me with your whiteness" (Hiába kísértesz hófehéren), "white" symbolizes the woman's perfection, a perfection that is impenetrable and thus impossible to love; it is virginity that awaits darkening by blood and dirt. Several poems associate dark colors or red and gold with passion and love, such as "The other two" (A másik kettő), "Léda on the boat" (Léda a hajón), and "Prayer to God Baal" (Ima Baál Istenhez). Other poems bring new elements, reinterpreting and even contradicting this meaning. For instance, in the poem "I am a burning wound" (Tüzes seb vagyok), "white flame" takes on the burning pain of torturing love. Then, in other poems, whiteness assumes a meaning almost opposite to its earlier sense. In the poem "Adam, where art thou?" (Ádám, hol vagy?), whiteness is the symbol of the radiant brightness of heaven ("In great, white light came God toward me"); in "White lotus flowers" (A fehér lótuszok) it symbolizes the purity of beautiful dream-thoughts ("And, see how they open suddenly, the white lotuses, . . . white thoughts, flowers").

With expressions such as "white silence," "white thoughts," and "mirrors of blessed miracles," Ady forces his readers to focus on the interacting symbolic content of words. Yet the more we immerse ourselves in this symbolism the more it resists our straightforward interpretation. Reading Ady, we have to approach each new poem as a complex web of potential symbolic meanings but remain open to project any or all previous connotations as well as new meanings onto a particular word. This attitude creates an ambiguity that becomes part of the message. A poem may exploit this ambiguity, as does "The castle's white woman" (A vár fehér asszonya). The framework of its symbolism appears in the first line, "My soul is an old, enchanted castle" (A lelkem ódon, babonás vár). The first three stanzas depict the enchanted castle (literally: the castle of superstitions): its sad walls looking down onto the valley, the wailing groans of enchanted spirits in the hollow, deserted halls. Interpolated into this description are rhetorical questions about the eyes of the poet, as asides to an unidentified listener: "My eyes, don't you see how big they are?" "See how tired are these eyes?" By associating the eyes with the windows of the soul-castle, the poem condenses the imagery: speaking out from the poem and looking out through the window are the same thing, and both are in turn metaphors of the motion of the soul reaching out to someone. To this longing the last stanza brings a new motif:

(Csak néha, titkos éji órán	(Sometimes, at secret night hours,
Gyúlnak ki e bús, nagy szemek.)	Suddenly, those sad eyes light up.)
A fehér asszony jár a várban	The white woman walks in the castle
S az ablakon kinevet.	And laughs out through the window.

This poem is so close to the symbolism of *Bluebeard's Castle*, both in its general conception and the details of the imagery, that it could almost be its model. As we shall see, it has many parallels in Hungarian modernist poetry, using the images of the night, the castle, a window, and darkness for capturing the perfection, the loneliness, and the secrecy of the soul. Who is the white woman of the castle? Clearly, the two women implied in the poem are one and the same: the woman to whom the poet is talking, trying to make her look into his eyes, and the one who walks inside the castle looking out through the eye-window. Her coolness and precise contours are antithetical to the darkness and mystery of the soul. Whiteness and laughter together are symbols of insensitivity in Ady's poetry, and this woman is indeed insensitive: she walks (apparently without fear) in those enchanted rooms, and she turns toward the outside, away from the soul (looking out laughing). Yet she is not a negative force. The last stanza symbolizes the meeting of two eyes (a metaphor for embrace): her looking out of the window is the same thing as the lighting up of the eyes. True, her whiteness is an intrusion into the sadness of the castle. But it is the intrusion of the beloved and loving Other, which is the only hope for a soul trapped in sadness.

In the poem "On Elijah's chariot" (Az Illés szekerén) Ady created an even more polarized and complex web of symbolism. This poem paints a fantastic vision of the chariots carrying off the prophets of Elijah to unknown heights:

Az Úr Illésként elviszi mind,	The Lord carries away the Elijahs,
Kiket nagyon sujt és szeret:	Those whom he punishes and loves:
Tüzes, gyors szíveket ad nekik,	He gives them fast, burning hearts,
Ezek a tüzes szekerek.	The fiery chariots.
Az Illés-nép Ég felé rohan	The Elijah-people race toward the Sky
S megáll ott, hol a tél örök,	And rest where winter is eternal.
A Himaláják jégcsúcsain	On the ice peaks of the Himalayas,
Porzik szekerük és zörög.	Dust rises behind their rattling carriage.
Ég s Föld között, bús-hazátlanul,	Between Earth and Sky, in sad-aimless
Hajtja őket a Sors szele.	wandering,
Gonosz, hűvös szépségek felé	They are chased by the wind of Fate,
Száguld az Illés szekere.	Toward wicked and cool beauties,
	Races Elijah's chariot.

Szívük izzik, agyuk jégcsapos,
A Föld reájuk fölkacag
S jég-útjukat szánva szórja be
Hideg gyémántporral a nap.

Their brains are ice, their hearts are
   burning,
From below, the Earth laughs at them,
And the Sun compassionately throws
Cold diamond dust onto their road of ice.

The magically beautiful, fantastic visions of this poem are the metaphor of the sensation of life, the feeling of the sameness of the most extreme opposites. The imaginary journey of the poet-prophets (*Illés-nép* [the people of Elijah]) evokes the image of fire and ice; it is at the same time speed and motionlessness. The rattling of the burning chariots mars the cold beauty of the eternal winter; the infinite wandering of the prophets chased by fate disturbs the motionlessness of the snow-covered heights of the highest mountain. Ady chooses his symbols from words that evoke associations of opposite feelings: sun, heaven, and sky are symbols of both hot and cold. Even at this abstract level, Ady ties metaphysical thought to real physical experiences: very hot is sometimes felt as cold, and transcendence is experienced as the coldness of the mind and the passion of the heart. The basic idea of this poem, and of Ady's philosophy in general, is the recognition of the sameness of polarized contrasts.

In a sense, each of Ady's poems is an experiment, a challenge to reveal new oppositions and then see them as part of an underlying unity. For Ady, life—the subject of poetry—and words—the material of poetry—are diffuse and chaotic "material." From it he had to "shape," in the mind and the heart, things of precise character so that both their opposition and their unity would become transparent. Yet his symbolism does not confuse us. Everything does not equal everything else, but everything has the potential of turning into its own opposite and also dissolving into other elements. The lack of distance between things is not a given, but an ideal. This expanding symbolism is the paradigm of what Ady means by being "alive"—that is, an endless journey to draw everything into the fundamental experience of life.

A TRANSCENDENTAL CENTER

With the volume *Az Illés szekerén* (On Elijah's chariot), Ady reached a level of metaphysical symbolism consisting of a few basic concepts: Nothing, God, Life, Sun, Light, Death. Ady's use of these words is not only contrary to convention but seems to lack consistent meaning, sometimes even in the context of one poem. At first encounter, we might easily assume that these poems are merely sketches of the fantastic images of a capricious mind. Ady would be the first to oppose the idea that his poetry contained a coherent system of thought. As he wrote to his supporter and friend Lajos Hatvany, in reference to one of his poems, "I would be glad if this poem would make you realize to what extent the only human and artistic justification [for my poetry] is lack of systematization."[19]

This reluctance to create a philosophy, in the narrow sense of the word, answered the need to descend to a "mystery beyond understanding."[20] Ady's ambivalence toward logical systems and even toward language originated in a skepticism, very similar to Bartók's, that discredited intellect as a means of grasping the essence of things. Ady's refusal to project a systematic worldview stemmed from the conviction that each moment of life should reflect the imperative demand of the soul. Feeling validated understanding, not the other way around: only what was intensely lived through really mattered.

In a sense, Ady's poetry transcends philosophy—as perhaps all real poetry does. The concrete and precise meaning of an individual poem, for its particular reader, shows an idea's extreme potential and gives way to its opposite meaning. Ady creates philosophical systems only in order to destroy them. But the foundation of his anarchy is not skepticism or confusion but belief: a fundamental trust that life somehow holds all ideas that can be felt or dreamt, and also the opposite of all these ideas. If Ady was committed to an idea, it was to a philosophic openness, the insistence that every feeling fully lived is a path toward the essence. At a time when very few people in Hungary understood Ady, his friend Hatvany clearly saw that this attitude, rather than an idea or theory, was the cohesive force in Ady's poetry:

Ady tried to dig to the bottom of every idea that occurred to him. When he was seized by a passing sentiment, he was not frightened but followed it with self-torturing seriousness to its deepest depth. Just as one can reach down to the center of the earth from every point on its surface—to the center of this "not systematized" reality—Ady was able to reach down, through every capricious idea, to the center: really, to God. The diagonals of the Ady-globe go through this center to reach from one pole to the other. . . . That is why Ady's poems can be understood better if read together, for in this way one can feel this center much as one can sense the radiating center of a star by gazing at the furthest points of the light beams emitted from it. . . . In Ady, one can find not only his own system but the opposing criticism of his system as well. Not because of cynicism or because of the lack of fanatically held beliefs; on the contrary, because [he believed that] even the broadest system is too narrow to capture the universe. His poems are often but stammering. . . . At the end of his career he is struggling with the inexpressible. He knocks on the door of the Unknown, what is beyond the capacity of comprehension. He wants to penetrate the secret of what is beyond everything, that he writes with a capital letter, out of trembling superstition: Minden [the all-encompassing Everything]. Here, for the first time in Hungary, man fights his fatal dragon-struggle with the mysteries that lie beyond our understanding.[21]

The metaphor for this invisible gravitational center (in Lukács's terminology, transcendental center) is God.[22] For Ady, God is an entirely secular concept. The works literary scholars called his "God-poems" are not the confirmation but rather the denial of any formal connection with religion: "Show yourself to us: you are not Christian, you are not Jewish. You are the frightful, terrible Lord."[23] His attitude rejects the imposition of conventional forms and insists on the inalienable personal nature of religious experience:

Oszlik lelkemnek barna gyásza:
Nagy, fehér fényben jön az Isten,
Hogy ellenségeim leigázza.
. . . .
Szivemben már őt megtaláltam,
Megtaláltam és megöleltem
S egyek leszünk mi a halálban.
                    ("Ádám, hol vagy?")

Slowly vanishes the brown mourning of
    my heart:
In great white light comes God toward me
To subjugate my enemies.
. . . .
At last I have found him in my heart
Found him and embraced him
And we will be one in death.
                    ("Adam, where art thou?")

Mikor elhagytak,
Mikor a lelkem roskadozva vittem,
Csöndesen és váratlanul
Átölelt az Isten.

When they abandoned me,
When, under the weight of my soul, I
    stumbled
Unexpectedly and calmly
I was embraced by God.

Nem harsonával,
Hanem jött néma, igaz öleléssel,
Nem jött szép, tüzes nappalon,
De háborus éjjel.

Not with trumpets,
He came with a soundless, true embrace,
He came not on a sun-lit, fiery day,
But on a night of war.

És megvakultak
Hiú szemeim. Meghalt ifjuságom,
De őt, a fényest, nagyszerűt,
Mindörökre látom.
                    ("Az Úr érkezése")

My vain eyes were blinded.
My youth had died,
But all my life, I'll see him
Wonderful and radiant.
                    ("The Lord's arrival")

The confusion of imagery is intentional: God comes to us but is already in our heart; God comes with light to subjugate our enemies but at the same time appears silently and simply with an embrace; God's embrace is caring and encouraging but is also an embrace of death. Ady's path toward God goes through his extreme egoism: he projects the infinite range of the soul's sensations, which resists systematization, into the image of God. The poet's feelings become the mirror through which he senses God, an inexplicable and incomprehensible center of all things. God is the center of everything and also the sensation of an all-encompassing totality:

Az Isten van valamiként:	Somehow or other there is God:
Minden Gondolatnak alján.	At the bottom of every Thought.
. . . .	. . . .
Az Isten nem jön ám felénk,	God does not come toward us
Hogy bajainkban segitsen:	To help in our troubles.
Az Isten: az Én és a kín,	God: Me and suffering,
A terv s a csók, minden az Isten.	The plan and the kiss, God is everything.
("Az Isten balján")	("On God's left")

These poems are expansions of the thought that existed from the very beginning of Ady's art in his insistence on the centrality of love. Now the idea of recapturing an undivided consciousness becomes the vehicle for a new sort of awareness of life. What Ady attempts here is nothing less than a modern vision of transcendental experience. The depth of the unconscious and lonely soul merges into the all-encompassing, objective universe. God cannot help us because he is the source of everything, even of our troubles; God cannot come toward us because he is already here, because he is at all places and in all things, because he has always been at the "bottom of every thought." The feeling of God is the feeling of life but also the withdrawal from life: seeing and blindness, victory and death, the noise of the trumpets and soundless embrace. God is but a sensation, a smell: "I was looking for something / following the smell of God."[24] God becomes here the metaphor for the essence of all things: He is morality, belief, optimism, ideal. Yet circumscribing or denoting this essence would banalize the idea itself: God is the center that can only be felt, not grasped or argued about. God is the concentration of all into one point, the world's withdrawal from the surface into itself; God is the all-governing "Nothing." This abstract essence that has no volume, form, or shape is, however, the foundation of the ever-present life and exists only for the sake of life:[25]

Batyum: a legsúlyosabb Nincsen,	I carry my load: the heaviest Nothing,
Utam: a nagy Nihil, a Semmi,	My path: the great Nihil, the None,
A sorsom: menni, menni, menni	My fate: to go, to go, to go,
S az álmom: az Isten.	And my dream is God.
("Álmom: az Isten")	("My dream is God")

Mert Isten: az Élet igazsága,	Because God is the truth of Life,
Parancsa ez: mindenki éljen.	His command: everyone shall live,
Parancsa ez: mindenki örüljön.	His command: everyone shall be joyful,
Parancsa ez: öröm-gyilkos féljen,	His command: the murderers of joy shall tremble,
Parancsa ez: mindenki éljen.	His command: everyone shall live.
("Az Isten harsonája")	("Trumpet of God")

Ő: Minden, de áldani nem tud,	He is everything but he cannot bless
Ő: Minden, de senkit se büntet,	He is everything but he does not punish
Ő teljesíti az Időt	He fulfills time
S nem érti meg a mi szivünket.	And does not understand our hearts.
. . . .	. . . .
Ő: a folyásnak akarója,	He is the will of flow
Melynek forrása s vége nincsen.	Which has no source and no end.
Ő: Minden és vigasztalan,	He is all and without consolation,
Egyetlen és borzalmas Isten.	He is the one and terrifying God.
("Isten, a vigasztalan")	("The God without consolation")

MYSTICISM AND DEVOTION TO LIFE

With the concept of God to express the spirit that radiates through everything but draws it toward Nothingness, and the concept of Life to encompass everything that is real, Ady expresses a worldview that we can call "mystic." The mystical experience eliminates distance, both between the unrelated things of the world and between the individual and the universe. Lukács considered Ady's mystical attitude one of his greatest achievements, a valid—and perhaps the only valid—response to the alienation of the self from society and the disintegration of modern life:

> Endre Ady is a mystic—what is the meaning of this term? Perhaps this: the mystic (and here I refer only to its emotional aspects and not its manifestations) does not know of the problem of distance. To put it differently: for the

mystic, there are no contradictions, there is no difference between "view-points," he is everything and at the same time the opposite of everything. This means that, for the mystic, there are no great things and small things, no sacred and profane, no "realities" and dreams. For him, the differences that we usually make between the concrete and the abstract, the subjective and the objective do not exist. In the Middle Ages, this was very simple and could have been easily understood: the mystic was someone for whom everything became religion, or perhaps better: for whom religion—the emotional essence of religion—embraced everything. But today, this is just as simple even if it is perhaps not so apparent. The difference between the old and the new mystic is only that the old possessed forms that the new no longer has. The old mysticism was given form through religion, the official framework of the Church, the Bible; these were forms with firm walls within which the hot lava stream of ecstasy could be freely poured. Today's mystic has no forms, he has to create everything from himself: God and devil, earth and afterworld, Redeemer and Antichrist, saints and damned souls; he himself has to write the Bible and everything else for the sake of which he would want to read it. Here the essence, in spite of its sameness, loses the purity of the type: it appears to be mere poetry. Because for the superficial onlooker, there is no difference between poetic "motive" or "object" and the mystical explanation of life. What once clearly separated poetry from mysticism has disappeared today, that is, that one had the character of game while the other appeared as positive truth. Mysticism today exists only as a form of feeling scattered all around. Because of that, today every real poet is more or less a mystic, much more and much more strongly than in the Middle Ages, perhaps because today most mystics become poets out of necessity.[26]

In spite of the fact that he chose examples of premodern mysticism from the Christian Middle Ages (as most other European modernists did), Lukács was aware that mysticism was one of the few human experiences not bound by space and time. For him, this aspect of mysticism made it particularly relevant to the modern era. Lukács saw that mysticism divorces itself from religion, in spite of its emphasis on piety, because it searches for what is indescribable and uncontrollable. It is thus always at the same time personal and communal: "It is a strange fact that it is precisely the most individual, the least 'scientific' and, for that reason, the least controllable manner of thought, that is, mysticism, shows also the most uniformity [among different cultures]."[27]

The particular form of mysticism found in Ady's poetry comes especially close to the spiritual thinking of East European Jews.[28] The similarity between Jewish mysticism and that of Ady and his modernist contemporaries deepens our understanding of spiritual tendencies at the turn of the century. Both sought a mystical orientation to counterbalance the materialization and fragmentation of modern life and transcend the intellect's domain of logic and verbal expression.

In Jewish thinking, the potential of language to express thought and the capacity of thought to grasp what is the most essential in life were cardinal issues. Here too the point of departure was the paradox that thought requires the logic of language, yet words do not lead to an understanding of the great essence. For the most spiritual members, it was a religious demand to overcome this duality, to focus attention on words but only in order to reach beyond them. Hasidic writers noted, "Speech is a garment of thought. . . . And thought is [written] in letters, which are vessels, while Wisdom is above letters, and no vessels are able to contain it."[29] Knowledge and understanding are sensations, nonlinear and without time. Another source taught, "Speech and action are within time, but thought is not within time. . . . For example, when a person has understanding he is able to understand a thing in one moment, but when he needs to recite it [i.e., explain it] he must recite it for an hour or more."

In Hasidic mysticism, the origin of all thoughts and things is God, and the highest level of understanding is when the soul unites itself with God; this level is called *devekuth*. The pious who reach the state of *devekuth* have no need for the intellect to control their speech; truth will spring naturally and spontaneously from their lips. Like Ady, the mystics also believed that transcendence is itself the token of truthfulness, that truth naturally expresses itself, in such moments, in unpremeditated, spontaneous speech: "When I attach my thoughts to the Creator, I allow my mouth to speak whatever it wishes." Here understanding comes with distance from life—stepping out of time—and "essence" is the ultimate concentration of things into "Nothing": the devout seeking transcendence through prayer should "enter into the attribute of Nothing, which is without end."

The conceptual similarity between Jewish thought and Ady's philosophical poetry is striking, yet it is not clear whether there was (or might have been) a direct influence.[30] It is a well-known fact that Jews were prominent among the creators and perpetuators of the modernist movement. But it is difficult to say exactly what interchange of ideas took place within Hungarian modernist circles, and to what extent even their Jewish members were aware of the relation between Jewish and modernist thought. Because even the modernist intellectual circles sometimes regarded the influence of Jewish tradition on Hungarian culture as pretentious and also dangerous, we cannot expect to find written documents on the relation. And since contemporary use of the adjective "Jewish" often had negative overtones of "cosmopolitan," "rootless," "antinational," or "decadent," emphasis on the "Jewishness" of modern art would reinforce the idea that it was alien to Hungarian society. But there was an additional reason to suppress the Jewish heritage—namely, the mistaken notion that the Jewish intellect was naturally oriented toward practical and material things. Lukács's opening sentence of his review of Martin Buber's translation of Jewish mystical writings alerts readers: "The greatest merit of these pieces is that they prove the falsity of that seemingly just prejudice that the metaphysical orientation in Jewish thinking must have dried out in the modern era, that [modern Jewish culture] produced only 'clever' and 'witty' minds and not original, creative geniuses."[31]

Lukács's passionate self-justifying claim shows us the atmosphere of the era. Modern-minded, rational intelligentsia needed to find a framework for a metaphysical (poetic) mode of thinking that transcended the contemporary materialistic attitude. The more spiritually oriented minds despised the materialism and rationalism of the secular world but regarded religious institutions as the bastion of superstition and conservativism. They had to reinvent the forms of mysticism and spirituality apart from any institution on the basis of personal experiences and instinct. The highly personal systems of thought that resulted, such as Bartók's pantheism or Ady's abstract concept of God, were full of paradox. Some assimilated Jews found the medieval cult and prophetic image of Jesus closer to their thinking than the reformed version of Judaism they knew. Paradoxically, a deeply Jewish belief manifested itself in the antiJewishness of these assimilated Jews: they turned away from Judaism in order to embrace a Jewish mystical idea in their new vision of Christianity.[32]

Naturally, these secular but spiritually oriented Jews felt at home in the Hungarian modernist circles whose members—both Jewish and Christian—sought spirituality and mysticism without conventional religion. They helped create this social milieu and in it they felt they could remain Jewish—even though its context does not entirely explain their feeling. What facilitated the symbiosis was the fact that the Hungarian romantic tradition anticipated several modernist ideas that came close to Jewish thought.

Ady was perhaps the most influential figure in creating this intellectual symbiosis, for he did not face the dilemma of whether to identify with the conservative but "genuinely Hungarian" middle nobility or with the modern but "Jewish" bourgeoisie. At the age of twenty-three he moved to Nagyvárad (today Oradea), the most important intellectual center of Hungary after Budapest. With this move he broke out from the conservative life of his previous home, Debrecen, an old Calvinist city. In Nagyvárad as well as Budapest, Ady sought out the company of Jews even though he felt sometimes lonely among them. He regarded the Jews as the "ferment" of society; his Jewish friends were those young and enthusiastic allies who, as one of them remembered, "on fiery nights made an oath to fight with [their] pen against the 'power of darkness.' "[33] Ady's clear stance—proclaiming Jewish ideals and associating Jewish symbols with morality, God, and prophecy—suggests awareness of the Jewish strands in his thinking.[34]

By the time Ady moved to Nagyvárad, his personality was formed and his thinking was already saturated with a Calvinist devotional attitude and the teachings of Hungarian romantic literature. Their essence, intensified by Ady's prophetic personality and attraction to a kind of secular mysticism, was very close to Jewish thought. His contacts with Jews might have deepened his vision of life and made him more aware of its meaning.

In this development József Kiss, a poet of the generation before Ady, might have had a significant role. Even though Ady felt that Kiss was a mediocre poet, he respected Kiss enormously for his solitary struggle to create modern poetry that was, nevertheless, rooted in tradition. Unlike most middle-class Jews, Kiss was close to the Orthodox tradition of Judaism that saturated his thinking and works. His poem "Jehovah," for instance, depicts the old, mysterious, spiritual Jew whose knowledge and humanity are sensed but not understood by the others. His eyes transmit the joy of life, whose pleasures he ignores by focusing only on study, for the essence of his study is the understanding of life.

The most important meeting point of Judaism and Hungarian romanticism in Ady's thought was his unique conception of life, and the best expression of its romantic source is Imre Madách's drama *The Tragedy of Man* (1860). The play's topic was the search for the meaning of spirituality, modeled on the romantic philosophical drama exemplified by Goethe's *Faust*. The test of spirituality was its relevance to social life; Madách's question was whether the development of human thinking, guided by morality and spirit, improved human conditions. The drama unfolds as Lucifer leads Adam through history; each scene represents a higher (and historically later) stage of social development. At the end Adam realizes that even the greatest thoughts do not make mankind happier or more elevated. Losing his faith, Adam wishes to leave earthly life through death in order to enter the world of pure spirit. But at the threshold of nonexistence he turns back. He chooses to live, not out of fear of death and not even simply because of his love for life but because he understands that spirit is not possible without life, that everything that is imaginable and attainable by the intellect and the soul is within earthly reality.

For Madách, this realization meant the failure of spirit. Adam accepts life and this acceptance is in a sense optimistic. But it is also a defeat: resignation to the thought that because spirit is tied to earthly life, there is no spirit in the strict sense of the word. Alienated from the Christian ideal that celebrated spirit at the expense of life, Madách's artistic atheism is still deeply rooted in the Christian desire to understand pure spirit.

Ady, and with him Hungarian modernists in general, drew the Madáchian idea closer to secular spiritualism: they refused the separation of spirit and life entirely. It is here that the modernist ideology came very close to Jewish philosophy. In Jewish thought, the emphasis was on the separation not of body from spirit but rather of the sacred from the vulgar. Because the concept of sacred could easily become something purely spiritual that would stand in opposition to everyday life, especially physical life, the distinction might mean little. But Jewish tradition typically failed to make this logical further step. The notions of sacred and secular clearly exist in Jewish religious thinking, yet no aspect of life could be considered entirely part of one or the other sphere. Although the Talmud demands the utmost concentration on spiritual matters—in fact, all possible sacrifices for the sake of attaining a spiritual state of mind—life is above this demand. Prayer and the study of the sacred texts, spiritual fulfillment in themselves, have no meaning if they deprive human beings of the joy of life, including physical and sexual life. The roots of this thinking go back to the Old Testament, which focuses on the varieties of lives. The moral message is embedded in life stories, and not even the great figures of the Old Testament show themselves to be perfect and righteous in all their deeds. The reader has to sense the guiding moral principle, some inexpressible goodness that shines through the complex and confusing stories. The Talmud sets this approach at the center of learning, in the form of debate that leaves the question of right and wrong open—and responsibility for the decision with the individual.

These conceptions of a sense of morality on the one hand and life on the other permeate Judaism as well as the thinking of the Hungarian modernists. In this thinking, life holds everything: spirit, nature, feeling, physical existence. Against the all-embracing concept of life stands the idea of an invisible, and never fully comprehensible, center. Jewish spiritual thinking regards all its basic notions—God, the Messiah, and spiritual life—as transcendental centers, and the modernists used these and other "religious" concepts as poetic metaphors in a similar vein. The concepts point toward something beyond everyday life but have meaning in their connection to life.

No other member of the modernist circles was as devoted as Ady to placing life above all other spiritual considerations:

It has been eight years that I have followed my self-imposed path. I left behind the old emotions. I believe and proclaim that there is nothing more valuable, greater, and more beautiful than life. Life is beautiful and it is beautiful everywhere. My soul groveled in the dust, in the mud many times. But there came new heights of life. Life is something sacred, something with great value and magnitude. It is beautiful in the mud and beautiful at the top of virgin mountains. For life is depth and heights.

I do not mourn for anything in my past. . . . There is nothing shameful in life of any sort. I only wanted to find myself. . . . I fought for ideals that were more sacred than any other ideals because I would have given my life for them. . . . When I loved, I loved deeply, when I hated, I hated deeply. When I suffered, I suffered terribly, when I fell, I fell from terrible heights. . . . I lived. And there is no other truth but life.[35]

Life was not merely a great adventure. Ady's reason for insisting on the experience of life as the only truth was his belief that there was no other path toward the apprehension of morality. Morality could no longer be based on tradition, since conventional norms proved themselves mendacious and immoral. The only way to a new vision of morality was to learn and feel it through the experience of life. For Ady, to learn to live meant to learn to live morally, to be able to enjoy life while not losing the "path." And because life became so complex and contradictory, it demanded total concentration to keep to the path in the midst of the confused world: "Even the strongest among us has to halt for a moment when he looks at the world in which we, the people of today, live. Never was there a world that was more confused, labyrinthine, and demanding. . . . With all our nerves tight, we have to gather all our strength so that we would not despair or lose the path, so that we would not fall down, *so that we would be able to live.*"[36]

Ady's determination to take all knowledge from the surrounding reality was in itself a political program. His contemporaries saw political declarations throughout his work, the conservative circles disdaining his love poems because they liberated sensuality from Christian morality and rejecting his "God-poems" as antireligious, even anti-Hungarian. Ady's poetry was comprehensive in a way no other poetry had been in Hungary. He spoke in the name of any and all segments of the society; he wrote about the misery of the proletariat and the peasantry, the revolutionary feelings of his compatriots, the pain of the Jews, the anger of the gentry, the desperation of the poet, the greediness of the nouveau riche, the carelessness of the bohemian. Even though he chose stylized poetic forms for these topics, he still spoke somewhat from the inside, in the lyric first person singular. This was a political stance asserting that nationalism did not mean the proclamation of Hungarian values but was an active program to try to understand and feel everything that could possibly be felt in Hungary:

> I have felt and desired everything with all my might and, because of this great life-desire, today my doctors look at me, shaking their heads in disapproval when they examine me. I have wanted to tell everything that may spring from the soul of the Hungarian man of today and all that drives him, as a belt drives a machine's wheels. By now I have the right to say what I believe to be the conscience of Hungarians and of the Hungarian culture of our day, and this conscience cannot always be clean.[37]

In Ady's symbolism, death is part of life. It is eternity and nothing, it is the soul's embrace of God, it is *devekuth*. Against the all-encompassing idea of Life stands not death but Silence; that is the metaphor for the denial of the joy of action and feeling, the state of an existence without really being alive. As Ady wrote to his parents asking their forgiveness for "his immoral life":

> [Whenever I go back home] I feel that silence crushes me to death, my body falls to pieces, my lungs rot away if I do not run into the noise, if I do not run against someone, if I too do not shout into the noise of the metropolis. . . . And then you and my mother mourn again over me. . . . And perhaps you are right. . . . This demon has an ever stronger power over me. The belief and love of life and of perfection is ever stronger. I have never hated and loved like this before. My dear father, do not mourn for your son any more because now he believes in life itself more than ever![38]

Ady's ultimate message is a will to life that conquers everything, in spite of everything. In the poem "In front of good Prince-of-Silence" (Jó Csönd-herceg előtt), this will conquers the fear felt in the midst of a dark forest. Life is an eternal journey. A lonely wanderer lost in the forest on a winter night is haunted by the fear of silence and is able to oppose it only with the will to live and to sing:

Holdfény alatt járom az erdőt,	I walk in the forest under the Moonlight
Vacog a fogam s fütyörészek.	My teeth are chattering and I whistle.
Hátam mögött jön tíz-öles	At my back comes ten-fathom high
Jó Csönd-herceg	Good Prince-of-Silence,
És jaj nekem, ha visszanézek.	And woe to me if I look behind.

Óh, jaj nekem, ha elnémulnék,	Oh, woe to me, if I become silent,
Vagy fölbámulnék, föl a Holdra:	Or look up to the Moon:
Egy jajgatás, egy roppanás,	One cry, one crunch,
Jó Csönd-herceg	With a single leaping step
Nagyot lépne és eltiporna.	Good Prince-of-Silence
	Will trample me.

ADY AND BARTÓK

No one has challenged the assertion of similarity between the art of Bartók and that of Ady. And no one has explained it either. As we look at their work, the differences between the two artists strike us first. They were working in different spheres of art that called for greatly different techniques and means of expression. Ady's art belongs to an ideology before the war while Bartók's main output dates from the period between the wars, even though his aesthetics was formed long before Ady's death in 1919. Their personalities were very different and what each artist achieved is unique; they resist categorization in terms of artistic trends. In his devotion to live fully Ady stood alone, as in his active involvement with everything, his energetic search to know Hungary, the prophetic boldness of his writings, and the integral worldview and personality he projected through all these activities. And no one achieved the artistic integration of multiple modernist ideals so perfectly and convincingly as Bartók did by his unique synthesis of extremely different styles.

However difficult it is to draw connections between poetry and music, the conceptual closeness of the aesthetics of Bartók and Ady is evident. Both were devoted to the idea of creating art from an intense encounter with social segments and lifestyles sharply different from their own: journalism in Ady's case and ethnomusicological work in Bartók's. Both Ady and Bartók believed these undertakings to be necessary for the sake of their art—a self-training in understanding and feeling that emerged in their work and social stance. Bartók's field trips gave him the experience to distance himself from the village movement of interwar Hungarian ethnology when it drifted toward the right wing. What was original in this movement was not a novelty for him: he had seen the life of the peasants and worked on their culture long before and much more intensely than most of the representatives of the movement.

An intensity of thought, action, and art—which contemporaries noticed in both of them—mirrored an enormous will to explore feeling. There was also something deeply similar in their development of a firm inner sense of morality and justice precisely through the insistence on feeling. True, Bartók appears an almost ascetic figure compared to Ady, but this asceticism was not the sign of lack of passion. Similarly, it is misleading to think of Ady only as someone engrossed in the bohemian life. He needed immense discipline to accomplish his monumental oeuvre within less than two decades.

In relating to their material in poetry and in music, each artist explored its traditional resources. The aim was to grasp an essence that words could not express, the full potential of feelings and representations, including even that of the distorted, the nostalgic, the sentimental, and the grotesque. Their mature styles drew endless possibilities from the material of their respective arts. They expanded, as if from the inside, the latent sources of the existing styles, superposing and interweaving various levels of symbolism and formal function. Thus Bartók and Ady created their own world of motives and topoi, with connotations and symbolism that could be really understood only from their works.

Ady's inventive use of the resources of language and his unique poetic world created a radically new attitude toward the symbolism of words, employing it for the sake of a mystical expression. Words and expressions and the content of a poem as a whole typically have several levels of meaning and evoke various spheres of associations. Bartók was able to merge many different styles in such a manner that each style could remain functional and often recognizable. His compositions have several superposed structural plans. At any given moment of the musical process, various formal functions might coincide, some distilled from traditional forms (e.g., sonata and variation), and some original (large-scale plans of thematic transformation, of variational techniques derived from folk music, of orchestration, texture, etc.). The symbolism of motives and topoi shows a flexibility similar to Ady's symbolism. The same musical motive (i.e., any kind of recognizable musical entity, whether of rhythmic, tonal, melodic, or ornamental pattern) may carry various symbolic meanings, each motive having the potential to take on, in the course of the piece, a sharply different character from what it originally expressed.

Both Ady and Bartók strove to express the greatest polarization and underlying unity of the material. The ultimate unifying force was an optimism, a heroic belief in life as an all-saturating governing principle of structure and artistic message. The intensity of their belief was somewhat unusual in the twentieth century; it appears romantic and even somewhat narrow-minded and conservative in the light of the many structural and conceptual innovations that occurred contemporaneously in other countries. For instance, Ady could never detach himself from the idea of personal lyricism, and Bartók believed in the romantic idea of the finale to bring everything into a higher perspective—both signs of a belief in an ideal demand of art. They reflect a fundamental idea of the Hungarian modernist movement that can be best summed up through the Lukácsian concept of form: "The essence of form is to defeat oppositions, to conquer opposing forces, to create coherence from every centrifugal force, from all that has been deeply and eternally alien to each other before and outside of this form."[39]

Although never denying Ady's importance, many of the generation after the First World War found themselves out of sympathy with his worldview. They grew suspicious of his projection of outer experience into the soul and belief in the wholeness of life because they saw life falling apart in front of their eyes and felt their personalities being deeply split. They were victims of a dual ideology: without renouncing the ethical implications of a vision of wholeness, they had no faith in its reality. Only the most creative minds of this generation arrived at a coherent artistic vision—either through projecting the immense pain felt at the world's disintegration (as Attila József and Bartók often did) or through reaffirming humanism but at the expense of suppressing aspects of reality (as Miklós Radnóti and Bartók did as well).

For the postmodernist generation, Ady's approach epitomizes all that is despicable. The heroism of genius that sees unity in the diversity of reality does not strike our generation as either necessary or possible. And the projection of the universe into the ego sounds pretentious and ultimately false. Today Ady's picture appears on Hungarian currency—on the 500-forint bill first printed in 1970 (Bartók graces the 1,000-forint bill of 1983)—signaling that he remains the symbol of a liberal social ideal, but few in Hungary choose him for their favorite poet.

But at the turn of the century, at least in Hungary, the situation was very different. Among the seriously concerned, Ady's worldview was doubtless the strongest motive for the creation of modern art. It coincided with the more general tendencies in social life and art in Hungary: the distrust of formalism and conservativism. Whatever we may think of this ideal today, it was the only morally acceptable position in face of the negative tendencies embedded in nationalism, social conservativism, and racism. It was an ideal that, for all its intellectual elitism, proclaimed the dignity and moral potential of the individual.

CHAPTER 7

Loneliness and Love

The Literary Context of *Bluebeard's Castle*

COMMUNICATION AND FRIENDSHIP

We have no equivalent for the metaphors of loneliness, love, and womanliness as they articulated existential questions in turn-of-the-century art, especially in literature. Throughout this time gendered metaphors figured in art and everyday speech in a quite stereotypical manner.[1] The connection between patterns of masculine and feminine behavior in everyday life and their quasi-philosophical metaphorical uses in some modernist literary works is by no means straightforward. The stereotype of the woman as a despotic and demonic creature who plotted man's destruction was as common as that of the naive and childlike woman; but an artist's use of one or both images in his works did not necessarily guide his everyday relation to women.

Many Hungarian artists of this era took inspiration from their love for and friendship with women. Such was the case for Ady in his relationship with Adel Brüll, for Lukács with Irma Seidler, for Bartók with Stefi Geyer and Emma Gruber, and for Attila József with Márta Vágó. Brüll, Gruber, and Vágó were largely responsible for introducing Ady, Bartók, and Attila József into an intellectual and artistic milieu.[2] Yet these male intellectuals, except perhaps Ady, were not at ease with the idea that a woman could take an important role in their development. Attila József and Bartók in particular felt awkward and out of place in the intellectual milieu of Vágó and Gruber, who were older and Jewish (Lukács, who was Jewish, and Ady, who generally felt comfortable with Jews and had many Jewish friends, were not troubled by the fact that these women were Jewish).

Most men of this era could not entertain the idea that women were equal to them emotionally and intellectually. Béla Balázs invariably approached women with the idea that he was on a higher plane intellectually and emotionally, and that it was his task to lead women in their quest for meaning in life. We read in one of his diary entries (left out of the published version perhaps because of its arrogant style): "They come to me, into the life-observing tower to look around a little bit . . . and to seek advice and encouragement. . . . They regard me as their general. It is not as though I knew the path but because my faith is stronger and I see things more clearly."[3] Such an attitude of outspoken superiority alienated several woman friends: "At some point she distanced herself from me, she closed up whenever I became curious. [She said] that she did not want to be exploited by me, 'because I take her only as a subject for study.' "[4]

Although few were self-assured enough to put down such ideas in writing, Balázs's attitude was the norm rather than the exception. To be sure, Bartók thought similarly in this matter. But the need to assert male superiority clashed with his natural inclination to open up toward women more easily than toward men. The fact that Bartók never found a close male friend only increased his anxiety and insecurity in his encounters with women. Bartók insisted on his superiority, assuming, like Balázs, that women needed his guidance in intellectual and emotional questions. Even in his letters to his mother and sister, or in his love letters to Geyer, he occasionally assigned them topics to think about, somewhat in the manner of a schoolteacher, and gently scolded or praised them depending on how well they did.[5] The idea that a woman, following her own initiative, could take up a task worthy of a man seemed incomprehensible and ridiculous to him. For all his passionate love for Geyer, he did not miss an occasion to caricature her for the suggestion that she could also start collecting folk songs. In one letter to her Bartók described a hypothetical report in the Sunday paper with ridiculous photographs of the young woman folklorist in her nice outfit, standing among the peasants on the muddy village road.[6] This tone changed little in the correspondence with his first wife, Márta Ziegler, until Márta, in her kind and quiet way, rebelled against it.[7]

The only woman to whom Bartók related differently was Emma Gruber, who seems to have been Bartók's only close friend. After she married Kodály in 1910, their friendship became somewhat more difficult to maintain, but no one took her place in Bartók's life. Bartók could never come to terms with the idea that his only friend was a woman, and moreover a Jewish woman considerably older than he. He tried to justify this situation in a somewhat speculative manner:

> So far, I only have one friend, and sometimes I need some self-deception to call her a friend; I can do so only if I do not look too straight into the eyes of truth. Because for me, friendship exists only when there is harmony in the conceptualization of essential things. Therefore true friendship is rare or impossible among independent men. Between a man and a woman it is more likely because, in such a case, one or the other acts according to some conventional norms of self-adaptation. In my case too, my only friend is a woman. By the way—she is only a friend! I have already resigned myself to the thought that I will not and cannot have a male friend. [For me, a male friend] would have to be an independent person, but this circumstance already precludes a harmony in conceptions. If such persons get together, they are like two cog wheels that do not fit; they begin to move and crash into each other, cracking and rattling, without any real result, only to fall apart again. A characteristic example: Wagner and Liszt.[8]

The fact that Bartók and Kodály found in each other ideological allies who had similar ideas in musical and cultural matters was of great importance to both men. They continued to maintain and defend their friendship throughout their lives.[9] But Bartók's pessimistic note about friendship between men indicates that he knew from the beginning of their relationship (as Kodály did) that, apart from artistic and intellectual issues, they had little to talk about.[10]

Something in Gruber's intellect, personality, and sensitivity attracted Bartók in a different way. Judging from the correspondence accessible to me, Bartók had a unique relationship with her; she was perhaps the only person to whom he was able to talk about himself.[11] Of course, he revealed his feelings to Geyer too, but there is great difference between confessing love to a woman and speaking about that love and about feelings in general to a third person. The letters to Gruber did not attempt to impress and conquer but to express, and come to terms with, his own self.

The intensity with which Bartók reacted to events released in him a great urge to share his feelings, but he had immense difficulty in opening up. His unusual shyness and unease with words complemented the obstacles and inhibitions inherited from the conventions of the older generation and hampered his relationship with Gruber. It appears that those instances when he was capable of speaking about himself eased but did not resolve the problem of communication. After they talked, Bartók often realized how partial the result was and doubted whether communication was possible or necessary at all. In one letter he asked Emma not to let anyone know what he told her and added his regret at saying anything at all.

Nevertheless, Gruber's sensitivity and consistent emotional support had its beneficial effect. At the very least it gave Bartók the chance to acknowledge and explore his own feelings. His diary, perhaps the only one he ever wrote, dates from this era and gives a moving account of the magnitude of his passion for Geyer.[12] Ultimately the whole of this youthful attempt at being understood amounted to the realization that communication was impossible. The ambivalent friendship with Gruber, the failure of his attempt to establish a relationship with Geyer, and the feeling of being misunderstood by his wife, Márta, perhaps reinforced Bartók's conviction that the only solution was resignation to loneliness.

Balázs's play *Bluebeard's Castle*, which Bartók got to know just after its completion in 1910, was a text that suited his emotional state.[13] Bartók found the play immediately appealing. Even at the first hearing, Bartók must have realized that Balázs's central motive was the loneliness and eternal secrecy of the soul that even the deepest love cannot reach. The fact that Bartók was able to treat this subject at all suggests that by 1911 he had somewhat overcome the crisis of the preceding years and was able to internalize it as art. And yet the opera, more than any other composition, springs from immediate passionate feelings. In 1915, convinced that the piece was not going to be performed in the near future, Bartók wrote to Márta:

> After all, what do I wish for? All impossible things! I would like to go to collect among my dear Romanians; I would like to go, but go far away, travel, I would like to go to hear some great music, but not in Budapest; I would like to go to the rehearsals of Bluebeard, to the performance of Bluebeard! Now I know that I will never hear it in this life.—You asked me to play it for you—I am afraid that I would not be able to play it through. Still I will try it once, so that we could mourn for it together.[14]

BALÁZS'S "MYSTERY PLAY"

Unlike Bartók, Balázs had a natural inclination to think and talk about emotional matters. And though he had no more success than Bartók in finding a companion, he was able to look at his experiences as a workshop for exploring, as an artist, the nature of life and art. The longing to be understood and the failure of communication—experiences Balázs too lived through very intensely—gave the impetus for a global conception of life and art as a "mystery play."

In order to interpret his emotions for himself, Balázs used literary symbols quite spontaneously and was most likely unaware, at first, of their dramatic potential. Years before the conceptualization of *Bluebeard's Castle*, he described the process of discovering the soul of the self and the Other as a journey through a secret and mystical landscape.[15] Images such as a house with closed doors or a cave with hidden recesses frequently appear as metaphors for the secrets of the soul and of life. In one of these passages, Balázs wrote down a dream in which he saw himself walking in the soul of his intimate friend, Aranka Bauer. He was walking in a "dim forest of dense and dark olive trees, of red thorn bushes of roses, black and silent caves" until, because he took a "wrong step, mines began to explode all around as if the whole thing wanted to collapse." "Life is closed behind many doors," he noted another time.[16] On 27 December 1906, after receiving a letter from Paula Hermann in which she talked about herself apparently for the first time, Balázs entered a note that anticipated several ideas of *Bluebeard's Castle*:

> It is a wonderful thing to enter a soul suddenly and yet immediately reach its deepest depth, as if opening the door into a room. Because I loved and understood her even before I knew her. To enter suddenly, no, not even as if into a room—because the soul has a past to which it is connected organically—rather to enter a life, as if into a cave and, softly and carefully, walk around within its small recesses whence its water and light spring.[17]

Several conceptual ideas of the libretto appear here. One begins to understand another person before entering the other soul, just as Judith essentially understands Bluebeard before seeing inside the chambers. One walks within the soul softly and with care (as Judith opens the doors softly, kindly); the light and water spring out from the hidden caves (as light flows from each opened door in the opera). The soul is a cave with secret recesses because it has a past and because it is organically connected to its past: Bluebeard's castle is the landscape of his past life.

On the basis of this passage, we may still entertain hope that Balázs believed in the possibility of knowing the Other. But another note makes it clear that even descent into the depth of the soul cannot overcome the distance between two persons: "We tell everything, even what only we know about ourselves, we open the most inner doors. . . . All this is an effort to bring someone close to ourselves or grow close to someone. But we pour out the many inner images in vain—we are alone. We might as well have stolen each other's diary from the drawer. We remain strangers."[18]

The realization that emotional isolation cannot be overcome opened, for Balázs, two paths toward metaphorical interpretation. The incapacity of the soul to make itself understood reflected the basic condition of life and art. "This piece has hundreds of hidden depths," he wrote after the production of a piece by Gerhart Hauptmann; "they are like shafts of a cave, and it is impossible to descend to their deepest depth where all of them flow into one another, just as [it is impossible to descend] either to the secret of art or to that of life."[19] The thought led Balázs to a symbolist conceptualization of life: "Life is a mystery play. Visions flickering in the mist, barely emerging. It is not self-evident that any of them exist. It is as if they appeared just now and are about to disappear in a second. Only the mist of life is constant in which the apparitions and visions float; it feels everything that it sees."

What interested Balázs was the contrast between distinct events and characters and the continuity of a faceless dark background. Constantly emerging and disappearing, events have precise boundaries in time and space; characters suffer their fate passively in a half-conscious state. Behind them is the compassionate main actor of the mystery, the indefinable "mist" that "feels everything that it sees." A feeling soul governs the entirety of life and manifests itself in the half-conscious actions of characters who have no will of their own and act out only the will of the mysterious force. Pondering the essence of drama in his diary and analyzing Maurice Maeterlinck, Balázs came to see in drama the paradigm of art:

> In the novel, people drift with the current of a great river. In the drama, this river is carried inside the people, it flows in their veins. Man is much *larger* in the drama. The hero of the drama has unknown inside parts, he has both clarity and darkness in him and he tells only a hundredth of what he could tell.

> The true hero of Maeterlinck's dramas is an invisible, all-powerful mystery. In the languid silence nothing seems to happen, yet an invisible force takes over and represses life, it is its motion that is depicted by this motionlessness. This is the great Unknown that embraces us like a dark forest and whose most visible and dramatic manifestation is death. Death is the hero of all these dramas. But Death here does not mean the terrifying and sad end, it is not "grave" and "skeleton" but a lurking dark secret. Death is only *the symbol of the great mystery*. It is an invisible *living* figure who walks amongst us, caresses [us,] and sits at our table as an uninvited guest. Nothing happens in these plays. Life happens.[20]

In spite of the ambiguity of these passages, their main idea is clear. The real actor of the drama is a mysterious force that is at once compassionate (it "feels") and destructive as it draws everything together in a central point. This force lives in the abstract and symbolic notion of death or, in the context of *Bluebeard's Castle*, eternal night. We must not equate Balázs's feeling soul with fate. The feeling soul of a mystery play is more than the necessity that leads life, in a linear fashion, toward a predestined future. This force is ambiguous and total; it is something against which the characters act but also something within them: it is both their life and their death.

Balázs probed the potential of all traditional aspects of drama. In his new concept of drama, figures, actions, and dialogues became resonances of a deeper dramatic movement. Balázs thought of drama as the "technique of overtones": "Let us imagine . . . a chord," he wrote about Maeterlinck, "from which the fundamental tones are missing, a chord composed entirely of barely audible nuances and overtones."[21] And yet these "overtones" were not secondary to the dramatic expression. On one side stood the ultimate governing force—invisible and imprecise—while on the other side stood the concrete actions, which were accidental and less essential but precise and visible: "[What deserves attention is] not the seed but the accompanying elements. . . . Because the seed manifests itself anyway but the overtones would get lost otherwise [that is, if we did not listen to them]. But it may perhaps turn out that these overtones are not merely accompaniments, that [by listening to them] we can discover new territories."[22] And in another place Balázs wrote: "Words can tell little of what should be said—but it is precisely for this reason that words mean more than what they actually say."

Thus the theater stage, according to Balázs, is not merely there to provide a surrounding to the actions of its characters; rather it is one with them. Their soul, in some ambiguous symbiosis with the all-inspiring force of life, occupies the entire space. This point of view, in which "man is much larger," relegates the actual dramatic events to the sphere of incidental fragments: "he tells only a hundredth of what he could tell." In practice this means that the main actor is present in a dual role, identified both with the whole and with one character. In this way drama (in principle, every drama) becomes the paradigm of existence: the enlarged soul acts similarly to the "feeling soul" as it governs the "mystery play" of life. Balázs's *Bluebeard's Castle* realizes this idea by superposing three dramatic developments: first, the drama of Prince Bluebeard as that of an actual character; second, the soul of Bluebeard, that is, the background force represented symbolically by the castle; and finally, the symbol of an all-encompassing force of life that leads everything from darkness to light and, then, back to darkness.

LONELINESS IN THE
HUNGARIAN MODERNIST EXPERIENCE

At the base of the symbolic tradition of Hungarian poetry was a feeling of loneliness. In the literature of the Western countries at the turn of the century, loneliness typically had a social connotation that often resonated in artists' withdrawal from society, into the "garden." It emerged directly in themes focusing on the individual's hopelessness against the faceless and dispassionate system, in works like Robert Musil's *Man without Qualities*, Franz Kafka's *Castle* and *Trial*, and Alban Berg's *Wozzeck*.

Even though loneliness was a basic experience in Hungary too, artists rarely lived it through as social isolation.[23] The majority of the intellectuals simply did not have the means to set up residences away from Budapest, and the intensity and public nature of their encounters in the city left little place for physical isolation. More important, however, even when they escaped from this environment, their loneliness could not be total. The politicized nature of modern art made artists aware of their responsibility "for the people" and "for the nation." Whether they wanted it or not, their art had political implications. For instance, in his home on the outskirts of Budapest as far away from the city as was at all feasible, Bartók worked on folk-music transcriptions, a project that had political implications on a national scale. Paradoxically, the expression of existential loneliness became a uniting, almost political, force among the modernists. It was an emphatically "modern" feeling, a rebellion against superficial socializing and materialistic attitudes of petty bourgeois life and against the official view of a shared "national character."

In the motives used for the expression of existential loneliness—such as circular motion, night, journey into the soul (the essential motives of *Bluebeard's Castle*)—Hungarian art parallels artistic trends in the West. The vision of life as an eternal circle comes very close to the universe of Arthur Schopenhauer, whose *World as Will* sets out an endless and meaningless rebirth of love and death. Circularity was a basic motive of art nouveau, imbued with philosophical meaning especially in the paintings of Gustav Klimt.[24] The magnification of the nocturnal landscape so that it would become the metaphor for the lonely soul is a Nietzschean thought that resonated in various works in the visual arts, poetry, and music, especially in the works of Wagner and Mahler. The abandonment of ordinary life for a journey of psychological or spiritual quest is also a common theme, transmitted to a Hungarian audience primarily from the poetry of Rainer Maria Rilke.[25] The Hungarian symbolist movement as a whole was also greatly influenced by the symbolist poetry and drama of Baudelaire, Rimbaud, and Maeterlinck.[26]

The difference in how Hungarian modernists expressed these ideas in art could be summed up in three attitudes or aspirations. Perhaps none were unique to Hungary but, appearing together as a consistent demand on modern art, they assured its specific character. First, the motive of loneliness—unless it referred to the loneliness of the Hungarian nation—almost always meant an existential state. Second, there was an intense effort to interpret the "lonely soul" as a totality, thus using the motive of loneliness as a metaphor for "wholeness." Third, the symbolic images often evoked a feeling of Hungarianness through the use of elements of folk and other traditional Hungarian art.

The varied artistic expressions and philosophical theorizing about loneliness provided both the broader context and, in some cases, the direct model for the conceptualization of *Bluebeard's Castle*. The opera, in turn, came to be viewed as the centerpiece of turn-of-the-century Hungarian modernist endeavors, particularly of its symbolist movement. In spite of the universal importance of the motive of loneliness for Hungarian art, for the sake of this discussion we rely on the works of three major poets, Endre Ady, Mihály Babits, and Dezső Kosztolányi, with additional reference to Lukács's theoretical writings and to the paintings of Gulácsy and Csontváry. Because of his associations with the *Nyugat* circle, Bartók had to be familiar with all these works, although it is likely that he was influenced directly only by Ady, possibly with some impetus from Lukács's artistic ideology transmitted to him by Balázs.

THE LONELY SOUL:
MAGIC CIRCLE AND MYSTERIOUS LANDSCAPE

What happens in Bluebeard's castle? There is night and darkness. Suddenly a door opens, and in the stream of light a man and a woman appear. They descend slowly into the dark hall. A short dialogue confirms for Bluebeard that he can trust Judith's love, and he orders that the door of the castle be closed. Judith's eyes open to the sight of the dark hall. She looks around, sees, feels the wetness of the walls, notices closed doors, and hears the sigh evoked by her desire to open the secret chambers: "Your castle is weeping . . . your castle sighed. Let us open the doors so there will be light." Bluebeard is hesitant. But then he places the first key into her hand: "Blessed are your hands, Judith."

One after another, Judith opens four doors and sees terrible and beautiful things: torture chamber, armory, treasury, garden of flowers. The objects are bloodstained, but through each door light pours out to the hall. The fifth door opens to an empire, its brilliant light blinding Judith. Darkness disappears, and the gentle light streaming from the other chambers dissolves in the bright light of happiness. But Judith cannot remain thus. She opens the sixth door to see a lake of tears. Standing before the last door, Bluebeard and Judith confront each other with tremendous passion. The seventh door opens, allowing Judith to see the chamber of the ones who never died: the women whom Bluebeard loved before her. Bluebeard adorns Judith with jewelry as he sings the tale of his loves, and Judith disappears behind the seventh door. And there will be night forever.

At the background of the struggle between man and woman, there is the most painful experience of the modern man—loneliness. Loneliness does not mean here only alienation from society. The dissolution of communal life led to the realization that loneliness is, in reality, an existential state. One is eternally alone with one's soul whose secrets are impossible to share with others. Mihály Babits wrote in his sonnet "The epilogue of the lyricist" (A lirikus epilógja [1904]),[27]

Csak én birok versemnek hőse lenni,
első s utolsó mindenik dalomban:
a mindenséget vágyom versbe venni,
de még tovább magamnál nem jutottam.

S már azt hiszem: nincs rajtam kívül
    semmi,
de hogyha van is, Isten tudja hogy' van?
Vak dióként dióban zárva lenni
s törésre várni beh megundorodtam.

Bűvös körömből nincsen mód kitörnöm
Csak nyílam szökhet rajta át: a vágy—
de jól tudom, vágyam sejtése csalfa.

Én maradok: magam számára börtön,
mert én vagyok az alany és a tárgy,
jaj én vagyok az ómega s az alfa.

I am the hero of my poems,
The first and the last of all songs:
I want to sing about the universe,
But cannot break through my own self.

Perhaps there is nothing outside of me,
And if there is: who and how? I am:
Blind walnut closed in its shell
Tired of waiting to be broken.

There is no way out from my magic
    circle.
Only my arrow flies through: the desire,
But false is the hope of longing.

I remain: a prison for myself,
For I am the object and the subject,
Alas, I am the omega and the alpha.

This poem sums up the most important themes of the era's lyric poetry: the tragic and magical beauty of the lonely soul; its longing to be loved and—through this love—make its secrets known; and the failure of love to resolve this longing. Humans seek what is eternal and real but their actions and words tie them to their subjective existence. The only connection with the outside world is the ambiguous desire to be "opened": the lonely soul awaits the intrusion of the other. The motives of longing, of opening up, of false desire imply the theme of love, but, remarkably, Babits's wording precludes sensual and even emotional associations. What matters for him in this poem is the connection between art and the feeling of longing, an existential state.

For Babits, the limitation of the ego was the source and sine qua non of lyric poetry, and lyricism the highest form of artistic expression. As opposed to narrative, the theme of the lyric poem is always a single, nondirectional, and self-contained idea: its topic is the self captured in a single gesture or image. Similar to Ady's inward-turning lyricism, Babits's egoism becomes, in the final analysis, the basis of a moral ideal (and its moral aspect was increasingly important to assert as the century wore on). Because each soul is infinite, each carries equal weight; every individual is the cause and the purpose of the universe. Babits expressed this idea with great power in his "Psalm for male voice" (Zsoltár férfihangra [1918]):[28]

> You know that everything happens for you—why despair?
> The eternal revolution of the stars—they spin for you
> and all things speak to you, all concern you, all are for you,
> for your sinful soul.
> . . . .
> Believe me, the goal is in you and you have the key.
> . . . .
> He who does not understand you, cannot understand God.
>
> Because it is for you that he created the earth and the heaven and the seas,
> so that they become whole in you; he gave you the history of epochs
> as your book of tales, and dipped his brush into the sun,
> to color your soul.
> . . . .
> For do not think that you are only what you seem to be for yourself.
> . . . .
> Perhaps you do not even think that the arbitrariness of your existence is born
>   from you,
> And you do not know that your strength pulsates in faraway Suns

and the planets bend, in front of your sphere,
the poles of adamant.

The closed world of the ego is a magic mirror that opens up toward the mysteries of life. The ego is the reflection of all totalities. It is a "magic circle"—the living focus of all that is circular: time and space and the renewal of life and the motion of earth and planets. The universe resonates in the abandoned and lonely soul because and only if it closes on itself. Despair over the limiting nature of loneliness gave way, in the poetry of Babits, to serenity and belief.

In symbolist poetry, the soul expanded into a magical landscape. It was night, forest, sea, lake, cave, abandoned castle—that is, images of the unknown. Night and dream express an undifferentiated possession of both the most intimate and the most distant; they symbolize the recapturing of the original feeling of oneness with the cosmic world. Things are both close and distant; the individual moves effortlessly between the concrete and the absurd, between reality and dream, between the inside and the outside view. The real landscape suddenly turns to a landscape of mysteries—a landscape that symbolizes the soul.

In the poetry of Ady and Babits there is a conscious ambiguity, a confusion in the use of images: a door may open on the surface of the sky (Babits, "Paysage intime: 3. Twilight"); the road of the poet, as he opens the door to meet death, is blocked by the night of death (Ady, "Insane, mad night"); the gold moon slipping though the dark sky is seen as the reflection of the dark boat slipping through the gold lake (Babits, "Symbols: Symbols about the moonlight").[29]

In Tivadar Csontváry Kosztka's painting *Trees in lamplight in Jajce* (1903), solid and fluid surfaces, light and darkness mix in a half-real, half-magical landscape (Figure 9). The men with the donkey are standing on the same shining green surface where a boat is gliding. Is it river, road, or meadow? Instead of the moon, the round plate of the lamp shines in the darkness. Night does not descend onto this landscape: between the brilliant colors of twilit sky and lamplit road, night's infinite darkness expands from the center of the canvas.

Dream is both escape and revelation; it is motion away from the world into the self, from daylight into night, from empirical reality into a deeper truth of life. In Babits's poetry the great questions of existence emerge at night ("Night," "Evening question"); the soul is free and inspiration comes only at

FIGURE 9. Tivadar Csontváry Kosztka, *Trees in lamplight in Jajce* [Villanyvilágított fák Jajcében], 1903. (Courtesy of Hungarian National Gallery, Budapest)

night ("Nocturnal song," "The prologue of twilight"); and only the sight of the stars makes us understand the infinite ("To the stars!").[30] The mysteries of life are revealed when they cannot be seen; understanding comes when it cannot be known:[31]

Húnyt szemmel bérceken futunk	With eyes closed, we run through the
s mindig csodára vágy szívünk:	mountains,
a legjobb, amit nem tudunk	our heart awaits miracles:
a legszebb, amit nem hiszünk.	the best is what we do not know,
	the most beautiful, what we do not
	believe.

Az álmok síkos gyöngyeit
szorítsd, ki únod a valót:
hímezz belőlük
fázó lelkedre gyöngyös takarót.

When tired of the real, hold
the slippery pearls of dreams,
weave them into an embroidered cover
for your freezing soul.

In his introduction to a volume of mystery stories, Kosztolányi pointed to the anxiety about materialistic life and to the increased awareness of the subconscious as the reason for modern poets' absorption in the soul. His description resembles the underlying idea and the imagery of Balázs's and Bartók's *Bluebeard's Castle*. And like Balázs's prologue, Kosztolányi's introduction places the emphasis on the "journey into the soul" without even mentioning the motive of conflict between man and woman, even though he is introducing a collection of what are essentially love stories:

> Our lives pass with the certainty of two times two. There are no witches anymore and there is no need to speak of beings who do not exist. The outside world is clear. But our inner world is full of mysteries. . . . What was once outside is now inside. We carry the ghosts in ourselves. It is in this era that psychology made the basic discovery that we know hardly anything about most of what happens in our souls; we do not know the vast territory of that enormous empire beyond the threshold of our consciousness. The brave conquistadors, conquerors, and missionaries of the soul are wandering in search of the land of forgotten impressions and memories, of discarded feelings and thoughts. We do not have secret rooms as medieval castles did. But in our souls there are still such rooms. Our era is romantic because it extends the limits of reality, the reality that has always been too small for man. But it extends it not the same way as the romantics of the past century did, who paraded colorful oriental people on exotic landscapes, but by showing the depth inside us. We extend the borders not toward the outside but toward the inside. . . . The solution is in our own selves.[32]

The expansion of the ego to the point where it may embrace everything is also a gesture of alienation. The idea of discovering the soul, as if looking at a distinct entity from the outside, allows its representation in stylized forms and situations. The mysterious landscape of the soul appears characteristically as something distant—an old faraway castle or a land of childhood memory. Here again, reality and dream merge. However distant and dreamlike these images of haunted castles and enchanted towns, the contemporary public recognized a real Hungarian countryside. Krúdy based the enchanted town that had been asleep for centuries in his *The Ghost of Podolin* (A Podolini kisértet [1900]) on an actual town of the same name, and the novel's enchanted castle in the mountains was like the abandoned castles found all over the countryside.

Stylization, especially in lyric poetry, was the means of expressing psychological depth: alienation allowed for the concentration of an intense feeling in a simple image. For instance, in his series "Complaint of a poor little child" (1910), Kosztolányi took the child's viewpoint to treat basic questions of existence (confusion over the limits of the self, fear of being similar and different, fear of death). The opening poem captures the moment of falling under a moving train. At the instant of death comes sudden understanding: simple things alone have value—butterflies, sweet dreams.[33]

Mint aki a sínek közé esett . . .	Like one who fell between the rails . . .
És általérzi tűnő életét,	And senses his fleeting life,
míg zúgva kattog a forró kerék,	as the hot wheels shriek, rattle and roar,
cikázva lobban sok-sok ferde kép	and awry images are flitting,
és lát, ahogy nem látott sose még:	he sees as he has never seen before:
Mint aki a sínek közé esett . . .	Like one who fell between the rails . . .
a végtelent, a távol életet	the infinite, the faraway life,
búcsúztatom, mert messze mese lett,	I think of all for the last time
mint aki a sínek közé esett:	for they are a tale now, distant,
	like one who fell between the rails:
Mint aki a sínek közé esett—	Like one who fell between the rails—
vad panoráma, rémes élvezet—	wild panorama, frightful delight—
sínek között és kerekek között,	between the rails and between the wheels,
a bús idő robog fejem fölött	mournful time rumbles over my head
és a halál távolba mennydörög,	and death thunders in the distance,
egy percre megfogom, ami örök,	for a moment, I seize the eternal,
lepkéket, álmot, rémest, édeset:	the butterflies, the dream, fearful and sweet:
Mint aki a sínek közé esett.	Like one who fell between the rails.

The view that the psyche contains the whole world—that "the solution is in our own selves"—placed the antagonism between man and woman inside the soul. *Bluebeard's Castle* explored this idea. The play's dramatic energy derives from capturing the opposing desires of the soul: its wish to remain hidden versus its urge to let itself be seen (an acutely personal struggle for Bartók). Neither impulse has anything to do with gender. Their antagonism, however, is sharp—much sharper than the contrast between the femininity of Judith and the masculinity of Bluebeard. Their behavior, in fact, blends conventional gender attributes. Interpreted in a traditional manner, Judith is hysterical, curious, and seductive (or, as a typical audience would see her, "feminine"), but she is also strong and steadfast ("masculine"). Bluebeard is withdrawn into his emotions and does not display passion ("masculine"), but at other times he is mild, hesitant, and susceptible to influence ("feminine").

Drawing out the consequences of this ambivalence into an artistic theme, Lajos Gulácsy created one of the best-known works of the era, *The magician's garden* (Varázsló kertje [1906–7]) (Figure 10). The painting's magic lies in the ambiguity of contours between the exterior and interior worlds, and between the gendered attributes of the figures. The colors and motives of the magical garden in the background blend with those of the people in the foreground; the lovers in embrace are lost in the flow of the textile (reflecting smoke or steam); a blooming branch of the tree shelters them. The disproportionately small, half-closed eyes of the man may suggest his independent and restrained nature, which stands in contrast to the woman's pleading gaze and to her almost frightened, gentle gesture of embrace. If we look at the painting in this way, the man represents security and firmness against the hesitant gentleness of the woman. But their expressions and gestures could be interpreted differently. The man's closed stance (he is fully clothed, his eyes are closed, and his arms are hidden) may suggest insecurity, while the woman's openness (expressed by her fully open eye, the clear motion of her arm, and the display of parts of her body) invokes stability.[34] The ambivalence of roles is dissolved in the meeting of their eyes, in their sad and beautiful mutual dependence—in love.

CIRCULAR MOTION AS THE PARADIGM OF LIFE

The nexus of the complex web of symbolism in turn-of-the-century lyricism is the reversible, reflecting, and overlapping character of extensions and contractions. Like a simple image becoming the mirror of a quasi-borderless universe and vice versa, time opens toward infinite ending and beginning in the motive of the circle. The circle is the symbol of eternal rebirth and indeed of

FIGURE 10. Lajos Gulácsy, *The magician's garden* [Varázsló kertje], 1906–7. (Courtesy Hungarian National Gallery, Budapest)

being itself. It captures motion both through its precision and through infinity; it is something dynamic and, in its ultimate result, static. Beginning and ending alike are halfway points; repetitiveness is at once eternal motion and deadly motionlessness. Babits expressed this idea through the sensation of looking, dazed by perfect sunshine, at a uniform series of medieval arcades in his poem "The eternal arcade" (Az örök folyosó [1906]). A line at the end of the poem indicates that it should in principle be repeated ad infinitum:[35]

A véghetetlen portikusznak	The uniform arches of
egyhangu oldalívei	endless columns
rejtett forrásu fényben úsznak.	float in the light of a hidden source.
Mi haszna széttekinteni?	Why look around?
A sima égnek semmi ránca	The smooth sky has no wrinkles
s szemed a földet nem leli.	And your eyes won't find the earth.
. . . .	. . . .
holt oszlopoknak méla tánca	The dazed dance of dead columns,
huzódva, mozdulatlanúl	pulling each other, motionless,
légtengelyén az üres űrnek,	through the pole of empty void,
s a külső sötétig vonúl,	reaches to the outer darkness,
. . . .	. . . .
futok gyáván, futok merészen,	bravely, cowardly,
habár előre jól tudom,	thus I run, knowing
nem érhetem végét egészen	I can never reach the end
s bárhol bukom, felén bukom,	wherever I fall, I fall midway
s e súlyos álmok összezúznak	these heavy dreams trample me,
s maradok majd féluton,	and I will be left halfway,
míg a végtelen portikusznak	as the uniform arches of
egyhangu oldalívei	endless columns
rejtett forrásu fényben úsznak.	float in the light of a hidden source.
(S megint elölről.)	*(And again, from the beginning.)*

In this poem Babits captured the dynamism of the circle in a simple static image. The spontaneous, urgent, and intense motion of running collapses into a decidedly lifeless, motionless, and heavy object: a medieval building. In contrast, Ady's symbolism is typically embedded in action. Bartók's lifelong interest in circularity (both as a theme and as a structure) attuned him to the deeper message in Ady's poems, often conventionally seen as the portrayal of a mood. The poem "My bed calls" (Az ágyam hívogogat [1909]) touched him so deeply that, as he wrote later, it was impossible for him even to mark it: "This [poem] is something entirely wonderful, a magical composition, the music of words. I cannot tear myself away from it. I would like so much to set it to music. I tried, it does not work. Perhaps someday I will succeed. [It is composed of] the most simple words and yet they are filled with eternal sorrow. 'Oh my bed, my coffin. . . . I lie down.' He ends with what he began with. Only the greatest poets of all times could write something like that. How happy we are to read such masterpieces in our own language."[36] In Ady's design, not only does the end return to the beginning, but the second half of each line repeats as the first half of the next one, suggesting that every motion flows from another and that each is at the same time beginning/anticipation and ending/afterthought:

Lefekszem. Óh, ágyam,	I lie down. Oh my bed,
Óh, ágyam, tavaly még,	Oh my bed, last year still,
Tavaly még más voltál.	Last year still you were different.
Más voltál: álom-hely,	You were different: dream world,
Álom-hely, erő-kút,	Dream world, well of strength,
Erő-kút, csók-csárda,	Well of strength, kisses' pub,
Csók-csárda, vidámság,	Kisses' pub, happiness,
Vidámság. Mi lettél?	Happiness. And today?
Mi lettél? Koporsó,	And today? Burial,
Koporsó. Naponként,	Burial. Ever more,
Naponként jobban zársz,	Ever more you clasp me.
Jobban zársz. Ledőlni,	You clasp me. To lie down,
Ledőlni rettegve,	To lie down terrified,
Rettegve fölkelni,	Terrified to get up,
Fölkelni rettegve,	To get up terrified,
Rettegve kelek föl.	Terrified, I get up.
Fölkelni, szétnézni,	To get up, to look around,
Szétnézni, érezni,	To look around, to feel,
Érezni, eszmélni,	To feel, to awaken,
Eszmélni, meglátni,	To awaken, to see,
Meglátni, megbujni,	To see, to withdraw,
Megbujni, kinézni,	To withdraw, to look out,
Kinézni, kikelni,	To look out, to arise,
Kikelni, akarni,	To arise, to desire,
Akarni, búsulni,	To desire, to despair,
Búsulni, elszánni,	To despair, to decide,
Elszánni, letörni,	To decide, to give up,
Letörni, szégyellni,	To give up, to be ashamed,
Szégyellni. Óh, ágyam,	To be ashamed. Oh my bed,

Óh, ágyam, koporsóm,	Oh my bed, my coffin,
Koporsóm, be hívsz már,	My coffin, you call me,
Be hívsz már. Lefekszem.	You call me. I lie down.

The intimate and quite unromantic moment of getting up and going to bed becomes the microcosm of life, concentrating into one image the opposing desires to live and to die, to act and to withdraw. The core of the poem, a series of infinitive verbs, depicts the circular movement from inertia to action and back to inertia—one day of life serving as the metaphor for life. In a few words, it says everything that may happen to people: feel, awaken, see, hide, rise, want, despair, decide, give up, be ashamed, and die. As always with Ady, words function on various planes, referring both to the immediate and to the universal situation. "To despair" may be the mood of the moment, a desperation that often follows intense actions, and it may be despair over the repetitiveness of everyday life and the aimlessness of existence. As Bartók noticed, the power of the poem lies in its music; these words, so full of meaning and associations, pile up in an almost neutral manner, with the boring uniformity of dripping water (all verbs of three syllables). The indifference of enumeration and the consistency of its rhythm become the symbol of infinite circularity.

MYSTERY OF THE OTHER AS THE PARADIGM OF LOVE

To explain what, artistically speaking, love meant for the modernists, and particularly for Bartók and Ady, we have to point toward those aspects in which "love" and "life" were seen to coincide: urgency for movement, circularity of form, and unresolvable tension between polarized forces (particularly between the contrasting desires for mystery and openness—all central themes of *Bluebeard's Castle*). For Ady, sensual love best symbolizes the necessity of being always halfway within an eternal motion. He captures this feeling in his poem "Kiss halfway kissed" (Félig csókolt csók [1906]):[37]

Egy félig csókolt csóknak a tüze	The flame of a kiss halfway kissed
Lángol elébünk.	Flares up before us.
Hideg az este. Néha szaladunk,	The night is cold. At times we run,
Sírva szaladunk	We run weeping,
S oda nem érünk.	And never arrive.

Hányszor megállunk. Összeborulunk,	At times we stop. We fall on each other,
Égünk és fázunk.	We burn and freeze.
Ellöksz magadtól; ajkam csupa vér,	You push me away: my lips are bleeding,
Ajkad csupa vér.	Your lips are bleeding.
Ma sem lesz nászunk.	We will not make love today.
Bevégzett csókkal lennénk szívesen	With a kiss, complete and full,
Megbékült holtak,	We could have peace in death,
De kell az a csók, de hí az a tűz	But the fire calls, we need the kiss,
S mondjuk szomorún:	And say sadly:
Holnap. Majd holnap.	Tomorrow. Tomorrow.

Incompleteness is both the inalienable attribute of love and the original manifestation of life. To be alive means to feel and to want; it is a constant desire for (e)motion, but the fulfillment of this desire would mean death. For Ady, motion—typically aimless motion—is the most profound way of experiencing life. Several of his short stories, such as "Flóra will not marry," "The millionaire Cleopatra," and "Juliette goes to Florence,"[38] unfold around the ambiguous urge to "go away." In the poem "Evening in the Bois" (Este a Bois-ban [1906]), aimless wandering becomes the ecstatic experience of "falling into the great night, into the wondrous world of infinity," which leads both toward new times and back to the past. As expressed in another poem by Ady, "I seek a miracle, a secret / A dream. And I do not know what I seek."

The pleasure of love lies in its incompleteness, which for Ady is symbolized by the ever-incomplete kisses and embraces. We can explore the elements of Ady's metaphor by turning to the philosophical theory of eros. In the theory put forward by Emmanuel Levinas, impatience is the single most important attribute of eros. The explosion that breaks forth at the moment of fulfillment leaves the participants with a feeling of void, which they experience with astonishment, but this void becomes instantly the source of a newly awakening desire: "In love there is no fulfillment in achieving, for the love temporalizes itself as a not-yet that lies outside the range of the possible."[39]

The source of impatience is the eternally secret nature of the Other. Love is an encounter, not even merely with the Other but with mystery itself; love springs from and lives only in this mystery. Erotic love, in which nudity suspends the body's natural inclination for modesty, does not reveal anything; it cannot erase the mystery of sensuality, which belongs to the domain of the unspeakable. The Other remains always in the distance, and renewed attempts to discover it inevitably fail. The presence of the Other as a mystery is a constant provocation to penetrate into its depth, but this discovery is never wholly successful; the beloved remains eternally a stranger:

> The pathos of love . . . consists in an insurmountable duality of beings. It is a relationship with what always slips away. The relationship does not ipso facto neutralize alterity but preserves it. The pathos of voluptuousness lies in the fact of being two. The other as other is not here an object that becomes ours or becomes us; to the contrary, it withdraws into mystery. . . . What matters to me in this notion of the feminine [i. e., the notion of the Other] is not merely the unknowable, but a mode of being that consists in slipping away from the light. . . . It is a flight before a light. . . . Alterity . . . [is] the absolutely original relationship of the eros, a relationship that is impossible to translate into powers and must not be translated. . . . The transcendence of the feminine [the Other] consists in withdrawing elsewhere, which is a movement opposed to the movement of consciousness. But this does not make it unconscious or subconscious, and I see no other possibility than to call it mystery.[40]

Levinas's interpretation is relevant to Hungarian modernism and especially to the art of Ady and Bartók. In many Ady poems and in *Bluebeard's Castle*, love is urgency that culminates in an explosion and then collapses back into void, which instantly turns into urgency again. Moreover, in several compositions by Bartók, circularity and the feeling of urgency moving toward explosion create an aesthetic demand, against which he posits the demand for an ending—that is, arrival in the dramatic sense.

Love thus becomes the metaphor for life. As life is the desire for the ever-escaping future, love is the desire for mystery. From the reality of fulfilled love, the soul desires to escape to the mystery of a love that remains eternally a dream. As in Ady's "I want to keep you" (Meg akarlak tartani [1906]),

Őrjít ez a csókos valóság,	It maddens me, this reality of kisses,
Ez a nagy beteljesülés,	This great fulfillment,
Ez a megadás, ez a jóság.	Submission, goodness.
Öledbe hullva, sírva, vágyva	Falling on your lap, crying, in desire
Könyörgök hozzád, asszonyom:	I beseech you my lady:
Űzz, kergess ki az éjszakába.	Chase me, drive me out into the night.
. . . .	. . . .
Maradjon meg az én nagy álmom	Let me have my great dream
Egy asszonyról, aki szeret	Of a woman who loves me
S akire én örökre vágyom.	And whom I eternally desire.

The artistic ideas discussed so far appear gender-free (or at least not gender-specific). The loneliness of the soul, the eternal circular motion of life reflected in love, the incapacity to open up, and the slipping away of the Other do not require an exclusively male perspective. Much of the lyricism of the time, even when its topic was love, suited the viewpoint of both genders or deliberately merged gender roles.

For instance, Balázs's conception of drama led unavoidably to a confusion of genders. If the mysterious force of life (the acting force of the drama) stands for the soul, it must be the soul of one character. Consequently the drama must have only one hero, an all-encompassing soul that contains both male and female, negative and positive forces, life and death. Forced by dramatic logic to identify it with a specific figure, Balázs had no choice but to magnify the importance of one gender—in *Bluebeard's Castle*, the male character—at the expense of the other. But he strove to symbolize the life of the human soul as such. Thus the association of the castle with Bluebeard's soul and the distribution of male and female roles were more an arbitrary choice than a concept. In his diary notes, he consistently associated himself with what became the role of Judith: in his dreams, it was always he who walked in the cave of the soul of the beloved.

Yet neither love nor emotional life could be gender-free. Turn-of-the-century art drew on traditional theories of man's superior spiritual and ethical being. In circumscribing femininity, Hungarians did not dissociate themselves from the common view that women are closer to animalistic biological life. In Vienna, Otto Weininger magnified this view into a theory that women were mindless, amoral, and purely materialistic beings who lacked individuality and were governed exclusively by their animalistic and impersonal sexual desires. He maintained that the exclusion of women and the erasure of any sign of the feminine were the token of moral and intellectual development.[41]

In contrast to Vienna, where this theory inspired such significant works in science and art as the psychological theories of Freud and Strauss's *Salome* and *Elektra*, in Hungary the impact of such theoretical doctrines appears limited, at least within the intellectual-artistic circles.[42] The reason was not at all that modernists opposed its basic premises: even such liberal thinkers as Lukács accepted this chain of thought without much hesitation. Women could never write tragedy, Lukács argued, because their "feeling of necessity" is still on the level of the "necessity of the life of plants, it is a necessity of those who are entirely one with community, who are without conflict."[43]

Hungarian intellectuals, however, did not advocate Weininger's doctrine. Balázs simply rejected Weininger, viewing him as "perverse."[44] As for Bartók, he was convinced of the necessity of giving equal rights to women and was quite aware of the social conditions that put women in a doubly difficult position when they tried to achieve something in the intellectual domain.[45] The reason behind this relative liberalism was again the backwardness of the Hungarian situation, more precisely, the weakness of the bourgeoisie as a social group. Coming from the periphery of society (as non-nobles and economically marginal segments) and being in opposition, the intelligentsia had no choice but to protect liberalism and suspect anything that was proclaimed to be an "eternal" common characteristic. After all, they encountered some of the same accusations (such as being sensual, mindless, and amoral) directed against them as modernists, as Jews, and as urbanites.

Ady's attitude was most interesting. He valued the feminine orientation toward life. For him, womanliness equaled "oversensitivity," that is the capacity to feel and the unconditional devotion to feeling. As such, the feminine was a positive force instrumental in the creation of art. In fact, it was even more: womanliness meant the basis of being really human. In a series of autobiographical articles that appeared in *Nyugat* during 1908 (published later as a separate volume that Bartók owned and read), Ady castigated the elements of "civilization" who posed as manly:

> I am a woman soul, an "âme féminine," even today when I am not chasing myself, with hysterical cries, along the triangle of Paris, Budapest, and Rome. I see more clearly in several matters, there are many things I once wanted terribly and do not need anymore, but I still have a thousand senseless outbursts daily. Suddenly I feel the pain of an old . . . wound and this pain overpowers me to such an extent that I am seized by madness, I remember an old thought and would like to cut some people into pieces with a sword. This is the *vitéz* [heroic] soul of the *Tas* [my ancestors] transformed into the feminine: it is the blood and the soul of the village but it is a feminine soul—a noble, cowardly, barbaric soul. Everything else is superfluous glitter on me: civilization, the display of manliness that I bear with difficulty, this cult of the I that overbids Nietzsche. All these: nobility and barbarism that together are feminine and naturally the negation of the whole of today's culture that is masculine or, better, a culture that is masculinizing all that is feminine, that [calls itself] democratic and socialist, a culture that is, above all, artificial. . . . [Because of this attitude] I became hated by those people who are important personalities, but whom I never regarded as being human, even though it felt good when they wreathed me with laurels.[46]

And yet, in spite of Ady's bold rejection of the masculinization of modern culture, the conventional view of woman persisted. What matters to us is not a stereotype of everyday discourse but a conceptualization of womanliness in its relation to intimacy and eros. In Hungary, this discourse grew from a romantic tradition to which the feminine was the synonym of life. It goes back to Madách's *Tragedy of Man*, which as we have seen challenged the belief that pure spirit was at all possible outside the sphere of empirical reality.[47] In the play the contrast of spirit and life translates to the opposition of Adam and Eve. Facing the woman who holds the token of future life in her body, Adam's rejection of life appears trivial and meaningless. According to the literary critic Antal Szerb, "The great struggle between Adam and Eve throughout history represents the eternal antagonism between spirit and life. . . . Adam is the clear, constructing consciousness that aspires to higher aims and collapses if it cannot achieve its goal. Eve represents the ambiguous, original instinct, the voice of nature in humans, who wants nothing but to live and who defies the power of spirit. She is the Schopenauerian Will, and compared to her the individualism of Adam is only a fragile illusion. Every god will die once, every principle will collapse, but life lives and hopes with hope."[48]

This interpretation was in a sense the reiteration of the conventional notion that women belonged to a lower, prehuman, biological world. But Madách's conclusion pointed toward a broader conceptualization of woman as a totality that at the same time opposed and contained pure spirit. The anxiety over this problem resonated in Lukács's essay on Kierkegaard: "When man first stood face to face with the world, everything around him was his, but the individual objects always eluded him, and his every step seemed to put a distance between himself and objects. And the tragicomic end would have been that he starves to death in the midst of all the plenty of the world, had it not been for woman, who knew from the first moment how to take hold of things, how to use them, and what their significance was. And woman saved man for life . . . but only so she could keep him attached to life, chained to its finitude. Real woman is first and foremost a mother and the deepest antagonist of all yearning for the infinite."[49]

To conceive of (finite) life as feminine and (infinite) spirit as masculine was a Pyrrhic victory. Lukács could not disguise that, by this assertion, he arrived at an absurdity: the unreality of both life and spirit. The man of pure spirit is far from being dignified; he is grotesque in his incapacity to know how to live.

What caused Lukács to reevaluate his ideas of life and spirit was his love for Irma Seidler. Lukács's preoccupation with the soul began in 1907 when he won the Kisfaludi Társaság prize for his first work in literary criticism and ended in 1911 with the suicide of Seidler. During these years Lukács wrote and published most of his uniquely personal literary essays in his first major book, *Soul and Forms*. This time frame coincides with Bartók's personal crisis, which began in 1907—with his love for Stefi Geyer, his first field trips, and his first pieces in the modern style—and ended with the composition of *Bluebeard's Castle* in 1911.

The overlap of these time periods may be a coincidence, but Lukács's and Bartók's attitudes toward emotional matters rested on a similar set of beliefs and expectations characteristic of the thinking of that time. Both men arrived at a deeper understanding of their selves and their creative works as a result of these emotional experiences. Awareness of the magnitude of their passion and its unhappy outcome had a decisive impact on them, facilitating a complex emotional and intellectual transformation. The experience led Lukács toward withdrawal from emotional life. It helped Bartók abandon the Nietzschean aspiration to "be above all things."

The most lasting effect of the emotional transformation on Lukács (and, to judge from *Bluebeard's Castle*, also on Bartók) was a new attitude toward emotional and spiritual fulfillment and perfection.[50] The mere possibility of man's longing for woman—his undeniable urge for intimacy with the Other—cast doubt on all the male theorizing about the pure spiritual soul as a manly quality, as well as the Nietzschean idea of being "above all things." Submission to passion was an attack on dignity and on the elevated state of loneliness.

The fundamental issue here was one of coherence: could the self ever be fully and only itself, coherent and whole in its isolation? The ideal of the inner harmony of the purely spiritual soul could be achieved only at the expense of forcing out everything that seemed to be incongruous with this totality. The individual has to erase all traces of sentimentality from the self to turn it into a work of art, coherent and self-sufficient. The life of such a man, as Lukács understood it, meant learning "how to live without limits. How to live with the knowledge that one only trespasses on one's own deeds . . . that the person one embraces remains a stranger forever."[51] The yearning for the Other was a dangerous challenge to this concept of wholeness:

What does it mean for someone to yearn? . . . Perhaps this: that he needs something that detaches itself from his self, that is separate and apart from his life and yet still his. . . . There is something somewhere, that perhaps I will melt into; there is a mirror perhaps that will reflect my rays; there is a deed in which I will discover myself. Is there really? I do not know what it could be. I only know that I am journeying toward it and everything is merely a wayfaring station along the way. . . . Perhaps it is death—who can tell?—that the soul will become whole; perhaps it is with death that the yearning stops.

This yearning within the soul, not the feminine Other, kept man from achieving the state of pure spirituality. It would be self-deception to suppress the urge to be seen by the Other, or even to minimize its importance for man. And yet this longing remained, unsatisfied and unresolved. Like Balázs and Bartók, Lukács was convinced that full understanding was not possible between man and woman. Happy love was something trivial and sentimental, another form of self-deception. Kierkegaard's decision to break off his engagement provided the occasion for Lukács to formulate his suspicion of happy marriage: "Perhaps something in him realized that happiness—even if it is attainable—would have paralyzed him and rendered him sterile for all time. Perhaps what he was afraid of was that happiness was not unattainable, that Regine's lightness could, after all, have redeemed his great sadness, and that they would both have been happy. But what would become of him if life had taken away from him his unhappiness?"[52]

In Lukács's case, the rejection of the idea of conventional marriage sprang primarily from a fear that a normal everyday existence would endanger the future of his creative work. He fashioned for himself the ideal of the intellectual man, an abstraction of life entirely free from emotional turbulence. For the sake of creative work, he imposed on himself the abstract conception of purely intellectual existence. As Lukács recognized, it was neither life nor pure spirit. It was a strange existential state somehow at the frontier of life, inert and unfruitful in the emotional sense, and yet not without feeling:

I am no longer afraid [of loneliness] but I do not believe that I will ever touch the living reality of life. . . . I realize this without distress. . . . I know that my love cannot find its way into your real lives, nor yours into mine—because I have no life. . . . There is some sadness mixed with pride in this knowledge—but there is much pride—and today at least much strength as well. . . . I believe that my genuine value as a thinker stems from this circumstance, one has to pay a price for it. I pay with "life"—one should not complain against the inevitable; it is vulgar.

The "ice age" has begun. I have died but she lives within me; to the extent that anything can live within me. Quietly. Without reproaches. Without pain. . . . In spite of everything, only she exists—even if I no longer love her, no longer desire her, no longer want her back. It makes no difference. The memory of one episode with her means more than a lifetime spent with someone else.[53]

In Lukács's concept, love is not infinite circularity. Growing from a state in which the ego is a totally coherent and perfect entity, love begins with the motion by the sovereign act of longing for the unknown. At its heights it reaches intimacy without complete resolution in happiness. The final stage is the "ice age" of eternal sadness, which is informed by the memory of the great love. Precisely because of the hopelessness of love, the lover is able to see beyond self and personal life. The "magic circle" closes into itself:

Love is hopeless precisely because of its cosmic dimensions. . . . It is through the feeling of love that man becomes conscious of [his] cosmic dimensions, that his everyday existence is destroyed and becomes the symbol of and the door to cosmic relations. Those waves which broke through the boundaries of individuality and poured their force onto empirical love, retreat into themselves and the circle closes into itself. . . . All is in vain. Man can never reach woman and woman can never reach man.[54]

Around the same time Ady gave a poetic expression to the emotional stages of this incomplete circle in his volume *Longing for love* (Szeretném, ha szeretnének), which appeared in 1909 and was especially dear to Bartók. In his conception too, the starting point of love is the destructive motion directed against the completeness of the ego. The choice of the title of the volume and its motto poem indicate his emphasis:

Sem utódja, sem boldog őse,	Nor descendant, nor happy ancestor,
Sem rokona, sem ismerőse	Nor relative, nor acquaintance,
Nem vagyok senkinek,	I belong to no one,
Nem vagyok senkinek.	I belong to no one.
Vagyok, mint minden ember: fenség,	I am, like every man: dignity,
Észak-fok, titok, idegenség,	North Pole, secret, alien,
Lidérces, messze fény,	Lonely, faraway light,
Lidérces, messze fény.	Lonely, faraway light.

De, jaj, nem tudok így maradni,	But, oh, I do not want to remain thus,
Szeretném magam megmutatni.	I would like to show myself,
Hogy látva lássanak,	And to be seen,
Hogy látva lássanak.	And to be seen.

Ezért minden: önkínzás, ének:	All are for this: self-torture, singing,
Szeretném, hogyha szeretnének	So that I would be loved and
S lennék valakié,	Belong to someone,
Lennék valakié.	Belong to someone.

Both the clarity and the final message of the poem are remarkable; there is a nondogmatic quality about this confession that distinguishes it both from conventional representations of longing for love and from theorizing about emotions in terms of gender. Ady captures here the real confrontation between the desire to be lonely and whole in one's own being, and the longing to break out from this wholeness. The primordial state of human beings is loneliness. Every spirit is alien to the world, and the source of its dignity lies precisely in its secrecy in distance: "I am, like every man: dignity / North Pole, secret, alien." Dignity is destroyed by the yearning to be loved. For Ady, this desire for intimacy is also the foundation of art: "All are for this: self-torture, singing."

What is happening here is something altogether beyond communication: the soul does not seek understanding and not even primarily love, but first and foremost it wants to be seen. It seeks understanding without words and thoughts, an understanding that comes about when the invisible becomes transparent: the lover looks at the other and is able to see. The "eye" is a basic symbol in Ady's love poetry: eyes are the "mirrors of blessed miracles" in the poem "Because you love me"; they are the windows of the soul in the poem "The castle's white woman" (mentioned in chapter 6). It is the moment of looking at each other that expresses love in Gulácsy's painting. In *Bluebeard's Castle*, the prologue stresses the act of looking, and, in the course of the play, Bluebeard refrains from explanation; he allows Judith only to see. In a letter written to a friend, Lukács confessed his yearning to be seen: "When I left you, something wept within me, wept after a great intimacy. I longed, if only for a moment to take off my impenetrable mask of cleverness, longed for someone to see me, if only for one moment, so that it could be said: I see you and love you."[55]

The loneliness that occurs in the aftermath of passionate love is described in Ady's poem "Even if the Moon is cold" (Hiába hideg a Hold [1909]):

Hiába hideg a Hold. Egyszer
A mi óránk forrón ütött
S szent láz verte az éjszakát,
Melybe két szép, nyomorult embert
Terelt be a véletlen Idő,
A sokféle Időnek eggye,
Irgalmas, bolond, dús Idő,
Mely asszonyommal összehajtott
S melynek azóta nincs mulása.

Égő sebek az Égen s fázva
Suhog itt a földön a palást,
Suhog utánunk a palást,
Szomorúságunk hosszú palástja,

. . . .

Úgy borulunk, úgy remegünk
Egymásba, mintha soha-soha
Kettő nem lettünk volna ketten.

Mindig ezt az asszonyt szerettem.
Szájában és szívében voltam
S ő volt a szám s az én szivem,
Mikor ittasan kóboroltam,
Kárhozottan, a váradi éjben,

. . . .

S akkor volt, amikor ő ment itt,
Hozzám-hajtott, édes némberem
S akkor volt, amikor nagy-ámulva
Tárta ki karját két szakadt
Egy-ember és megint egy lett újra.
És nem is volt ez szerelem,
Csak visszaforrás újra itt,
E választó, bitang időben.

Even if the Moon is cold. Once
Our time came with warmth and heat
And sacred fever was beating the night,
Into which two beautiful, miserable
   beings,
Were herded together by the arbitrary
   Time,
One of the many-faced Times,
Merciful, mad, rich Time,
That brought me together with my
   woman,
And that has not passed ever since.

Burning wounds on the Sky, coldly
Rustles here on the earth the cape,
Rustling flies behind us the cape,
The cape of our sadness,

. . . .

Thus we fall, thus we tremble
Into each other, as if never-never
We two had been two.

It was this woman I always loved
I was in her mouth and in her heart
And she was my mouth and my heart
When I wandered drunken and
Accursed in the nights of Várad,

. . . .

It was then when she walked here,
And came to me, my dear woman
It was then when with great amazement
Two torn one-beings opened their arms
For embrace, and became one again.
It was not love,
But the return of the spring into itself,
   here, again
In this merciless time of separation.

The first line, "Even if the Moon is cold," gives the key to the interpretation of this poem. It does not suggest that the cold emotionlessness of the present is only appearance, but rather that even if the great passion is over, it remains perpetually in suspension. Ady intentionally superposes here different times and different concepts of time: time is "arbitrary" and "many-faced," it "herded" people together but is also the "merciless time of separation." Most of the narration is in past tense but refers to a past that "has not passed ever since." There is tension between the actual moment of embrace and the memory of that embrace. Real embrace is confused; it is everything and the opposite of everything: burning and cold, separation and coming together, oneness being torn apart and two separate beings becoming one, embracing the Other and becoming one with the self ("return of the spring into itself"). The memory of embrace is eternal and clear: it is sadness born from the certainty of memory: "It was this woman I always loved." Two symbolic associations of "night" oppose each other: the night is the symbol of the greatest passion and of the state of eternal sadness.

Images that haunt the poem also permeate the symbolism of *Bluebeard's Castle*. The lovers are covered by the cape of sadness just as Bluebeard clothes Judith with a cape when she is about to retreat into memory. The line "It was this woman I always loved" (which reminds us of the closing line of the poem "Because you love me") might be the model for the ultimate line of Bluebeard's aria to Judith; Bartók added the line to Balázs's original text. Most important, this poem stresses the polarity of love as being both separation and union, both the instance of becoming one with the other and that of returning to the self.

THE POETIC IDEA OF *BLUEBEARD'S CASTLE*

In explaining the opera's symbolism, the prologue offers a clue:

> The curtains of our eyelids are raised:
> Where is the stage, within or without,
> Fair ladies and lords?

This introduction defines the stage of the play as the soul of Bluebeard, and its topic as the transformation of feelings within this soul. All analyses accept this interpretation, and yet all minimize the fact that the plot is a metaphor and reabsorb the message of the prologue into a traditional concept of drama as the playing out of conflict between characters. Sándor Veress's interpretation was among the first to popularize the idea that the opera is about the "eternal tragedy of the dualism of man and woman," and that Judith's curiosity brings catastrophe to both of them. Because most scholars today share Veress's opinion, I summarize it here:

> Bluebeard and Judith represent the eternal tragedy of the dualism of man and woman, the heavenly and earthly perspective of their souls. Here is the drama of man's loneliness seeking complete fulfillment in woman and finding only partial satisfaction, and of woman, who, in her devotion to man, sacrifices her whole being. . . . [Bluebeard will] find in Judith the most beautiful one, the final fulfillment . . . whom he adorns with his most precious jewels; but he has to lose her, too, because Judith desires the disclosure of the secret behind that last door. It is in vain that he begs her not to open it. . . . Judith insists . . . , and with this her fate is sealed.[56]

Taking this interpretation as a starting point, critics usually describe Bluebeard as wise and rational and Judith as passionate and narrow-minded. György Kroó associates Bluebeard with the "heroes of legends," a man of "wisdom and great experience in emotional life" who is capable of integrating into his life his "past experiences and eternal problems." In contrast, Judith is "chased by her passion into total tragedy"; she is "impatient, curious, jealous, and stubborn."[57] Carl Leafstedt's recent study complements this image by looking at the metaphorical representation of Judith in twentieth-century art. He suggests that Balázs might have been consciously evoking the character of the heroine of Hebbel's play *Judith* since "both Judiths are placed into conflict with an extremely masculine man against whom they must apply all their feminine cunning to obtain what they desire."[58]

Such characterizations are valid to some extent and reflect a plausible contemporary interpretation of womanliness. We have no reason to suppose that such ideas could not occur to Balázs and Bartók as well. The transgression of the prohibition against questioning was a well-known motive of art—notably in Wagner's *Lohengrin*, an opera Bartók admired. Maeterlinck's play and perhaps Paul Dukas's opera were known in Hungary before 1910. Nevertheless, in the light of the complex philosophical and artistic tendencies of the time, it would be difficult to view the opera merely as the perpetuation of an already exploited romantic theme, namely the story of the demonic woman who, in her narrow-mindedness, manipulates man in order to satisfy her curiosity and thereby brings about her own destruction.

Underlying the entire design of the play is the realization that the self does not know its secrets and that these can be revealed only if the soul is opened—by the Other. Before Judith comes to the castle and after she has departed from the active life of Bluebeard, all the doors are locked; there is darkness. Bluebeard does not lock the rooms so that Judith will not see behind them; in her absence no door will open and no light exists. The normal state of being is ignorance and dark ambiguity in the soul. Light—that is, knowledge—comes only with the help of the Other.

Bluebeard does not confront Judith with a premeditated firm decision as to which doors should be opened and which should remain closed, or even as to in what order they are to be shown. It is as though he himself does not quite know what is behind the doors or is unsure of the effect of revealing their secrets or, at least, has no power to decide how to reveal them. Only his lack of self-knowledge explains why he is, at the beginning, against opening any door at all, whereas in fact he could have every reason to want Judith to see several or perhaps even most of them. Bluebeard's indecisiveness is really the ambiguous fear of, and ambivalence toward, his own secrets. Judith's intrusion answers his need to be seen, and it is her blessed capacity to be able to see. As Bluebeard says to her, after having placed the first key into her hand: "Blessed are thy hands, Judith."

In the original plan, Balázs included the castle as the third character. Even though he abandoned the idea for obvious practical reasons, it indicates a fundamental aspect of the dramaturgy. The castle is the metaphor for the concentrated point where the actions of the two characters are conjoined in a common essence—in darkness and death, to use the Balázsian metaphor. It is the ambiguous all-encompassing soul that acts behind their will and gives their abstraction precise shapes. Like characters in a conventional play, Judith and Bluebeard suffer. But their suffering becomes meaningful only as a metaphor, a metaphor for the opposing desires of the soul to see (and to be seen) and to allow its mystery to slip away. If the opera is a tragedy at all, it is certainly not that of either Bluebeard or Judith. It is the drama of the eternal condition of love, the impossibility of fulfilling and resolving the infinite yearning for intimacy. In this, the motive of love becomes also the metaphor for life, which is nothing other than the urge to find an unknown future and push back its boundaries.

It is significant that the opera opens with darkness and ends with darkness. In Bluebeard's last phrase, "And there will be night forever" (the composer's addition to the original text), "night" is a symbolic center into which everything collapses. Night is the symbol of coldness and emotionlessness, and it is the symbol of fiery love. It is the night that comes after love and is thus distant from and saturated with the memory of love. Furthermore, night is the traditional symbol of womanliness (here emphatically of Judith, who was found by

Bluebeard at night), but also the symbol of the mystery of existence (here emphatically of the soul of Bluebeard). And finally, total darkness is the symbol of wholeness; it is the darkness of the cosmos, the source and the end of everything.

Bluebeard's Castle is an abstract drama: in the form of a sequence of clashes between man and his Other, it projects into time the timeless dynamic force of love. Bluebeard is the absolute self whose ultimate nature is to be only itself, to return to its own soul. His story is both of the past (it is an old tale) and of the ever-present moment of intimacy. The form of the piece evolving from darkness and returning into darkness as it folds inward suggests both eternal circularity and completeness. Its microcosm is the mirror of overlapping circularities and totalities: it is one monumental embrace that begins and dies; it is the story of love; and it is the drama of finding the self with the help of another. Bluebeard is led back by Judith's love to his origins so that he can be one within the self in complete and beautiful loneliness.

CHAPTER 8

Bartók's Stylistic Synthesis

The Dramatic Music of *Bluebeard's Castle*
and Its Antecedents

THE NEW IDEAL OF NATIONAL MUSIC

Bartók's task after his experiences in 1907 was no longer to find an aesthetic ideal but to create a musical language that corresponded and gave weight to that ideal. The elevation of Hungarian tradition into something universal was not enough for Bartók and other modernists. New artworks had to embody the reality of modern life, thus expressing a "more true Hungarianness," and they had to be structurally coherent. As we have seen, the demands led these artists of the beginning of the century to a new conception of folklorism.

The integration of structural aspects of folk (popular) art into high art already characterized some nineteenth-century works (for instance, those of Liszt), and not all the modern artists went beyond the eclectic use of folk themes. But the modernists intended to synthesize elements of Hungarian and universal art in a new way. While the issue of nationalism remained an essential ingredient of their preoccupation with folk art, they looked less to its surface elements than to what they thought to be enduring and universal themes and structural patterns, which they called "the phenomena" or "original facts of life."

Bartók's experience illustrates the transition from an older view of nationalist art to a new one. The impetus to create a national style came to him around 1903, when he suddenly and unexpectedly joined the chorus of turn-of-the-century chauvinist propaganda. His fascination with political nationalism lasted only a short while. Artistically and ideologically, nationalism proved to be a dead end, and his disillusionment made Bartók a staunch opponent of the doctrine for the rest of his life. Yet he came to a new concept of national music during that time and as a result of his nationalist enthusiasm. The young Bartók began to dream of a music where there would be no split between folk and universal styles. He noted the split in the works of several romantic composers who relegated folkloristic tone to lighter genres or to lighter movements of multimovement pieces. Bartók was impelled toward an ideal of coherent and serious national style as a reaction against the rigid attitude of his composition teacher, Hans Koessler, a Brahms disciple and firm defender of musical classicism. To Koessler, national style was a peripheral issue of composition. He equated the language of music with the style of the great German composers, considering anything that did not accord with this tradition to be "dialect," useful for coloristic episodes only.[1]

The symphonic poem *Kossuth* was Bartók's first attempt to transcend the view that national style was an exotic color unsuitable for expressive music. Hungarian, serious, and modern throughout—such was Bartók's ideal style in 1903 and for the rest of his life, with one significant modification of his youthful attitude. Later he would believe he had discovered the source of modern style in folk music; but at this time he associated modernism exclusively with the new developments of German music. His task, as he saw it, was to combine one style that was modern but foreign with another that was Hungarian but conservative. In *Kossuth*, he would merge aspects of the Straussian symphonic poem with elements of romantic Hungarian symphonic music.[2]

During the compositional period that spans 1903 (the composition of *Kossuth*) to 1907 (the composition of the *Fourteen Bagatelles*) and includes such different pieces as the Piano Quintet, the Rhapsody op. 1, and the two orchestral suites, Bartók returned to a somewhat more conventional Hungarian tradition. The musical material became more homogeneous than in *Kossuth* and the movements often followed existing musical types. Even in their time, these compositions failed to elicit the same enthusiasm as *Kossuth* had; contemporary critics found the rhapsody "monotonous."[3] But the more unified style reflects Bartók's decision to break with the technique and musical ideal of *Kossuth*. Disenchanted with the narrative aspect of Strauss's music, he also rejected literary inspiration as the governing principle behind the form. Characteristically, Bartók regarded the Marche funèbre as the only section worth publishing from *Kossuth*, since it had no story attached to it but continued a traditional type. He experimented for several years to discover how he might continue a Hungarian tradition: rather than rework romantic style, he changed the underlying structural ideas of art music as a whole.

COHERENCE AND FOLK STYLE

In the encounter with folk music Bartók uncovered unusual tonal and rhythmic structures, such as modal scales, pentatonicism, rubato rhythm, and rhythmic ostinato. However, the first, and perhaps most important, lesson of peasant music had less to do with melody, tone, rhythm, and other technical elements than with a general concept of musical expression: folk music was disciplined, simple, and restrained musical discourse. The terse, sometimes even painful concentration of feelings that Bartók sensed in the peasant performance gave him the impulse for a new relation between musical structure and its expressive content:

> According to the way I feel, a genuine peasant melody of our land is a musical example of perfected art. I consider it quite as much a masterpiece, for instance, in miniature, as a Bach fugue or a Mozart sonata movement is a masterpiece in larger form. A melody of this kind is a classic example of the expression of a musical thought in its most conceivably concise form, with the avoidance of all that is superfluous. It is true that this pitiless terseness, as well as the unfamiliar mode of expression of these melodies, results in their not appealing to the average musician or music lover. . . . In a peasant melody . . . all that is incidental is entirely missing—we have only what is fundamentally essential. . . . So, above all, from this music we have learned how best to employ terseness of expression, the utmost excision of all that is non-essential—and it was this very thing, after the excessive grandiloquence of the Romantic Period, which we thirsted to learn.[4]

But the point was to blend these two influences—an artistic model of terse form on the one hand and concrete structural discoveries on the other—into a modern style. The discovery of folk music did not resolve the problem of style, it deepened it.

The *Fourteen Bagatelles* illustrate the achievements and also the compositional problems of the years that followed the encounter with folk music. If Bartók sought to create pieces that were concentrated, coherent, and original, the *Bagatelles* answered this demand. He painstakingly avoided any conventional type, unless he could display it as a "neoclassical" stylization. Almost all pieces contained a compositional idea that was strikingly modern at the time; some of these reappeared in later works. Bartók shaped several pieces as if to depict an organic development: the evolution of a rhythmic or tonal idea defines the formal process.[5]

The cost of this uncompromising modernity and coherence was the fragmentation of style. Neither an abstract demand for intensity nor the newly discovered tonal and rhythmic ideas suited the actual material of folk music. A comparison of the *Bagatelles* nos. 2 and 4 (Examples 17 and 18) illustrates the difficulty. The fourth *Bagatelle* is a folk-song arrangement with a harmonic accompaniment that is modern only inasmuch as it uses modal harmonic progressions. The second exemplifies the opposite direction. The ostinato and some of the rhythmic patterns may reflect Hungarian swineherd songs (*kolomeika*): the pattern ♫ ♫♫ | ♩ is its metrically displaced form, and the pattern ♩ ♫ ♫♫ is its inversion (mm. 7–8, 11–12). But nothing in the intervallic progressions, the tonal design, or the melodic development resembles folk song, and furthermore, the piece has a somewhat sarcastic tone—hardly the character that Bartók associated with folk music.

These pieces represent the split between a somewhat conservative musical framework using actual folk music on the one hand and modern tonal and rhythmic ideas mostly without folk material on the other. Several of the *Bagatelles* were conceived as a sort of musical free-association on the basis of an isolated melodic, rhythmic, or formal element of folk song. Experimenting with one single musical idea—a different idea in each piece—allowed for hitherto unknown solutions and a remarkable variety of stylistic inventions. But Bartók had not yet found a governing force to bring these diverse ideas together into a coherent large-scale form. He imagined a style in which the isolated folk elements were recombined to function differently than in folk music while keeping something of its spirit—the technique of his mature composition. In spite of significant achievements, the compositions of the following years still fall short of a real stylistic synthesis. The last movement of the First String Quartet indicates Bartók's frustration with this problem. In this movement, a pseudo-folk song appears, interrupting the musical process as if holding it up against the rest of the musical material as an ideal object.

The split would not be worth considering had Bartók arrived at his personal modern style without elements of folk music. But the idea of achieving modernity and coherence by integrating folk music—an idea hardly relevant to any other composer of the twentieth century—was an absolute demand for Bartók. To separate the issue of modernity from that of Hungarianness would mean to fall back on the use of national material as an exotic color. This

EXAMPLE 17. *Fourteen Bagatelles*, no. 4. (Béla Bartók, *14 bagatell zongorára* [Budapest: Editio Musica, 1969])

EXAMPLE 18. *Fourteen Bagatelles*, no. 2. (Béla Bartók, *14 bagatell zongorára* [Budapest: Editio Musica, 1969])

decision contradicted his ideal of national style and precluded coherence as well. If, as Bartók believed, coherence in art meant that the piece grew organically and spontaneously from the mind of the composer, then folk music could be part of a coherent artwork only if the subconscious resources of the composer's mind had absorbed it. For Bartók, a modern and personal style was inevitably a style derived from folk music. The more his style developed, the deeper and more constant became the relations among the typically Bartókian and folk-derived elements of his music—indeed the two became one and the same thing.

VOICES FOR JUDITH AND BLUEBEARD

At the turn of the century, opera had general esteem as the most representative work of a composer and of national style—it was the musical repertoire's best candidate to express nationalism. To compose a dramatic piece for stage was among the highest aspirations of those composers who hoped to establish themselves as national composers. Yet Bartók, planning to create an art that was specifically Hungarian and true to modern life but free from the conventions of political nationalism, had no model to rely on. He needed to reinvent the genre of national opera in Hungary.

Balázs's text was so unlike anything Bartók might encounter in the operatic repertoire (though it had points of similarity to Debussy's *Pelléas et Mélisande*) that it called for unique solutions. Perhaps the exceptional demands themselves inspired Bartók, giving him a free hand in creating a large-scale work in a radically new style, something that he could not yet achieve within the constraints of more traditional genres. In *Bluebeard's Castle* we find a certain freedom in the flow of the music. There is an exuberance of ideas: many that are unique to the piece and all the basic elements of his later style (without the rigorous and concentrated treatment that we see in most of Bartók's work composed after the second half of the 1920s).

Bartók's stylistic inventions in *Bluebeard's Castle* fall roughly into two categories. The orchestral music is essentially a large-scale one-movement symphonic form that creates the stylistic synthesis similar to Bartók's later music. The vocal style, however, had no continuation either in the pieces of Bartók or others, even though this invention was no less original and was, in fact, the only attempt to create a modern Hungarian vocal style.

Whereas he based the orchestral material on a generic Hungarian instrumental type (the slow *verbunkos*/pastorale—as we will see later), he drew the style of the vocal parts from a specific type found only in vocal music and in the peasant tradition, namely the old-style peasant songs. With the idea of modeling the vocal parts on a traditional vocal style and the orchestral parts on a traditional instrumental style, Bartók imposed on himself a compositional constraint that would characterize his attitude for the rest of his life. He would derive new structures from elements of traditional styles by extending their original functions. The goal was to draw into the work as many musical traditions as possible—not randomly, but by realizing hidden potentialities of and similarities among conventional styles.

Bartók's choice to derive the vocal lines from the old-style folk songs, and the material of the orchestra from the type of the Hungarian instrumental pastorale, solved in one stroke the problem of national music and the problem of modernity in opera. The choice of the Hungarian pastorale for the orchestral material was a logical solution that nevertheless allowed him to create a new type of dramatic music. Transforming the pastorale from a light intermezzo-like movement to a dramatic form, thus pulling it to the center from its peripheral place in the repertoire, allowed Bartók to break with the romantic tradition in several respects. First, he was positing a novel view of nationalism, opposing the convention that Hungarianness equaled heroism. Second, the emphasis on the pastorale meant the assertion of the primacy of lyricism, even in dramatic form, over the narrative approach. The idea of expressing drama through lyricism paralleled the modernist trend of Hungarian literature and reflected the philosophical and aesthetic attempt to condense all the related and contrasting things of the world into simple images that were at once personal and universal. Similarly, the singing style Bartók created was a sort of Hungarian recitative and thus perfectly logical in opera but was so different from any traditional operatic style that its use challenged operatic conventions.

Traditionally, much of the dramatic energy in opera derived from the flexibility of vocal styles. It allowed the composer to contrast various singing types, often making the vocal lines similar to instrumental melodies. Bartók's plan, however, sharply separated the music of the actors onstage from the music of the orchestra; furthermore, it restricted the expressive potential of the singers. The performing style of the Hungarian old-style songs is rather uniform and not really dramatic. Although transformed for the sake of dramatic expression, the vocal parts still strike us as stylized folk singing with simple, sometimes almost primitive, melodies and rhythms. This stylization leaves little space for traditional opera's virtuosic display.

In fact, depriving the vocal lines of their potential for operatic virtuosity and limiting their interaction with the orchestra reflect the dramatic idea that

Balázs was particularly attached to and that evidently was meaningful to Bartók as well. If, fundamentally, the function of language is to name—to raise up a representation or point it out as though with a finger—the speech, music, and action of the characters function perfectly, their role being language.[6] Rather than compete with the melodic sophistication and variety of the orchestral material, the vocal lines give this material sharper meaning both musically (clarifying or expanding tonality, marking structural dividing points) and texturally (interpreting with key sentences the themes of the orchestra or the visual images). This role corresponded to Balázs's idea that "words can tell little of what should be said—but it is precisely for this reason that words mean more than they actually say."[7] The separation of orchestral and vocal styles became the musical metaphor for the contrast between the ambiguous world of the soul and its expression in words.

Bartók's choice of Hungarian old-style songs as the model for the vocal parts created an insurmountable problem that helps explain the opera's relative neglect outside Hungary. What Bartók envisioned here was a revolutionary new style of operatic singing dependent on the knowledge of Hungarian accentuation. The inspiration came from his analysis of the so-called parlando-rubato performance of the Hungarian old-style songs. For Bartók and Kodály, the term "parlando-rubato" was not simply a performing instruction calling for some kind of speechlike performance, but a specific performing style that they believed to be inherent to the oldest stratum of Hungarian folk music. It was this style that Bartók hoped to transfer, obviously with substantial modifications, to opera.

In order to understand how Bartók imagined the performance of the vocal parts, we need to consider his approach to the performance of peasant music. The conceptualization and notation of rubato raised the same question in both cases: the relation between the constant enduring essence of a melodic line and its actual individual performance. It was necessary to decide what constituted the "melodic-rhythmic essence" of the piece in order to determine the level of precision with which the details of the performance were to be notated. As an ethnomusicologist, Bartók encountered the common and the unique together in any individual performance of a song; he had to separate the piece's typical features from its personal and/or improvisatory aspects. The performance represented three different things: the immediate musical object that came to life there and then; the piece that existed in the mind of the singer as an abstraction and always came out in performance somewhat differently; and the variant of a general idea of the song, a type that was part of a collective tradition. Bartók attempted to separate these layers, at least in principle, and hoped to find the essence of the song (type) that was worth being notated. During his field trips, he notated only the core melodic line, as in Figure 11 (second staff).[8] This notational practice indicates that an analytical approach colored his aural experience even at the first encounter: as he was listening to the complex, perhaps richly ornamented melodic line, he immediately conceptualized it as a melodic-rhythmic scheme.

This manner of notation, used in the early ethnomusicological publications of both Bartók and Kodály, served as the model for the notation of the vocal parts in *Bluebeard's Castle*. The meaning of this notation becomes evident if we compare Bartók's different transcriptions of the same folk song (Example 19). Its first published notation is almost identical with the spontaneous notation Bartók made on the spot, except that it is transposed and the bar lines are placed differently (see Example 19a).[9] The theoretical basis for publishing such minimal notation was the assumption that only the melodic-rhythmic type was worth preserving in writing, since the subtleties of ornaments and rhythm were incidental additions of the singer.

In the later publications, however, he notated rhythm and ornamentation with meticulous precision—a difference that reflects the change in Bartók's conceptualization of rubato (see Example 19b).[10] He came to this new view sometime after 1908. He based the evolutionary chain of folk rhythms in his *Hungarian Folk Song* (1924) on this concept, already taking it for granted.[11] As early as 1911, Bartók suggested that the categories of "rubato" and "metric" were only theoretical constructs, and in 1918 he concluded: "The style of performance is always parlando, poco rubato. Single notes are often diminished or augmented by rational, or still more often, by irrational values. . . . The augmentations, especially those of a rational value, are constant at certain tones of the melody . . . and are to be considered as a hardened rubato."[12] Here Bartók conceived of rubato less in terms of the singer's freedom in executing rhythm than as a specific performing and rhythmic style that is expressed within the framework of fixed rhythms. "Hardened rubato" meant metric rhythm that was not subject to substantial change in performance but still gave the impression of rubato—supposedly because of the irregular rhythmic formations and a certain subtle rubato quality of the performing style.[13]

Balázs's verse is identical in form to the old-style eight-syllable folk songs, one of the most ancient and typical forms of Hungarian folk poetry. Bartók's notation of the melodies for this text, like his earlier notation of old-style folk songs, indicates that he wished them to be performed in a manner similar to the parlando-rubato performance of these songs. However, Bartók probably wanted this rubato to manifest itself only in very subtle modifications of the

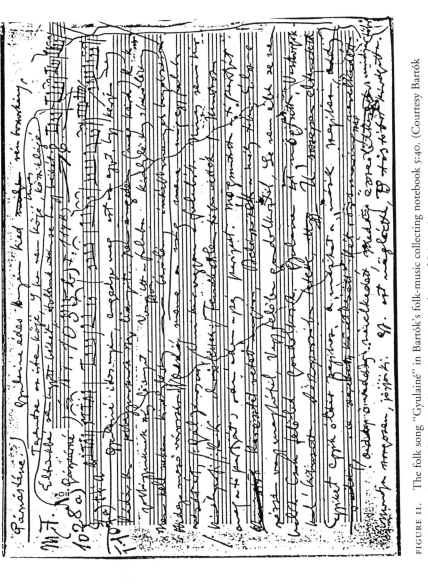

FIGURE 11. The folk song "Gyulainé" in Bartók's folk-music collecting notebook 5:40. (Courtesy Bartók Archive, Institute for Musicology, Hungarian Academy of Sciences)

EXAMPLE 19. Bartók's notation of the song "Gyulainé" in publications from 1908 and 1933.

a.

b.

rhythm, essentially in the speechlike quality of the singing, without substantial change to the notated rhythms. What mattered was that the singers feel comfortable and thus follow their natural inclinations in articulating the phrases. Bartók's ideal was most likely an effortless, speech-centered singing, similar in spirit to what he had heard among the peasants and later attempted to recreate in his folk-song arrangements.[14] The composer was remarkably tolerant in answering the needs of singers who performed this piece: in order to accommodate them, he often changed the vocal lines significantly, thus modifying the tonal structure of certain passages. The performance of *Bluebeard's Castle* demanded the close collaboration of composer and imaginative singers who, on the basis of their feel for the Hungarian language, could recreate a vocal character that defied exact notation. (The absence of such creative collaboration after Bartók's death in 1945 helps us understand why the work did not pave the way toward a new Hungarian operatic style.)

A performance that executed vocal lines without speechlike rubato, as a series of even eighth notes—as they are notated—would destroy Bartók's idea of separating the vocal and instrumental spheres of the opera through different performing styles. In a number of cases that minimal difference of rhythmic execution creates the dramatic tension. For instance, when Judith looks around the dark castle, her melody has the same rhythm as the uniform eighth notes of the orchestral ostinato (see Example 30, no. 9, on p. 259). The same rhythms superposed on each other but executed in somewhat different manner (evenly by the strings, and with slight rubato by Judith) give the musical metaphor for the dramatic situation of that scene: Judith's voice translates into the language of emotions the motionless, dark sight of the castle represented by the ostinato background.

With too much rubato, however, a performance of lines notated with even-note values would similarly contradict Bartók's idea. In the dialogues of Bluebeard and Judith, melodic lines moving in undifferentiated, even eighth notes represent their relatively neutral voice; they signal their emotional closedness or their motion to close themselves up. By writing out rhythmic modifications of the basic pattern in the score, Bartók also indicated an emotional, warm singing style for both Judith and Bluebeard. For Judith, he intensified the rubato aspect of the melody and ornaments with slight elongations or shortenings of the even eighth-note rhythms. At moments of emotional outburst, such minor rhythmic changes give way to precise rhythms, often to sharp dotted-rhythm patterns that make her singing sound like harsh exclamations. Unlike the folk character of Judith's emotional singing style, Bluebeard's warm voice is represented by waltzlike triple-meter rhythmic patterns. The waltz, an important musical type at the turn of the century, had a specific connotation for Bartók; it evoked the feeling of passionate love, sensual and perhaps even decadent.

These differences in the manner of singing become especially transparent in the confrontation between the characters. For most of the opera, both Judith and Bluebeard remain within the framework of the rubato of old-style songs, which means, symbolically speaking, that they are ultimately part of the same musical world. Within this framework, Bartók maximizes the contrast between more neutral and more emotional singing styles. Typically, the characters move in opposite directions: if Judith's voice becomes more emotional, Bluebeard's retreats into neutrality, and when Bluebeard opens up, Judith confronts him in a cold voice.

An example of this technique appears in the section when Judith tries to orient herself in the darkness, after the outer door of the castle has been closed.

Under the weight of her first impressions, she can only echo the voice of the castle: her lines add nothing tonally or rhythmically essential to the background ostinato (see Example 30, no. 9). At the text "Ki ezt látna, jaj, nem szólna, suttogó hír elhalkulna," whose exact English translation is "Whoever would see this would not be able to speak of it, whispering rumors would fade away" (see Example 31, p. 262), she "comes forward": her melodic lines become warmer and more passionate (poco espressivo). The larger intervallic movements and emphatic ornaments lend her voice an emotional quality suggesting the dramatic presentation of a ballad (which her text in fact alludes to). At her next phrase, Judith's melody opens up the framework of the ostinato, by adding the note A (no. 10 m. 8), which eventually leads the music toward a new tonality. In her next line the pentatonic melody is replaced by wide, descending motives leading to an emotional climax: "Your castle is weeping! Your castle is weeping!" (Sír a várad! Sír a várad!; no. 11 mm. 5–8; unfortunately, the English libretto translation is "Walls and rafters, all are weeping").[15] These melodic changes are paralleled by the gradual transformation of the even eighth-note rhythm into an emphatic dotted-rhythm pattern.

The more emotional Judith becomes, the sharper the contrast between her voice and that of Bluebeard. As long as she restricts herself to echoing the ostinato of the castle, Bluebeard remains in the background, only repeating Judith's key words (see last measure of Example 30). Once she moves toward more expressive singing, Bluebeard's role changes: he repeatedly interrupts, trying to pull her back to the level of simple rubato. The ostinato halts when he speaks, the tempo slows down, and there is a return to a dry and unemotional flow of even eighth notes (see Example 31: Molto adagio at n. 10 m. 5: "Hírt hallottál?"; and Molto andante at no. 11 m. 9: "Ugye Judit").

As the opera unfolds, the roles of Bluebeard and Judith change. The pivotal point is the fifth chamber, whose door opens to Bluebeard's kingdom, almost blinding Judith ("Dazzled by the radiance, Judith shields her eyes with her hands"). Bluebeard's voice, "quasi parlando ma sempre grave," yields to Judith's unaccompanied soft lines of even eighth notes, "senza espressione" (see Example 43, pp. 282–83). On the following pages, Bluebeard's waltzlike singing contrasts with Judith's even eighth-note lines (Example 20). Just as the halt of the ostinato in the previous example represents the idea that Bluebeard's questions are really interruptions opposing Judith's emotions, here too the musical structure makes apparent the opposition between Bluebeard's and Judith's emotional states. Judith's uniform duple meter clashes with Bluebeard's waltz: she superposes four quarter groups on Bluebeard's music in ¾ meter (a rhyth-

EXAMPLE 20. The dialogue of Bluebeard and Judith during the fifth door scene.

mic modification of the waltz; a similar rhythmic clash occurs a few measures later at no. 83 m. 5).

This plan of rhythmic contrast, which is consistent throughout the opera, translates Balázs's poetic idea that the confrontations of the characters onstage should play out the soul's opposing desires. Judith and Bluebeard are not so different, in that both have emotional and neutral voices. Yet the motion of one toward warmth always meets coldness on the part of the other. The constant tension (or balance) between these behaviors symbolizes the opposition between the belief that love can bring happiness and the awareness that complete happiness is not possible, that it is self-deception. But the deeper meaning of this rhythmic contrast emerges in the context of the symbolism expressed by the orchestral material.

SOURCES OF THE ORCHESTRAL
MATERIAL: *VERBUNKOS* AND PASTORALE

Bartók's turn to the pastorale tradition as the model for new Hungarian style was a logical choice. At the turn of the century, pieces entitled Divertimento, Serenade, or Pastorale accounted for a large proportion of the compositions in the national style. The tradition continued throughout the first half of the twentieth century and even after the Second World War; virtually all the members of the generation active in the 1950s and 1960s composed serenades at some point in their careers.[16] Kodály's first works in the modern style, such as the Adagio for violin and piano (1905) and the *Summer Night* (Nyári este [1906]), grew out of this tradition. He returned to it in several of his later pieces, including the First String Quartet (op. 2 [1908–9]), the Sonata for Solo Cello (op. 8 [1915]), Serenade for two violins and viola (op. 12 [1919–20]), and various piano pieces and choruses (including the *Mountain Nights* [1923]). The serenade-pastorale permeates the compositional world of both Ernő Dohnányi (Serenade for violin, viola, and cello op. 10 [1902] and *Ruralia Hungarica* [1923–24]) and Leó Weiner (Third String Quartet op. 26).

"Divertimento," "serenade," and "pastorale" did not quite mean the same thing but each relied on essentially the same set of musical types, combined in varied ways in the multimovement form. What unites these various types are, first, a common emphasis on lyricism over the expression of energy and dynamism and, second, a tendency toward stylization and archaization of Hungarian and other historical musics. Dohnányi's Serenade op. 10, as well as Weiner's Third String Quartet op. 26, is composed of a series of stylized movements based on types of baroque, classical, and romantic music (Marcia, Romanza, Scherzo, Tema con variazioni, and Rondo in the case of Dohnányi; and Pastorale, Phantasie, and Fugue in the case of Weiner). When Bartók revitalized the pastorale, he often stylized historical types for the sake of dramatic expression, as in the Divertimento for string orchestra and the grotesquely exaggerated conventional types in the Sixth String Quartet.

The continuous revitalization of the pastorale during the twentieth century appears inevitable if we consider that it connected three Hungarian modernist desires: an emphasis on Hungarianness, the stylization of old forms, and lyricism. At the turn of the century, however, modernists considered nothing less logical than dramatizing the types of this tradition, at least not to the extent of making them the main vehicle for a composer's expressive voice. In this respect, Bartók's solution was unique, even though Kodály moved toward that direction as well.[17]

The suggestion that Hungarian instrumental tradition gave Bartók significant techniques for his new style clashes with what Bartók himself claimed and what had been the consensus about his development so far. After his first encounter with the old-style peasant songs, Bartók turned against Hungarian instrumental styles, whether from the art or the folk music tradition. His attack was directed most emphatically against gypsy music, which he criticized with the enthusiasm typical of a new convert. Bartók's sharp separation of "folk" and "gypsy style" was not entirely without meaning—at least within the paradigm he created for himself. When Bartók spoke of "real Hungarian peasant music" he meant primarily a vocal repertoire unique to the peasants. What he called "gypsy music" was a more or less distinct urban popular instrumental style performed mostly by Gypsies and commonly associated with them.

In the performance of slow pieces by the restaurant gypsy band, a particular performing practice had developed that relied heavily on rubato, ornamentation, tempo changes, and display of virtuosity. While the general public held up this rhapsodic rubato style as the most representative music of the Hungarians, Bartók rejected it: "[The Gypsies] transformed [all the] melodies to some parlando-rubato, their excessive rubato playing crowded with overflowing and exuberant embellishments to the point where the songs became unrecognizable."[18]

But the urban gypsy style was not an isolated phenomenon within Hungarian musical traditions. In one form or another, elements of gypsy music figured in the style of *verbunkos* and romantic art music as well. Nor was the rhapsodic rubato style unique to the gypsy performance. This performing tradition derived from a structure common to a type of Hungarian instrumental music that I call here "slow *verbunkos*." It existed in the most varied contexts of folk, popular, and art music during various eras. As examples from an early-nineteenth-century and a modern folk source (Examples 21 and 22) show us, there were substantial differences in its performance. But the overall form remained the same in all subtypes: a uniform slow motion in the background (repetitive rhythmic pattern or sustained chords) gave the harmony, and a solo instrument (in the gypsy tradition, typically the violin or the clarinet) played the melody, often based on a strophic song, freely with many ornaments.

In an exuberant performance, the ornamentation could reach the point where the piece as a self-contained and coherent entity fell apart, a phenomenon probably well known throughout the nineteenth century; it inspired Liszt to conceive his rhapsodies. Examples 23 and 24 contain a popular song in the style of the nineteenth-century *magyar nóta* and its elaboration by a Gypsy clarinetist, Sándor Burka, as he played it in 1979 in a Budapest restaurant. Al-

though they are modern examples, they are unlikely to differ substantially from the style that was widespread since the latter part of the nineteenth century. Burka's approach to ornamentation is strikingly different from what is usual in Western music: he does not simply ornament the melody but replaces some parts of it entirely. Let us consider, for instance, the rendition of the second line of the song (measures 3–4 of the song = lines 3–4 of the transcription). First there is an embellished statement of the first note as if it were an anticipation, then the first six notes are played, melodically and rhythmically modified and, on the whole, faster than usual when the piece is sung—as if this were yet again an anticipation. The figuration beginning at this point seems to be, at first, the ornamental elongation of the seventh note of the melodic line (D). But as it continues, we gradually lose this functional connection; the virtuoso passage no longer impresses us as ornaments around a note but as a statement in its own right. We realize only retrospectively that this figuration replaces the rest of the melodic line. The rhythmic outline disappears, and the only signal for the end of the melody is a dotted-rhythm pattern (♪♪.), replacing the original cadential formula (♪♩. ♩) and standing on its own detached from the passages that precede it.

The effect of such a performance is by no means as fragmented as it seems to be on paper. The audience recognizes the melody, or at least its highly stereotypical structure, and the conventions of the performance suggest its shape.

EXAMPLE 22. *Lassú* [Slow], played by the Ferenczi ensemble of Szék. (László Lajtha, *Széki gyűjtés* [Budapest: Zeneműkiadó, 1954], 87)

Nevertheless, its exaggeration blurs the formal function of ornamental patterns. Most parts of the melody may be replaced by ornaments, and those ornaments may or may not indicate the melody, the rhythm, or the formal function of the section it replaced.

Perhaps what interested Bartók in this performing style was that it isolated elements of melody and rhythm, to make them stand on their own. As a logical extension of this technique, a composer could detach and recombine elements clearly belonging to a certain musical entity, to form unusual structures.

Although Bartók did not fully explore the consequences of this technique before the composition of *Bluebeard's Castle*, he recognized some of its potential several years earlier and used it to make the slow *verbunkos* type more dramatic. In the second movement of the Suite no. 1, for orchestra, he isolated three traditional elements of the slow *verbunkos*—the scalar upbeat that normally introduces the melody, the chordal accompaniment, and the ornamental melody—and played them off against one another (Example 25). He changed the scalar upbeat into an unfinished, expressive upward gesture. The neutral, continuous chordal accompaniment became forte pizzicato chords, responding to the violins' gesture with what sound like heartbeats. And he dramatized the melody: instead of an ornamented song, a short circular motive became a painful outcry on the English horn.

RHYTHMIC VARIATION IN THE NEW DRAMATIC STYLE

The lyrical and emotional tone of the orchestral music of *Bluebeard's Castle* may strike us as somewhat romantic. Yet its essential tonal, rhythmic, and for-

EXAMPLE 24. Gypsy performance of the same song. (Bálint Sárosi, *Folk Music: Hungarian Musical Idiom* [Budapest: Corvina, 1986], 56)

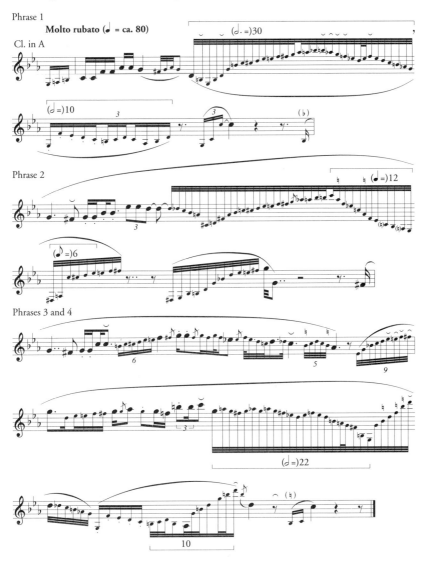

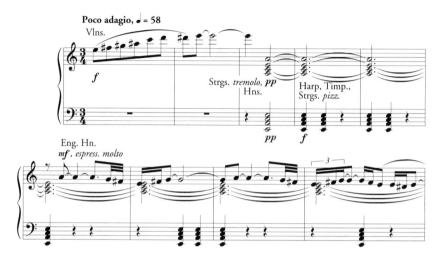

mal ideas show it to be a radical step away from classical and romantic music. It is important to emphasize this shift because Bartók did blend classical elements into his conception of dramatic form, although the underlying principles of his dramatism would seem to preclude such a synthesis. In classical music, dramatic motion derived from the contrast between conventional and unusual musical passages. Conventional patterns—"filling," as Charles Rosen calls them—prepared, contrasted, or enhanced the dramatic moment. Some late romantic music, like some of Bartók's previous compositions, departed from this concept. But in *Bluebeard's Castle* Bartók reenvisioned dramatic form in a manner entirely new to him and to his time. He attempted to create a music that is thematic throughout, thereby eliminating the notions of background, accompaniment, or "filling." His quasi-monothematism called for new solutions for most traditional principles of form, such as recapitulation, development, and thematic contrast.

The new style kept many features of the common symphonic and/or operatic tradition, such as symmetrical phrase structures for themes, gradual decomposition and intensification of motives in developmental sections, and sustained chords or static background movement accompanying recitative-like passages. The novelty involved two aspects of the musical style: tonal relationships on the one hand, and a variational system that ensures motivic and thematic coherence on the other. Since Lendvai's pathbreaking work, there has been extensive analysis of the Bartókian tonal system.[19] But the second innovation, no less significant for his modern style, has almost entirely escaped the attention of scholars.

Bartók faced three central problems in the composition of the orchestral material of the opera. How would he create a form to reconcile the threefold demand of expressing individual feelings, the "original facts," and Hungarianness; a form at once representational (corresponding to the text and dramatic action) and expressive; and a form of utmost contrast (corresponding to the needs of drama) and stylistic unity? Bartók cut the Gordian knot when he realized that the use of extremely minimal motives as a base for the thematic material would allow him to vary and combine the motives into an infinite number of themes and make infinite connections among them. As we shall see, this structural approach was necessary also for dramatic reasons: the complex symbolism of the piece needed music in which each element related to every other.

Bartók based this musical symbolism on a variational technique in which the smallest alteration in the form of the motive might change its meaning entirely. In some cases, motives transform themselves into one another gradually and logically, in a linear fashion—a technique Bartók could have learned from Wagner and even from classical music. More typically, however, the connection between subsequent themes is not at all evident. Different rhythmic and tonal structures contrast and overlap each other, their connection being apparent only when the listener considers all the variants of the original motive and reconstructs, theoretically, the chain of transformation. In the music, the subsequent steps of this process may appear several minutes apart or at entirely different points in the opera. In the meantime the dramatic action has moved forward, thus the varied theme acquires a new context to represent something radically different, leaving the thematic connection hidden.

In the ornamental style of *verbunkos* Bartók found the inspiration to make a system of rhythmic thematic transformations that refer back to the most elementary fragment of music, the single note. The technique distinguishes the "main note" (a long and/or melodically significant note of the melody) from notes that are "ornamental" (shorter and melodically less significant). However, through some change of emphasis or of phrasing, ornamental notes may become main notes and vice versa—thus we have an endless series of thematic variants. The connections between themes form a chain of rhythmic variations that move in a circle, taking a main melodic note as the point of departure, turning it into new motives by way of ornamentation, and then transforming these motives back into a single note (Example 26). Any main note of a

EXAMPLE 26.   The chain of *verbunkos*-derived rhythmic variations.

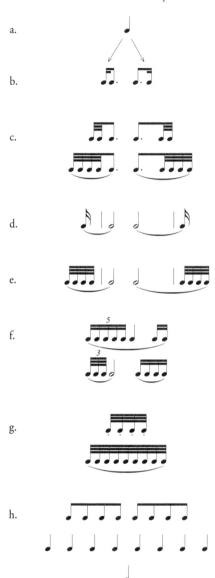

melodic progression (Example 26a) can develop into several rhythmic patterns: various dotted-rhythm note pairs (b), dotted rhythm dissolved in ornamentation (c), unaccented preceding or following grace note (d), or unaccented ornaments (e)—all heard as variants of the given note. With metric displacement, the patterns based on dotted rhythm and on ornaments can turn into each other—(b) turning into (d) and (c) into (e). These dotted-rhythm and ornamental figures can be combined into various complex ornamental motives (f); the ornaments, then, separate from the long note to appear as motives in their own right (g). Finally, ornaments can slow down to become a series of main notes of a melody, any note of which can serve as the starting point of a new series of variations (h = a).

This technique gave Bartók a musical metaphor with which he could simultaneously represent dramatic motion and superpose a symbolic interpretation on this representation. One theme, invested with a particular symbolism, changes into a different theme with potentially different, even contrasting symbolism. Thus the music simultaneously clarifies the dramatic events and—by means of thematic connections—superposes on such an interpretation several, possibly contradictory layers of symbolic meaning.

DRAMATIC DESIGN AND SYMBOLISM

An analysis of key moments from the first scene up to the opening of the first door (from beginning to no. 30) shows us this dramatic design at work. The opera opens with two contrasting themes (Example 27). They are the themes of the castle and of night: we hear them while "the stage is in total darkness." The music emerges as if from far away, from the background—the narrator is reciting the end of the prologue.[20] The two themes differ in tonality, rhythm, harmonization, dynamics, melodic style, phrase structure, orchestration. The first theme—henceforth "pentatonic theme"—played on the lower strings, is in F sharp minor pentatonic scale and resembles what Bartók often notated for himself as the "melodic essence" (the main notes) of an old-style pentatonic folk song.[21] There is no variety in the rhythm, no ornamentation, no dynamic change; the melody moves in unison throughout, the symmetry of the phrases is undisturbed until the second theme enters superposed on the last note. The second theme—henceforth "dolce-marcato theme"—is based on a two-measure thematic idea that is repeated, varied, and then dissolved into a developmental continuation. The thematic idea is itself composed of three motivic repetitions, its basis being a note pair outlining the motion from a longer

EXAMPLE 27.   The beginning of the opera: pentatonic theme and dolce-marcato theme.

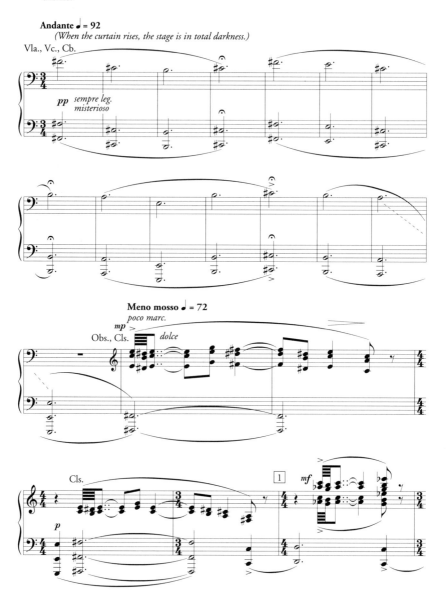

EXAMPLE 28. The motivic basis of the dolce-marcato theme.

to a shorter note (Example 28). Contrary to the empty sound of the fourth and second intervals of the first theme, this theme is based on "sweet" thirds in both the melody and harmony and performed dolce with changing dynamics. The theme uses the minor scale with augmented second—the most chromatic of the traditional scales, often associated with *verbunkos* and gypsy style (G, F sharp, E, D sharp, C; and B, A in the lower voice).[22] In fact, this theme, based on circular motion, belongs to a slow *verbunkos* thematic type that we encountered in the slow movement of the Suite no. 1 (see Example 25).

Both themes are enigmatic in their content. The first impresses the listener as something perfect, beautiful, and peaceful but also cold, abstract, and lifeless. If this is the main theme of the castle—as every interpreter thinks—then why is the spoken prologue superposed on it? The character and function of the second theme are also unclear. What are we to make of Bartók's instruction that this theme is "dolce" but also "poco marcato"? Should the mordentlike sixty-fourth-note pattern at the beginning be played as an ornament or as a sharp accent representing shuddering? The first interpretation would endow the melody with a gentle, human character; the second would make it seem more an intrusion to the calmness of the castle. The tonal symbolism is similarly ambiguous. Throughout the opera, F sharp (minor) is associated with darkness and C (major) with light. Here, however, there is a prominent statement of C tonality at the beginning of the dolce-marcato theme while the stage is still completely dark.

In a sense, the entire opera is built around these two themes. The orchestral music is the story of their metamorphoses, the story of the struggle for bringing them into connection with each other. At first they are both presented as being of the castle, of darkness, and yet of opposing characters. But continuous transformations will make this opposition yield to a complex web of thematic relationships that bring them ever closer to each other and relate all the themes of the opera to them. Thematic transformation begins immediately after the presentation of the dolce-marcato theme. Its development

EXAMPLE 29.   The opening of the outer door: gesture motive.

Meno mosso ♩ = 72

(Suddenly the small iron door at the head of the stairs is flung wide and in the dazzling white opening appear the black, silhouetted figures of Bluebeard and Judith)

leads to a new theme that depicts the opening of the outer door of the castle (Example 29).

According to the stage directions, "suddenly the small iron door at the head of the stairs is flung wide, and in the dazzling white opening appear the black silhouetted figures of Bluebeard and Judith." This design has dramatic significance. The spectators, by now used to staring into the darkness, are blinded by the dazzling light pouring from the back of the stage where they can see only the silhouettes of the main characters—the viewer of the drama experiences the same discomfort that Judith will when the light at the opening of the fifth door blinds her. Our first experience with light in this drama is unpleasant and gives us little to see. The music captures the violent motion, in the one-measure theme, by the widening of the space between upper and lower voices: the ascending motion of the higher voices is superposed on the descending motion of the lower ones. The expanding register, the crescendo, and the final dissonant sforzando chord signal passion as if it were the musical rendering of an unfinished gesture.

This motivic type—henceforth "gesture motive"—will recur throughout the opera. It usually consists of a one-measure-long (ascending and/or descending) melodic progression from one (usually longer) note to another (usually shorter) one; occasionally there is a circular or ornamental melodic movement preceding or connecting the notes. That this motivic type is intended to depict "gesture" is indicated also by instructions calling for an expressive performance (markings of crescendo, decrescendo, sforzando, espressivo, etc.). The stage directions associate such motives with a dramatically significant simple motion, such as the closing or the opening of a door, or an embrace.[23]

After the dialogue in which Bluebeard provokes Judith to express her devotion, we arrive at another key moment: the closing of the door behind the actors. It marks the end of the opera's introductory section and the beginning of what we may consider its first scene (Example 30). This scene begins with Bluebeard's embrace. The motive of the first measure, with its ornamented first note, depicts an outgoing and energetic gesture; it recurs in the second measure. In the following two measures, metric displacement and the addition of eighth notes transform this motive into its variant that further emphasize incompleteness and impatience (the ending eighth notes' function being to lead toward a continuation). These are answered by an ornamental figure (in the fifth and sixth measures) that is a stereotypical cadence of *verbunkos* and gypsy music. Dramatically speaking, this six-measure phrase incorporates the sequence of outgoing passion, impatience, and resolution—its last measure overlapping with the first measure of the phrase's varied repetition. Bartók's choice to represent Bluebeard's embrace with such dynamic music bespeaks subtle dramatic planning: embrace here is not calm resolution but the expression of passion, anxiety.

This is the first of three dramatic actions that function as introductions to the scene: Bluebeard embraces Judith, then he orders the closing of the door to the outside world, and finally Bluebeard and Judith remain in the darkness. There is tonal movement from D major (no. 7) toward a quasi Dominant–Tonic closure (C sharp–F sharp, mm. 10–11) leading back to F sharp (which proves to be a pivotal pitch toward D sharp minor pentatonic, the tonality of the first part of the following longer scene). The music shifts between emotional states rapidly, paralleling the shifts in musical and formal functions: the representation of passion expressed by the gesture theme (Sostenuto–climactic statement), through moments of suspense depicted by the reverberations of this motive as the door closes (Andante–transition), to a state of (e)motionlessness, depicted by the return of the pentatonic theme in the form of an undifferentiated eighth-note movement of the ostinato (Sostenuto–quasi recapitulation).

The three sections differ in tempo, texture, phrase structure, tonality, and technique of musical development, and they represent different types of dramatic events. The first—Bluebeard's embrace—is a gesture of the actor on-stage; the second—the closing of the door—is the motion of an object, in the spatial layout, rather far from the actors. The third is not precisely an action but the beginning of a new stage situation: the return of darkness and the hesitant motions of the actors in that darkness. As is characteristic for the entire opera, the music functions on three levels. First it represents the motions and images on the stage—indeed in such a vivid manner that it seems almost visual in the sense of program music. At the same time, this representation is the

EXAMPLE 30. The closing of the outer door.

EXAMPLE 30   *(continued)*

9

(She fumbles her way along the left wall, keeping hold of Bluebeard's hand)

Judith ***pp***

Ez   a kék-sza-kál – lú   vá –   ra!
Is this real-ly Blue-beard's cas – tle?

sempre ***pp***

Judith

Nin – csen   ab – lak?   Nin – csen   er – kély?
Why   no   win-dows?   No sweet day-light?

Bluebeard ***pp***

Nin – csen.
Nev – er.

vehicle for expressiveness. The motions and images reflected in the music are also emotions: for instance, the darkening of the stage and the music depicting this darkening create the visual and musical metaphor for an emotional state, a feeling of growing insecurity and hesitation. Finally, the motives used for such local visual and expressional representation form part of a thematic design with overarching symbolism for the drama.

At first sight, it seems surprising that Bartók represented such different events (motion of a character onstage, motion of an object, and darkness) by the same musical motive and rendered the succession of these events by a continuous process of thematic transformation. This compositional choice shows how Bartók combines static and dynamic forces, integrating what may appear to be representational music with merely local significance into the strict thematic system and symbolism of the opera. The first six-measure phrase connects several hitherto separate themes, investing them with new symbolism. The motive of the first measure relates both to the dolce and to the marcato aspects of the dolce-marcato theme of the opening: the mordent on the first note is essentially the variant notation for the sixty-fourth notes of the dolce-marcato theme, and the melodic motion connecting a note pair is reminiscent of the gesture motives (compare it to Examples 28, 29). The gesture motive, which originally developed from the dolce-marcato theme and represented the opening of the outer door, becomes here the musical symbol for both Bluebeard's embrace and the closing of the same door. In evoking Hungarian style, the ornamented *verbunkos* cadential figure is somewhat unexpected. Yet structurally, it is a logical response to this gesture: the upward motion from the ornamented F sharp to C is answered by an ornamented melody descending from B to ornamented F sharp to B. (The cadential character of this motive is evident even though its last note becomes the first note of the next motive.)

In the Andante section the subsequent statements of the gesture motive with different intervallic contents function as a transition, as if searching for the proper interval for the beginning of a theme; this interval is finally defined as the opening fourth motion of the recapitulating pentatonic theme (no. 8 mm. 4 ff.). The circle has been completed: the gesture theme, derived from the dolce-marcato theme and originally a contrast to the pentatonic theme, is transformed in a few simple steps into the beginning of the pentatonic theme itself.

Thus transformation and rearrangement of small thematic elements open up the dolce-marcato theme to a variety of new thematic types, logically connecting all the themes heard so far. In retrospect, the entire section up to this point appears to be circular, beginning with the pentatonic theme and leading back to it through variations of the dolce-marcato theme. The rhythmic design changes from an even-note theme to rhythmically more complex gesture themes, and back to the even-note motion. The pentatonic melody—the theme of the castle—returns as background to the action of the characters: the castle, which was the only "actor" at the beginning, is now the stage for the drama.

The rest of the scene, which lasts until the opening of the first door, holds only two dramatic actions: Judith's noticing the closed doors and her demand that they be opened. From the closing of the outer door until the opening of the first inner door, the stage should be as dark as possible: according to the instructions, "only bright enough for the two figures and the seven huge black doors to be just visible." The main dramatic event of this scene is merely that Judith's eyes gradually become accustomed to darkness, and she begins to see the castle. This stage situation, again, is an expressive metaphor: as we noted, in Hungarian modernist literature the act of "seeing" is a metaphor for love.

By looking and being able to see, the loving Other brings to the foreground the secrets of the soul—this poetic idea defines the developmental process of the music (see end of Example 30, and Example 31). The scene is structured by moments when, after some distractions, Judith turns her eyes again toward the castle. As she comes to see more things, new musical motives appear, evolving naturally from the preceding material, leading the listener from the complete darkness of the ostinato toward a rich texture with polyphonically interacting voices. The first time she looks at the castle anew occurs after Bluebeard's interruption, "You heard rumors?" (Hirt hallottál?; in the libretto's translation, "Do you know them?" Example 31: Molto adagio at no. 10 m. 5). The ostinato, which stopped during Bluebeard's phrase, continues as before (Judith turns her face back to the castle), but there are two new musical motives added (she begins to see objects in the darkness). It is characteristic of Bartók that he chose motives that are composed essentially of a single note (or interval) to function as the seed for development. The motive of the clarinet highlights the tonal center of the pentatonic background (first D sharp, later C sharp as the ostinato moves toward a new tonality), repeating the same note in each measure with a neighboring note's embellishment (Example 31, no. 10 mm. 6 ff.). This brings little tonal or melodic novelty. But its typical *verbunkos* ornamental upbeat, its dolce dotted rhythm, and its use of the clarinet—the typical melody instrument of gypsy ensembles—suggest that this motive may be the seed of an ornamental melody. The dotted-rhythm upbeat at its seventh repetition (one measure before no. 11) suggests its potential extension.

Superposed on this melody, woodwinds and horns intone—pianissimo and without accent—a minor second (G sharp–A), the "blood motive" (no. 11). The reiteration of the dissonant unornamented chords for three measures strikes us as a hocket-like countervoice, each chord echoing the other and the note repetitions of the clarinet, whose upbeat functions now as the introduction to the blood motive. The ornamented, lyrical clarinet melody and the dissonant blood motive, which will come to represent contrasting forces both against each other and against the motionlessness of the castle, first appear here softly, without accent and in connection with one another, growing naturally from the ostinato, as if they were objects that belonged naturally to the castle.

Judith immediately perceives and understands the meaning of these

EXAMPLE 31   *(continued)*

"objects." She intones the pitch A *before* it actually appears in the orchestra (no. 10 m. 8)—this A, superposed on the G sharp of the orchestral pentatonic ostinato, foreshadows the blood motive. And it is her voice that interprets for us the meaning of the clarinet motive, repeating it on the words "Your castle is weeping!" (Sír a várad!; no. 11 mm. 5–6).[24]

During the following section, the clarinet motive is developed and varied until it is transformed into an emphatic gesture motive that, played fortissimo, signals the first climax of the scene (Example 32: Molto vivace). The rhythmic outline reminds us of the clarinet motive, with the beginning long note extended for three measures. At no. 18 the motive is transformed into a four-note descending pattern with the addition of two eighth notes at the beginning, emphasizing the urgency and energy of the "gesture." A few measures later, with the bass moving from C sharp to B natural, the retransition to the ostinato begins. This extended moment of climax is captured by harmonic stagnation: the C sharp organ point lasts ten measures.

The passage offers Judith's answer to Bluebeard's question "Why did you come to me, Judith?," a question that demands the reply "Because I love you." But this is not how Judith answers. Her reply is a long tirade listing all the things that she would like to do in order to make the castle brighter and happier. Her central theme is light: "Your castle will not be dark, we together will open the walls" (Nem lesz sötét . . .). These words sum up the clash between the opposing forces in Judith's love: she will bring light into the castle even at the expense of destroying its walls.

That Judith's aggressivity in insisting on her role of changing things in the castle appears to Bartók as an act of passionate love is obvious from both the thematic and the harmonic designs. The harmonic basis for these ten measures is a minor chord with raised seventh note: C sharp–E–G sharp–B sharp.[25] In a letter to Stefi Geyer, Bartók spoke about how love made him sensitive to deep feelings (a state of mind that, as he wrote, was "exactly what is needed" for composition and that could only be poured out into music). He notated for Geyer the piece he composed at the inspiration of this feeling and marked a motive composed of the same notes as the chordal accompaniment to this section as being her leitmotiv (C sharp–E–G sharp–B sharp).[26] This chord connects two tonal centers, bringing them into relationship with the F sharp tonality of the castle: C sharp is its dominant, and the pitch C, the symbol of light, is its polar opposite on the same axis (a tritone apart on the minor third axis of F sharp–A–C–E flat). It is significant that the notes C–D–E, emphasizing C tonality—the symbol of light—appear in Judith's part.

This design exemplifies the dual function of Bartók's musical symbolism

EXAMPLE 32.   The first climax of the first scene.

both to clarify the meaning of a dramatic moment and to contradict this clarification by superposing on it a complex web of multiple associations. In Bartók's opera, light is a positive symbol associated with positive tonal direction (toward C major), and yet Judith's light is not the symbol of resolution and happiness. She speaks of light on a passionate and exalted tone (fast tempo, fortissimo, high register), her voice being superposed on the chromatic gesture-motive and the sustained augmented minor seventh chord. This passion belongs to both Judith and Bluebeard; it belongs to the castle, to love itself. The most straightforward interpretation would be, of course, to regard it as the representation of Judith's passion, since we see her expressing feelings, whereas Bluebeard stands silent and supposedly motionless on the stage. But we cannot forget that the thematic elements of the orchestral accompaniment derive from the clarinet motive of the castle and are reminiscent of Bluebeard's embrace motive, and also that Bartók regarded this chord as the musical symbol of (his own) love toward a woman.

Bluebeard's laconic response, "My castle is not bright" (Nem tündököl az én váram), is a natural reaction to Judith's outburst (Example 33). Her percep-

EXAMPLE 33.   The section following the first climax of the first scene.

tive vision of the castle and willingness to brighten it obviously provoke resistance; Bluebeard protects his solitude. It is paradoxical that Bluebeard insists on the darkness of the castle even though he knows that, in fact, his castle is bright and seems dark only because the doors are closed. Yet his statement brings forth a more melodic and ornamental variant of the clarinet melody (now played by the English horn at Ancora più tranquillo). Both the pentatonic accompaniment and the melody emphasize C-major sonority (with the G sharp—raised fifth—to make it even brighter); a few measures later, C becomes the organ point of what is the lengthy cadence to this dramatic dialogue (no. 20 mm. 7 ff.). Songlike melody, dolce character, and C tonality are all symbols of tenderness and/or light. Perhaps the mere presence of Judith is enough to brighten the castle, or perhaps she can foresee the light behind the doors. Or perhaps it is Bluebeard who, although insisting on the darkness of his castle, thinks secretly of the light that will penetrate its halls. Whatever interpretation we choose, the direction of the drama is evident: as Bluebeard and Judith spend time together in the castle, they move toward light from darkness—even without their opening the doors.

The most significant formal division of this scene occurs when the motive that represented Judith's passion at the previous climax changes into one that renders her hammering on the door as she demands that it be opened (Example 34; compare the motive [a] to the one in Example 32, no. 18). The musical motive that represented her gesture of passionate love becomes the motive of "hammering" by the transformation of the rhythm: first, the motive is metrically displaced (b), and then the eighth notes are collapsed into two sixteenth notes representing the resonating sound of her beats (c). The orchestra stops playing as this sound is "answered by a cavernous sighing, as when the night wind sighs down endless gloomy labyrinths." Such a halt in the musical process would normally announce either the entry of a contrasting new theme or the recapitulation.

What follows is a musical solution that meets the demands of three formal functions projected into one melody, a melody that is simultaneously new theme, culmination of the preceding thematic transformations, and recapitulation (Example 35). The theme intoned on the clarinet—henceforth "lament theme"—is a slow-moving, florid melody whose long notes are encircled by shorter ornamental notes. This theme—its sudden lyricism, gentleness, the sadness and beauty of its fluid ornaments—is one of the most moving moments of the opera. The melodic type comes from the Hungarian tradition and is associated with a weeping, lamenting mood—the type I called slow *verbunkos* (see Example 22). After Bluebeard's interruption "Are you afraid?"

EXAMPLE 34.   The transformation of Judith's gesture motive into the motive of hammering on the first door.

EXAMPLE 35.   The lament theme.

(continued)

EXAMPLE 35 *(continued)*

EXAMPLE 36. The ornamental continuation of the lament theme.

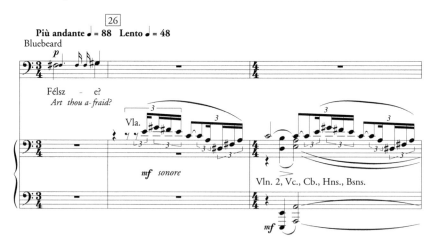

(Félsz-e?), the theme continues on the viola (Example 36), transformed into a flow of exuberant ornaments that follow on one another without direction, encircling merely the sustained C note that defines the tonality until the end of this scene.

As the scene proceeds, the lament character gradually gives place to that of the pastorale (Example 37). Moving in triple meter and composed of descending third intervals, the melody of this section is an example of traditional pastorale themes (henceforth, "pastorale theme"). Its character is best expressed by Judith's kind words sung to this melody: "I will open them sofly, softly and calmly" (Szépen, halkan fogom nyitni, halkan puhán). The triple-meter motion of this section is interrupted only once, when Judith, losing her patience, demands the keys (Andante: no. 28 mm. 2–3). The even eighth-note melody and the halt of the pastorale background mark this moment as an emotional opposition similar to what we have seen in the confrontation of the two characters at various points of the piece, except that here it is the opposition of Judith's own aggressive voice to *her* words of kindness.

What is the musical and dramatic function of this scene? When the lament theme first occurs, it is superposed on the pentatonic theme—the main theme of the opera, the theme of the castle, which, as at the beginning, is played here on the strings (see Example 35, m. 3). The relationship between the lament theme of the clarinet and the pentatonic theme of the lower strings is neither melody accompaniment nor theme and countertheme texture. The two voices present essentially the same theme: the strings "play the song," as it were, and the clarinet plays an ornamental fantasy based on that song. This technique is common in both the village and the urban gypsy tradition of Hungarian music: the singers perform the piece without much ornamentation and, simultaneously, the instrumentalist plays its ornamented elaboration. Bartók's version is a modification of this pattern. Instead of moving together with the strings, the clarinet ornaments the melodic essence of the first half of the pentatonic theme by emphasizing its main notes (playing them as long notes and/or metrically accented notes): E–F sharp–E–C sharp–B–C sharp.

Ornamentation proves to be the connecting force among the various thematic elements. The choice of the original themes even seems to anticipate their transformation into ornamental variants. Looking at it retrospectively, we may see the pentatonic theme as a "theme" in variation form with its bareness virtually calling for melodic elaboration. Its potential to be developed in two directions—as a background and/or bass line and as an ornamented version—has been foreshadowed throughout this scene, by the pentatonic ostinato on the one hand and the earlier clarinet melodies on the other. The

EXAMPLE 37.   The pastorale theme.

connection between the lament theme and the gesture theme is also apparent. Since the individual segments of the ornamental lament melody typically contain a motion toward or away from an emphasized note, the melody becomes a series of gesturelike motions. These motions, some circular and some unidirectional, are filled in with ornaments, creating a series of ornamental gestures (see especially the motive at Example 35, no. 25). The dolce-marcato theme is integrated into this ornamental surface as well. Its sixty-fourth-note motive appears as a natural response to the florid ornamentation (last measure of Example 35), and the pastorale theme is identical with its note pairs (compare the motive of the first measure of Example 37 to Example 28). Thus two motivic ideas—ornamentation and gesture—connect all the varied thematic ideas. Example 38 offers some of the themes that derive from the gesture motive.

A formal recapitulation requires some ingenuity if it is to move to the operatic stage; the resolution and symmetry natural in instrumental form must reflect the novel dramatic situation of the moment. The scene's dramatic demands inspired Bartók to find a solution that became the "Bartókian type" of recapitulation in many of his later instrumental works. Recapitulation is seen here not as a return to something previously heard but the synthesis of earlier ideas and thematic elements. This section does not simply reiterate themes, it brings them onto a higher plane, so to speak. It is the culmination of the tendency to move toward ornamentation, the arrival at a stable C tonality and the transfiguration of the opening themes as entirely new thematic types: "*verbunkos* lament" and "pastorale." Putting it in organicist terms, we could say that the recapitulation makes transparent those hidden connections and meanings that were inherent at the beginning and have been gradually evolving since then. This hidden meaning surfaces in a transformation that is both logical and surprising: the recapitulation appears to be the result of a gradual process and yet strikes the listener as something unexpected.

However, the dramatic function of this design is not self-evident. Nothing seems to be less natural than gentle pastorale music after the frightening, "cavernous sighing." And it is also hard to interpret why the scene immediately before the opening of the first door—that is, the actual plot of the opera that depicts struggle—lacks dynamism but evokes instead a feeling of sad resignation. Bartók's solution appears less enigmatic if we regard the first scene not as introduction but as exposition in the dramatic sense: it encapsulates the essence of the entire play. What is the theme of the drama? That love is the capacity of the Other to see the hidden realms of the soul and share its solitude for a moment, but that the capacity alone cannot bring lasting and complete

EXAMPLE 38.   Gesture motives.

a. Opening of the outer door.

b. Bluebeard's embrace.

c. Judith's passion.

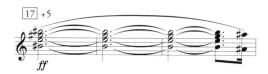

d. End of the lament theme.

e. Climax of the struggle between Judith and Bluebeard.

happiness to either. "Seeing" in this context means the intuition and insight that illuminate the soul of the Other and comprehend its inner forces. This seeing does not equate with understanding by means of logic and argument; it is the flash of inspiration, when everything becomes suddenly transparent: the idea of Bartókian recapitulation.

No other part of the play emphasizes seeing as the essential aspect of love more clearly than the first scene. It is customary to interpret the opera as the story of Bluebeard's destruction so that, as the opera proceeds and strips him of his secrets, it leaves him naked. Yet if there is a scene in the opera that can be interpreted as a metaphor of nakedness, it is this first scene. In love, standing naked is the passive state of waiting to be seen, then to be discovered and forgiven. The gesture of opening up once and for all, allowing another to see all that was hidden and secret, is an irreversible dramatic act, something that cannot be undone. By closing the outer door, Bluebeard makes the most decisive step: he allows Judith to learn to see things in the darkness. At this point, Bluebeard is powerless; he can only wait, in fear, hoping that Judith will be able to see and understand—his sensitive, self-protective, and self-reassuring brief responses to Judith are signs of this fear. Here both Bluebeard and Judith are helpless and at the mercy of the other, but they can no longer turn back; they have stepped over the threshold of empirical reality into the world of the soul. Hence the first scene is the story of Judith's gradual discovery and understanding. The dark stage is, in a sense, already Bluebeard's whole self, so that Judith is indeed able to discover his deepest secrets; she notices the coldness and darkness, "hears" and feels the blood, the tears, and the sighs. She learns the melodies of the castle, copies Bluebeard's gesture, and makes it into her own expression of passion and aggressivity.

The lament theme and the following pastorale represent the soul as an eternal, sad, and beautiful landscape. They translate into music a poetic metaphor common to modernist lyric poems. The nocturnal landscape—for Hungarians, naturally, a Hungarian landscape—is the metaphor for the mystery, the loneliness, and the perfection of the soul. It is the gentleness and resolution of eternal sadness. Judith understands it all. Bluebeard's question "Are you afraid?" she leaves unanswered as irrelevant; fear has nothing to do with this mystery. Judith's question "What was that? What sighed? Who sighed?" is one she herself answers: "It was your castle! Your castle sighed out!" Judith is no longer using the logic of an everyday world or of legend, she is following the rules of the soul. She knows that the sighs come not from the ghosts of captured women but from the castle itself because everything that is real in the drama of love and life belongs only to the soul.

Lament and gentle pastorale are the starting point for the drama of love. They represent Judith's acceptance of the castle as it is—as a beautiful but sad landscape. Tears and sighs are to end in consolation, darkness is to give way to light: the universal symbols of this scene make it imperative that Judith proceed in the direction she will in the course of the play. But the representation of darkness and tears as something self-contained signifies that even though the soul desires to move away from sadness, this moving away is bound to lead back to the point of departure. It is gentleness that unites Judith and Bluebeard in a struggle in which they are fated to destroy their happiness but will be able to preserve gentleness. The motive of embrace depicts the opening and closing of the outer door, and the music of pastorale expresses Judith's attempts to open the doors calmly and softly. Bluebeard's last dramatic actions—his aria to Judith and his clothing her in rich garments—are a return to this gentleness.

EXPANDING SYMBOLISM

If we accept that the intricate web of motivic connections based on rhythmic variation defines the opera's dramatic and musical symbolism, we begin to understand the relations among its themes and appreciate their symbolic meaning. The piece uses only a few basic melodic-rhythmic elements throughout, constantly varying and recombining them into different themes that, in turn, form thematic types. In the symbolic language of the opera, the human world is represented most clearly by an "ornamented gesture theme." This thematic type, usually marked "dolce" or "espressivo," contains (often begins with) a melodic motion that highlights the intervallic leap between two notes, and this melodic movement is elaborated with ornaments. Ornamented gesture themes occur at the two "positive" chambers, namely the treasure house and the garden of flowers (Examples 39 and 40).

The gentle and emotional character of these themes is obvious, but this character does not come from their motivic elements. Neither the gesturelike note pair nor its ornamentation consistently symbolizes the opera's human world. The ingenuity of the symbolism of Bartók's music lies precisely in that, although we isolate recurring motivic elements in themes, these elements are so basic that, in themselves, they signify nothing. In particular, ornamentation belongs to both the "positive" and the "negative" world and, in fact, may take on opposite meanings. For instance, the motivic basis for the armory's cruel opening theme (Example 41e) is an ornamental *verbunkos* figure that occurs also in themes with markedly different characters (Example 41): the end of the

EXAMPLE 39.   The theme of the treasury.

EXAMPLE 40.   The first theme of the garden of flowers.

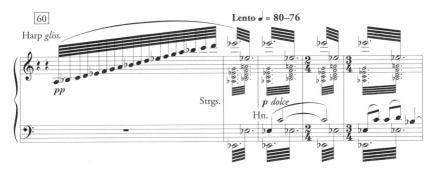

pastorale theme (a), the lament theme (b), the second theme of the garden (c), and—in an inverted and augmented form—the lamenting theme of the last door (d). Only slight modification was necessary in order to achieve a different character. Unlike in the other versions, in the theme of the armory the figuration is not part of a melodic progression; it is an independent, "frozen" melodic fragment that encircles a sustained F sharp–C sharp open fifth. The use of wind instruments, the "allegro risoluto" tempo marking, the repetitions of the same motive in "forte" without any change in the manner of performance transform this ornament from an emotional gesture into something like a military signal (which is exactly what this scene calls for).

   In the musical process, there is little to guide the listener to realize connections such as those among the themes of Example 41. But there are a few instances where the new form arrives in a linear process, as in the transitional

EXAMPLE 41.   Themes containing the *verbunkos* cadential figure.

a.

b.

c.

d.

e.

section that leads from the pastorale of the introduction to the first door (Example 42). The pivotal motive here is an ornamental cadential figure (the same type of ornament as in the motive of the armory [Example 41a = first measure of Example 42]). At its second occurrence in Example 42 (m. 3), the motive is accompanied by a different chord. Then it changes into another figure with similar tonal function (that is, leading to the note C of the previously heard chord: Andante). However, this figuration no longer alludes to the pastorale; it is merely a trill that represents, according to the stage instruction, the noise of the key turning in the lock. This trill leads directly to the theme of the torture chamber, which combines a continuous trill and fragments of scalar motives representing the noise of rattling chains (Sostenuto). What makes the trill and the scalar motive sound "inhuman" in this scene is essentially that these figures are cut off from a melodic progression. This minimal modification changes their character entirely: they no longer strike us as ornaments but rather as background noise.

With their very long and very short notes, the ornamental themes symbolize gentleness and positive force, while those themes in which there is no rhythmic differentiation belong to the "inhuman" sphere of the opera, symbolizing negative force. It is significant that Judith's outburst that leads to the opening of the last door, thus ending their passionate love, is based on themes that move in even-note values. But in the symbolism of the opera, negative and positive are not directions on an imaginary line whose ends never meet. The dramatic process is rather a circle moving from darkness to light and back to darkness, and any movement on the periphery of a circle is always both positive and negative at the same time. The opening of the first five doors is a movement toward light, but this movement also brings the drama closer to its unavoidable end in darkness. Similarly, the opening of the last two doors appears to be negative only because it follows the positive pole of the circle. The natural continuation of the same road (the opening of the doors) has now become a motion toward the negative direction. This duality marks the symbolism for the images of each chamber: each includes the motive of blood (negative), and the opening of each door brings forth a stream of light (positive).

The connecting force between themes is the technique of thematic-rhythmic variation whose focal point is the rhythm of undifferentiated note values. Simple even-note themes become ornamented, then the ornaments detached from the melody become even-note patterns—the rhythmic design reinforces the opera's circular motion. The thematic types of even-note melodies moving in quarter or eighth notes on the one hand and even-note ornamental passages on the other present the motion back to night and back to the source

EXAMPLE 42. Transition from the pastorale section to the first door scene.

at some imaginary center. Characteristically, the pentatonic theme of the castle is one without rhythmic differentiation. Throughout the piece, the eight-syllable, even eighth-note folk-song verse remains the rhythmic framework for the vocal parts, acting as the meeting point of the vocal and instrumental melodic styles. At the other end of the rhythmic pole, ornamentation acts as a cohesive force among themes and as a sonorous background texture connecting scenes. Its ornamental motives unite the themes of the first four chambers, and ornament appears in these scenes also as a continuous background ornament (trill or a continuous figuration). This ornamental background transfigures the eighth-note ostinato that provided the background to the scene before the first door. The speeding-up of the even-note patterns appears to symbolize a motion inward to the castle: the pentatonic theme moving in dotted half notes at the beginning of the opera, the pentatonic ostinato in eighth notes in the first scene, and fast (typically, sixty-fourth-note) figuration as the background for the inner chambers. The sixty-fourth-note ornament of the dolce-marcato theme at the beginning of the opera foreshadows this development.

The dramatic meaning of this system of thematic relations lies in the dialectic of unity and utmost opposition. The possible link between any two themes is as important as their unique individual form. Similarly, the conceptualization of direction of the drama as motion on the periphery of a circle does not contradict the fact that, in the immediate context, specific actions strike us as negative or positive. Bartók's underlying idea here was to establish a framework in which all things are potentially alien to one another even though all derive from the same source. The thematic basis of this system is in fact extremely simple. Most of the themes consist of the varied repetition of short—most commonly one-measure-long—motives that are "dynamic": they easily lend themselves to continuation, development, and transformation. The motives belong essentially to four types: ornament, dotted rhythm, even notes, and gesture.[27] The process of thematic variation gradually moves a theme from one motivic type toward another: gesture theme becomes ornamental theme, ornamental theme becomes even-note theme, and so on.

This system breaks down at the fifth door (Example 43). The scene has a theme unlike any earlier one: it is a "normal" rhythmic sequence within the basic duple metric system, containing exclusively half and quarter notes without ornaments, dotted rhythms, tied notes, or any other rhythmic complication. Even though the match between rhythm and melody is unconventional, its repetitiveness is striking. In both melody and rhythm, the same pattern recurs three times within four measures, and each note of the melody is harmo-

EXAMPLE 43. The fifth door.

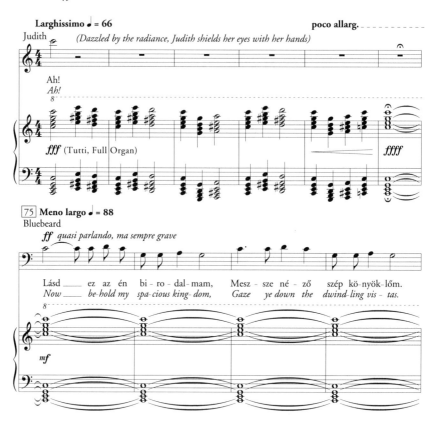

nized with a major chord. For all its majestic air, the theme strikes us as some-what primitive. (Bartók returned to this idea of combining simple melodic and rhythmic units many years later in the easiest pieces of the *Microcosmos*, al-though the motivic play is usually more intricate there than it is here.) After several static repetitions of this theme and its fragments, there is a transition toward a series of waltzlike themes that express Bluebeard's exuberant mood and his urgent desire to embrace and kiss Judith.

The majestic and yet simple tone of this scene has a tremendous effect in the performance—nothing in the music anticipates it. Yet after a few repeti-tions and Judith's interjections, the effect loses some of its power. Is this happy and carefree Bluebeard identical with the man whose complex inner world emerges from the images of the previous chambers? Could the castle (the soul) of Bluebeard be a place of eternal dazzling light, a place without tears, mem-

EXAMPLE 43 *(continued)*

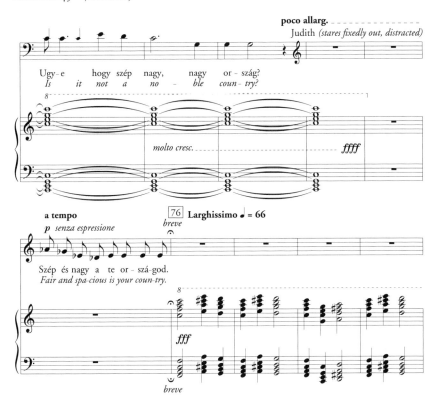

poco allarg.

Judith *(stares fixedly out, distracted)*

Ugy-e hogy szép nagy, nagy or-szág?
Is it not a no-ble coun-try?

molto cresc.

ffff

a tempo
p senza espressione

76 Larghissimo ♩ = 66
breve

Szép és nagy a te or-szá-god.
Fair and spa-cious is your coun-try.

fff

breve

ory, and sadness (without the sixth and seventh chambers)? Judith's answer to both questions is a definitive No. At the sight of Bluebeard's kingdom, she covers her eyes almost as if blinded by the light, and a moment later she answers Bluebeard "senza espressione," "staring fixedly out, distracted," in A flat, as if she is out of tune with the rest of the music. Here she spends no time looking at the things now visible in the chamber, as she had done in all the earlier scenes. Nor does she respond to Bluebeard's gesture to embrace her. For Judith, all this is self-deception and emptiness; she knows that the simple and happy Bluebeard who wants to forget about sorrow, tears, and darkness is no longer his true self. Her simple even-note, pentatonic parlando melody is a close variant of the pentatonic theme, combining the melodic motion of its first two lines. Judith posits against *this* happiness the theme of the castle itself.

If the section that extends from the beginning to the opening of the first door functions as an introduction and first scene (quasi-exposition), then the corresponding closing section (quasi-recapitulation) begins after the fifth door, when Judith first demands the opening of the last two doors (no. 85). The themes that appear at this point are rearrangements and transformations of motives from the first scene. The central part of that scene had an even eighth-note ostinato motion derived from the pentatonic theme; the corresponding musical element in the recapitulation is the chromatic even eighth-note motion that dominates the music before and after the sixth chamber until the opening of the last door.[28]

The sixth chamber is, in a sense, an interruption of this progression.[29] The preceding measures, leading to the opening of the door, correspond to the long halt of the first scene: a series of harsh chords are followed by rest, and then by the sigh of the castle (which appears here also in the orchestra's glissando). As the sigh in the introduction led to a static image that functioned as a recapitulation in the Bartókian sense, the sixth door is also a static dramatic and musical situation that brings, nevertheless, the rearrangement, synthesis, and transformation of previous themes (Example 44). Several basic tonal and thematic elements recapitulate here: Judith's melody recalls the pentatonic ostinato, the glissandi and trills remind us of the noise effects of previous chambers, and tonally, one figurative passage combines the pentatonic theme and the minor second blood motive. The gesture theme recapitulates as a melodic line in unison (a texture characteristic so far only of the pentatonic theme) outlining the minor second (blood motive). There is recapitulation in the visual symbolism as well: in the first scene Judith spoke of the weeping castle; here she actually sees those tears. As in the first scene Judith simply reflected on what she saw of the castle, here too she describes only what she sees, and Bluebeard likewise repeats only her observations.

Memory defines this scene. Things once lived through as contrast, pain, and action reappear here without tension or (e)motion. It is the mirror image of Judith's passionate struggle preceding and following this scene. The section leading to the sixth door forms a continuous movement by intensifying its short motives, shifting occasionally to a one-measure minor-second descending motive (Example 45). The sixth door scene offers a static variant of this design. Instead of the alternation of energetic chromatic movement and passionate descending gestures, here we have the alternation of a pianissimo broken chord and a slow gesture motive played dolce and piano.

This transition from the emotional world to the world of motionlessness defines the place of this scene in terms of the opera as a whole. Whereas before the musical material was for the most part dynamic—building from themes

EXAMPLE 44. The sixth door.

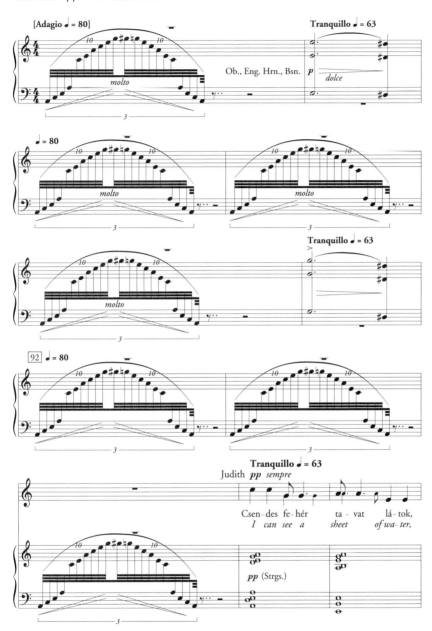

EXAMPLE 45. The section before the sixth door.

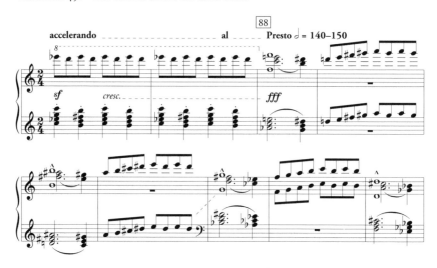

that continuously opposed each other and moved toward or away from one another—here contrasting melodic and rhythmic elements appear as unrelated, "frozen" fragments without tension and opposition. In the previous scenes, ornamentation always carried a precise meaning, being the metaphor alternately for the human or the inhuman world. Similarly, the gesture motive had precise meaning as the expression of passion, of gentleness, or, together with ornament, of the human world. Here ornament and gesture are independent motives unrelated to each other, each deprived of its previous emotional potential. This is the moment when emotions freeze—the threshold of eternal night.

The development of the chromatic ostinato continues after the sixth chamber and reaches its climax with the reiteration of the chromatic motive as a monumental tragic outcry (Example 46, no. 117: Molto sostenuto). At this moment the even-motion chromatic ostinato slows down and transforms into a gesture motive built on the minor second—the blood motive. As Bluebeard's embracing gesture led to an ornamental cadential figure at the closing of the outer door, the repetitions of this motive conclude in a slowed-down version of the *verbunkos*-like cadence (Andante: no. 117 mm. 7–8).

In a sense, the entire opera has been moving toward this culmination point. In the previous scenes the minor-second blood motive provides sharp contrast to other themes, then in the section after the fifth door it becomes

EXAMPLE 46.   Before the seventh door: climax of the chromatic theme.

(continued)

EXAMPLE 46   *(continued)*

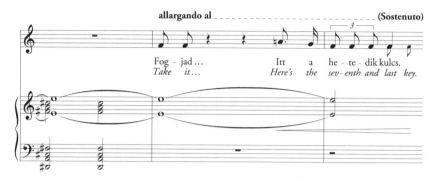

integrated into themes with variant expressive characters: passion (in the continuous chromatic eighth-note motion), sadness (in the gesture theme of the sixth door), and finally, here, a desperate gesture, as if a last embrace. This theme expresses the grandness and humanity as well as the cruelty and self-destructive passion of Judith.

Like everything else in this drama, destructive passion does not belong solely to Judith. Its motives come from the music of the castle—from Bluebeard's world. The minor second of the blood motive, which has been foreshadowed by the dolce-marcato theme already at the very beginning of the opera, assumes here a new significance. It becomes the symbol of "love at the moment of separation," meaning the most intense awareness of imminent loss. A gesturelike minor-second motive expresses this love at the end of the opera when Bluebeard and Judith look at each other for the last time (Example 47: Largo).

Looking back now at the beginning of the piece, we discover symbolic meaning in the ambiguity of the dolce-marcato theme. This motive represents motion as opposed to the motionlessness of the pentatonic theme of the castle. Motion away from darkness and perfection is a direction both positive and negative, it is intrusion into the solitude of the soul but also an opening to emotion. That is why the dolce-marcato motive appears in constant modulation at the end of the opera, as if floating without direction above the pentatonic theme (Example 48). In the course of these scattered repetitions, the motive gradually diminishes to an ornamental gesture motive, then to a gesture motive, then to a chord, and finally to two notes, as if falling gradually from sight. The last statement of the piece is the fragment of this motive shrunk into the notes A–B sharp (= C), faintly pointing toward C tonality. At the same

EXAMPLE 47. The theme as Judith and Bluebeard look at each other for the last time.

time, the pentatonic theme in the bass also diminishes, until only its first melodic motion remains. This quasi Tonic–Dominant opening gesture moving from F sharp to C sharp fades away until at the very end of the piece a single note, a C sharp, remains. These motions toward the dominant C sharp and the polar opposite C are similar to what we heard at the beginning of the piece. The story of Bluebeard and Judith opens up toward eternal circularity: Bluebeard will live in darkness, but somewhere in a cosmic universe the motion of love continues.

EXAMPLE 48.   The end of the opera.

THE MUSICAL MIRROR
OF THE DRAMATIC IDEA

Balázs's ideal of drama was a "mystery play" in which the actual dramatic elements, such as dialogue, stage, and action, were only the overtones of the fundamental motion of the all-encompassing feeling soul. In *Bluebeard's Castle* Balázs took this concept to the extreme. The lack of precision in the dramatic development of characters and the awkwardness of the dialogues were its outcome. Balázs's neglect of the language reflects his belief in the superiority of the concept over verbal expression. The insistence on this idea undermined the play's theatrical potential—the piece had no success as theater. Yet the concept, which deemphasized both the verbal and theatrical aspects in favor of some grandiose invisible movement, found its natural expression in the medium of music. Even though it was not Balázs's original intention, the play became really functional as a libretto.

The play's emotional and expressive content caught Bartók's imagination because it reflected his own experience, yet in the end the text became something much more than the vehicle for his personal expression. The dramatic concept of the play came to serve as a model for a new musical style. Whether Bartók only clarified the basic conception of his new style as he wrote the opera, or whether he actually created it as a response to the text, is impossible to say. What is certain, however, is that the composition did not simply set the text to music but formulated a new musical system through its mirroring of the dramatic design of Balázs's play. With this sudden and complete achievement, Bartók assembled the essential elements of his style, but he worked through their consequences only several years later. In many ways, the *Wooden Prince* and the piano compositions of the 1910s represented a step backwards, a period for processing the opera's structural ideas. And then the *Miraculous Mandarin* followed a different path. Only during the early 1920s, beginning with the sonatas for violin and piano, and then the compositions of 1926, did Bartók continue the stylistic innovations of the opera.

The first significant innovation was a new conception of national music—in this respect Balázs's works were an important experiment, in spite of their obvious shortcomings. With *Bluebeard's Castle*, he hoped to create a work that would eliminate the separation of "high" from "folk" on the one hand and that of "universal" from "national" on the other. In this spirit he chose a folk tale in order to express a philosophical thought of particular relevance to the modern world. The choice of the genre is significant in itself. For the Hungarian modernists, the folk tale manifested the most original form of art, born from primordial human consciousness. Moreover, the story of Bluebeard was an archetypal folk tale known all over Europe from both the art and the folk traditions, with versions also in Hungarian folk poetry.[30] To highlight the folk-music connection, Balázs used the poetic meter and rhyme scheme of Székler ballads, held to be the most ancient and original stratum of Hungarian folk music. As he recalled the idea behind the creation of the play, Balázs wrote, "I was striving to develop a Hungarian dramatic style. I endeavored to enlarge the dramatic vein of Székler folk ballads for the stage. I wanted to delineate modern souls with the plain primitive colors of folk song."[31]

To expand a primeval poetic theme and form it into a complex philosophical modern drama was a bold experiment and one that was not entirely successful. The text's oversimplified pseudo-folk style does not match its author's complex philosophical ideas and sophisticated dramatic design. But the underlying thought is profound and brilliant. Balázs intended to erase the borderlines between national and universal, folk and modern by focusing on a few basic elements inherent to all of them. This thought became the underlying principle of Bartók's folklorism as well.

A critical element in Balázs's dramatic design was the idea of a play as a uniform and unbroken entity in which things reflected each other as in a mirror. It made no clear separation between outside and inside, stage and emotions, lighting and words. The stage was an imaginary landscape of mysterious objects and images with continuously changing symbolic associations, and similarly, the dramatic action was both concrete and symbolic, functioning at various levels of symbolic associations. The play's intimate connection between representational and expressive aspects inspired Bartók's music and perhaps reinforced his belief that music was capable of expressing those fundamental primeval human motions (or gestures) in which bodily movement and fluctuations of speech and emotions become one and the same.

Most important, the polarization of symbols as the central dramatic idea perhaps gave Bartók the impetus to create a musical style based on that same principle. In 1964 Ernő Lendvai recognized that Bartók's tonal system based on polarized formations was the reflection of a poetic theme:

> What differentiates Bartók's piece from Tristan's yearning for night, and from Wagner's and Nietzsche's belief in the redeeming power of the idea of nirvana, is precisely the balance between the conceptions of light and darkness, day and night, life and death. The pessimism of the piece (if it is pessimistic at all) lies not in the power of the night that swallows up everything but rather in the thought that the dialectic unity of dark and light is a necessity. . . . Bartók's world is a world of polarity: it is neither "dark" nor "light" but it is dark *and* light. Both are always together, in inseparable unity as if polarity were, for him, the only framework in which a conceptual and dramatic message could manifest itself.[32]

As we have seen, Bartók's system of polarization goes much further than that of the opposition of two poles. In his music everything is variation and, potentially, the polar opposite of everything else. Consequently, no musical statement functions as theme in the sense that it would be the most perfect formulation of the central idea. For instance, the relations between the pentatonic theme and the lament theme are not simply those of theme and ornamental variation, even though Bartók's design incorporates this scheme. In the end they express an opposition between stillness or perfection and compassion or gentleness—that is, both of them are polarized manifestations of something that the play never quite states.

The idea of polarization derives from the dramatic concept. Each door of the castle opens to a different world, confronting us with a new and unexpected realm in Bluebeard's soul. These realms are extreme in their emotional and symbolic meaning: torture chamber, garden of flowers, dazzling light, or lake of tears. Where does the personality of Bluebeard lie among these many images? Which is his real or most typical face? The play annihilates such questions: the soul has an essence, but no single image can hold it. The soul becomes transparent only in its contradictions.

The assumption that coherence manifested itself not in consistency and continuity but in polar oppositions became the foundation of Bartók's conceptualization of modern style. Balázs's play might have given him the final impetus to devise the musical structure expressing this aesthetic principle, but Bartók had been moving toward it instinctively since 1907. Many turn-of-the-century artists shared the ideal, but Bartók and Ady gave it expression in their works. Like Bartók, Ady drew everything into his intense experience of life. In his poetry even the simplest gesture can reveal a great essence. Any event of empirical life has the potential to assume meaning, to move from a peripheral position to the center of poetic symbolism with remarkable ease. And in this expanding and open-ended system any word can symbolize a wide array of ideas, even entirely opposite ones, forming part of a complex web of potential symbolic associations. Bartók's all-encompassing thematicism, connected to a system of motivic transformation, is the musical parallel to Ady's poetic symbolism. Like Ady's poetry, Bartók's music moves with ease between variant structures and symbolic meanings. It transforms the musical material expressing one character into something that expresses another or changes insignificant elements into themes or themes back into the background. A strict system controls this continuous flow of variant ideas: for Ady, a few absolutely stable conceptual principles and symbols, and for Bartók, an underlying plan for tonality and for melodic and rhythmic ideas.

For Bartók and Ady, each work was a challenge to create a framework in which the unity of the most polarized elements becomes inevitable. At the foundation of such an art lies the belief in an aesthetics, or more precisely, in a human attitude. It is a belief that, as Lukács put it, "lies vividly beyond all proofs, the belief that the scattered multidirectional roads of the soul do meet at the end; they have to meet because they departed from the same center. And the form [in art] is the only proof of this belief, because it is its only realization, a realization more vivid than life itself."[33]

Afterword

As readers of this book will recognize, all its chapters tell somewhat the same story about early-twentieth-century Hungary. In architecture and art, social studies and politics, aesthetics, psychology, literature, journalism, music, poetry, popular culture, and other parallel and seemingly independent domains, the subject of "wholeness" or its absence fascinated the intellectual modernist circles and oriented their activities. Artists and intellectuals placed the ideal of a meaningful life above all other goals. In their era as today, almost a century later, a meaningful life did not mean the piling up of accomplishments or the indulgence in the pleasures of life. It meant rather a continuous effort to penetrate the mysteries of existence, to achieve transparency by living intensely, by deepening feelings.

Transparency did not equate with intellectual (verbal) interpretations, and despite the influence of Freud, psychoanalytic tools were of limited use on the journey to the depths of the soul. Facing its mysteries, artists of our era found few words to describe their feelings or relieve their loneliness. But loneliness now had meaning, it contained knowledge and a sense of life's essence. This loneliness did not mean alienation in the social sense. On the contrary, it was the outcome of shared experience. Only individuals who saw and suffered in life's immediate, close-to-earth, communal form could understand the self.

The highest of all forms of life experiences was the intimacy of love because it brought the realization of the self (and with it, true loneliness). Love encompassed the intensity of passion and the opening up toward the Other in the moment of intimacy; it gave the lover access to the depths of the soul and transcendence over the self. Nothing—not art or philosophy or religion—equaled its power.

The modernists did not have a manifesto to explain their philosophical orientation in the manner I describe here. Art, especially the art of a loosely connected group, often does without philosophical systems. Yet the creators of this art shared a basic attitude, even if each of them shaped his or her personal interpretation of it—as if forming different buildings from the same set of building blocks and for the same purpose. The fact that a writer was sensitive to one particular social problem and that another was sensitive to something else does not mean that their aspirations and ideas were necessarily different. By selecting different details, they related to the same underlying problem in a manner that suited their personalities. In the context of their art and lives, the philosophical and aesthetic principles underlying Bartók's markedly nonreligious attitude were very similar to Ady's aesthetics, in which the notion of God is crucial.

In the work the modernists left behind, a series of conceptual ideas recurs with remarkable consistency. Because I discuss these in detail in this book, I simply list them briefly here:

- There is an essence in all things (a moral essence, the essence of life, of character) that an artist strives to comprehend and obey. This essence corresponds to nothing in real life and is impossible to render in words. The moment of perceiving it is like a revelation, and its aftereffect is a generally positive feeling that, however ambiguous it may seem, determines the course of the individual's life.

- The artist reflects this essence through emphasis on its distance from everyday reality: by exaggerating, distorting, blurring, transforming, or annulling, through magic, the themes of everyday life. Distortion and exaggeration have another, deeper role. Only by living to life's limits and by showing the most extreme potential of things does the artist convey their real nature.

- The more diversity an artwork encompasses, the more meaningful its coherence. For in life as well as in the structure of the artwork, everything is potentially (but only potentially) equally important. The background may become foreground and an irrelevant fragment may prove to be the central idea or connecting force between things. The work must show the oppositions of things and the multiple nature of elements: everything is also its opposite.

- Thus the work is symbolic on every level because its contrasts and resolutions are the symbolic representation of wholeness. Landscape, ornaments, background, actors, plot—all serve to reveal a higher connection. Art does capture real situations, but these have meaning only inasmuch as they are also symbolic.

- Each new step, each new work is a transformation, even metamorphosis, but essence, truth, and morality are always out of reach. There is no attaining a moral life and no avoiding it—there is only continuous motion toward the abstract ideal of morality.

- Wholeness is not uniformity, nor is it harmony without tension. Unity in art means the capacity to make transparent the presence of the inner governing force that unites all elements in spite of their fragmentary nature, even opposition.

- Unity is awareness of the fact that all the antagonistically opposing things ultimately contain the same essence; and the moment when such a connection becomes transparent is a moment of catharsis.

- The essence of art and life—the truth—resides in what is most particular and unique because—paradoxically—the personal, communal, and local (Hungarian) experience ensures its universality. Art and life rest on elementary, immediate, and real feelings and acts—on the phenomena.

The consistency with which these ideas recur in diverse spheres of Hungarian intellectual culture should not surprise us. At the turn of the century, the passionate search for life's essence in its diverse facets challenged intellectuals to deal with subjects far from their everyday occupations. Being an intellectual has little to do with specialized knowledge and with control of a wide range of information; it means rather the capacity to passionately engage in the discovery of various spheres of the surrounding world. We notice in writings of this period that intellectuals were by no means well informed about the whole of cultural life or entirely prepared to treat most of the things they tackled. They immersed themselves in subjects quite far from their expertise because they believed that all things would eventually reflect back on the general questions they dealt with in their lives.

As far as art is concerned, this attitude was rooted in the aesthetic tradition, deeply ingrained in artists' thinking, that the same essence manifested itself in different forms of art. Bartók, for his part, believed that he was able to capture the "spirit of folk music" within his compositions, in spite of their distinctive musical structure, because of their shared expressive content. And he regarded Ady's poetic world as the form closest to what he attempted to convey in music. The same belief in art's shared expressive content gave Bartók reason to insist that those who wished to know his music should accompany him on his field trips so that they could actually partake in the atmosphere of folk music. And he considered it similarly important that his friends read the poetry of Ady.

The intellectual environment the modernists constructed in this way was the juxtaposition of various and somewhat eclectically selected aspects of life.

They probed each aspect and saw their own faces, as well as the totality of life, reflected there. Rather than assemble a starkly objective view of contemporary reality, they created an image of the surrounding world in which the significant problems of their time come into especially sharp focus. This book is an attempt to recapture their image of life.

Notes

All translations of Hungarian texts—prose and poetry—are mine unless otherwise noted.

INTRODUCTION

1. Zoltán Horváth, *Magyar századforduló: A második reformnemzedék története, 1896–1914* [Turn-of-the-century Hungary: The history of the second reform generation, 1896–1914] (Budapest: Gondolat, 1961), 7, 10. The translated excerpt is much shorter than the original text.

2. *Kakania*, a term Robert Musil invented, meant the Habsburg empire during its last decades. On the surface, it derives from the initials K.K. or K.u.K. (*kaiserlich und königlich*, or "imperial and royal"), which designated all the major Habsburg institutions. But we cannot miss the pejorative meaning of Musil's coinage: *Kaka* is the international nursery word for "shit," *Kakania* is "shitland."

3. The best comprehensive summary of Bartók's encounters with other artists and members of the intelligentsia is still János Demény, "Bartók Béla művészi kibontakozásának évei" [The years of Béla Bartók's artistic development], in *Zenetudományi tanulmányok* [Musicological studies] ed. Bence Szabolcsi and Dénes Bartha (Budapest: Akadémiai, 1955, 1959), 3:286–459 and 7:5–425. See also Béla Bartók, Jr., *Apám életének krónikája* [The chronicle of my father's life] (Budapest: Zeneműkiadó, 1981).

4. Denijs Dille, "Bartók et Ady," in *Béla Bartók: Regard sur le passé*, ed. Yves Lenoir, Études Bartókiennes no. 1 (Namur: Presses universitaires de Namur, 1990), 297.

5. To Márta Ziegler, Darázs, 4 February 1909, in Béla Bartók, Jr., *Bartók Béla családi levelei* [Béla Bartók's family letters] (Budapest: Zeneműkiadó, 1981), 187.

CHAPTER 1

1. It is not feasible to summarize the extensive literature in musicologists' debates over modernism. The dismissal of neoclassicism and the hailing of the Viennese modernism as the new musical style go back to Theodor W. Adorno's theory, *The Philosophy of Modern Music*, trans. Anne G. Mitchell and Wesley V. Blomster (New York:

Seabury, 1973). Studies written in the 1960s and 1970s essentially follow Adorno's interpretation but usually judge Stravinsky's "conservativism" less severely. See, for instance, Donald Mitchell, *The Language of Modern Music* (New York: St. Martin's, 1987). Most studies dealing with Schoenberg regard him as a revolutionary composer because of his serialist invention and treat his adherence to classical forms as a secondary issue. See for instance Ethan Haimo's insistence that "Schoenberg was not engaged in a superficial recycling of classical forms" in his *Schoenberg's Serial Odyssey: The Evolution of His Twelve-Tone Method, 1914–1928* (Oxford: Clarendon, 1990), 108. Studies today increasingly take into account the novelty and modernity of neoclassicism. See, for instance, Robert P. Morgan, *Twentieth-Century Music: A History of Musical Style in Modern Europe and America* (New York: W. W. Norton, 1991). The most recent contributions to this discussion have been Richard Taruskin, "Revising Revision," *Journal of the American Musicological Society* 46, no. 1 (1993): 114–38; Kevin Korsyn, "Towards a New Poetics of Musical Influence," *Music Analysis* 10 (1991): 3–72; Joseph N. Straus, *Remaking the Past: Musical Modernism and the Influence of the Tonal Tradition* (Cambridge, Mass.: Harvard University Press, 1990); Alan Lessem, "Schoenberg, Stravinsky, and Neo-Classicism: The Issues Reexamined," *The Musical Quarterly* 68 (1982): 527–42.

2. See part three of Leonard Stein, ed., *Style and Idea: Selected Writings of Arnold Schoenberg*, trans. Leo Black (Berkeley: University of California Press, 1984), 161–84.

3. Theodor W. Adorno, "Über Béla Bartók: Aufsätze und Auszüge aus Kritiken, zusammengestellt von Rainer Riehn" [1925], in *Béla Bartók*, ed. Heinz-Klaus Metzger and Rainer Riehn, Musik-Konzepte no. 22 (Munich: Edition Text + Kritik, 1981), 128.

4. Carl Dahlhaus, "Nationalism and Music," in *Between Romanticism and Modernism*, trans. Mary Whittall (Berkeley: University of California Press, 1980), 99–100. See also his chapter "The Symphony after Beethoven," in *Nineteenth-Century Music*, trans. J. Bradford Robinson (Berkeley: University of California Press, 1989), 157–58. Among articles generating Schoenberg's and Adorno's view and leading to Dahlhaus's argument see esp. Manfred Bukofzer, "The New Nationalism," *Modern Music* 23 (1946): 244; Pierre Boulez, "Béla Bartók" (1958), in *Relevés d'apprenti*, ed. Paule Thévenin (Paris: Éditions du Seuil, 1966), 304–5; Igor Stravinsky and Robert Craft, *Conversations with Igor Stravinsky* (New York: Doubleday, 1959), 82.

5. "The Influence of Peasant Music on Modern Music" (1931), in *Béla Bartók Essays*, ed. Benjamin Suchoff (Lincoln: University of Nebraska Press, 1976) 344; see also 332–33.

6. Arnold Schoenberg, "Folkloristic Symphonies" (1947), in *Style and Idea*, 166.

7. Béla Bartók, "A magyarországi modern zenéről" [On modern music in Hungary] (1921), in *Bartók Béla írásai I* [The writings of Béla Bartók, I], ed. Tibor Tallián (Budapest: Zeneműkiadó, 1989), 118; see "On Modern Music in Hungary" (1921), *Bartók Essays*, 474.

8. Schoenberg, "Folkloristic Symphonies," 165. Schoenberg speaks here only about the "static treatment of folk song." But elsewhere the article shows his belief that folk music in compositions was inevitably incoherent and static.

9. Anton Webern, *The Path to the New Music* (1932–33), ed. Willi Reich (Bryn Mawr: Theodore Presser, 1963), 42, 40.

10. Johann Wolfgang von Goethe, *Italian Journey*, trans. W. H. Auden and Elizabeth Mayer (San Francisco, 1982), 383 (6 September 1787). Webern referred to this paragraph by Goethe in his first lecture of the series on new music (*The Path to the New Music*, 11; original emphasis).

11. A good summary of the development of German organicism can be found in M. H. Abrams, *The Mirror and the Lamp* (London: Oxford University Press, 1953). The influence of organicism on music criticism in the romantic and the modern eras respectively can be seen in such central works as Eduard Hanslick, *The Beautiful in Music: A Contribution to the Revival of Musical Aesthetics* (1885), trans. Gustav Cohen (New York: Da Capo, 1974); and Ferruccio Busoni, "Sketch of a New Aesthetic of Music," in *Three Classics in the Aesthetic of Music*, trans. Theodore Baker (New York: Dover, 1962).

12. Edward Young, "Conjectures on Original Composition" (1759), quoted in Abrams, *The Mirror and the Lamp*, 199; original emphasis.

13. Quoted in Tzvetan Todorov, "The Romantic Crisis," in *Theories of the Symbol*, trans. Catherine Porter (Ithaca: Cornell University Press, 1982), 153.

14. Ibid., 161.

15. See, for instance, Goethe's description of "Herder's God" in his letter of 8 October 1787 from *Italian Journey*.

16. W. H. Wackenroder, "The Remarkable Musical Life of the Musician Joseph Berglinger" (1797), in *Source Readings in Music History: From Classical Antiquity Through the Romantic Era*, comp. Oliver Strunk (New York: W. W. Norton, 1950), 752.

17. Quoted in Carl Dahlhaus, *The Idea of Absolute Music*, trans. Roger Lustig (Chicago: University of Chicago Press, 1989), 5.

18. Quoted in Todorov, "The Romantic Crisis," 189. Schoenberg too regarded the difference between the "morbid heart" and the "poetic mind" essential. Following Schopenhauer, he talked of the contrast between "sentimentality" and "true sorrow" (Arnold Schoenberg, "Gustav Mahler" [1912, 1948], in *Style and Idea*, 457).

19. See Carl Dahlhaus, "The Metaphysics of Instrumental Music," in *Nineteenth-Century Music*, 88–95.

20. Samuel Taylor Coleridge, *Theory of Life: Biographia Literaria*, ed. George Watson (London, 1965), 1:174, 2:12. See also Ruth A. Solie, "The Living Work: Organicism and Musical Analysis," *19th-Century Music* 4 (1980): 148.

21. Quoted from Herder's *Von Deutscher Art und Kunst* (1773), in Abrams, *The Mirror and the Lamp*, 205.

22. Carl Dahlhaus, "Poetic Music," in *Nineteenth-Century Music*, 144; see also Dahlhaus, *The Idea of Absolute Music*, 11.

23. It is clear from the correspondence and writings of Schoenberg, Webern, and Bartók that they knew about the works of those literary figures, music historians, and philosophers who generated the organicist discourse in aesthetics, such as Busoni, Goethe, Hanslick, Hofmannsthal, Kraus, Nietzsche, Schopenhauer, and Strindberg. Although perhaps these works were significant at a certain stage of the composers' development (e.g., the influence of Nietzsche on the young Bartók), ideas of organicism became deeply engrained in their artistic awareness, generated mostly not by theoretical writings but through informal conversations.

24. Schoenberg, "Folkloristic Symphonies," 165, 166.

25. Arnold Schoenberg, "New Music, Outmoded Music, Style, and Idea" (1946), in *Style and Idea*, 123.

26. Georg Wubbolt, "Weberns Goethe-Rezeption: Ein Beitrag zum Thema Natur und Kunst," in *Opus Anton Webern*, ed. Dieter Rexroth (Berlin: Quadriga, 1983), 107.

27. Allen Forte, "Heinrich Schenker," in *The New Grove Dictionary of Music and Musicians* (London: Macmillan, 1980), 16:628.

28. See Nicholas Cook, "Schenker's Theory of Music as Ethics," *Journal of Musicology* 7 (1989): 415–39. See William A. Pastille, "Schenker, Anti-Organicist," *19th-Century Music* 8 (1984): 33–34.

29. Janet M. Levy, "Covert and Casual Values in Recent Writings about Music," *Journal of Musicology* 5 (1987): 3–27.

30. Colin Mason, "An Essay in Analysis: Tonality, Symmetry, and Latent Serialism in Bartók's Fourth Quartet," *Music Review* 18 (1957): 189–201.

31. In Carl Dahlhaus, *Schoenberg and the New Music*, trans. Derrick Puffett and Alfred Clayton (Cambridge: Cambridge University Press, 1987), 32–44.

32. See for instance Liszt's 1856 letter to Louis Köhler, in *Briefe*, ed. La Mara [Ida Maria Lipsius] (Leipzig: Breitkopf & Härtel, 1893–1904), 1:225. Liszt's distinction between *Formen* (forms in harmony with their inner expressive power) and *Formeln* (formulae, or inherited formal devices) is very similar to Friedrich Nietzsche's distinction between "unpretentious truth" and "forms" (see aphorism 3 in *Human, All Too Human: A Book for Free Spirits* [1878, 1886], trans. R. J. Hollingdale [Cambridge: Cambridge University Press, 1986], 13–14). See also his letter from 2 December 1852, in ibid., 1:120–25. These sections are translated in Winklhofer, *Liszt's Sonata in B minor: A Study of Autograph Sources and Documents* (Ann Arbor: UMI Research Press, 1980), 122–23. For a discussion of Liszt's Weimar period see Alan Walker, *Franz Liszt: The Weimar Years (1848–1861)* (New York: Alfred A. Knopf, 1989). See also H. G. Schenk, *The Mind of the European Romantics: An Essay in Cultural History* (Garden City, N.Y.: Doubleday, 1969), 204–5.

33. There exists a large literature on the concept of "decadence": see Ellen Moers, *The Dandy: Brummel to Beerbohm* (New York: Viking, 1960); Bernard Bergonzi, *The Turn of the Century: Essays on Victorian and Modern English Literature* (New York: Barnes and Noble, 1973); Osbert Burdett, *The Beardsley Period: An Essay in Perspective* (London: John Lane, The Bodley Head, 1925); Ian Fletcher, ed., *Decadence and the*

1890s (London: Edward Arnold, 1979); Matei Calinescu, *Faces of Modernity: Avant-Garde, Decadence, Kitsch* (Bloomington: Indiana University Press, 1977); Graham Hough, *Image and Experience: Studies in a Literary Revolution* (London: Gerald Duckworth, 1960); Janko Lawrin, *Aspects of Modernism: From Wilde to Pirandello* (Freeport, N.Y.: For Libraries Press, 1968).

34. Allan Janik and Stephen Toulmin, *Wittgenstein's Vienna* (New York: Simon and Schuster, 1973), 64–65.

35. Friedrich Wilhelm Nietzsche, "The Case of Wagner" (1888), in *Basic Writings of Nietzsche*, ed. and trans. Walter Kaufmann (New York: Random House, 1968), 626.

36. Hugo von Hofmannsthal, "The Letter of Lord Chandos," in *Selected Prose*, trans. Mary Hottinger and Tania and James Stern (New York: Pantheon, 1952), 134.

37. Of course, the situation was far more complex, since German avant-garde circles often viewed opera (especially works by Puccini and Verdi) as something popular.

38. Karl Kraus, "In These Great Times" (1914), in *In These Great Times: A Karl Kraus Reader*, ed. Harry Zohn, trans. Joseph Fabry et al. (1976; reprint, Manchester: Carcanet, 1984), 74.

39. Arnold Schoenberg, *Theory of Harmony* (1911), trans. Roy E. Carter (Berkeley: University of California Press, 1983), 1–2.

40. Schoenberg and Webern often referred to Kraus in their writings. (The opening idea of Webern's lecture series on new music, that of the "moral gain" in dealing with disciplines of art, comes from Kraus.) On the importance of Kraus in turn-of-the-century Viennese culture see recent studies: Janik and Toulmin, *Wittgenstein's Vienna;* Edward Timms, *Karl Kraus, Apocalyptic Satirist: Culture and Catastrophe in Habsburg Vienna* (New Haven: Yale University Press, 1986); Carl E. Schorske, *Fin-de-Siècle Vienna: Politics and Culture* (New York: Random House, Vintage Books, 1981); see also Cook, "Schenker's Theory of Music as Ethics."

41. Karl Kraus, "My Ambivalence," in *In These Great Times*, 149.

42. Arnold Schoenberg, "Problems in Teaching Art" (1911), in *Style and Idea*, 368.

43. Carl Dahlhaus, "The 'Obbligato Recitative,' " in *Schoenberg and the New Music*, 144–48.

44. Schoenberg, "New Music, Outmoded Music," 121.

45. For instance, in his *Theory of Harmony*, 10.

46. In some of his writings Schoenberg refuted the idea of "natural law" in music, as in the preface to the *Theory of Harmony* (8–9), where he referred to rules traditionally called "laws of harmony," such as the avoidance of parallel fifths. These he considered mere practices, not "natural laws." He did not question the idea that certain universal laws existed in music, but these were more general principles of structure and tonality, as expressed in Webern's lecture series.

47. Arnold Schoenberg, *Arnold Schoenberg Letters*, ed. and comp. Erwin Stein, trans. Eithne Wilkins and Ernst Kaiser (Berkeley: University of California Press, 1987), 146–47.

48. Webern, "The Path to the New Music," 10, 15, 18.

49. Ibid., 18.

50. Ibid., 11.

51. "At a very early stage it was found necessary to bring another dimension into play [that is, of more than one voice]. . . . The first person who had this idea—perhaps he passed sleepless nights—he knew: it *must* be so!" (ibid., 19).

52. Schoenberg, *Theory of Harmony*, 8.

53. "Nobody has yet appreciated that my music, produced on German soil, without foreign influences, is a living example of an art able most effectively to oppose Latin and Slav hopes of hegemony and derived through and through from the traditions of German music" (Arnold Schoenberg, "National Music" [1931], in *Style and Idea*, 173).

54. Schorske, *Fin-de-Siècle Vienna*, 292–93.

55. Hermann Broch, *Hugo von Hofmannsthal and His Time: The European Imagination, 1860–1920*, ed. and trans. Michael P. Steinberg (Chicago: University of Chicago Press, 1984), 60–61.

56. Quoted in Schorske, *Fin-de-Siècle Vienna*, 282.

57. Webern, "The Path to the New Music," 10.

58. Schorske, *Fin-de-Siècle Vienna*, 304.

59. Ibid., 363.

CHAPTER 2

1. Reprint, Budapest: Pesti Szalon, 1993.

2. An English translation of the story is found in Frigyes Karinthy, *Grave and Gay: Selections from His Work*, trans. István Kerékgyártó (Budapest: Corvina, 1973), 122–28. For analysis of Karinthy's art see László Halász, *Karinthy Frigyes alkotásai és vallomásai tükrében* [Frigyes Karinthy in his works and confessions] (Budapest: Szépirodalmi, 1972).

3. See András Lányi, *Az írástudók áru(vá vá)lása: Az irodalmi tömegkultúra a két világháború közti Magyarországon* [The treason of the literate/the literate as industrial products: Literary products of mass culture between the two world wars in Hungary] (Budapest: Magvető, 1988), 178–94.

4. Miklós Szabolcsi, ed., *A magyar irodalom története 1905-től 1919-ig* [The history of Hungarian literature between 1905 and 1919] (Budapest: Akadémiai, 1965), 306–33, especially 319–22. Several of Karinthy's short stories express the duality of identity in a similar manner, but humorously: "Ego and Little Ego" (Én és énke) and "Meeting with a Young Man" (Találkozás egy fiatalemberrel). The English translations of these stories are in Karinthy, *Grave and Gay*.

5. The Compromise of 1867 was an agreement between the Habsburg court and Hungary, following the Hungarian revolution and war of independence of 1848–49. Within the Dual Austro-Hungarian Monarchy (which lasted until 1918), Hungary en-

joyed full internal independence, while common ministries dealt with foreign affairs and defense. Its first decades brought considerable economic progress.

6. The data on working-class life come from Zsuzsa Ferge, *Fejezetek a magyar szegénypolitika történetéből* [Chapters from the history of Hungarian politics concerning the poor] (Budapest: Magvető, 1986). Agricultural servants normally worked sixteen hours a day for little pay and might be required to work also at night and on holidays. A moving account of their life is the autobiographical novel by Gyula Illyés, *The People of the Puszta*, trans. G. F. Cushing (Budapest: Corvina, 1967). Domestic servants also had very little pay, received a minimal amount of food and a room to sleep in, and had at most one afternoon off per week (Ferge, *Fejezetek*, 31). The life of a domestic servant and her treatment by members of the middle class is captured in the novel *Anna Édes* by Dezső Kosztolányi (Édes Anna [1926]).

7. Quoted in Oszkár Jászi, *The Dissolution of the Habsburg Monarchy* (Chicago: University of Chicago Press, 1929), 392.

8. Jürgen Kocka, ed., *Bürgertum im 19. Jahrhundert: Deutschland im europäischen Vergleich* (Munich: Deutscher Taschenbuch Verlag, 1988), 16; Károly Halmos, "Polgár—polgárosodás—civilizáció—kultúra: A társadalomtörténet alapvető kategóriáiról a XIX–XX. századi lexikon- és szótárirodalom tükrében" [Bourgeoisie—bourgeois development—civilization—culture: Basic categories of social histories represented in 19th-century encyclopedias and dictionaries], *Századvég* 2–3 (1991): 131–66 [special issue, The bourgeoisie in Hungary]. In the same issue see Zoltán Tóth, "A rendi norma és a 'keresztyén polgárisodás': Társadalomtörténeti esszé" [The norms of the feudal estates and the ideal of the Christian bourgeoisie: An essay in social history], 75–130; see also Éva Somogyi, ed., *Verbürgerlichung in Mitteleuropa: Festschrift für Péter Hanák zum 70. Geburtstag* (Budapest: MTA Történettudományi Intézet, 1991).

9. People with the first or highest category of salaries had the title *Kegyelmes Úr;* those in the second category had the title *Méltóságos Úr,* and in the third category, *Nagyságos Úr;* below that, *Tekintetes Úr.* In titles *Úr* is the equivalent of the German *Herr.* The full titles mean something like "Your Excellency" or "Right Honorable." See Péter Hanák, ed., *Magyarország története 1890–1918* [A history of Hungary, 1890–1918] (Budapest: Akadémiai, 1983), 1:454.

10. See Kodály's letter to Emma Gruber, Charlottenburg, 21 March 1907, in Dezső Legány, ed., *Kodály Zoltán levelei* [Zoltán Kodály letters] (Budapest: Zeneműkiadó, 1982), 34; Bartók's letter to his mother, Budapest, 3 November 1901, in Béla Bartók, Jr., ed., *Bartók Béla családi levelei* [Béla Bartók's family letters] (Budapest: Zeneműkiadó, 1981), 50. See also the first chapter of my dissertation, "Béla Bartók and Hungarian Nationalism: The Development of Bartók's Social and Political Ideas at the Turn of the Century (1899–1903)" (Ph.D. diss., University of Pennsylvania, 1989).

11. This situation within the Lukács circle is discussed in Mary Gluck, *Georg Lukács and His Generation, 1900–1918* (Cambridge, Mass.: Harvard University Press, 1985), 44–48.

12. English-language introductions to this period of Hungarian history are István

Deák, "Hungary: A Brief Political and Cultural History," in *Standing in the Tempest: Painters of the Hungarian Avant-Garde, 1908–1930* (Santa Barbara, Calif.: Santa Barbara Museum of Art, 1991), 21–45; Ferenc Eckhart, *A Short History of the Hungarian People* (London: G. Richards, 1931); Peter I. Hidas, *The Metamorphosis of a Social Class in Hungary During the Reign of Young Franz Joseph*, East European Monographs no. 26 (New York: Columbia University Press, 1977); Paul Ignotus, *Hungary* (New York: Praeger, 1972); Andrew C. János, *The Politics of Backwardness in Hungary, 1825–1945* (Princeton: Princeton University Press, 1982); Jászi, *The Dissolution of the Habsburg Monarchy;* Domokos G. Kosáry, *A History of Hungary* (Cleveland and New York: Benjamin Franklin Bibliophile Society, 1941); Carlisle Aylmer Macartney, *The Habsburg Empire, 1790–1918* (London: Weidenfeld and Nicolson, 1968); Carlisle Aylmer Macartney, *Hungary: A Short History* (Edinburgh: Edinburgh University Press, 1962); Carlisle Aylmer Macartney, *Hungary and Her Successors: The Treaty of Trianon and Its Consequences, 1919–1937* (London: Oxford University Press, 1937); Arthur James May, *The Hapsburg Monarchy, 1867–1914* (Cambridge, Mass.: Harvard University Press, 1951); William O. McCagg, Jr., *Jewish Nobles and Geniuses in Modern Hungary* (New York: Columbia University Press, 1972); Armin Vambery, *The Story of Hungary* (New York, 1886); Steven Béla Várdy, *Modern Hungarian Historiography*, East European Monographs no. 17 (New York: Columbia University Press, 1976); Gábor Vermes, *István Tisza: The Liberal Vision and Conservative Statecraft of a Magyar Nationalist*, East European Monographs no. 184 (New York: Columbia University Press, 1985).

13. About this period, see chaps. 1–7 of Hanák, ed., *Magyarország története 1890–1918;* Gusztáv Gratz, *A dualizmus kora: Magyarország története 1867–1918* [The era of dualism: A history of Hungary, 1867–1918], vol. 1 (Budapest: Magyar Szemle Társaság, 1934); Péter Hanák, *A dualizmus korának történeti problémái* [Historical problems of the era of dualism] (Budapest: Tankönyvkiadó, 1971); József Galántai, *A Habsburg monarchia alkonya: Osztrák-Magyar dualizmus 1867–1918* [The twilight of the Habsburg Monarchy: Austro-Hungarian Dual Monarchy] (Budapest: Kossuth, 1985).

14. This problem is discussed in detail in István Fried, *Kelet- és Közép-Európa között* [Between Eastern and Central Europe] (Budapest: Gondolat, 1986); and in Jenő Szűcs, *Vázlat Európa három történeti régiójáról* [A sketch of the three historical regions of Europe] (Budapest: Magvető, 1983).

15. I developed the ideas summarized in this subchapter, with documentation, in "Béla Bartók and the Concept of Nation and *Volk* in Modern Hungary," *The Musical Quarterly* 78, no. 2 (1994): 255–87.

16. This legend is very similar to the myth of ethnogenesis found in other European nations. See Jenő Szűcs, "A nemzet historikuma és a történelemszemlélet nemzeti látószöge (Hozzászólás egy vitához)," in his *Nemzet és történelem: Tanulmányok* [Nation and history: Essays] (Budapest: Gondolat, 1984), 11–188 (German translation, *Nation und Geschichte: Studien* [Budapest: Akadémiai, 1981]). See also Gyula Szekfű, *Magyar történet* [Hungarian history], ed. Bálint Hóman and Gyula Szekfű (Budapest: Királyi Magyar Egyetemi Nyomda, 1936), 5:156, 558–62.

17. This concept goes back to the *Tripartitum Juris Consuetudinari inclyti Regni Hungariae*, the fundamental work on Hungarian common law, compiled by István Werbőczy in the sixteenth century, which listed the rights and codified the equality of barons and common nobles (*köznemes*) and summarized the laws about the servitude of the peasantry.

18. Hanák, ed., *Magyarország története 1890–1919*, 1:426–35, 449–63.

19. János, *The Politics of Backwardness in Hungary*, 14?.

20. [Pál Engelman], "A magyar földmives-munkásosztály történetéhez" [Essay on the history of the Hungarian agrarian proletariat]," *Huszadik Század* [Twentieth century] 8, no. 4 (1903): 919.

21. Dezső Malonyay, *A magyar nép művészete II: A székelyföldi, a csángó és a torockói magyar nép művészete* [The art of the Hungarian people, vol. 2: The art of the Hungarians of the Székely, Csángó, and Torockó areas] (Budapest: Franklin Társulat, 1909), 4. The writer of this letter points out the social, ethnic, and territorial distance between the gentleman-folklorist and the Székler peasant: between the higher and the lower class, the culture of the mainstream Hungarian and that of the Székler, the inhabitant of the capital and that of the country's periphery.

22. Quoted in Gyula Ortutay, "Folk-Life Study in Hungary," in *Hungarian Folklore: Essays* (Budapest: Akadémiai, 1972), 28. See also Catherine Károlyi's account of the tulip movement in *Együtt a forradalomban* (Budapest: Európa, 1967), 19; Tamás Hofer, "Construction of the 'Folk Cultural Heritage' in Hungary and Rival Versions of National Identity," *Ethnologia Europaea* 21 (1991): 145–70.

23. Because of the specific historical context, I use the term "Gypsy" rather than "Roma," now considered more appropriate. Zoltán Ács, *Nemzetiségek a történelmi Magyarországon* [Nationalities in historical Hungary] (Budapest: Kossuth, 1986); Ferenc Glatz, *Magyarok a Kárpát-medencében* [Hungarians in the Carpathian Basin] (Budapest: Pallas Lap- és Könyvkiadó Vállalat, 1988); László Kósa and Antal Filep, *A magyar nép táji-történeti tagolódása* [The geographical and historical stratification of the Hungarian people] (Budapest: Akadémiai, 1978); Pál Engel, "Beilleszkedés Európába a kezdetektől 1440-ig" [Hungary's acculturation into European society from its beginnings to 1440], in *Magyarok Európában* [Hungarians in Europe], vol. 1 (Budapest: Háttér Lap és Könyvkiadó, 1990); Viktor Szombathelyi and Gyula László, eds., *Magyarrá lett keleti népek* [The assimilation of oriental people into the Hungarians] (Budapest: Panoráma, 1988). For an English summary see Katherine Verdery, *Transylvanian Villagers: Three Centuries of Political, Economic, and Ethnic Change* (Berkeley: University of California Press, 1983). See also relevant sections of historical surveys in nn. 12 and 24.

24. In this respect, Hungarian nationalism shared traits of European nationalism in general. My analysis of Hungarian nationalism in this and the other chapters benefited greatly from modern works on this issue. See Benedict Anderson, *Imagined Communities: Reflections on the Origin and Spread of Nationalism* (London: Verso, 1983); Ernest Gellner, *Nations and Nationalism* (Oxford: Oxford University Press, 1983); E. J. Hobsbawm, *Nations and Nationalism since 1780: Programme, Myth, Reality* (Cam-

bridge: Cambridge University Press, 1990); Hans Kohn, *The Age of Nationalism* (New York: Harper, 1962); Hugh Seton-Watson, *Nations and States: An Enquiry into the Origins of Nations and the Politics of Nationalism* (Boulder, Colo.: Westview Press, 1977); Anthony D. Smith, *The Ethnic Origins of Nations* (Oxford: Blackwell, 1986); Szűcs, *Nation und Geschichte;* Larry Wolff, *Inventing Eastern Europe: The Map of Civilization on the Mind of the Enlightenment* (Stanford: Stanford University Press, 1994).

25. See the remembrances of Dezső Szabó and Zsigmond Kende, quoted in *Magyarország története 1890–1919*, 1:172–73.

26. Bartók's father also composed such a poem. For translation of part of this poem and the nationalist tradition in Bartók's family background see my dissertation, "Béla Bartók and Hungarian Nationalism," 37–44.

27. On the historical sources of the *verbunkos*, see Bence Szabolcsi, *A XIX. század magyar romantikus zenéje* [Hungarian romantic music in the nineteenth century] (Budapest: Zeneműkiadó, 1951); László Dobszay, *Magyar Zenetörténet* [A history of Hungarian music] (Budapest: Gondolat, 1984); Bálint Sárosi, *Gypsy Music* (Budapest: Gondolat, 1975); Bence Szabolcsi, *A magyar zenetörténet kézikönyve* [A concise history of Hungarian music] (1947; reprint, Budapest: Zeneműkiadó, 1979), in English translation: *A Concise History of Hungarian Music*, 2d ed., transl. Sara Karig, Fred Macnicol, and Florence Knepler (Budapest: Corvina, 1974); *Hungarian Dances: 1784–1810*, ed. Géza Papp, vol. 7 of *Musicalia Danubiana* (Budapest: Magyar Tudományos Akadémia Zenetudományi Intézet, 1986).

28. I follow here the unpublished hypothesis of Bálint Sárosi, to whom I am grateful for sharing his research and thoughts on the origin of new-style folk songs.

29. On professional music making and the role of the Gypsies in Eastern European peasant society, see William Noll, "Economics of Music Patronage among Polish and Ukrainian Peasants to 1939," *Ethnomusicology* 35 (1991): 349–80; Bálint Sárosi, "Professionelle und nichtprofessionelle Volksmusikanten in Ungarn," *Studia instrumentorum musicae popularis* 7 (1981): 10–16; Bálint Sárosi, "An Instrumental Melody," *Yearbook for Traditional Music* 17 (1985): 198–205; Judit Frigyesi, "Hungarian Folk Music," *Garland Encyclopaedia of World Music—Europe* (in progress). The origin, style, and national character of Hungarian gypsy music are still a controversial issue. The best English language summaries are Bálint Sárosi, *Gypsy Music* (Budapest: Corvina, 1970); and Bálint Sárosi, *Folk Music: Hungarian Musical Idiom* (Budapest: Corvina, 1986).

30. Gypsy musicians were often joined by Jews, thus creating the strange situation of the most genuinely Hungarian music being performed by non-Hungarians. See my "Jews and Hungarians in Modern Hungarian Musical Culture," in *Modern Jews and Their Musical Agendas*, vol. 9 of *Studies in Contemporary Jewry*, ed. Ezra Mendelsohn (Oxford: Oxford University Press, 1993), 40–60.

31. Typically, a history of music published by the Hungarian Academy of Sciences in 1908 considered virtually all Hungarian monophonic vocal compositions since the Middle Ages "folk song" (Bertalan Fabó, *A magyar népdal zenei fejlődése* [The musical

development of Hungarian folk song] [Budapest: Magyar Tudományos Akadémia, 1908]). György Kerényi edited a volume of *magyar nóta* collected from the peasants in the twentieth century. Mór Jókai, a famous Hungarian novelist, referred to about 450 Hungarian tunes in his works and was supposedly able to sing many of them even at the age of seventy-five. In his childhood Bartók too was fascinated by gypsy music; in fact, the first concert he heard featured orchestral elaborations of *magyar nóta*, and at the age of four he could already play 40 tunes on the piano. See Szabolcsi, *A XIX. század magyar romantikus zenéje*, 139–49; Tibor Tallián, *Béla Bartók: The Man and His Work*, trans. Gyula Gulyás (Budapest: Corvina, 1981), 15–17.

32. Szabolcsi, *A XIX. század magyar romantikus zenéje*, 10.

33. Ibid., 14. The first chapter of this work is entitled "A magyar zenei romantika eszmevilága: mámor és kijózanodás" [The conceptual framework of Hungarian musical romanticism: Euphoria and disenchantment].

34. Szekfű, *Magyar történet*, 5:335. The people referred to in this paragraph are well-known personalities of the Hungarian aristocracy of the nineteenth century.

35. Kornél Abrányi, *A magyar zene a 19-ik században* [Hungarian music in the nineteenth century] (Budapest: Rózsavölgyi és társa, 1900), 131.

36. A Hungarian "rejoices with tears" (sírva vígad), according to a popular saying, and the sad sweetness of slow gypsy music embodies the Hungarian's "weeping-rejoicing Asian soul." See Bálint Sárosi, "Merry-making in Tears," in *Folk Music*, 83–85.

37. *Magyar történet*, 5:517. Szekfű's words in the last sentence are literally "into the hand of the *prímás*." The leading violinist of the gypsy ensemble, the *prímás*, is the one who normally receives the payment.

38. Neither the radical intelligentsia nor the conservative circles called into question the Hungarianness of any of these styles.

CHAPTER 3

1. Zoltán Horváth, *Magyar századforduló: A második reformnemzedék története, 1896–1914* [Turn-of-the-century Hungary: The history of the second reform generation, 1896–1914] (Budapest: Gondolat, 1961).

2. Carl E. Schorske, *Fin-de-Siècle Vienna: Politics and Culture* (New York: Random House, Vintage Books, 1981), 295.

3. Among its representative political figures we find Count István Széchenyi, Baron Miklós Wesselényi, Lajos Kossuth, Ferenc Kölcsey, Ferenc Deák, László Lovassy, Count Aurél Dessewffy, and Count Lajos Batthyány. The activities of Count György Festetics and Sámuel Tessedik prepared the reform of agriculture. Poets, writers, and musicians contributed to the national movement, especially Sándor Kisfaludy, Mihály Fazekas, József Katona, Mihály Vörösmarty, Sándor Petőfi, and János Arany in literature, and in music János Bihari, János Lavotta, and Ferenc Erkel.

4. Mihály Babits, "Széchenyi István," *Mai magyarok—régi magyarokról* [(special

issue) The Hungarians of today—about the Hungarians of old times], *Szép Szó* [Beautiful word] 1, nos. 1–3 (1936): 146–54.

5. József Eötvös, "A zsidók emancipációja" [The emancipation of the Jews (1840)], quoted in *Nemzeti Olvasókönyv* [Readings about nation and nationalism], ed. Sándor Lukácsy (Budapest: Gondolat, 1988), 144.

6. Oszkár Sashegyi, "Széchenyiről röviden" [About Széchenyi briefly], afterword to *Széchenyi István válogatott művei* [István Széchenyi's selected works], ed. György Spira (Budapest: Szépirodalmi, 1991), 3:1228.

7. *Széchenyi István válogatott művei*, 1:267.

8. Ibid., 1:86.

9. Gyula Szekfű, *Magyar történet* (Budapest: Királyi Magyar Egyetemi Nyomda, 1939), 5:315.

10. Zsigmond Móricz, "Bethlen Gábor," *Mai magyarok—régi magyarokról*, 84.

11. Jenő Péterfy, "Báró Eötvös József, mint regényíró" [Baron József Eötvös as a writer of novels], in *Péterfy Jenő válogatott művei* [The selected works of Jenő Péterfy], ed. István Sőtér (Budapest: Szépirodalmi, 1983), 539, 547.

12. Gábor Egressy, "Indítvány a szellemhonosítás ügyében" [Proposal for a nationalization of spirit (1848)], quoted in *Nemzeti Olvasókönyv*, 119.

13. The idea that the Hungarian nation was destined to disappear originated with Herder. See Johann Gottfried Herder, *Outline of a Philosophy of the History of Man* (1784), trans. T. Churchill (New York: Bergman, n.d.), 476.

14. I thank Andras Hamori for the translation of these lines by Vörösmarty. In the surrealistic imagery of "Foreword" [Előszó (1850–51)], another poem influenced by Catholic imagery of the apocalypse, disaster comes in the shape of a monster ravaging the earth, playing with human heads, trampling on hearts. In the middle of the poem cosmic nothingness is captured by one line that emptily lists words symbolizing death: "Now is winter, and stillness, and snow, and death" (Most tél van és csend és hó és halál).

15. The two lines are from Vörösmarty's poem "Thoughts in the library" [Gondolatok a könyvtárban (1844)], in *Az ember élete: Vörösmarty Mihály válogatott művei* (Budapest: Kozmosz, 1986). On " 'and yet' morality" (*de mégis*) see Péter Hanák, *The Start of Endre Ady's Literary Career (1903–1905)* (Budapest: Akadémiai, 1980), 28–30. See also István Király, "The 'and yet' morality," and "Hungarian existence as a mission: the *kurucz*-poems," in *Ady Endre* (Budapest: Magvető, 1972), 1:198–206, 2:701–12.

16. "Poesy" [Költészet (1847)], translated in *His Entire Poetic Works*, by Sándor Petőfi, trans. Frank Szomy (Boca Raton, Fla.: Petőfi Publications, 1973), 436.

17. Béla Bartók Jr., *Bartók műhelyében* [In Béla Bartók's workshop] (Budapest: Szépirodalmi, 1982), 14–15. The translation of a stanza of this poem comes from my "Béla Bartók and Hungarian nationalism: The development of Bartók's social and political ideas at the turn of the century (1899–1903)" (Ph.D. diss., University of Pennsylvania, 1989).

18. Béla Bartók, Jr., ed., *Bartók Béla családi levelei* [Béla Bartók's family letters] (Budapest: Zeneműkiadó, 1981), 110.

19. The significance of reading newspaper reports as "mass ceremony in creating national spirit" is interestingly described in Benedict Anderson, *Imagined Communities: Reflections on the Origin and Spread of Nationalism* (London: Verso, 1983), 35.

20. Gyula Szekfű, *Három nemzedék: Egy hanyatló kor története* [Three generations: The history of an era of decline] (Budapest: "Élet"-kiadás, 1920–22), 51, 52, 57.

21. Béla Balázs was among those who were disappointed by the aestheticism of intellectual circles in Berlin: "This entire cultural milieu in which I find myself appears somehow outdated. . . . I feel it to be claustrophobic. . . . Where is that famous West European culture which is still fresh and unknown, into which I can enter and from which I can draw sustenance? . . . Everything I meet appears to consist of empty noise and verbosity; I feel decadent weakness here, not the freshness of spiritual energy" (Mary Gluck, *Georg Lukács and His generation: 1900–1918* [Cambridge, Mass.: Harvard University Press, 1985], 117). See Gluck's book for a good summary of the crisis of aestheticism at the beginning of the century. The problematic relation of art to social and political issues remained an open question throughout the first half of the century, as illustrated by the debate in the 1920s between Babits, Osvát, Ignotus, and others about the "responsibility of the literate."

22. Other significant figures who published in *A Hét* included Bernát Alexander, Zoltán Ambrus, Lajos Bíró, Viktor Cholnoky, Miksa Fenyő, Andor Gábor, Ferenc Herczeg, Zsigmond Justh, Dániel Papp, Gyula Reviczky, Ernő Szép, Dezső Szomory, Zoltán Thury, Lajos Tolnai, István Tömörkény, and János Vajda.

23. The circle was frequented by Bernát Alexander, Béla Balázs, Hilda Bauer, Béla Fogarasi, Lajos Fülep, Imre Kner, Anna Lesznai, Karl Mannheim, Emma Ritoók, Leo Popper, Károly Tolnai, and Béla Zalai.

24. Chapters 7 and 8 discuss the new and deeper meaning of traditional poetic images. For the possible influence of the *Jugendstil* on Bartók's style see János Kárpáti, "A Typical Jugendstil Composition: Bartók's String Quartet No. 1," *The Hungarian Quarterly* 36, no. 137 (spring 1995): 130–40.

25. Disenchantment with the broader public's response to modern music also gave Bartók the impetus for these pieces; he wanted to create a repertoire that would lead the public toward his serious pieces.

26. György Bölöni called Reinitz's performances of his Ady songs "Ady-rituals" (László Flórián and János Vajda, *Reinitz Béla* [Budapest: Zeneműkiadó, 1978], 34).

27. Endre Ady, "A nacionalizmus alkonya" [The fall of nationalism], in *Ady Endre válogatott cikkei és tanulmányai* [Endre Ady's selected articles and essays] (Budapest: Szépirodalmi, 1954), 113.

28. "We dream without dream" in the poem "Hungary in winter" [A téli Magyarország (1907)].

29. Ady, "Betlehem néma" [Bethlehem is silent], in *Ady Endre válogatott cikkei*, 34.

30. Ignotus, "Gyulai Pál" (1906), quoted in Horváth, *Magyar századforduló*, 184.

31. Quoted in Ilona Fodor, "Babits Mihály és a Jónás könyve" [Mihály Babits and his Book of Jonah], *Kortárs* 11, no. 2 (February 1967): 302.

32. József Révai, *Ady* (Budapest: Szikra, 1949), 109–10.

33. The journalist is quoted in Gluck, *Georg Lukács*, 113. Tisza wrote in 1912, "The incomprehensible bombast [of the literature represented by *Nyugat*] is nothing more than the chaotic exterior of spiritual anarchy and an emptiness of mind and heart" (quoted in Gluck, *Georg Lukács*, 114).

34. The following points are discussed in more detail in my article "Béla Bartók and the Concept of Nation and *Volk* in Modern Hungary," *The Musical Quarterly* 78, no. 2 (1994): 255–87.

35. "Cigányzene? Magyar zene?" (Magyar népdalok a német zeneműpiacon) [Gypsy music or Hungarian music? (Hungarian folk songs in German music publications), 1931]; in *Béla Bartók Essays*, ed. Benjamin Suchoff (Lincoln: University of Nebraska Press, 1976), 207.

36. Kodály had significant influence on Bartók's conception of Hungarian folk music. Although the two composers shared many of the ideas outlined below, their ideas and the social significance of their works differed in several ways. I deal here only with Bartók's attitude.

37. This and the following quote come from Béla Bartók, "Mi a népzene?" [What is folk music? (1931)], in *Bartók Béla összegyűjtött írásai* [The collected writings of Béla Bartók], ed. András Szőllősy (Budapest: Zeneműkiadó, 1966), 672–73; Tibor Tallián, ed., *Bartók Béla írásai I* [The writings of Béla Bartók, I] (Budapest: Zeneműkiadó, 1989), 138–39; and *Bartók Essays*, 5–6.

38. Béla Bartók, *The Hungarian Folk Song* (1924), ed. Benjamin Suchoff, trans. M. D. Calvocoressi (Albany: New York State University Press, 1981).

39. "The Folk Songs of Hungary" (1928), in *Béla Bartók Essays*, 332–33; and "The Influence of Peasant Music on Modern Music" (1931), in ibid., 341.

40. Count Géza Zichy commented on the national song competition in 1912: "Unfortunately, national feeling has disappeared almost entirely from our modern music. But it is alive in the song and spread enthusiastically by [our] singers" ("Országos Dalosverseny" [National song competition (1912)], quoted in Horváth, *Magyar századforduló*, 461).

41. Emil Haraszti, "Cigányzene—parasztzene—hivatalos zene" [Gypsy music, peasant music, official music], *Budapesti Hirlap*, 1 May 1929, 1–3; original emphasis. My article "Nation and *Volk*" explains that Haraszti did raise relevant issues: his comment on the elitist intelligentsia's rejection of gypsy music has more than a grain of truth.

42. It is obvious from Haraszti's rhetoric that its focus was Bartók and Kodály; the article mentions Bartók.

43. Gyula Illyés, *Magyarok* [Hungarians] (1939), reprinted in *Itt élned kell* [Here is where you have to live] (Budapest: Szépirodalmi, 1976), 1:16.

44. Pál Ignotus, "Népiség" [The folk movement (1959)], reprinted in *Századvég* [Turn of the century] (The journal of social studies of the College István Bibó, Budapest, 1988), 6–7:325. Pál Ignotus took as his surname the pseudonym of his famous father, Hugo Veigelsberg.

45. Ignotus, "A magyar kultúra és a nemzetiségek" [Hungarian culture and the nationalities], *Nyugat* 1, no. 4 (1908): 225.

46. Ignotus's answer to Kálmán Mikszáth in "Hazafiság és irodalom—Egy kis polémia" [Patriotism and literature—polemics] (1904), reprinted in *A Hét: Politikai és irodalmi szemle, 1900–1907* [The week: Political and literary observer, 1900–1907] (Budapest: Magvető, 1978), 215; "Utóirat a perzekútor-esztetikáról" [Afterword about the aesthetics of persecution], *Nyugat* 1, no. 4 (1908): 227–28.

47. To Irmy Jurkovics, 15 August 1905, in *Bartók Béla levelei* [Béla Bartók letters], ed. János Demény (Budapest: Zeneműkiadó, 1976), 97; see also *Béla Bartók Letters*, ed. János Demény, trans. Péter Balabán and István Farkas (New York: St. Martin's, 1971), 50.

48. Zoltán Kodály, "Confession: A Lecture Given to the Nyugat Circle of Friends (1932)," in *The Selected Writings of Zoltán Kodály*, ed. Ferenc Bónis, trans. Lili Halapy and Fred Macnicol (London: Boosey and Hawkes, 1974), 210.

49. Among the works created by this movement were scholarly studies by Lajos Kiss, Gyula Ortutay, Géza Kiss, and Ferenc Erdei and autobiographical novels by Péter Veres, József Darvas, Gyula Illyés, and Géza Féja.

50. István Vas, *Nehéz szerelem: Harmadik rész* [Difficult love: Third part] (Budapest: Szépirodalmi, 1984), 1:101.

51. See, for instance, Babits's high praise for Karinthy's primarily "oral" oeuvre, quoted in László Halász, *Karinthy Frigyes alkotásai és vallomásai tükrében* [Frigyes Karinthy in his works and confessions] (Budapest: Szépirodalmi, 1972), 11.

52. Károly Lyka, *Festészeti életünk története a milleneumtól az első világháborúig* [The history of our visual arts from the millennium to the First World War] (Budapest: Corvina, 1953), 21.

53. Quoted in Sándor Scheiber, "A magyar zsidóság szellemi élete a századfordulótól: Kitekintéssel Bartók Bélára" [The intellectual life of the Hungarian Jews from the turn of the century: With an outlook on Béla Bartók], in *Folklór és tárgytörténet (Folklore und Motivgeschichte)* (Budapest: A Magyar Izraeliták Országos Képviseletének kiadása, 1984), 3:209.

54. Béla Zsolt, *Kilenc koffer* [Nine suitcases], ed. Ferenc Kőszeg (Budapest: Magvető, 1980), 368–70.

CHAPTER 4

1. Ignotus [Hugo Veigelsberg], "Költés és való" [Poésie and the real], in *Ignotus válogatott írásai* [The selected writings of Ignotus] (Budapest: Szépirodalmi, 1969), 542–44. Originally published in the journal *Nyugat* in 1926.

2. Mihály Babits, *Keresztül-kasul az életemen* [Through and around my life] (Budapest: Pesti Szalon, 1993), 96–97.

3. The quote from Lajos Fülep's "A művészet útvesztője" [The labyrinth of art] and the following quote from Krisztina Passuth's *A Nyolcak Festészete* [The art of "the Eight"] occur in Mary Gluck, *Georg Lukács and His Generation: 1900–1918* (Cambridge, Mass.: Harvard University Press, 1985), 112 and 116.

4. Ignotus, "Hadi készületek" [Preparations for war], *Nyugat* 1, nos. 24–26 (1908): 451.

5. Béla Tábor, *A zsidóság két útja* [The two roads of the Jews] (Budapest: Pesti Szalon, 1990), 23; originally published in 1939. I translate the Hungarian *faj* as "ethnicity" throughout this and the following quotations because its more precise meaning, "race," connotes what we now term "ethnicity."

6. Béla Balázs, *Napló 1903–1914* [Diary 1903–1914] (Budapest: Magvető, 1982), 1:164 and 133.

7. See *A modern dráma fejlődésének története* [History of the development of modern drama] (Budapest: Magvető, 1911), 27–62, esp. on drama as mass art and on its universality and necessity.

8. "A tragédiának metafizikus teóriája a német romantikában és Hebbel Frigyes" [The theory of the metaphysical nature in German romanticism and Friedrich Hebbel], *Nyugat* 1, no. 2 (1908): 89.

9. Bernát Alexander, "Irodalmi bajok" [Literary troubles] (1890), reprinted in *A Hét: Politikai és irodalmi szemle, 1890–1899, Válogatás* [The week: Political and literary observer, 1890–1899, selections] (Budapest: Magvető, 1978), 22 and 23.

10. Denijs Dille, "Bartók, lecteur de Nietzsche et de La Rochefoucauld," in *Béla Bartók: Regard sur le passé*, ed. Yves Lenoir, Études Bartókiennes no. 1 (Namur: Presses universitaires de Namur, 1990), 87–105; András Batta, "Gemeinsames Nietzsche-Symbol bei Bartók und bei R. Strauss" [Common Nietzsche symbols in Bartók and R. Strauss], *Studia Musicologica* 24 (1982): 275–82. I thank László Somfai, director of the Bartók Archives of the Institute for Musicology, Budapest, for letting me consult the markings Bartók made in his copies of Nietzsche's works.

11. Friedrich Nietzsche, *Human, All Too Human: A Book for Free Spirits*, trans. R. J. Hollingdale (Cambridge: Cambridge University Press, 1986), 13–14; original emphasis.

12. Arnold Schoenberg, *Theory of Harmony*, trans. Roy Carter (Berkeley: University of California Press, 1983), 8.

13. György Lukács, "Az utak elváltak" [The roads parted], *Ifjúkori művek (1902–1918)* [Youthful writings (1902–1918)] (Budapest: Magvető, 1977), 284, 286.

14. Gluck, *Georg Lukács*, 152.

15. Letter to Stefi Geyer, 17 July 1907, in *Béla Bartóks Briefe an Stefi Geyer, 1907–1908* (Basel: Paul Sacher, 1979), document 3. On the context of these lines, see the discussion in chapter 5.

16. György Lukács, "Balázs Béla: Hét mese" [Béla Balázs: Seven tales], in *Ifjúkori művek*, 710. We will see (in chapter 7) that Lukács associated this definition of the "primordial" condition with the feminine.

17. György Lukács, "A vándor énekel: Balázs Béla költeményei" [The wanderer sings: The poems of Béla Balázs], in *Ifjúkori művek*, 473.

18. Ödön Lechner, "Magyar formanyelv nem volt, hanem lesz" [Hungarian language of form (architecture) did not exist in the past, but it will in the future], quoted in János Gerle, Attila Kovács, and Imre Makovecz, *A századforduló magyar építészete* [Hungarian turn-of-the-century architecture] (Budapest: Szépirodalmi, 1990), 125.

19. Both buildings are standing today: Földtani Intézet (the Institute of Geology) is located at Budapest XIV, Népstadion út 14; and Posta-takarékpénztár (the Postabank, which Lechner designed with Sándor Baumgarten) is located at Budapest V, Hold (Rosenberg házaspár) u. 4.

20. Ady based this style on Kálmán Thaly's editions of real and pseudo-*kurucz* poems. The *kurucz* claimed descent from the peasant army of György Dózsa, the leader of the greatest peasant uprising that took place in the sixteenth century. Legends surround the activities of these soldiers who carried on guerrilla warfare against the Habsburgs. They symbolize the poor abandoned fugitive and the freedom fighter—both metaphors of Hungarian fate. On the fugitive-image see my article "Can nationalism and modernism co-exist?—The case of the hero-figure in Hungarian modernism" (forthcoming).

21. László Somfai, "The Influence of Peasant Music on the Finale of Bartók's Piano Sonata: An Assignment for Musical Analysis," in *Studies in Musical Sources and Style: Essays in Honor of Jan Larue*, ed. E. K. Wolf and E. Roesner (Madison, Wis.: A-R Editions, 1990), 537.

22. "The Folk Songs of Hungary" (1928) and "The Relation of Folk Song to the Development of the Art Music of Our Time" (1921), both in *Béla Bartók Essays*, ed. Benjamin Suchoff (Lincoln: University of Nebraska Press, 1976), 338 and 326.

23. "The Folk Songs of Hungary," 332.

24. "Mi a népzene?" [What is folk music?] (1931), in *Bartók Béla összegyűjtött írásai* [The collected writings of Béla Bartók], ed. András Szőllősy (Budapest: Zeneműkiadó, 1966), 672–73; original emphasis (see also English text in *Bartók Essays*, 5–6).

25. "The Relation of Folk Song," 321; original emphasis.

26. This and the following quote are from ibid., 321–22.

27. "Volkmusik und ihre Bedeutung für die Neuzeitliche Komposition" [The influence of peasant music on modern music (1932)], in *Bartók Béla írásai I* [The writings of Béla Bartók, I], ed. Tibor Tallián (Budapest: Zeneműkiadó, 1989), 256; and *Bartók Essays*, 342.

28. See "The Folk Songs of Hungary," 334–35.

29. Anton Webern, *The Path to the New Music*, ed. Willi Reich (Bryn Mawr: Theodore Presser, 1963), 34.

30. The recognition of melodic-harmonic unity inspired Heinrich Schenker to develop his analytical method. See his *Harmony*, ed. Oswald Jonas, trans. Elisabeth Mann Borgese (Cambridge, Mass.: MIT Press, 1973), 173, 212.

31. Among the numerous examples are the transposition of the folk-song-like pentatonic theme by a fifth, which occurs in the polyphonic first theme of the Prima parte of the Third String Quartet; the use of two choruses in the *Cantata profana*, which is a symbolic synthesis of the performing apparatus of Romanian colindas and Bach's *St. Matthew Passion*; and the Marcia movement of the Sixth String Quartet, a tragically sarcastic magnification of the march that combines the type used in Beethoven's string quartets with Hungarian *verbunkos*.

32. Gyula Krúdy, *A vörös postakocsi* (Budapest: Editorg, 1992), 7–8.

33. Bartók struggled throughout his career with the large-scale form of his pieces, and especially with the problem of the ending. Unlike Stravinsky or Webern, Bartók did not like to leave his pieces "open"—to end with a question mark or with an unresolved contrast. Nor did he want the resolution to come about in a simple or easy manner. In several cases, he changed the shape of the finale at the suggestion of performers, as in the Sonata for Solo Violin (the last movement of which exists in two versions) and the Concerto for Orchestra. He made major cuts in the finale of the Sonata, 1926, during the compositional process and discarded the entire conception of the last movement of the Sixth String Quartet at a relatively late stage of the composition.

34. Carl E. Schorske, *Fin-de-Siècle Vienna: Politics and Culture* (New York: Random House, Vintage Books, 1981), 317.

35. "Molnár Ferenc Andorja" ["Andor" by Ferenc Molnár], in György Lukács, *Magyar irodalom, magyar kultúra: Válogatott tanulmányok* [Hungarian literature, Hungarian culture: Selected essays], comp. and ed. Ferenc Fehér and Zoltán Kenyeres (Budapest: Gondolat, 1970), 146.

36. See Allan Janik and Stephen Toulmin, "Language, Ethics, and Representation," in *Wittgenstein's Vienna* (New York: Simon and Schuster, 1973), especially 155–64.

37. György Lukács, "Trisztán hajóján" [On the ship of Tristan], in *Magyar irodalom, Magyar kultúra*, 96–97.

38. Ibid., 97.

39. Attila József, "Miért legyek én tisztességes? Kiterítenek úgyis! / Miért ne legyek tisztességes! Kiterítenek úgyis" (1936).

40. Milán Füst, *Napló* [Diary] (Budapest: Magvető, 1976), 2:74.

41. This and the following passage occur in Miklós Lackó, "Osvát Ernő," in *Szerep és mű: Kultúrtörténeti tanulmányok* [The role and the artwork: Essays in cultural history] (Budapest: Gondolat, 1981), 26, 29.

42. Füst, *Napló*, 2:38.

43. Lukács, "Trisztán hajóján," 102.

44. Quoted in László Halász, *Karinthy Frigyes alkotásai és vallomásai tükrében* [Frigyes Karinthy in his works and confessions] (Budapest: Szépirodalmi, 1972), 115–19.

CHAPTER 5

1. "The Folk Songs of Hungary" (1928), in *Béla Bartók Essays*, ed. Benjamin Such-off (Lincoln: University of Nebraska Press, 1976), 332–33.

2. To Márta and Hermina Ziegler (Darázs, 4 February 1909), in Béla Bartók, Jr., ed., *Bartók Béla családi levelei* [Béla Bartók's family letters] (Budapest: Zeneműkiadó, 1981), 187–88.

3. Tibor Tallián, ed., *Bartók Béla írásai I* [The writings of Béla Bartók, I] (Budapest: Zeneműkiadó, 1989), 181.

4. As Bartók proceeded with the series of lectures planned for Harvard, he changed parts of the outline but not the general concept. On the basis of Bartók's handwriting, Tallián believes that the idea of the last lecture was a later addition (see ibid., 181).

5. An example of this is the pentatonic melody in the last movement of the First String Quartet.

6. For example, Bartók used the scheme of four-line strophic songs as the model for the first theme of the first movement of the Violin Concerto (no. 2), the first theme of the first movement of the Sonata for two Pianos and Percussion, and the first theme of the second movement of the *Music for Strings, Percussion, and Celesta*.

7. "Népzenénk és a szomszéd népek népzenéje" [Our folk music and the folk music of the neighboring people] (1934), in *Bartók Béla összegyűjtött írásai* [Collected writings of Béla Bartók], ed. András Szőllősy (Budapest: Zeneműkiadó, 1966), 416. Both the Hungarian swineherd melodies and the *kolomeika* form part of a broad and more universal dance music tradition whose origin could be traced back to sixteenth-century dance music, and perhaps even to the Middle Ages. See Bálint Sárosi, *Folk Music: Hungarian Musical Idiom* (Budapest: Corvina, 1986), 158.

8. In Hungarian ethnomusicological conventions, folk songs that are not performed parlando-rubato have the tempo marking "giusto," which means metric performance with some flexibility in the execution of beats and rhythmic patterns.

9. In that respect, Bartók's compositional process differs from Stravinsky's. Except for his folk-song arrangements and some exceptional cases like the folk-song quote of the First String Quartet, Bartók did not derive his themes from an actual folk song. Among the thematic sketches and drafts, it is rare to find a theme that went through crucial changes between its first sketch notation and final form. There are some alterations—usually to make the theme more structural in the final context—but they involve minor aspects (typically the notation) and rarely bring change in character, melody, and rhythm. See László Somfai, ed., *Black Pocket-book: Sketches 1907–1922, by Béla Bartók* (Budapest: Editio Musica, 1987); László Somfai, *Béla Bartók: Composition, Concepts, and Autograph Sources* (Berkeley: University of California Press, 1996); Richard Taruskin, "Russian Folk Melodies in 'The Rite of Spring,'" *Journal of the American Musicological Society* 33, no. 3 (1980): 501–43.

10. The technique of "distorting" folk-song themes by means of unusual combi-

nations of folk elements is typical of Bartók. Other examples are the rondo theme of the last movement of the Sonata for Piano, 1926, and the theme of the recapitulation of the Prima parte of the Third String Quartet.

11. See Bartók's letter to Geyer, 21 December 1907, facsimile in *Béla Bartóks Briefe an Stefi Geyer, 1907–1908* (Basel: Paul Sacher, 1979), document 21.

12. These sections are discussed in my article "Between Rubato and Rigid Rhythm: A Particular Type of Rhythmical Asymmetry as Reflected in Bartók's Writings on Folk Music," *Studia Musicologica* 24 (1982): 327–37.

13. Somfai, *Béla Bartók,* 169.

14. This theme appears first as a penciled notation in the continuity draft for *Out of Doors* (between the movements With Drums and Pipes and Barcarolla) in almost exactly the same form used in the piece. See László Somfai, "Manuscript versus Urtext: The Primary Sources of Bartók's Works," *Studia Musicologica* 23 (1981): 30; Somfai, *Béla Bartók,* 57.

15. The thematic transformation I summarize here is explained in detail in László Somfai, "Analytical Notes on Bartók's Piano Year of 1926," *Studia Musicologica* 26 (1984), esp. 38, 39, 53, 58.

16. This is one of the two themes Bartók sketched for the composition, the other being the theme of the development. See Somfai, *Béla Bartók,* 52.

17. László Somfai, "A Characteristic Culmination Point in Bartók's Instrumental Forms," in *International Musicological Conference in Commemoration of Béla Bartók 1971,* ed. József Ujfalussy and János Breuer (Melville, N.Y.: Belwin Mills, 1972), 53–64. Somfai regards the pentatonic theme of the First String Quartet as the prototype of the idea of culmination. Examples from a variety of movements and pieces include the first and second movements of the Divertimento, the third movement of *Music for Strings, Percussion, and Celesta,* the first movement of the Second String Quartet and the first two piano concertos, and the Prima parte of the Third String Quartet. Like the caricature theme of the Fifth String Quartet, these themes come from the thematic material of the movement.

18. One such book, for instance, contained the short story "Jozafát" by Kristóf Schmid. It is an outwardly moralizing story, in twenty chapters, "for young people," celebrating Christian piety, asserting the superiority of Christianity over all other religions, and representing the Christian faith as something that automatically turns all bad people into good-hearted ones who (even if they are excessively rich) "wish nothing but the well-being of the people" (88). Bartók received this book for his "excellent work and good behavior" at the Nagyszőllős Middle School in 1891. The book is presently at the Bartók Archives of the Institute for Musicology, Budapest.

19. See my dissertation, "Béla Bartók and Hungarian Nationalism: The Development of Bartók's Social and Political Ideas at the Turn of the Century (1899–1903)" (Ph.D. diss., University of Pennsylvania, 1989).

20. See the letter to his mother, 10 September 1905, in *Bartók családi levelei,* 139–40.

21. Bartók got to know Stefi Geyer in 1907, perhaps during the opening celebrations for the Academy of Music, at which they both performed. Geyer was a child prodigy from the violin school of Jenő Hubay. By 1908 it was obvious to Bartók that Geyer did not return his affection, and Bartók was so deeply shaken that he decided not to have any contact with her for many years. In the thirties they met again, and during Bartók's last years spent in Europe they were close friends (Tibor Tallián, *Béla Bartók: The Man and His Work*, trans. Gyula Gulyás [Budapest: Corvina, 1981], 64–65).

22. This and the following quotes come from the same letter written in Csíkkarcfalva, 27 July 1907, in *Briefe an Stefi Geyer*, document 4.

23. Csíkkarcfalva, 17 July 1907, in ibid., document 4.

24. Here Bartók notates three measures of the first violin's part from no. 2, Allegro molto vivace (%, pianissimo) of Beethoven's String Quartet op. 131, without indicating where the theme comes from. Similarly, later in the letter he notates but does not name the Tristan chord and the motive leading to it.

25. 8 December 1907, in ibid., document 20.

26. 27 July 1907, in ibid., document 4.

27. Ibid., document 3.

28. Letters to Philip Heseltine, in János Demény, ed. *Bartók Béla levelei* [Béla Bartók letters] (Budapest: Zeneműkiadó, 1976) 262, 264.

29. 21 December 1907, in *Briefe an Stefi Geyer*, document 21.

30. This and the following quote come from his letter written to Irmy Jurkovics on 15 August 1905, in *Béla Bartók Letters*, ed. János Demény, trans. Péter Balaban and István Farkas (New York: St. Martin's, 1971), 50–51.

31. To Stefi Geyer, Vésztő, 6 September 1907, in ibid., 82.

32. To Irmy Jurkovics on 15 August 1905, in ibid., 50–51.

33. "The Folk Songs of Hungary," 332.

34. To Márta and Hermina Ziegler, Darázs, 4 February 1909, in *Bartók családi levelei*, 188.

35. Csíkrákos, 14 July 1907, in *Briefe an Stefi Geyer*, document 3; see also the letter of 26 November 1907 (document 17). Kodály wrote in a similar manner about the difficulty of collecting folk music. See, for instance, "Bartókról és a népdalgyűjtésről" [About Bartók and folk-music collecting] (1950), in *Visszatekintés: Összegyűjtött írások, beszédek, nyilatkozatok* [Looking back: Collected writings, speeches, interviews], by Zoltán Kodály, ed. Ferenc Bónis (Budapest: Zeneműkiadó, 1979), 2:457–58.

36. Bartók's letters and writings contain several sections illustrative of this situation and of his attitude. See "A magyar népzene," in *Bartók összegyűjtött írásai*, ed. András Szőllősy (Budapest: Zeneműkiadó, 1966), 580; *Bartók családi levelei*, 188. The same attitude is apparent in Kodály's writings about folk music in his letters and travel diary. See *Voyage en Hongrie*, ed. Márta Sz. Farkas (Budapest: Múzsák, n.d.).

37. "I would be very glad if you became interested in the collecting of folk songs although this is not really a musical but rather a scholarly undertaking" (Csíkrákos,

14 July 1907, in *Briefe an Stefi Geyer*, document 3). "Here are three more Székler folk songs. A bit too similar (boring)" (postcard, Gyergyó-kilyénfalva, 7 August 1907, in ibid., document 5). On other occasions Bartók refused the idea of collecting folk music only out of scholarly interest. See letter to Frederick Delius, in János Demény, ed., *Bartók Béla levelei* [Béla Bartók letters] (Budapest: Zeneműkiadó, 1976), 168.

38. See his letters written to Tango and Delius in Demény, *Bartók levelei*, 239–41, 168, and 170.

39. Here Bartók notates an old-style folk song. Csíkrákos, 14 July 1907, in *Briefe an Stefi Geyer*, document 3.

40. Whatever the political regime in Hungary, the culture of ethnic minorities was a popular topic for research, which displeased the minorities: they felt it treated their culture as an inferior object. Even though Bartók's original experience related to this ideology, he later conceived of peasant culture in somewhat different terms (see chapter 3).

41. Bertalan Pethő, *Bartók rejtekútja* (Budapest: Gondolat, 1984); shortened version in English: "The Meaning of Bartók's Secret Path," *Studia Musicologica* 24 (1982): 465–73.

42. Csíkkkarcfalva, 27 July 1907, in *Briefe an Stefi Geyer*, document 4.

43. The following two quotes are from Friedrich Nietzsche, *Human, All Too Human: A Book for Free Spirits*, trans. R. J. Hollingdale, 7th ed. (Cambridge: Cambridge University Press, 1993), 29, 30; original emphasis.

44. To Márta Ziegler, n.d. (probably from the beginning of 1915), in *Bartók családi levelei*, 235.

45. Rákospalota, 20 August 1907, in *Briefe an Stefi Geyer*, document 7. See undated letter (probably 1907) Rákospalota, in ibid., document 2.

46. Dezső Kosztolányi, "Bartók Béla" (1925), in *Bartók breviárium*, ed. József Ujfalussy and Vera Lampert (Budapest: Zeneműkiadó, 1980), 590.

47. To Stefi Geyer, 11 September 1907, in *Briefe an Stefi Geyer*, document 11.

48. *Bartók breviárium*, 590.

49. Somfai distinguishes two types of sketches. In some cases, Bartók worked out on paper difficult, usually polyphonic sections; these sketches belong to the working process and complement the compositional work Bartók carried out in his head. The other type involves true sketches: notes to preserve a musical idea. In Somfai's terminology, these are "thematic sketches." See Somfai, "Manuscript versus Urtext," 26–30.

50. In Hungarian usage at the time (and to some extent today), women dropped their names entirely after marriage. Thus Emma Schlesinger (her name at birth) became Mrs. Henrik Gruber—not "Emma Gruber" or "Gruber," both of them inventions I use here for the convenience of readers. (After her marriage to Kodály in 1910, she became Mrs. Zoltán Kodály.)

51. This and the following passage from letters to Emma Gruber, 26 July 1908 and

13 May 1907, come from Dezső Legány, ed., *Kodály Zoltán levelei* [Zoltán Kodály letters] (Budapest: Zeneműkiadó, 1982), 44 and 35.

52. Béla Balázs, *Napló* [Diary] (Budapest: Magvető, 1982), 1:264.

53. To Emma Gruber, Nagyszombat, 26 October 1906, in *Kodály levelei*, 26. Balázs's experience with folk music was much less intense and more frustrating (perhaps because he was a writer and a Jew). Yet he too captured something of the same feeling (*Napló*, 1:337).

54. *Napló*, 1:413.

55. Ibid., 326.

56. Ibid., 192. See also notes on 218, 265, 311, and 328.

57. The following four quotes come from ibid., 234, 335, 359, and 200.

58. To Emma Gruber, 5 January 1907, in *Kodály levelei*, 31.

59. *Napló*, 1:342.

60. Ibid., 1:255.

61. See letter to Emma Gruber, 13 July 1907, in *Kodály levelei*, 39.

62. *Napló*, 1:394.

63. Letter to Emma Gruber, 5–6 January 1907, in *Kodály levelei*, 32. See also ibid., 43, and Balázs, *Napló*, 1:394 and 372.

64. "The Metaphysics of Tragedy," in *Soul and Form*, by Georg Lukács, trans. Anna Bostock (London: Merlin, 1978), 156.

65. This and the following quote come from "The Metaphysics of Tragedy," 156, 158.

66. "Esztétikai kultúra" [Aesthetic culture], in *Ifjúkori művek (1902–1918)* [Youthful works], by György Lukács, ed. Árpád Tímár (Budapest: Magvető, 1977), 424, 434.

67. Ibid., 434–35.

68. An example of the first technique is the recapitulation in the first movement of the Sonata for two Pianos and Percussion. An example of the second technique is the recapitulation of the Prima parte of the Third String Quartet.

CHAPTER 6

1. Virág Móricz, *Apám regénye* [The story of my father], quoted in Zoltán Horváth, *Magyar századforduló: A második reformnemzedék története, 1896–1914* [Turn-of-the-century Hungary: The history of the second reform generation, 1896–1914] (Budapest: Gondolat, 1961), 287.

2. See Béla Balázs's poems "Ady Endrének" [To Endre Ady] and "Ady Endre halálára" [In memory of Endre Ady] in his *Az én utam: Összegyűjtött versek* [My path: Collected poems] (Budapest: Athaneum, 1945), 12, 127. For Ady's influence on Lukács, see Árpád Kadarkay, *Georg Lukács: Life, Thought, and Politics* (Cambridge: Basil Blackwell, 1991), 7, 11; Lee Congdon, *The Young Lukács* (Chapel Hill: University of North Carolina Press, 1983), 56–57. See also Lukács's remembrance describing Ady's effect in

György Lukács: His Life in Pictures and Documents, comp. and ed. Éva Fekete and Éva Karádi (Budapest: Corvina, 1981), 28–29.

3. Denijs Dille, "Bartók et Ady," in *Béla Bartók: Regard sur le passé,* ed. Yves Lenoir, Études Bartókiennes no. 1 (Namur: Presses universitaires de Namur, 1990), 293–302. In this article Dille quotes from a 1916 letter to which he stated he had access (but not pemission to reveal its intended recipient or where it was stored).

4. None of the major Bartók biographies—such as Ujfalussy's, Stevens's, or Tallián's—devote attention to Ady's influence on Bartók.

5. Bartók often prepared readings for his wife, Márta Ziegler. The markings in the volume *Új versek* (New poems) are meticulously done at the same point on each page (and probably not during the enthusiasm of a first reading). Several of the Ady volumes in Bartók's library contain more than one set of markings, made evidently during different readings and perhaps with different objectives. I am greatly indebted to László Somfai and Adrienne Gombócz of the Bartók Archives, Budapest, where these volumes are presently housed, for easing my access to them when they were part of a permanent exhibition.

6. This and the two following quotations come from Dille, "Bartók et Ady," 296–97.

7. On Ady's early development see especially György Belia, introduction to *Ady Endre levelei* [Endre Ady letters], 3 vols. (Budapest: Szépirodalmi, 1983); Erzsébet Vezér, *Ady Endre alkotásai és vallomásai tükrében* [The oeuvre and confessions of Endre Ady] (Budapest: Szépirodalmi, 1971); Péter Hanák, *The Start of Endre Ady's Literary Career (1903–1905)* (Budapest: Akadémiai, 1980).

8. See Ady's criticisms of nationalism and racism in Gyula Földessy, ed., *Ady Endre válogatott cikkei és tanulmányai* [Endre Ady's selected articles and essays] (Budapest: Szépirodalmi, 1954), 39, 46, 50, 63, 113; Sándor Koczkás and Erzsébet Vezér, ed., *A nacionalizmus alkonya* [The twilight of nationalism] (Budapest: Kossuth, 1960).

9. Endre Ady, "A társadalmi viszonyok" [The social conditions] (1902), in *Ady válogatott,* 37.

10. "Curriculum vitae" (1913), in ibid., 9.

11. On the influence of the European symbolist movement on Ady, see Péter Pór, "The Symbolist Turn in Endre Ady's Poetry," in *The Symbolist Movement in the Literature of European Languages,* ed. Anna Balakian (Budapest: Akadémiai, 1982), 361–80.

12. See the poems "Evening in the Bois" and "My bed calls," both of which I discuss in chapter 7.

13. The poems in this chapter come from Ady's first four volumes: *Új versek* [New poems (1906)], *Vér és arany* [Blood and gold (1907)], *Az Illés szekerén* [On Elijah's chariot (1908)], *Szeretném, ha szeretnének* [Longing for love (1909)], later collected in *Ady Endre összes versei* (Budapest: Osiris-Századvég, 1994).

14. Előd Halász, *Ady és Nietzsche* [Ady and Nietzsche] (Budapest, 1942); Pór, "The Symbolist Turn," 365–66.

15. Gyula Földessy, "Ady költészetének külső és belső formái" [The outer and inner forms of Ady's poetry], in *Esszépanoráma, 1900–1944* [Selection of essays, 1900–1944], ed. Zoltán Kenyeres (Budapest: Szépirodalmi, 1978), 1:269–89.

16. Of the two commonly used words for woman—*nő*, meaning female person in general, and *asszony*, meaning older or married woman—Ady chooses *asszony*.

17. György Lukács, "Ady Endre," in *Magyar irodalom, magyar kultúra: Válogatott tanulmányok* [Hungarian literature, Hungarian culture: Selected essays], comp. and ed. Ferenc Fehér and Zoltán Kenyeres (Budapest: Gondolat, 1970), 50.

18. In his foundational study of Ady's symbolism, János Horváth uses the term "surplus" to designate what words cannot express. See János Horváth, "Ady szimbolizmusa" [The symbolism of Ady], in *Esszépanoráma*, 1:522–36, esp. 526.

19. Quoted in Lajos Hatvany, *Ady: Cikkek, emlékezések, levelek* [Ady: Articles, remembrances, letters], comp. and ed. György Belia (Budapest: Szépirodalmi, 1974), 99. Ady is referring to his poem "Hunn, új legenda."

20. Ibid., 101.

21. Ibid., 100–101. Lukács recognized this aspect of Ady's poetry: "Ady is everything and the opposite of everything: his lyricism is the fixation of every momentary mood for eternity" ("Ady Endre," 50).

22. The following interpretation of Ady's mystical symbolism, most evident in his "God poems," differs from Király's (István Király, *Ady Endre*, 2 vols. [Budapest: Magvető, 1972]) but agrees on most major points with the (much less detailed) analyses of Lukács and Horváth. Király regarded Ady's metaphor of God as a peripheral phenomenon, essentially a dead end that gave way, in Ady's development, to a "return to life" (2:385–86). As I will show, the concept of life was an essential part of Ady's mystical attitude from the beginning.

23. "Mutasd meg, hogy nem vagy keresztyén, / Nem vagy zsidó: rettentő Úr vagy," from the poem "A nagy Cethalhoz" [To the great whale].

24. " Éreztem az Isten-szagot / S kerestem akkor valakit," from the poem "A Sionhegy alatt" [Beneath Mount Sion].

25. See also "Szeress engem, Istenem" [Love me, my God] and "A vidám Isten" [The joyful God].

26. Lukács, "Ady Endre," 48.

27. György Lukács, "Zsidó miszticizmus" [Jewish mysticism] (1911), in *Ifjúkori művek (1902–1918)* [Youthful works], ed. Árpád Tímár (Budapest: Magvető, 1977), 556–57.

28. On Jewish mysticism and the spirituality of East European Jewish life, see Abraham Joshua Heschel, *The Earth Is the Lord's: The Inner World of the Jew in Eastern Europe*, 3d ed. (Woodstock, Vt.: Jewish Lights, 1995); Gershom S. Scholem, *Major Trends in Jewish Mysticism*, 6th ed. (New York: Schocken Books, 1972); Rifka Schatz Uffenheimer, *Hasidism as Mysticism: Quietistic Elements in Eighteenth-century Hasidic Thought*, trans. Jonathan Chipman (Princeton: Princeton University Press, 1993).

29. This and the following three quotes come from Schatz Uffenheimer, *Hasidism as Mysticism*, 181, 211, 184, 172.

30. I discuss an aspect of this interchange, with a more detailed introduction to the problem, in my "Jews and Hungarians in Modern Hungarian Musical Culture," in *Studies in Contemporary Jewry: Jews and Music*, ed. Ezra Mendelsohn (Oxford: Oxford University Press, 1993), 9:40–60.

31. Lukács, "Zsidó miszticizmus," 556.

32. See Balázs's opinion on this subject, as expressed in his diary (Béla Balázs, *Napló* [Budapest: Magvető, 1982], 1:281–82). See also István Vas, *Nehéz szerelem: Harmadik rész* [Difficult love: Third part] (Budapest: Szépirodalmi, 1984), 1:17.

33. See his letter to Adél Brüll, Nagyvárad, 30 September 1903, in *Ady levelei*, 1:89. The expression "idők kovászai" (the ferments of time) appears in the fourth stanza of Ady's poem "A bélyeges sereg" (The branded host). Endre Nagy's comment comes from *Várad—Pest—Párizs* (Budapest: Szépirodalmi, 1958), 34.

34. Ady consistently associates "eternal going" with prophecy, a recurring image of several poems quoted in this chapter.

35. "Itthon vagyok" [I am at home], in *Ady válogatott*, 64–65.

36. "Az élet szobra" [A monument of life] and "Finale" [about the Dreyfus trial], in ibid., 89 and 124 (both original emphasis).

37. "Curriculum vitae," *Nyugat* (1909): 513–14.

38. "Levél az apámhoz" [Letter to my father], in *Ady válogatott*, 58.

39. György Lukács, "Esztétikai kultúra" [Aesthetic culture], in *Ifjúkori művek*, 434; I quote this sentence in context in chapter 5.

CHAPTER 7

1. For a summary of Hungarian feminist studies see Nanette Funk and Magda Mueller, eds., *Gender Politics and Post-Communism: Reflections from Eastern Europe and the Former Soviet Union* (New York: Routledge, 1993).

2. György Belia, introduction to *Ady Endre levelei* [Endre Ady letters], ed. György Belia (Budapest: Szépirodalmi, 1983), 1:14–25; Erzsébet Vezér, *Ady Endre alkotásai és vallomásai tükrében* [The oeuvre and confessions of Endre Ady] (Budapest: Szépirodalmi, 1971); Mary Gluck, "The Crisis of Aestheticism" in *Georg Lukács and His Generation: 1900–1918* (Cambridge, Mass.: Harvard University Press, 1985), esp. 119–31; Lee Congdon, *The Young Lukács* (Chapel Hill: University of North Carolina Press, 1983); Miklós Szabolcsi, *Kemény a menny* [Heaven is hard] (Budapest, 1992), 25–121; Márta Vágó, *Attila József* (Budapest: Szépirodalmi, 1975); several sections in Iván Horváth and Tverdota György, ed., *"Miért fáj ma is?" Az ismeretlen József Attila* ["Why does it still hurt today?" The unknown Attila József] (Budapest: Balassi kiadó, 1992).

3. Diary, MS 5023/12, 14–15, Manuscript Department, National Széchenyi Li-

brary. The text preceding this entry is found in Béla Balázs, *Napló* [Diary] (Budapest: Magvető, 1982), 1:344.

4. Diary, MS 5023/16, 13–14. The preceding text is found in *Napló*, 1:460.

5. See, for instance, the letters to his sister, Elza, on 26 December 1904 and 5 February 1905, and to his mother, ca. 9 September 1906 (Béla Bartók, Jr., ed., *Bartók Béla családi levelei* [Béla Bartók's family letters] [Budapest: Zeneműkiadó, 1981], 123–28, 165–67).

6. Csíkkarcfalva, 27 July 1907, in *Béla Bartóks Briefe an Stefi Geyer: 1907–1908* (Basel: Paul Sacher, 1979), document 4.

7. Writing to Márta when she was in a sanatorium, Bartók filled pages inquiring about her diet, going into minute details about the size of butter portions, etc. Even though his attitude was justified to some extent by Márta's sickness and by wartime shortages of food, we note its tone of the caring husband checking on his naughty wife. Perhaps the tone irritated Márta much as letters Bartók received from his mother (focusing on all the details of his meals) had irritated him a few years earlier, when he was a student. I did not have access to the letter Márta wrote to Bartók, but some of what happened can be deduced from Bartók's response of 27 March 1917, in *Bartók családi levelei*, 264–65.

8. To Stefi Geyer, 20 August 1907, in *Briefe an Stefi Geyer*, document 7.

9. See Bartók's *Nyugat* article on Kodály (1921), in Benjamin Suchoff, ed., *Béla Bartók Essays* (Lincoln: University of Nebraska Press, 1976), 469–70.

10. Dezső Legány, ed., *Kodály Zoltán levelei* [Zoltán Kodály letters] (Budapest: Zeneműkiadó, 1982), 39.

11. I am greatly indebted to Mrs. Zoltán Kodály (the former Sarolta Péczely) and to István Kecskeméti of the Kodály Archive for allowing me to see photocopies of some of Bartók's letters to Emma Gruber. I was not given permission to copy the letters and had access to them only for about two hours; thus I base the following summary on my general impressions gained through this one brief encounter with the texts.

12. The diary was published in facsimile in *Briefe an Stefi Geyer*.

13. Balázs finished the piece during the spring of 1910. The prologue was published in the 20 April issue of Artúr Bárdos's journal *Színjáték;* the entire piece appeared in vol. 1, nos. 16–17, of the same journal, giving 13 June as the date of completion. According to the reminiscence of the musicologist Bence Szabolcsi, Balázs originally intended it for Kodály and read it to him some time in 1910. Bartók was present at this reading (György Kroó, *Bartók színpadi művei* [Budapest: Zeneműkiadó, 1962], 26–27). Balázs seems to have designed it originally as a play but probably thought of the possibility of its use for an opera by Kodály or Bartók soon after its completion. Later, in his own writings he alternately referred to it as a libretto or drama. See Carl Leafstedt, "Music and Drama in Béla Bartók's Opera *Duke Bluebeard's Castle*" (Ph.D. diss., Harvard University, 1994), 7. In a 1966 interview, Kodály recalled that Balázs

thought of using the text for opera but had no preference as to whether Kodály or Bartók would write the music. Kodály confessed that the topic of the play was so far from him that he never thought of composing music for it, but he recalled that Bartók felt very close to it from the beginning and started the composition shortly after he read it (Zoltán Kodály, "A Kékszakállú herceg váráról" [About *Bluebeard's Castle*] in *Visszatekintés: Összegyűjtött írások, beszédek, nyilatkozatok* [Looking back: Collected writings, speeches, interviews], ed. Ferenc Bónis [Budapest: Zeneműkiadó, 1979] 3:479, 481). According to Bartók, he "composed the music for the mystery play *Duke Bluebeard's Castle* from March to September 1911" (Bartók, " 'A Kékszakállú herceg vára': Az Operaház újdonsága," *Magyar Színpad* 21, no. 143 [1918]: 1; English translation under the title "On Duke Bluebeard's Castle," in *Bartók Essays*, 407).

14. Undated letter from the beginning of 1915, in *Bartók családi levelei*, 235–36; original emphasis.

15. None of the passages that I quote below refer to the play in any direct manner. In the section entered on 4 August 1908 Balázs outlined, in a few sentences, a short play that would have used the characters of Don Juan and Barbe-Bleue (*Napló*, 1:477). This sketch gives the first sign that Balázs was preoccupied with the story of Bluebeard, but its only similarity to the final play is the use of the name Barbe-Bleue. Leafstedt, however, found that one element of this sketch foreshadowed the concept of the piece (see "Music and Drama," 25–26).

16. 26 September 1905 and 22 August 1906, in *Napló*, 229 and 337.

17. 27 December 1905, in ibid., 284. Paula Hermann was a student of the Hungarian and German Department and later became a teacher in a gymnasium. She belonged to the small circle of Balázs, Kodály, and Aranka Bauer.

18. 20 July 1906, in ibid., 325.

19. This and the following passage were written on 31 December 1905 and 19 May 1907, in ibid., 291 and 425; original emphasis.

20. The first paragraph of this extract from 23 August 1906 comes from ibid., 338. The second comes from Balázs, "Maeterlinck," *Nyugat* 1, nos. 1–15 (1908): 448. My translation of Balázs's somewhat poetic and grammatically loose text draws on Ivan Sanders, "Symbolist and Decadent Elements in Early Twentieth-Century Hungarian Drama," *Canadian-American Review of Hungarian Studies* 4 (1977): 27; original emphasis.

21. This entire paragraph from Balázs's Maeterlinck essay is quoted in Leafstedt, "Music and Drama," 59.

22. This and the following quote: late March 1907 and 17 July 1906, in *Napló*, 408, 322.

23. Péter Hanák, "A kert és a műhely," in *A kert és a műhely* [The garden and the workshop] (Budapest: Gondolat, 1988), 161.

24. Carl E. Schorske, *Fin-de-Siècle Vienna: Politics and Culture* (New York: Random House, Vintage Books, 1981), 228–31.

25. See Robert Hass, introduction to *The Selected Poetry of Rainer Maria Rilke*, ed. and trans. Stephen Mitchell (New York: Random House, Vintage Books, 1982), xviii–xxii.

26. G. Béla Németh, *A magyar szimbolizmus kezdeteinek kérdéséhez (Nyelvi és stílusproblémák)* [On the beginnings of Hungarian symbolism (Problems of language and style)] (Budapest: Magvető, 1970); B. André Karátson, "The Translation and Refraction of Symbolism: A Survey of the Hungarian Example," and Miklós Szabolcsi, "On the Spread of Symbolism," in Anna Balakian, ed., *The Symbolist Movement in the Literature of European Languages* (Budapest: Akadémiai, 1982), 165–82, 183–90; Sanders, "Symbolist and Decadent Elements."

27. The poem first appeared in *Levelek Irisz koszorújából* [Leaves from the laurel of Iris], which contains poems Babits wrote between 1902 and 1908; later published in *Babits Mihály összegyűjtött versei* [Mihály Babits's collected poems] (Budapest: Szépirodalmi, 1977).

28. The subtitle of the poem is "Consolatio mystica." It first appeared in the volume *Nyugtalanság völgye* [The valley of anxiety], a collection of poems Babits wrote between 1917 and 1920; then collected in *Babits versei*.

29. Babits, "Paysage intime: 3. Alkony"; Ady, "Bolond, halálos éj"; Babits, "Szimbolumok: Szimbolum a holdvilágról."

30. Babits, "Éjszaka!," "Esti kérdés," "Éji dal," "Alkonyi prológus," "Csillagokig!"

31. Babits, "Húnyt szemmel" [With eyes closed; 1906]. The poem first appeared in *Levelek Irisz koszorújából*.

32. Aladár Bálint, comp., *Éjfél: Magyar írók misztikus novellái* [Midnight: Mysteries by Hungarian writers] (1917; reprint, Gyoma: Gyomai Kner nyomda, 1992). Written in 1917, Kosztolányi's text predates the first performance of Bartók's opera but not the publication of Balázs's play (1910), which Kosztolányi might have read.

33. The poems in Dezső Kosztolányi's series "Complaints of a poor little child" [A szegény kisgyermek panaszai (1910)], in *Kosztolányi Dezső összegyűjtött versei* (Budapest: Révai, 1943), do not have separate titles even though they are recognizably separate units. They are normally referred to by first line.

34. Béla Szíj suggests that Baudelaire might have influenced Gulácsy's attempt to connect the motive of love with that of the mysterious garden. In his analysis of the painting, Szíj comes up with the second interpretation I offer concerning the relationship of the two figures (Géza Csorba, Anna Szinyei Merse, and Margit Egry, eds., *20. századi magyar festészet és szobrászat* [Twentieth-century Hungarian painting and sculpture] [Budapest: Képzőművészeti Kiadó, 1986], 173).

35. The poem appeared in *Levelek Irisz koszorújából*.

36. Denijs Dille, "Bartók et Ady," in *Béla Bartók: Regard sur le passé*, ed. Yves Lenoir, Études Bartókiennes no. 1 (Namur: Presses universitaires de Namur, 1990), 296–97.

37. Bartók marked this poem in the volume he owned. The same idea is expressed in Ady's "Three Baudelaire Sonnets" [Három Baudelaire-szonett (1906)].

38. Endre Ady, "Flóra lány marad" (1907), "Milliomos Kleopátra" (1910), and "Juliette Firenzébe megy" (1907), in *Sápadt emberek és történetek* [Pale people and stories] (Budapest: Athaneum, n.d.).

39. Edith Wyschogrod, *Emmanuel Levinas: The Problem of Ethical Metaphysics* (The Hague: Martinus Nijhoff, 1974), 119; see also 116–20.

40. Emmanuel Levinas, *Time and the Other*, trans. Richard A. Cohen (Pittsburgh: Duquesne University Press, 1987), 86–89. To Levinas, the Other is synonymous with the "feminine," and "mystery" with "virginity." In the section from which the quote comes he uses alternately "feminine" and "Other" to refer to the same thing. For a feminist criticism of his work, see Luce Irigaray, "Questions to Emmanuel Levinas: On the Divinity of Love," in *Re-reading Levinas*, ed. Robert Bernasconti and Simon Critchley (Bloomington: Indiana University Press, 1991), 109–18.

41. Otto Weininger, *Geschlecht und Charakter* (1903); in English translation: *Sex and Character* (London, n.d.).

42. See Lawrence Kramer, "Culture and Musical Hermeneutics: The Salome Complex," *Cambridge Opera Journal* 2 (1990): 269–94; Lawrence Kramer, "Fin-de-Siècle Fantasies: Electra, Degeneration and Sexual Science," *Cambridge Opera Journal* 5 (1993): 141–65.

43. György Lukács, "Kaffka Margitról" [About Margit Kaffka], in *Ifjúkori művek (1902–1918)* [Youthful works], ed. Árpád Tímár (Budapest: Magvető, 1977), 277.

44. See Balázs's diary entry for 19 March 1905, in *Napló*, 162. Nevertheless, as even this entry makes clear, Balázs held to his conviction that women were, by nature, less developed than men both emotionally and intellectually.

45. See letter to his sister, 5 February 1905; and to his mother, 10 September 1905; in *Bartók családi levelei*, 126–27, 139–40.

46. Endre Ady, "A magyar Pimodián (Vallomások és Tanulmány)" [The Hungarian Pimodian (Confession and essay)], *Nyugat* 1, nos. 1–15 (1908): 182.

47. See my discussion of Madács's play in chapter 6, in the section on mysticism and devotion to life.

48. Antal Szerb, *Magyar irodalom történet* [The history of Hungarian literature] (Budapest: Magvető, 1934), 385–86.

49. Lukács's Kierkegaard essay, quoted in Mary Gluck, *Georg Lukács and His Generation: 1900–1918* (Cambridge, Mass.: Harvard University Press, 1985), 121. I am greatly indebted to this work by Gluck, which provides valuable insight into Lukács's development. The following discussion relies on her selection and translation of Lukács's works.

50. In the following, I describe the concept of love as it emerges from the writings by men and take their point of view. Looking at women's writings, we find points of overlap but also crucial differences. For many male artists, a life lived in happy love was unimaginable because love meant the most intense, revelatory experience—one that, by its very nature, cannot last. Women took a more pragmatic (and honest) approach. The divergence of opinions resulted in tragic endings of relationships, leading in the

case of Lukács and Seidler to Seidler's suicide. See Ágnes Heller, "Lukács György és Seidler Irma," *Portrévázlatok az etika történetéből* [Sketches of portraits from the history of ethics] (Budapest: Gondolat, 1976), 385–422.

51. This and following passage are quoted in Gluck, *Georg Lukács*, 122–23.

52. Ibid., 125.

53. Lukács wrote the first passage to his friend Leo Popper; the second comes from his diary (both quoted in ibid., 125–26).

54. Lukács, "A vándor énekel" [The wanderer sings], in *Ifjúkori művek*, 474.

55. Gluck, *Georg Lukács*, 122.

56. Sándor Veress, "Bluebeard's Castle," *Tempo* 5, no. 13 (1949): 33.

57. Kroó, *Bartók Béla színpadi művei*, 83.

58. Leafstedt, "Music and Drama," 132.

CHAPTER 8

1. Zoltán Kodály, "Bartók the Folklorist," in *The Selected Writings of Zoltán Kodály*, ed. Ferenc Bónis, trans. Lili Halapy and Fred Macnicol (London: Boosey and Hawkes, 1974), 102–3.

2. On Bartók's attitude toward merging Hungarian and foreign styles see my dissertation, "Béla Bartók and Hungarian Nationalism: The Development of Bartók's Social and Political Ideas at the Turn of the Century (1899–1903)" (Ph.D. diss., University of Pennsylvania, 1989), 138–39, 233.

3. See the summary of this compositional period in Tibor Tallián, *Béla Bartók: The Man and His Work*, trans. Gyula Gulyás (Budapest: Corvina, 1981), 42–52; he discusses the rhapsody's reception history on 47.

4. "The Folk Songs of Hungary," in *Béla Bartók Essays*, ed. Benjamin Suchoff (Lincoln: University of Nebraska Press, 1976), 333.

5. Among the novel ideas are the bitonality of *Bagatelle* no. 1; the harmonic plan (based on expanding intervals leading to symmetrical formations) of no. 2; the use of the triton as the main melodic interval in nos. 2, 6, and 10 (as well as in other pieces); the combination of pentatonicism, tritons, and symmetrical formations and the use of ostinato and folk-like rhythms in no. 10; and the unusual rubato rhythms in no. 12. Some of these ideas, such as the rubato aspect of no. 12 or the bitonality of no. 1, Bartók did not develop. *Bagatelles* nos. 13 ("Lento funebre"), 14 ("Valse"), and 3 ("Andante") are stylized pieces modeled on traditional types. See Elliott Antokoletz, "The Musical Language of Bartók's *14 Bagatelles* for Piano," *Tempo* 137 (June 1981): 8–16; Allen Forte, "Béla Bartók Number VIII from Fourteen Bagatelles, Op. 6," in *Contemporary Tone-Structures* (New York: Columbia University Press, 1955), 74–90, 167–70.

6. A similar conception of language is in Michel Foucault, *The Order of Things: An Archeology of the Human Sciences* (New York: Random House, Vintage Books, 1994), esp. chap. 4, section on speaking.

7. Diary note on 17 July 1906 in Béla Balázs, *Napló* [Diary] (Budapest: Magvető, 1982), 1:322.

8. Bartók's collecting notebooks, 5:40. I thank László Somfai, director of the Bartók Archives, Budapest, for permitting me to reproduce this page.

9. Béla Bartók, "Székely Balladák" (1908), in *Bartók Béla összegyűjtött írásai* [Collected writings of Béla Bartók], ed. András Szőllősy (Budapest: Zeneműkiadó, 1966), 23. The barline division of this published version was a mistake on Bartók's part: in this article the eight-syllable poetic lines of all the pieces are structured metrically as 6 + 2 syllables—probably because of the elongation of the last two syllables in the performace, which seemed to suggest a new metric unit. In his first notation on the spot, Bartók instinctively felt the correct poetic division (4 + 4 syllables) and returned to this pattern, keeping it even in the rhythmically complicated transcriptions in the later publications.

10. This notation from Bartók's "Ungarische Volkmusik" [Hungarian folk music] (1933) is almost identical with the transcription that appeared in "Ungarische Bauermusik" [Hungarian peasant music] (1920), except that the metrome number is given in quarter notes there and in eighth notes here. Bartók had arrived at a satisfactory transcription by 1920 but further refined the rhythm in the 1930s. These transcriptions were reprinted in *Bartók összegyűjtött írásai*, ed. Szőllősy, 383 and 88; *Bartók Essays*, 311 and 86.

11. See my article "Between Rubato and Rigid Rhythm: A Particular Type of Rhythmical Asymmetry as Reflected in Bartók's Writings on Folk Music," *Studia Musicologica* 24 (1982): 327–37, esp. 328.

12. Béla Bartók, "The Melodies of the Hungarian Soldier's Songs," in *Bartók Essays*, 51.

13. What Bartók attempted to capture by the term "hardened rubato" is a peculiar, little researched phenomenon of Hungarian folk music (and most likely of other rubato performances as well). The performance of old-style songs gives the impression of rubato even though the rhythmic duration of the notes is almost entirely even. The folk-music tradition sometimes superposes different types of rubato performances (instrumental and vocal rubato) on pieces used for dancing, while the feeling of meter remains clear (this performing style is typical of the *Lassú* dances from Szék). In my article on rubato and rigid rhythm I discuss Bartók's discovery of hardened rubato (that is, a performance that strikes the listener as rubato even though it has fixed metric rhythms) and its effect on his compositional style.

14. The simple singing style of Mária Basilides, a famous Hungarian singer of oratorios and songs, may help us recreate the opera's vocal style from the folk-song recording Bartók made with her. See *Centenary Edition of Bartók's Records (Complete)*, (6) LPX 12328-B, nos. 1–2. The point was not to imitate the style of folk singers but to find an art-music parallel to the simplicity and clarity of their style. Basilides performed these songs as she performed baroque oratorios, in a clear, unpretentious, spontaneous singing style devoid of vibrato, emphasizing the text. There was a radio broadcast of

the opera (or at least a plan for one) in the mid-1930s in which Basilides was to perform Judith. I believe nothing survived of this performance—apart from a piano score partly marked by Bartók, containing changes (supposedly at her request). On Bartók's changes at the request of singers see György Kroó, "Data on the Genesis of Duke Blue-beard's Castle," *Studia Musicologica* 23 (1981): 79–123, esp. 120–23. Perhaps frustration with the creation of a Hungarian vocal style made Bartók turn toward folk-song ar-rangements instead of modernist experiments in his later years.

15. The following discussion gives a precise translation of the text under analysis, together with the Hungarian (as a reference point). This English text usually differs from the libretto's translation.

16. László Lajtha, Three Nocturnes for Soprano, Harp, Flute, and String Quartet op. 34 (1941); Tibor Sárai, Serenade for String Orchestra (1946); Endre Szervánszky, Serenade for String Orchestra (1947–48); Pál Kadosa, Serenade for Chamber Orchestra op. 65 (1967).

17. The tendency to dramatize the serenade can be seen in Kodály's *Summer Night* and in the slow movement of the Sonata for Solo Cello.

18. Béla Bartók, "A magyar népzene" [Hungarian folk music] (1921), in *Bartók ösz-szegyűjtött írásai*, ed. Szőllősy, 100. See also *Bartók Essays*, 70. Bartók's objection to gypsy music also related to its political associations. See my "Béla Bartók and the Concept of Nation and *Volk* in Modern Hungary," *The Musical Quarterly* 78, no. 2 (1994): 255–87.

19. Among the most significant works focusing on the tonal structure of the opera are György Kroó, *Bartók Béla színpadi művei* [Béla Bartók's stage works] (Budapest: Zeneműkiadó, 1962); Ernő Lendvai, *Bartók dramaturgiája: Színpadi művek és a Can-tata profana* [Bartók's dramaturgy: Pieces for stage and the *Cantata profana*] (Budapest: Zeneműkiadó, 1964); Elliott Antokoletz, "Bartók's *Bluebeard:* The Sources of Its 'Modernism,' " *Journal of the College Music Society* 30, no. 1 (spring 1990): 75–95; Carl Leafstedt, "Music and Drama in Béla Bartók's Opera *Duke Bluebeard's Castle*" (Ph.D. diss., Harvard University, 1994).

20. Although most modern performances omit the prologue, Bartók's idea was to superpose its last part on the pentatonic theme—only this design explains the theme's extremely slow tempo.

21. The literature customarily assigns a name to each theme of the opera, as for a Wagnerian leitmotiv. For the "pentatonic theme" and the "blood motive," I follow the practice of the existing literature; to others I give new names. On the motives' sym-bolic meaning see especially Antokoletz, "Bartók's *Bluebeard*"; Kroó, *Bartók színpadi művei;* and György Kroó, "Monothematik und Dramaturgie in Bartóks Bühnenwer-ken" [Monothematism and dramaturgy in the stage works of Béla Bartók], *Studia Mu-sicologica* 5, nos. 1–4 (1963): 449–67; Lendvai, *Bartók dramaturgiája;* Sándor Veress, "Bluebeard's Castle," *Tempo* 13 (1949): 32–38.

22. Antokoletz analyzes the tonal content of this motive somewhat differently in "Bartók's *Bluebeard*," 81.

23. The concept of "gesture" meant more to Bartók than simply representational

music. Bartók considered the gesturelike quality of music fundamental to its universal nature and expressive quality. He might have felt reassured in this belief by Nietzsche's view; in his copy of Nietzsche's *Human, All Too Human*, he marked the section that explained the connection of gesture, language, and music in this manner. Nietzsche believed that the gestural aspect of music and language was the manifestation of some fundamental motions pertaining to the mind and the soul. See the section underlined by Bartók and his marginal notes as quoted in Denijs Dille, "Bartók, lecteur de Nietzsche et de La Rochefoucault," in *Béla Bartók: Regard sur le passé*, ed. Yves Lenoir, Études Bartókiennes no. 1 (Namur: Presses universitaires de Namur, 1990), 87–108; English translation in Tallián, *Bartók*, 22

24. In Lendvai's interpretation, this section is a transition from the tonic axis (D sharp, F sharp, A), with momentary emphasis on "major" sounding chords (as the F sharp major at the text "Sír a várad") leading toward a G-major sonority complemented with notes of the acoustic scale (major with raised fourth, and lowered seventh), that is, what Lendvai calls the dominant axis (Lendvai, *Bartók dramaturgiája*, 71–74). Antokoletz finds that the minor second was foreshadowed in Judith's vocal lines already at the very beginning of the opera, thus anticipating this development ("Bartók's *Bluebeard*," 83).

25. Lendvai calls this chord "hyper-minor" and associates it with the pain and the passion of love at various instances in the opera.

26. To Stefi Geyer [11 September 1907] in János Demény, ed., *Bartók Béla levelei* [Béla Bartók letters] (Budapest: Zeneműkiadó, 1976), 131.

27. For the sake of brevity, in this analysis I ignore the symbolic meaning of dotted-rhythm motives, even though this motivic type is no less important than ornamentation.

28. To contrast pentatonic (diatonic) and chromatic scales is a typical Bartókian technique symbolizing the contrast of light and darkness. On this aspect of Bartók's music see the works of Elliott Antokoletz, Ernő Lendvai, and János Kárpáti.

29. Leafstedt's analysis of this scene (focusing primarily on the tonal design) differs somewhat from the discussion here. See his "Music and Drama," 207–42.

30. György Kroó summarizes the variants of the Bluebeard theme in European literature and art music in his *Bartók Béla színpadi művei*, 9–36. In nineteenth-century collections a Hungarian variant of this theme, the ballad "Anna Molnár," was a popular piece of Hungarian folk poetry, first notated around 1840 in Klézse (Romania). See type 3 in Vargyas, *A magyar népballada és Európa* [The Hungarian folk ballad and Europe] (Budapest: Zeneműkiadó, 1976), 2:44–65, with a bibliography of European ballads on this theme.

31. Balázs's 1922 article in the *Vienna Hungarian News* is quoted in Kroó, "Duke Bluebeard's Castle," 277–78; and also in Leafstedt, "Music and Drama," 27.

32. Lendvai, *Bartók dramaturgiája*, 66.

33. György Lukács, "Esztétikai kultúra" [Aesthetic culture], in *Ifjúkori művek (1902–1918)* [Youthful works (1902–1918)] (Budapest: Magvető, 1977), 435. I discuss this essay at the end of chapter 5.

Index

aesthetics, 4, 5, 13, 14, 15, 162–67; Ady's, 5, 6, 76, 103–4, 150, 157, 176, 193, 293–94, 296; Balázs's, 13, 157–61; of folklorism, 23, 78, 98–109; Hofmannsthal, 111; Hungarian modernist, 15, 89–115, 172–73, 297; Lukács and, 5, 10–11, 13, 99–103, 111–13, 157, 162–67, 204, 294; positivist, 30; road toward new, 144–48; romantic, 25–30, 161. *See also* Ady: aesthetics; aestheticism; art; Bartók's aesthetics; coherence; literature; music; organicism

A Hét (The week), 71, 72, 95; contributors, 71, 311n22; Kiss as editor of, 71, 82, 110

Alan, ethnic, 54

Alexander, Bernát, 81, 95, 311nn22,23

alienation: Austrian artist, 41; in Hungarian literature, 44, 205, 210; vs. loneliness, 205, 295; Nietzschean, 174. *See also* detachment; isolation; loneliness

Ambrus, Zoltán, 311n22

Angyal, Dávid, 81

"Anna Molnár" ballad, 332n30

Antokoletz, Elliott, 331n22, 332n24

Arany, János, 5, 58–59, 173, 309n3; *Gypsies of Nagyida*, 59

Arányi family, 81

architecture: Austrian social status and, 40; and folklorism, 11, 100–102; Kós's, 102, 103 (fig. 4); Lechner's, 11, 100, 101 (fig. 2), 102 (fig. 3), 315n19

aristocracy: Austrian, 40, 41. *See also* Hungarian aristocracy; nobility

Armenians, 54

armory theme, *Bluebeard's Castle*, 276, 277, 279

art: abstract, 20, 26–27, 40, 99; for art's sake (aestheticism), 69–70, 95, 311n21; coherence in, 6, 24–40, 95, 106–15, 164–65, 195, 235, 296; Hungarian (general), 10, 49–50, 89–115, 230–32; and imitation, 26–27; and "infinite," 32–33; Jewish support for, 81–82, 84–87; and life, 67, 160, 162–65; and morality, 40, 41, 49, 67, 111–15; natural laws of, 27, 37–38, 97; organicist theory of, 89–115; and politics, 10, 12–13, 51, 65, 69–70, 92, 203; realism, 12, 24, 31, 35, 120–21, 165, 296; of simplicity, 98, 99, 173. *See also* aesthetics; creation; litera-ture; music; national art; popular art; true art; truthfulness; universal art; visual arts

art music: Bartókian aesthetics and, 16, 23, 122, 143; and folklorism, 22–23, 109, 122, 125, 152, 230–32; popular, 78; romantic, 78, 245. *See also* classicism; national music (Hungarian)

art nouveau, 72, 100, 203

"art song." See *magyar nóta*

As, ethnic, 54

Ascher, Oszkár, 86 (fig. 1)

Austria: Dual Austro-Hungarian Monarchy, 3, 4, 45–46, 55, 304–5n5; politics of, compared with Hungarian, 50–51; romanticism in, compared with Hungarian, 61–62; social context of art, 40–42. *See also* German-Austrian culture; Habsburg empire; Vienna

avant-garde, 20, 35, 91, 303n37

Babits, Mihály, 5, 86 (fig. 1), 311n21; background, 47; "The epilogue of the lyricist" (A lirikus epilógja), 205–6; "The eternal arcade" (Az örök folyosó), 213; and loneliness, 204, 205–9; and night, 207–9; in *Nyugat*, 72; and politics, 63, 76; "Psalm for male voice" (Zsoltár férfihangra), 206–7; and universal vs. national art, 91; "With eyes closed" (Húnyt szemmel), 208–9

Babits, Sophie Török, 86 (fig. 1)

Bach, J. S., *St. Matthew Passion*, 316n31

Balázs, Béla, 5, 8, 15, 157–62; and Ady, 170; aesthetics of, 13, 157–61; background, 48; Bartók and, 11, 71, 146, 157, 158 (fig. 6), 291–92, 325–26n13 (see also *Bluebeard's Castle*); *Bluebeard's Castle* play, 199–203, 209, 218, 226–28, 290–93, 325–26nn13,15, 327n32; and *Bluebeard's Castle's* vocal/orchestral separation, 236–37; Communist party, 98; diary, 94–95, 160, 161, 197, 201, 328n44; and gender stereotypes, 197, 219, 328n44; and German aestheticism, 311n21; Jewish, 82; and life, 158, 160–61, 200–201, 218; and Lukács's ideology, 204; mystery play, 199–203, 290–91; in *Nyugat*, 72; poetry, 5, 8, 99–100, 102–3; short

Bartók's music (*continued*)
Fifth String Quartet, 318n17; First String Quartet, 233, 317n5, 318n17; *Five Songs* op. 16, 11, 70, 73, 170; *Fourteen Bagatelles*, 2, 231, 232–33, 234 (exs. 17, 18), 329n5; Fourth String Quartet, 32; and love for Geyer, 149, 264; *Hungarian Folk Song* (1924), 238; *Hungarian Folksongs* (1906), 72; *Kossuth*, 231–32; large-scale form, 135, 143, 148–49, 194, 233, 235, 316n33; *Microcosmos*, 282; The *Miraculous Mandarin*, 44, 72, 84, 291; *Music for Strings, Percussion, and Celesta*, 317n6, 318n17; *Out of Doors*, 318n14; piano compositions (1910s), 291; Piano Quintet, 231; Rhapsody op. 1, 2, 231; Second String Quartet, 318n17; Sixth String Quartet, 244, 316nn31,33; Sonata for Piano, 1926, 316n33, 318n10; Sonata for Solo Violin, 316n33; Sonata for Two Pianos and Percussion, 317n6, 321n68; Sonata for Violin and Piano no. 2, 157; sonatas for violin and piano (1920s), 291; style (general), 2, 7, 9–10, 15, 23, 194; stylistic synthesis, 104, 121, 193, 230–94; Suite no. 1, for orchestra, 248, 250 (ex. 25), 255; Third String Quartet, 22, 316n31, 318nn10,17, 321n68; two orchestral suites, 2, 231; Violin Concerto (no. 2), 157, 317n6; *The Wooden Prince*, 152, 291. *See also* Bartók's aesthetics; Bartók's composition; Bartók's folklorism; *Bluebeard's Castle;* First Piano Concerto; themes; tonal systems; *verbunkos*
Bartók's writings, 8, 9, 15; on Budapest, 83, 84; diary, 199; on field trips, 154; on folklorism, 104; on individualism, 120–21; letters to Geyer, 98, 144–56 passim, 197, 264; letters to Gruber, 198, 325n11; letters to Jurkovics, 145, 149; letters to women (general), 145–46, 197; letters to Ziegler, 120–21, 145, 165, 197, 199, 325n7; on music, 11; on spirit, 120; on stylistic coherence, 23; youthful letters, 68. *See also* Bartók's composition
Basilides, Mária, 73, 330–31n14
Batthyány, Lajos, 309n3
Baudelaire, Charles, 91, 204, 327n34

Bauer, Aranka, 200, 326n17
Bauer, Hilda, 311n23
Baumgarten, Sándor, 315n19
"beautiful object," romanticist, 26–27, 28
beauty: garden of, 40, 41; power of, 111; spiritual, 97
Beck, Fülöp Ö., 82
Beethoven, Ludwig van, 20, 56, 129, 133, 316n31; Piano Concerto in G major, 138; String Quartet op. 131, 147, 319n24
Benedek, Marcell, 71, 82
Berény, Róbert, 82
Berg, Alban, *Wozzeck*, 203
Berglinger, Joseph, 28
Berlin aestheticism, 311n21
Berlin Phonogramm-Archiv, 153
Berlioz, Hector, *Symphonie Fantastique*, 121
Bihari, János, 56, 309n3
Bildung, 41
Biró, Lajos, 86 (fig. 1), 311n22
blood motive, *Bluebeard's Castle*, 261–64, 279, 284, 286–88, 331n21
Bluebeard's Castle, 2, 15, 167, 196–294; Balázs play, 199–203, 209, 218, 226–28, 290–93, 325–26nn13,15, 327n32; Bluebeard's voice, 241–43, 243 (ex. 20); dramatic style, 235–43, 248–76, 279, 290–94; end of, 288–89, 289 (ex. 47), 290 (ex. 48); fifth door scene, 281–84, 282–83 (ex. 43); first climax of first scene, 264, 265 (ex. 32); first door scene, 279, 280 (ex. 42); first scene/transition, 257–76, 258–59 (ex. 30), 262–63 (ex. 31), 265 (ex. 32), 266 (ex. 33), 284; gender in, 210–11, 218–20, 226–29; identity in, 44; introduction, 253–57, 281, 284; Judith's voice, 241–43, 243 (ex. 20); loneliness in, 199, 203, 204–5, 226, 227; love in, 217–29 passim, 261, 264–66, 273–75, 279, 288–89; "main notes" and ornamentation, 245–61 passim, 271–73, 276–77, 279–81, 286, 288; musical style, 16, 235–43; "negative"/inhuman world, 276, 279, 281, 286; orchestral music, 235–37, 241, 244–53, 255–56, 281; performance requirements, 240–41; plot of, 273; poetic idea of, 226–29, 243, 261, 292; "positive"/human world, 276, 279, 281, 286; section before sixth door, 284, 286 (ex. 45);

circularity, 203, 211–15, 217; *Bluebeard's Castle* motive, 203, 204, 255, 273, 279, 289; eternal circle, 203, 211–13, 289; First Piano Concerto and, 135; love and, 223, 289; magic circle, 207, 223; new modernism and, 72, 74

"civic virtue," 47, 63–64

civis, of *mezőváros*, 46

class. *See* social status

classicism, 20; Bartókian aesthetics and, 20, 143, 166, 231; *Bluebeard's Castle* and, 250, 251; First Piano Concerto and, 133, 134, 135, 138, 142; Koessler's, 231; pastorale and, 244; and poetry, 55; Schoenberg and, 39, 300n1. *See also* neoclassicism

coherence, 44; Ady's poetry and, 182, 293; in art, 6, 24–40, 95, 106–15, 164–65, 195, 235, 296; Bartók and, 22–26 passim, 106–9, 232–35, 250, 293; and love, 221; modernism and, 14, 19–24 passim, 30–35; and realism, 109–15; romanticism and, 23–30; structural, 28–32, 37, 95, 106–9, 112, 164, 230. *See also* organicism; truthfulness; unity; wholeness

Coleridge, Samuel Taylor, 25; *Theory of Life*, 29

colors: in Ady's poetry, 179. *See also* darkness; whiteness

Comenius lodge, 70

comfort, Schoenberg on, 35–36

communication: failure in, 198–201. *See also* friendships; language; writings

Communist party, Hungarian, 50, 98, 155

composition, 38–39; organicism and, 24–32 passim, 38–39, 104–9; pastorale tradition of, 244; twelve-tone, 26, 32, 37–38, 93, 108–9. *See also* Bartók's composition; creation; musical style

Compromise of 1867, 45, 304–5n5

concerts, salon, 81

conservatism: Austrian social, 64–65; Bartók's, 1–2; Stravinsky's, 300n1. *See also* Hungarian conservatism

constitutions, conservatives and, 64–65

cosmopolitanism, 2–3, 49, 53, 66, 83–84

creation, 26–27, 38–39; and attitude on life, 149–50; happiness vs., 222; from inside/inner self, 24–25, 36–37, 39, 94–95, 104,

164–65, 191–92; in isolation, 156, 160; and phenomena of life, 96–97, 104. *See also* art; composition

"creation-music," First Piano Concerto, 134

critics, music, 72

Croatians, 54

csárdás dance, 57

Csáth, Géza, 72

Csermák, 56

Csík mountains, Bartók's field trip, 146, 150, 154, 166

Csók, István, 71

Csokonai, Mihály, 58, 173

Csontváry Kosztka, Tivadar, 10–11, 204; *Trees in lamplight in Jajce*, 207, 208 (fig. 9)

cultural environments: Berlin, 311n21; European, 19–21, 33, 311n21; Viennese, 23–30, 33, 40–42. *See also* art; German-Austrian culture; Hungarian cultural environment; intellectual milieu; mass culture; modernism

Cuman ethnicity, 54

Czóbel, Béla, 71

Dahlhaus, Carl: "Nationalism and Music," 22–23; "New Music and the Problem of Musical Genre," 32–33; "Poetic Music," 29, 31

dance: First Piano Concerto themes, 135, 139; folk, 56; music for, 55–59, 128, 317n7, 330n13; swineherd, 123, 317n7

darkness: in Ady's poetry, 180; *Bluebeard's Castle*, 255, 257–61, 267, 275–76, 289, 292, 332n28. *See also* night

Darvas, József, 313n49

Deák, Ferenc, 309n3

death: Ady's, 5; in Ady's thought, 176, 192; in Balázs's thought, 201, 202; "national death" theme, 67, 75; romanticism and, 67

Debrecen, Ady from, 188–89

Debussy, Claude, *Pelléas et Mélisande*, 235

decadence, 33–34, 91

decorativeness, Vienna, 40–41

Delius, Frederick, 152

democracy, 3; Ady and, 10, 171; Bartók and, 10, 12; Hungarian republic, 50; radicals and, 87

Dessewffy, Aurél, 309n3

detachment: Nietzschean, 149, 153–54, 156, 174. *See also* alienation; isolation

Deutch publishing house, 82

devekuth, 187, 192

development: of *Bluebeard's Castle*, 250, 261; of First Piano Concerto, 129, 133–38, 136–37 (ex. 10), 142, 318n16; in symphonic/operatic tradition, 250

diaries: Balázs's, 94–95, 160, 161, 197, 200–203, 328n44; Bartók's, 199

disorder, social. *See* social disorder

distortion: in Ady's poetry, 176; folk music, 128, 138, 143, 317–18n10; modernism and, 296

divertimento, tradition of, 244

Dohnányi, Ernő: *Ruralia Hungarica*, 244; Serenade for violin, viola, and cello op. 10, 244

dolce-marcato theme, *Bluebeard's Castle*, 253–56, 254 (ex. 27), 255 (ex. 28), 260, 273, 281, 288

domestic servants, 45, 305n6

Dózsa, György, 315n20

drama: Balázs's *Bluebeard's Castle* play, 199–203, 209, 218, 226–28, 290–93, 325–26nn13,15, 327n32; Balázs's "mystery play," 199–203, 290–91; *Bluebeard's Castle*'s new style of, 235–43, 248–76, 279, 290–94; Lukács and, 95, 162–65, 166; of Madách, 189, 220; of Maeterlinck, 201, 202, 227; pastorale and, 244. *See also* musical drama; theater

Dual Austro-Hungarian Monarchy, 3, 4, 45–46, 55, 304–5n5

duality: in *Bluebeard's Castle*, 276, 279, 286; gender, 226–27; of identity, 304n4. *See also* polarization

Duke Bluebeard's Castle. See *Bluebeard's Castle*

"East European School," 119

eccentricity, decadence and, 34

economics: abolition of feudalism and, 45–46, 51, 52; middle class, 4; political conservatives and, 50, 55; radicals and, 76; and titles of address, 47, 305n9. *See also* capitalism; social status

education: Austrian, 41; by modernist circles, 72–73; musical, 41, 73, 144, 319n21; painting, 71, 82, 91

educational works (Bartók's Harvard lecture topic), 121, 122

ego: Ady and, 173–77, 184, 195; Babits and, 206–7; Kosztolányi and, 209; love and, 223. *See also* identity

Egressy, Gábor, 66, 94

Eight, the (Nyolcak), 71, 91–92

elitism, 37, 73, 195, 312n41. *See also* intellectual milieu; social status

emotions: Ady's, 176; analyzing, 161; Balázs and, 199–201; in Bartók's compositions (general), 2, 10, 11, 13, 148–50; in Bartók's field trips, 150, 152–54; in Bartók's first decade in Budapest, 9; in Bartók's First Piano Concerto, 126, 128, 135; in Bartók's letters, 145–46, 148, 198; in Bartók's relationships with women, 145–46, 198–99, 221; *Bluebeard's Castle*, 241–43, 248–53, 257–59, 264, 276, 286; complexity in, 147–48, 152; feeling soul, of Balázs's "mystery play," 201–2; form and, 149, 165; in Kodály's field trips, 160; Lukács's attitudes toward, 221–22; music and, 119–23, 146–50; organicism and, 28, 30, 31, 90. *See also* intensity; loneliness; love; passion; sentimentality

empathy: Ady's, 172; of artist, 20; Bartók's, 148

Enlightenment, 19, 66

entertainment, art vs., 35, 67

Eötvös, József, 63, 64, 65–66

Eötvös college, 48

equality: gender, 197, 219; social, 48–49. *See also* social inequities

Erdei, Ferenc, 313n49

Erdélyi, József, 86 (fig. 1)

Erkel, Ferenc, 23, 56, 309n3

eros: philosophical theory of, 216–17. *See also* love

essence: Ady and, 182, 184; Bartók's search to express, 148–49; Jewish mystics and, 187; modernists and, 296, 297; moral, 113–15. *See also* soul

eternal circle, life as, 203, 211–13, 289

eternal night, in *Bluebeard's Castle*, 202, 205

German-Austrian culture, 13, 24–30; avant-garde, 303n37; and folklorism, 21, 22–25, 301n8; musical superiority claimed, 23; national/universal art, 40; organicism, 21–42, 90, 92–93, 96–97, 302n23. *See also* Adorno, Theodor W.; Austria; Dahlhaus, Carl; Germany; Kraus, Karl; Schoenberg, Arnold; Vienna; Webern, Anton

German Hungarians: ethnicity, 54; urban, 46, 49, 73, 83–84

Germany: Berlin aestheticism, 311n21; Berlin Phonogramm-Archiv, 153; Hungarian nationalism and, 66–67; romanticism, 24–30, 61–62, 67, 161. *See also* German-Austrian culture; Prussia

gesture motive, *Bluebeard's Castle*, 256–57, 256 (ex. 29), 260, 264, 268 (ex. 34), 273–88 passim, 274 (ex. 38), 331–32n23

Geyer, Stefi, 319n21; Bartók's letters to, 98, 144–56 passim, 197, 264; Bartók's love for, 145, 146, 170, 196, 198, 199, 221, 319n21; Bartók's piece on feelings for, 149, 264

giusto folk songs, 123, 124 (ex. 1), 317n8

Gluck, Mary, 14

God: Ady and, 182, 183–85, 188, 189, 296; Goethe's, 25, 27; Jewish spirituality and, 187, 190

God-poems, Ady's, 183–85, 191, 323n22

Goethe, Johann Wolfgang, 25, 27, 90, 302n23; *Faust*, 189; Wilhelm Meister, 28–29

Goldziher, Ignác, 81

Gratz, Gusztáv, 70

"great tradition," modernism and, 30

growth, organicist, 24, 26, 27, 31

Gruber, Emma, 145, 157–58, 160, 196–99; Bartók's friendship with, 9, 10, 145, 157–58, 197–99; Bartók's letters to, 198, 325n11; on field trip, 159 (fig. 7); and Kodály, 9, 10, 157–58, 160, 197–98, 320n50; marriages, 197–98, 320n50; names, 320n50

Gruber family, 81

Grünwald, Béla Iványi, 71

Gulácsy, Lajos, 204, 327n34; *The magician's garden* (Varázsló kertje), 211, 212 (fig. 10), 224

Gypsies, 54, 245, 307n23

gypsy music, 57–60, 244–48, 308nn29,30, 309nn31,36,37; Bartók's objection to, 78, 245, 331n18; *Bluebeard's Castle* and, 245–48, 255, 261, 271; intelligentsia's rejection of, 312n41; as national music, 55–60, 78, 79, 80; notation of, 247, 249; performance style, 245–48, 246 (ex. 21), 249 (ex. 24); *verbunkos* and, 55, 244–48

Habsburg empire: Compromise of 1867, 45, 304–5n5; Dual Austro-Hungarian Monarchy, 3, 4, 45–46, 55, 304–5n5; Hungarian reform, 62–63, 65; Hungarian revolution, 57, 62, 68, 304n5; *Kakania*, 299n2; police, 62–63. *See also* Austria; Hungary

Haimo, Ethan, 300n1

hammering motive, *Bluebeard's Castle*, 267

Hanák, Péter, 67

Hanslick, Eduard, 25, 302n23

happiness: Bartók's on field trips, 150, 152–54; Budapest, 4; in love, 222, 223; middle-class, 4; Vienna, 4, 34, 40

Haraszti, Emil, "Gypsy music, peasant music, official music," 80, 312nn41,42

Harvard lectures, Bartók's, 121–22, 317n4

Hasidic Jews, 187. *See also* Jews

Hatvany, Lajos, 72, 81–82, 87, 182–83

Hatvany family, 81

Hauptmann, Gerhart, 201

Haydn, Franz Joseph, 56, 133

Hebbel, Friedrich, *Judith*, 227

Hegedűs, Lóránt, 70

Heltai, Jenő, 71, 82

Herczeg, Ferenc, 311n22

Herder, Johann Gottfried, 25, 29, 310n13

Hermann, Paula, 200, 326n17

heroes: *Bluebeard's Castle* and, 236; genius, 195; nationalist, 67–68

Hevesi, Sándor, 71, 82

history: and Hungarian modernism, 3–4, 14–15, 43–60; Hungarianness in, 54; of music, 38

Hoffmann, E. T. A., 29, 31

Hofmannsthal, Hugo von, 34, 302n23; and garden, 40; and inexpressible things, 33, 34; and Lukács, 111; and style, 93

Hollósy, Simon, 71, 91

hopelessness: loneliness and, 203; of love,

intimacy: in love, 221, 223, 224, 228, 295; poetry of, 173, 177, 224. *See also* love

introductions: Bartók's typical, 166; *Bluebeard's Castle*, 253–57, 281, 284; First Piano Concerto, 134–38, 134 (ex. 9), 139

isolation: artist in, 35–37, 40–42, 69–71, 92, 203; Balázs and, 160, 200–201; Bartók and, 7–8, 9, 156. *See also* alienation; detachment; loneliness

Iványi-Grünwald, Béla, 82

Janik, Allan, *Wittgenstein's Vienna*, 14

Jász, ethnic, 54

Jászi, Oszkár, 70, 73

Jenő, Rejtő, 44

Jews, 54, 81–84; Ady and, 82, 186–90, 197; Bartók and, 7, 81, 82, 84, 197, 198; in Budapest intelligentsia, 49, 73, 81–85, 87, 189, 197; and Christians, 64, 94, 188; in conservative middle nobility, 74; East European, 186–87; and Gypsies, 308n30; Hasidic, 187; liberal politics and, 50; middle-class, 46, 81–85, 189; and modernism, 187–88, 190; mysticism of, 113, 186–88, 190; racism against, 84, 87; reform and, 64, 65; in Sunday circle, 48; women friends of artists, 197, 198

Jókai, Mór, 49, 71, 82, 309n31

journalism: Ady's, 98, 171–72, 193

journals: *Ma*, 7; *Pesti Hírlap*, 62; *Szép Szó*, 7; *Szinjáték*, 325n13; *Twentieth Century*, 70. See also *A Hét;* journalism; *Nyugat* journal

József, Attila, 88, 115; poetry, 5, 113; relationships with women, 196–97; and social disorder, 195

Judaism, 188–90; Orthodox, 189. *See also* Jews

Jugendstil. See art nouveau

Juhász, Gyula, 71

Jurkovics, Irmy, 145, 149

Justh, Zsigmond, 311n22

Kaffka, Margit, 47–48, 71

Kafka, Franz, *The Castle*, 203; *The Trial*, 203

Kakania, 4, 299n2

Karinthy, Frigyes, 72, 86 (fig. 1), 114, 115, 304n4; "Loneliness" (A magány), 43–44

Károlyi, Mihály, 50

Katona, József, 309n3

Kerényi, György, 309n31

Kern, Aurél, 71

Kernstock, Károly, 71

Kierkegaard, S., 220, 222

Király, István, 14, 323n22

Kisfaludi Társaság prize, awarded to Lukács, 221

Kisfaludy, Sándor, 309n3

Kiss, Géza, 313n49

Kiss, József, 71, 82, 110, 189

Kiss, Lajos, 313n49

Klimt, Gustav, 203

Kner, Imre, 311n23

Kóbór, Tamás, 71, 82; *Budapest*, 43

Koch, Heinrich (Christoph), 29

Kodály, Emma. *See* Gruber, Emma

Kodály, Zoltán, 4, 15, 155, 157–59, 326n17; Adagio for violin and piano, 244; and Ady, 170; aesthetics, 157–61; artistic materialism, 161–62; background, 48; Balázs and, 11, 48, 157–62, 325–26n13; Bartók's friendship with, 7, 9, 10, 157, 198; on Budapest, 83–84; field trips, 98, 159 (fig. 7), 160, 319n35; first modern-style pieces, 10; First String Quartet, 244; and folk music, 10, 72, 73, 78–79, 80, 160, 237, 312n36, 319n35; Gruber and, 9, 10, 157–58, 160, 197–98, 320n50; *Háry János*, 80; *Hungarian Folksongs* (1906), 72; and life, 157–61; *Mountain Nights*, 244; and parlando-rubato singing, 237; and pastorale style, 244; and peasants, 53, 78–79; public life, 73; Serenade for two violins and viola, 244; Sonata for Solo Cello, 244, 331n17; *Summer Night* (Nyári este), 244, 331n17; Thália theater, 71; UMZE association, 91; and *verbunkos* style, 56

Koessler, Hans, 231

Kohner family, 81

Kokoschka, Oskar, 41

Kölcsey, Ferenc, 59, 309n3

kolomeika rhythm, 123–26, 124–25 (ex. 1), 126 (ex. 2), 128, 135, 233, 317n7

Kós, Károly, 102, 103 (fig. 4)

Kossuth, Lajos, 61–68 passim, 309n3; *Congressional reports* (Országgyűlési Tudósítások), 62

minimal element, Bartókian basic, 143

mirror, *Bluebeard's Castle* play, 292–93

modernism, 14, 296–97; and aestheticism,
69; anxiety, 33–35, 44–46; and Bartók's
aesthetics, 119; and coherence/incoher-
ence, 14, 19–24 passim, 30–35; European,
1, 19–21, 22, 91; irritation with art of, 77;
Jews and, 187–88, 190; outside mainstream, 19–24; and organicism, 14–15, 30–
33, 37–39, 69, 89–115; and romanticism,
14, 20–21, 30–33, 38–39, 48–49, 60–88,
188–89; second reform generation, 61,
68–77; Viennese, 14–15, 22–26, 30–42,
96, 299–300n1. *See also* Hungarian modernism

modernist circles, 14–15, 47, 70–72, 91–92;
Budapest, 7, 14–15, 72, 86 (fig. 1), 91;
MIÉNK, 71, 91, 92; *Nyugat*, 72, 86 (fig.
1), 91, 155, 204; radicalism of, 51, 70–72,
74, 85–88; Sunday circle, 14, 48, 71, 157,
311n23; and wholeness, 295

modernization: political conservatives and,
51; radicals and, 74; reform and, 63–64.
See also industrialization; progress

modes (Bartók's Harvard lecture topic), 121

Molnár, Ferenc, 71, 82

Molnár, Géza, 71

monarchy: Austro-Hungarian, 3, 4, 45–46,
55, 304–5n5; under Horthy, 3, 50

monothematism, Bartókian, 10, 139, 143,
250

Montesquieu, Charles Louis, 19

morality, 296; Ady and, 171, 189, 191, 194;
"and yet," 67, 111; art and, 40, 41, 49, 67,
111–15; Babits and, 206; Bartók and, 9,
44, 144–45, 194; Christian, 48, 64, 144,
318n18; form and, 165; Hungarian search
for identity and, 43, 44; intellect vs., 114;
Jewish tradition and, 189, 190; mass culture and, 34–35, 49; organicism and, 34–
35, 40, 41, 92, 111–15; radicals and, 75–76,
112; reform and, 63–64; "sense" of, 112

Móricz, Virág, 168, 170

Móricz, Zsigmond, 47, 65–66, 72, 86 (fig. 1)

Moritz, Karl Philipp, 25, 26–27, 28

Mosonyi, 56

motives: Ady and, 194; Bartókian (general),
122–23, 165, 194, 293; First Piano Con-

certo, 123, 129, 132, 135, 139, 142; of loneliness, 203–11; *Microcosmos*, 282; organicism and, 29, 31; in symphonic/operatic
tradition, 250. See also *Bluebeard's Castle*
motives; themes

Mozart, Wolfgang, 56, 133

Munkácsi, Bernát, 81

music: absolute, 28; abstract, 11–12, 20, 21;
Bartók's abandoning language for, 8, 166;
in Bartók's library, 7; critics, 72; for
dance, 55–59, 128, 317n7, 330n13; education in, 41, 73, 144, 319n21; and emotion,
119–23, 146–50; forum for modern, 155;
genres, 32–33, 39; German's claim of superiority in, 23; history of, 38; laws of,
38, 303n46; natural laws of, 38, 303n46;
post-tonal, 13; program, 28; publishers,
82; reformers in, 309n3; representational,
259–60; romantic, 28–30, 39, 56, 58–59,
78, 244, 245; salon concerts, 81; structural
approach to, 30; theory, 32; Vienna, 4,
21; Western, 32, 56, 246. See also art music; Bartók's music; classicism; composition; folk music; form; gypsy music; instrumental music; *magyar nóta;* musical
entries; new music; popular music; singing

musical drama: symphony as, 29, 31. *See also*
opera; operetta

musical language: Bartók's, 12, 142–44, 230–
32; dissolution of common, 32, 35; peasant, 79–80; Western European, 39

musical style: Bartók's (general), 2, 7, 9–10,
15, 23, 194; Bartók's synthesis, 104, 121,
193, 230–94; folk music and, 55–60, 78,
232; fragmentation of, 233; national music and, 55–60, 78, 232, 291–92; *style galant*, 35; Viennese modernism and, 37–40,
299–300n1. *See also* aesthetics; folk music;
tonal systems

Music Directorate, Bartók on, 155

Musil, Robert: and *Kakania*, 4, 299n2; *The
Man Without Qualities*, 203

mystery, 295; in *Bluebeard's Castle*, 199–203,
229, 290–91; landscape, 207, 209–10; of
the Other, 215–17, 328n40

mystery novels, 44

mystery play, 199–203, 290–91

mystery stories, 209
mysticism: Ady's, 182, 185–93, 323n22; Jewish, 113, 186–88, 190. *See also* transcendence

Nádor, Kálmán, 82
Nagy, Endre, 73
Nagybánya painting school, 71, 82, 91
Nagyszőllős Middle School, 318n18
Nagyvárad (today Oradea, Romania), 4, 87, 188–89
names, women's after marriage, 320n50
Napoleonic Wars, 64
national art, 55–60, 95; and universal art, 40, 89–92, 98–99, 230–32, 291–92. *See also* national music
"national death," theme of, 67, 75. *See also* fate, Hungarian
nationalism: opera and, 235; and transcendence of art, 39–40. *See also* Hungarian nationalism; patriotism
"Nationalist Composition," 119
national music (Hungarian), 3, 54, 55–60, 78–80, 93; *Bluebeard's Castle* and, 230–35, 236, 291–92
natural laws: of art, 27, 37–38, 97; of music, 38, 303n46
nature: organicism and, 26–27, 31, 37–38, 64–65, 91–92, 105–8, 112; peasant culture as, 105–8, 153; and social inequities, 64–65. *See also* natural laws; organicism
neoclassicism, 20, 299–300n1; Bartók and, 232–33; French, 21; Kodály and, 162; Stravinsky and, 148, 300n1; Viennese and, 36–37
neorealism, 20
new art, 96–98
new music, 37–38. *See also* twelve-tone composition; Webern, Anton
"new objectivity," 20
Nietzsche, Friedrich, 154, 292; Ady and, 11, 174; Balázs and, 11; Bartók and, 8, 10, 11, 96, 146, 148–57, 160, 221, 302n23; and decadence, 33–34; detachment, 149, 153–54, 156, 174; folklorism and, 21, 148–57; and gesture, 332n23; *Human, All Too Human*, 96, 154, 332n23; Hungarian art and, 90, 96–97; Kodály and, 160; and

loneliness, 203–4; Lukács and, 11, 164; organicism, 25, 302nn23,32
night: in Ady's poetry, 180; in *Bluebeard's Castle*, 202, 203, 205, 228–29, 253–56, 275, 292; loneliness metaphor, 203–4, 205, 207–9, 226. *See also* darkness
nobility, 51–55; gentlemen, 53, 60; in Jókai's novels, 49; landless/gentry, 52–55, 59–60, 79–80, 94; landowners, 3, 48, 52; legal, 51, 307n17; middle, 3, 46, 48, 51, 52–55, 74; and national music, 59–60, 79–80; reform and, 62, 65, 66. *See also* aristocracy
notation: on Bartók's field trips, 238, 239 (fig. 11), 330nn9,10; in *Bluebeard's Castle*'s vocal parts, 238–40; "Gyulainé," 239 (fig. 11), 240 (ex. 19). *See also* scoring
Novalis, 25, 28
novels: Kosztolányi, 44; Krúdy, 110, 209–10; Thomas Mann, 135; about modern Hungary, 43, 44, 49; Rejtő's mysteries, 44
Nyolcak (the Eight), 71, 91–92
Nyugat (West) journal, 7, 11, 72, 76, 77; Ady articles, 219; circle, 72, 86 (fig. 1), 91, 155, 204; Jews and, 81–82; and moral essence, 113–14; organicism, 89–90; Osvát editing, 71, 72, 82, 113–14; Tisza and, 77, 312n33

objectivity: Ady and, 171–72, 174, 175; "new," 20. *See also* realism
Old Testament, 190
opera: avant-garde and, 303n37; Debussy's, 235; Dukas's, 227; and nationalism, 235; symphony as instrumental, 29; traditional vs. *Bluebeard's Castle*, 236–37, 250; Wagner's, 227. See also *Bluebeard's Castle*
operetta: genre of, 35; singers, 73
optimism: First Piano Concerto, 128; unity expressed as, 194
orchestral music, *Bluebeard's Castle*, 235–37, 241, 244–53, 255–56, 281
order: Austrian garden symbol and, 40, 41; new art and, 97. *See also* coherence; social disorder
organicism, 19–42, 89–115, 302n23; Bartók and, 15, 24, 25, 96, 98, 104–9, 133–34, 273, 293, 302n23; and folklorism, 25, 26, 104–9; German, 21–42, 90, 92–93, 96–97, 302n23; modernists and, 14–15, 30–33,

organicism (*continued*)
37–40, 69, 89–115; revival of, 90–115; romantic, 23–30, 31, 64–65, 66. *See also* coherence; truthfulness
original facts, 15, 105, 142, 230, 251. *See also* phenomena
"original" human existence, Ady's poetry and, 175
originality, organicism and, 26, 32–33, 37, 90, 93, 94, 99–100, 104
"original material," 104, 123–24
ornamentation, *Bluebeard's Castle*, 245–61 passim, 271–73, 276–77, 279–81, 286, 288
Ortutay, Gyula, 313n49
ostinato: *Bluebeard's Castle*, 242, 261, 264, 271, 281, 284, 286; First Piano Concerto, 138–39, 166; *Fourteen Bagatelles*, 233
Osvát, Ernő, 71, 72, 82, 113–14, 311n21
Other, 328n40; love of the, 180, 215–17, 221–26, 227–28, 273–75, 295
otherness: of peasant society, 79; of Western European art, 90
overtones, drama and, 202

painting: abstract geometrical representation, 99; Csontváry, 10–11, 207, 208 (fig. 9); Gulácsy, 211, 212 (fig. 10), 224; Jews in, 82; Nagybánya school, 71, 82, 91; radicals in, 71
Palots (Palóc) ethnicity, 54
pantheism, Bartók's, 188
Papp, Dániel, 311n22
Paris: Bartók's trip to, 145; peace treaty of (1815), 64
parlando-rubato, 237–42, 317n8
Parliament, Hungarian, 50, 53, 62, 65
Pártos, Gyula, 100
passion: of Ady, 171–72, 193–94; of artist, 20, 121; of Bartók, 161–62, 194, 199; *Bluebeard's Castle*, 199, 266, 267, 288; in *The Miraculous Mandarin*, 44; of reformers, 65. *See also* love
pastorale: in *Bluebeard's Castle*, 235–36, 244–48, 271–79 passim, 272 (ex. 37), 280 (ex. 42); tradition of, 244. *See also* verbunkos
patriotism: conservatives and, 69; gentry and, 52–53; literature and, 91; and multe-

ity, 94; reform and, 63, 65, 66. *See also* Hungarianness; nationalism
peace treaty, of Paris (1815), 64
peasant music: Bartók's discovery of, 77–80, 152; Bartók's folklorism and, 10, 23, 77–80, 104–7, 123–24, 152–57, 232–45 passim, 271, 309n31; in narrow sense, 78–80; "new-style folk songs," 56–58
peasants: Bartók's views of, 7, 10, 53, 150–56, 193, 320n40; conservatives and, 50, 80; gentlemen folklorists and, 53, 152, 307n21; gypsy music, 57; and Hungarianness, 53–54; legal status, 307n17; migration of, 57; naturalness of, 105–8, 153; reform and, 62, 65; revolt against Habsburgs (1500s), 315n20. *See also* folklorism; peasant music; serfs
pentatonic melody, in First String Quartet, 317n5
pentatonic themes: *Bluebeard's Castle*, 253–64 passim, 254 (ex. 27), 271–73, 281–93 passim, 331nn20,21, 332n28; First String Quartet, 318n17
percussion effects (Bartók's Harvard lecture topic), 121
performance: *Bluebeard's Castle*, first, 152; *Bluebeard's Castle*, requirements for, 240–41; gypsy, 245–48, 246 (ex. 21), 249 (ex. 24). *See also* dance; singing
Perlmutter, Izsák, 82
Pesti Hírlap (Pest journal), 62
Péterfy, Jenő, 65
Pethő, Bertalan, 153
Petőfi, Sándor, 5, 61, 66–68 passim, 173, 309n3
phenomena, 96–98, 104–9, 142, 230, 297. *See also* original facts
philosophy: Ady and, 181, 182; art and, 30, 295–96; and disorder, 19, 34; eros theory, 216–17; "popular," 30; positivist, 30; romantic music and, 30. *See also* aesthetics; metaphysics; modernism; Nietzsche, Friedrich; organicism; romanticism; worldview
physical exercise, Kodály and, 158
pianist, Bartók as, 145
piano: Bartók's Harvard lecture topic, 121. *See also* First Piano Concerto

Picasso, Pablo, 99
Pikler, Gyula, 70
plays. *See* drama
poetic idea, of *Bluebeard's Castle*, 226–29, 243, 261, 292
poetry, 5, 66–68, 90; Arany, 5, 58–59, 173; Babits, 5, 47, 205–9, 213; Balázs, 5, 8, 99–100, 102–3; Bartók's father, 308n26; Csokonai, 58, 173; folk, 103–4, 173, 238, 291, 332n30; Hofmannsthal, 34, 111; of intimacy, 173, 177, 224; József, 5, 113; Kiss, 189; Kosztolányi, 5, 210, 327nn32,33; Lukács on, 113, 177; lyric, 205–6, 210, 275, 323n21; nationalism and, 5, 55, 58, 91; Petőfi, 5, 67, 68, 173; romantic, 173; United States, 5; Vörösmarty, 5, 58, 67, 173, 310n14. *See also* Ady's poetry; poetic idea; symbolism; symphonic poems
polarization: Ady and, 194–95; in Bartók's compositions, 135, 139–42, 143, 149, 165–66, 194–95, 292–93; of Hungarian public life, 3–4, 5, 74–77, 88. *See also* duality
polgár, 46–47. *See also* middle class
police, Habsburg, 62–63
politics: Ady's, 171; European compared with Hungarian, 50–51; freedom in, 41, 63–64. *See also* democracy; Hungarian politics; modernism; monarchy; nationalism
polymodality (Bartók's Harvard lecture topic), 121
polyphony, discovery of, 38
Popper, Leo, 311n23
popular art, 73, 230
popular music, 16, 56–59, 73, 78, 107, 248 (ex. 23), 303n37. *See also* folklorism; songs
popular philosophy, 30
population, Hungary, 45
populus, nobility as, 52, 53
positivism, 30
Postabank building, 100, 102 (fig. 3), 315n19
postmodernists, 195
post-tonal music, 13
poverty, 45, 51. *See also* peasants; serfs; servants; workers
power: of art, 111; of logic and reason, 64–66; of poetry, 66–68
press. *See* foreign press; journals
primeval cell, 29–30, 31

"primeval plant," Goethe's, 25
primitivism: First Piano Concerto and, 135; folklorism and, 21, 98–100; of peasants, 152
primordial condition, 98–99, 224, 314n16
progress: nationalism and, 80, 82–83; radicals and, 74–75. *See also* modernization
prophecy, Ady and, 189, 324n34
Protestants, 47–48, 74, 189
Prussia, 64
psychoanalysis, 295. *See also* Freud, Sigmund
psychological quest, 204
public life: artist in, 41, 69–73, 92–93. *See also* communalism; Hungarian public life
publishing houses, Jewish, 82
Pulszky, Ágost, 70
purposelessness: of life, 34, 149. *See also* hopelessness; meaninglessness

quest, psychological/spiritual, 204

racism: Ady alienated from, 171; European, 51; Hungarian, 7, 55, 76, 84, 87
radicals, 5–6, 61–88, 168–73, 309n38; Ady, 3, 168–73; awareness of social problems creating, 46; Bartók, 3–4, 5, 7, 12, 77–88 passim; birth of, 68–74; heterogeneity, 73–74; loosely defined, 74; modernist circles, 51, 70–72, 74, 85–88; and morality, 75–76, 112; as second reform generation, 3–4, 61, 68–88, 309n3
Radnóti, Miklós, 195
railroad, reform and, 62
real art, 24, 31, 35, 120–21. *See also* true art
realism: Ady's writings and, 171, 173, 174, 175; Bartók on, 120–21, 165; coherence and, 109–15; and folklorism, 105–6, 121; modernism and, 15, 65–66, 90, 92–95, 296; in modern music, 120–21; reform and, 65–66. *See also* life; neorealism; social disorder
reason, power of, 64–66
recapitulation: *Bluebeard's Castle*, 250, 273, 284; First Piano Concerto, 132, 133 (exs. 7, 8), 137 (ex. 11), 138, 142; Sonata for two Pianos and Percussion, 321n68; Third String Quartet, 321n68

reform: Ady and, 171; first generation, 48–
49, 50, 61–69 passim, 75, 76; second generation, 3–4, 61–88, 168–73, 309n3; slow,
62. *See also* radicals; revolution
Reihe, idea of, 38, 108–9
Reinitz, Béla, 11, 70, 73, 82, 311n26
religion: Ady and, 183, 186, 188; of Jews,
188–90; liberal politics and, 50; middle-
class differences in, 47, 48; modernists
and, 188; and morality, 48, 64, 113, 144,
189, 190, 318n18; true art and, 67. *See also*
Christians; God; mysticism
representational art, 27
representational music, 259–60
research. *See* ethnography; field trips
Révai, József, 76–77
Révai publishing house, 82
Reviczky, Gyula, 311n22
revolution: Bartók's Harvard lecture topic,
121; France and, 48; Hungarian bourgeois, 3, 48–49; Hungarian spiritual, 82;
Hungarian war of independence (1848–
49), 57, 62, 68, 304n5. *See also* reform
rhythm: Bartókian (general), 143; Bartók's
Harvard lecture topic, 121; *Bluebeard's
Castle*, 237–38, 241–43, 248–53, 261, 276,
279–82, 286; in folk music, 232, 237–38;
Fourteen Bagatelles, 233; *kolomeika*, 123–
26, 124–25 (ex. 1), 126 (ex. 2), 128, 135,
233, 317n7. *See also* rubato
right wing: Hungarian, 7, 84, 193. *See also*
Hungarian conservatism
Rilke, Rainer Maria, 91, 204
Rimbaud, Arthur, 204
Rippl-Rónai, József, 71
Ritoók, Emma, 311n23
Roman Catholic Main Gymnasium, Pozsony (now Bratislava), 144
Romania: "Anna Molnár" ballad, 332n30;
field trips, 152; folk songs, 123; Hungarian
ethnicities of, 54; Oradea (Nagyvárad), 4,
87, 188–89
romanticism, 20, 61–88, 90; Ady and, 173,
189, 194–95; aesthetics, 25–30, 161; Bartók's break with, in *Bluebeard's Castle*,
236, 248–50; and Bartók's finale, 195; in
Bartók's writings, 11–12, 68, 150; "civic

virtue," 47, 63–64; and folklorism, 21, 53–
54, 98, 173, 231–32; and Judaism, 188, 189;
and modernism, 14, 20–21, 30–33, 38–39,
48–49, 60–88, 188–89; in music, 28–30,
39, 56, 58–59, 78, 244, 245; and nationalism, 55, 56, 58–59, 66–69, 80; organicism
of, 23–30, 31, 64–65, 66; about peasant,
53–54; poetry, 173; sentimentality of, 30,
78; symphonies, 138; and unity, 25, 27,
28–30, 31; and womanliness, 220
Rosen, Charles, 250
Rousseau, Jean-Jacques, 19
Rózsavölgyi, 56, 82
rubato, 237–42, 245, 317n8, 329n5, 330n13;
hardened, 238, 330n13
Russia, and revolution of 1848–49, 62
Ruthenians, 54

sadness: Ady's poetry, 180; *Bluebeard's Castle*, 288; sentimentality and, 301n18. *See
also* tragedy
salary category, and titles of address, 47,
305n9
salons, Jewish, 81
sarcasm, in *Fourteen Bagatelles*, 233
Schenker, Heinrich, 32, 36, 315n30
Schoenberg, Arnold, 13, 300n1, 301n18,
304n53; and folklorism, 22–25, 301n8;
"Folkloristic Symphonies," 24; *Fundamentals of Musical Composition*, 39, 97;
Harmony, 35–36; *Jacobsleiter*, 42; *Kol
Nidre*, 42; and Kraus, 36, 303n40; *Moses
und Aron*, 42; and natural law in music,
38, 303n46; "obbligato recitative," 37; organicism, 22–42 passim, 90, 97, 105, 107–
9, 302n23; *Survivor from Warsaw*, 42; and
twelve-tone composition, 26, 37, 38, 93,
108–9
Schopenhauer, Arthur, 90, 301n18, 302n23;
World as Will, 203
Schöpflin, Aladár, 86 (fig. 1)
Schorske, Carl E., 111; *Fin-de-Siècle Vienna*,
14, 40, 41
Schubert, Franz, 20
Schwabians, 54
scoring: Bartók's Harvard lecture topic, 121;
organicism and, 32–33. *See also* notation

sculpture, Jews in, 82
secessionist movement, 100
second reform generation. *See under* reform;
    see also modernists; radicals
Second Viennese School, 25–26, 32
seeing: in *Bluebeard's Castle*, 224, 261, 275.
    See also eyes
Seidler, Irma, 196, 221, 329n50
self-discovery: intellectuals and, 146, 295;
    and love, 149, 229, 295
self-identity: search for, 19. *See also* ego;
    identity; inner self; soul
sentimentality: and coherence, 221; folklor-
    ism and patriotism as, 91; romantic, 30,
    78; vs. true sorrow, 301n18. *See also* emo-
    tions
Serbians, 54
serenades, tradition of, 244
serfs: Hungarian, 51, 52, 53, 62. *See also* peas-
    ants; workers
serialism, 22–23, 119, 300n1
servants: agricultural, 45, 305n6; domestic,
    45, 305n6
Shakespeare, William, *Hamlet*, 28–29
short stories: Ady, 216; Balázs, 160; Karin-
    thy, 43–44, 304n4; mystery, 209
simplicity: of artworks, 98, 99, 173; Bartók's
    Harvard lecture topic, 121, 122; in poetry,
    173, 178
Singer and Wolfner publishing house, 82
singers, 73, 330–31n14
singing: *Bluebeard's Castle*'s style, 235–43,
    281, 330–31n14; cabaret, 73; choral pro-
    gram, 73; vs. instrumental music, 28, 29,
    236–37, 245; national song competition
    (1912), 312n40; parlando-rubato, 237–42,
    317n8. *See also* musical drama; singers;
    songs
skepticism: Ady's, 182; Bartók's, 182; poet
    and, 67; reformer and, 67
sketches, Bartók's, 156–57, 320n49
Slav culture, Hungarian nationalism and,
    66–67
slaves, Hungarian, 52
Slovakia: folk songs, 123; Hungarian ethnic-
    ities, 54
Slovenians, 54

social disorder, 19–20, 33–35, 44–46, 109–11;
    Ady's popularity and, 195; awareness of,
    19, 45–46, 49, 195
social inequities, 45, 48–49, 64–65, 197, 219
socialists, 50
social justice: Ady and, 171–72. *See also*
    democracy; social inequities
social status: and Austrian art, 40; inequi-
    ties, 45, 48–49, 64–65, 197, 219; in mod-
    ern Hungary, 43, 45–49, 51–55, 82; and
    nation, 54–55. *See also* aristocracy; middle
    class; nobility; peasants; poverty; ser-
    vants; soldiers; workers
society: abstraction and, 42; Ady's signifi-
    cance, 10, 168–73, 195; and art, 6, 40; and
    art music, 122; and Austrian art, 40–42;
    Bartók's significance, 10, 12–13, 87; Bar-
    tók's view of, 145, 153; Christian, 64;
    Hungarian, as fragmented, 43–46; and
    Hungarian modernism, 14–15, 43–60;
    Western, 19, 46; wholeness in, 6, 34. *See
    also* communalism; cultural environment;
    politics; public life; social *entries*
Society for Social Studies (Társadalomtu-
    dományi Társaság/TT), 70, 73
Society of Free Thinkers (Szabadgondolko-
    dók Magyarországi Egyesülete), 70
soldiers, Hungarian, 52, 57
Somfai, László, 104–5, 135, 143, 318n17,
    320n49
Somló, Bódog, 70, 73
songs: gypsy performance, 245–48, 246 (ex.
    21), 249 (ex. 24); and instrumental vs. vo-
    cal music, 28, 29, 236–37, 245; *kurucz*,
    123; modern styles, 56–57; national com-
    petition (1912), 312n40; Reinitz's, 11, 70,
    73, 311n26; swineherd, 123, 233, 317n7. *See
    also* folk songs; lyricism; singing
soul: "all-animating," 29; Balázs and, 200–
    202, 209, 218, 290–91; *Bluebeard's Castle*,
    199–211 passim, 226–28, 237, 243, 261,
    275, 290–91, 293; creation from, 94–95,
    164–65; Hungarian, 55–56, 58, 60, 80;
    Hungarian modernists and, 29, 295;
    Kosztolányi on, 209; lonely, 199, 203–11,
    224; Lukács and, 221–22; morality and,
    41, 63, 165; mystery play, 201–2. *See also*

soul (*continued*)
    essence; inner self; "transcendental cen-
    ter"
Spiessbürger, 47
spirit: Bartók's Harvard lecture topic, 121,
    122; in Bartók's music, 13, 119–23, 143; of
    folk music, 119–23, 143; and life, 190,
    220–22
spirituality: Ady and, 186–90; in art enjoy-
    ment, 28; cell, 29–30; in expression of
    Urlinie, 32; Hungarian revolution in, 82;
    Jewish tradition and, 190; of new art's
    beauty, 97; quest, 204. *See also* God; mys-
    ticism; religion
spontaneity: in Ady's language, 177–78;
    twelve-tone composition and, 37, 108–9
stage, *Bluebeard's Castle* play, 292
stage directions, *Bluebeard's Castle*, 256–57
state bureaucracy, Hungary, 45–52 passim,
    76, 90–91. *See also* Hungarian conserva-
    tism; Hungarian politics; monarchy
Stephen, Saint, 54
Stevens, Halsey, 322n4
Stifter, Adalbert, *Der Nachsommer*, 40, 41,
    61, 64
Strauss, Johann, 4
Strauss, Richard, 30, 148, 161, 231; *Elektra*,
    218; *Heldenleben*, 121; *Salome*, 161, 218;
    Zarathustra, 148
Stravinsky, Igor, 148, 300n1, 316n33, 317n9
structure: and aesthetics, 166; Bartók's com-
    positional (general), 143–44, 194; coher-
    ence in, 28–32, 37, 95, 106–9, 112, 164,
    230; First Piano Concerto and, 128, 142.
    See also form; organicism
style: Ady and, 194; exodus from, 91; mass
    culture and problem of, 33–40; organic
    development of, 104–9; organic or com-
    munal, 19–42, 93; as unacceptable no-
    tion, 37, 39. *See also* aesthetics; coherence;
    musical style
style galant, 35
stylization, for psychological depth, 210
subjectivity: Ady and, 174. *See also* ego
suffering, creation from, 94–95
suicides: Austrians, 34; Seidler, 221, 329n50;
    Széchenyi, 62, 63

Sunday circle, 14, 48, 71, 157, 311n23
swineherd songs, 123, 233, 317n7. *See also*
    kolomeika rhythm
symbolism: Ady's poetic, 14, 15, 168–95, 213–
    15, 293, 323n22; Balázs's, 201, 203; in *Blue-
    beard's Castle*, 180, 226–29, 243, 251–76,
    292–93; European movement, 173, 204;
    expanding, 177–81, 276–90, 293; Hun-
    garian movement, 203, 204; for loneli-
    ness, 203–4; for Lukács, 164–65; modern-
    ism and, 296. *See also* circularity; garden;
    metaphors
symphonic poems: *Kossuth*, 231–32; Strauss-
    ian, 231
symphonies: heroic romantic, 138; as musi-
    cal dramas/operas of instruments, 29; tra-
    ditional features, 250
syncopation, First Piano Concerto, 125, 126,
    128, 135, 136, 138
synthesis, Bartók's stylistic, 104, 121, 193,
    230–94
Szabolcsi, Bence, 58, 59, 325n13
Szalay, László, 59
Széchenyi, István, 10; *Hitel* (Credit), 62;
    and reform, 48–49, 59–69 passim, 75, 76,
    309n3; suicide, 62, 63
Szék: Ferenczi ensemble of, 247 (ex. 22);
    Lassú (slow) dances, 330n13
Szekfű, Gyula, 59, 60, 309n37; *Three Gener-
    ations*, 69
Székler (Székely) people, 54, 102, 291, 307
Szép, Ernő, 82, 86 (fig. 1), 311n22
Szép Szó (Beautiful word) journal, 7
Szerb, Antal, 220
Szíj, Béla, 327n34
Szinjáték journal, 325n13
Szinyei Merse, Pál, 71
Szomory, Dezső, 82, 311n22

Tábor, Béla, 94
tale, folk, 99, 291
Tallián, Tibor, 317n4, 322n4
Talmud, 190
Tango, Egisto, 152
taxation, reform and, 62
terseness, in music, 232–33
Tessedik, Samuel, 309n3

Designer:	Sandy Drooker
Compositor:	Impressions Book and Journal Services, Inc.
Music setter:	Rolf W. Wulfsberg
Text:	10.5/13 Adobe Garamond
Display:	Bodoni Classic
Printer:	Edwards Brothers, Inc.
Binder:	Edwards Brothers, Inc.